INVITATION *to* SOCIAL WORK

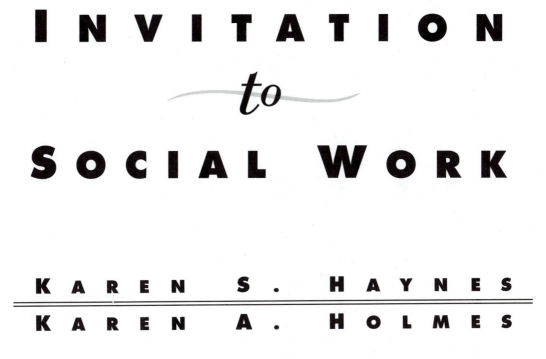

KAREN S. HAYNES
KAREN A. HOLMES

University of Houston

With contributions by Holly Van Scoy

Longman
New York & London

Invitation to Social Work

Longman, 10 Bank Street, White Plains, N.Y. 10606

Associated companies:
Longman Group Ltd., London
Longman Cheshire Pty., Melbourne
Longman Paul Pty., Auckland
Copp Clark Pitman, Toronto

Senior acquisitions editor: David M. Shapiro
Sponsoring editor: David J. Estrin
Development editor: Virginia L. Blanford
Production editor: Linda W. Witzling
Cover design, text design, and text art: Keithley and Associates
Cover illustration: Mural created for the WPA Social Security Administration Building
    competition, 1942 (200 Independence Avenue, Washington, DC) by Seymour Fogel
    (1911–1984). Fine Arts Collection, Public Building Service, General Services Adminis-
    tration, U.S. Federal Government. Photo by Albert E. Peterson.
Additional photo and illustration credits appear on page 442.
Photo research: Jack Adams
Production supervisor: Anne Armeny

 This book is printed on recycled paper.

Library of Congress Cataloging-in-Publication Data

Haynes, Karen S.
    Invitation to social work / Karen S. Haynes, Karen A. Holmes.
        p.   cm.
    Includes bibliographical references and index.
    ISBN 0-8013-0405-9
    1. Social service. 2. Social service—United States. 3. Social
case work—United States. 4. Social service—Vocational guidance—
United States. I. Holmes, Karen A. II. Title.
HV40.H37 1993
361.3'2'0973—dc20   93-15189
                                                                  CIP

1 2 3 4 5 6 7 8 9 10-MU-9796959493

The ability to think straight, some knowledge of the past,
some vision of the future, some skill to do useful service,
some urge to fit that service into the well-being of the community—
these are the most vital things education must try to produce.

Virginia Gildersleeve, *Many a Good Crusade*

Gildersleeve (1877–1965) dean of Barnard College from 1911 to 1947, was
an advocate for women's education and the only female delegate to the
UN founding conference.

CONTENTS

v

PREFACE

Social work educators write textbooks for any number of reasons: professional commitment and idealism, pragmatism born of frustration at not finding the "ideal" text, ego, the lure of recognition, and perhaps even a royalty check. Perhaps not surprisingly, we have at various times been motivated to varying degrees by all of these reasons.

In our divergent professional careers, we each found that what we believed to be significant educational and philosophical perspectives were noticeably missing from introductory or foundation social work texts. We also found that many texts were not organized as we would like, nor were many what we—or our students—considered "reader friendly." As a result, we became interested in this project because we believed we could add some of those missing perspectives, provide content not always included elsewhere, and write in an engaging fashion.

We have both been social work educators in undergraduate and graduate programs for more than two decades. We are both committed strongly to the importance of a generalist perspective as a foundation for social work practice and our own training, teaching, and professional interests support this. However, we diverge with respect to methodologies as one of us (Holmes) tends toward the micro view and the other (Haynes) tends toward the macro view. More importantly, we share a commitment to a particular "world view," which includes three specific perspectives that have influence beyond our work in this book.

Our Approach

We have three overarching perspectives that are relevant to the reader in understanding our approach in this text:

> our support for the generalist perspective on social work practice;
>
> our belief in advocacy as a central mission that underlies all of what we do as social workers; and
>
> our commitment to a personally integrated feminist world view.

The Generalist Perspective

We have used the generalist perspective on social work practice as a guide to the organization and content of this text. We believe that a focus on the commonalities of practice, and a focus on the transferability of social work knowledge, values, and skills is central to a foundation text like this one. We also believe strongly that these common and transferable elements are at the very core of the durability and strength of our profession. A generalist perspective prepares students to become professionals within and across fields of practice during the course of a career. A solid generalist foundation can transcend traditional social work settings by providing an infinite variety of professional choices over time. We do not necessarily accept the notion that the differences between and among practice settings—outpatient mental health clinics, nursing homes, public schools, hospitals, children's or adult protective services, probation departments, employee assistance programs—require separate bodies of knowledge, values, or skills for effective practice. In fact, we would argue that the focus on separate fields of practice represents a somewhat artificial distinction. Our approach, not surprisingly, is to focus on the commonalities across and among diverse practice settings.

Advocacy

We see advocacy as essential to the central mission of all social work, and as connected to and integrated with the generalist perspective. We have framed advocacy as a necessary role for all social workers because we must advocate on behalf of our clients, on behalf of our profession, and on our own behalf. We have attempted to demonstrate how advocacy has been a mainstay of our profession through its early development to the present. We have also tried to highlight the unique and particular contributions that women have made to the evolution and development of social work practice and education. As we address professional issues, we have attempted to highlight the importance of advocacy on our own behalf as members of a profession that is still (regrettably) misunderstood. Equally important, we have addressed advocacy as a necessary skill for all practitioners on behalf of their clients. Advocacy has been and continues to be a part of what we each do in our professional roles as educators and administrators.

A Feminist World View

Currently, no major social work texts (with the exception of those designed for "women's issues" courses) include a conscious and consistent feminist perspective. Certainly there are texts that address the concerns of women, and texts that include data about women, but neither necessarily suggests the inclusion of a feminist perspective. As we look toward the twenty-first century, we believe that a feminist perspective is needed to inform, to frame, and to enlighten not only social work practice, but public policy as well. In the political arena, 1992 was hailed as the "Year of the Woman," with an unprecedented number of women running for public office. Patricia Aburdene and John Naisbitt's new book, *Megatrends for Women*, hit the bookstores with its predictions of women having increasingly important and visible leadership roles in all walks of life.

These represent important accomplishments for women, but they do not reflect all the potential inherent in the feminist world view that we have integrated throughout this text. Our feminist perspective is not only about or for the benefit of women. Rather, the view that we hold is inclusive and encompasses potential benefits for all persons. Inequality—whether based on gender, race/ethnicity, sexual orientation, or any other difference—carries a price for both the "have nots" and for the "haves." We see no gain in social arrangements that serve to separate rather than to connect people. The feminist perspective we use in this text has guided each of us professionally and personally. At times, this has not been without a cost, both professionally and personally. Nonetheless, we have been, and continue to be, enlightened and empowered by a feminist world view, and by the contributions of women to our profession. In turn, we hope that we can share that with others.

Special Features of the Text

We realize that there is no perfect way to organize any text for the many faculty who will be using it. Everyone has a slightly different way of structuring a course, and many of you probably try to organize your courses to fit the needs and interests of your particular students. Those of us who have taught introductory or foundation courses, for example, realize that the Elizabethan Poor Laws, historically important though they may be, can put students into a comatose state. We also realize that we may be addressing a new generation of students who may have different learning styles from those of earlier students.

Recognizing this, we have created an ongoing cast of students who first appear in detail in Chapter 1, but who stay with us throughout the text. These students, although hypothetical, are representative of some of the individuals who enroll in introductory courses and who go on to become professional social workers. We have also created several former students whose career paths over a 10-year period are detailed in order to give your current students an understanding of the potential that social work may hold for them. By using these casts of characters, we have attempted to bring the content to life and to inform students about the profession, its history and development, and the practice of social work. We also hope that this approach will help to engage your students more actively in their own learning process.

Diversity

Many social work texts include separate chapters on selected groups, or "special populations." Our approach is different. We remain unconvinced that treating African Americans, or the aged, or gays and lesbians as special groups will enhance our understanding of those groups. We believe that, no matter how much information is provided about differences, that information will not be "heard" unless we understand that differences—diversity—can be a positive force in our society and in our own lives. Therefore, instead of offering discrete chapters on client groups, we provide an approach to diversity in Chapter 5. And because we believe that the client population of social workers represents a series of individuals and families, each representing many "special" characteristics, we integrate information on social work with a multiracial, multiethnic, multipreferenced population throughout this text.

Organization of the Text

This text is divided into four units comprised of 14 chapters. Unit One includes three chapters that serve as a contextual overview. The first chapter is devoted to presenting our perspective and to meeting our cast of current and former students. We have also provided selected definitions of social work that serve as reference points throughout the text. Chapters 2 and 3 focus on the historical development of social welfare and social work as the basis on which the profession and practice of social work has evolved. In these two chapters we have included time lines that provide easy reference to significant dates and events in social welfare.

Unit Two includes four chapters that frame the social work perspective and differentiate the social work profession from other helping professions. Chapter 4 addresses several ways in which the practice of social work is often organized, then presents a matrix model that we believe more effectively captures the infinite variety of practice opportunities in social work. Unlike most texts that provide separate chapters on selected fields of practice, or on specific social problems, we have discussed social work practice as integrated opportunities that evolve from our generalist perspective. Chapter 5 also represents an approach that is different from other texts in addressing so-called special populations. We believe that an inclusive perspective, founded on a philosophical base of appreciating and valuing difference, is essential for preparing students for practice in a world increasingly characterized by diversity. Chapter 6 builds on our approach to diversity, and presents the profession's values and ethics in some detail. Case material is included to highlight selected real-life practice issues, and we follow our cast of students as they attempt to work through their own questions and issues. Finally, Chapter 7 presents a delineation of the social work knowledge base, including a brief explanation of social work curricula that is intended to help students understand the structure and content of their own educational experiences.

Unit Three focuses on social work practice. Chapter 8 includes an overview of systems theory and the "person-in-environment" perspective that informs and guides our practice. Chapter 9 provides a brief discussion of BSW and MSW roles, presents selected generalist practice skills in some detail, and includes a section devoted to selected practice roles for BSWs. Chapter 10 briefly examines advanced micro and macro practice skills, including the influence of gender. As in Unit Two, we follow our students and former students through a variety of case illustrations and dialogues intended to highlight relevant points from each chapter.

Unit Four is devoted to professionalization. Chapter 11 traces the evolution of social work practice and education, and highlights the role of women in the profession. We have also included a time line to provide quick reference to significant dates and events in the profession's development. Chapter 12 helps students to identify and understand practitioner concerns, organizational issues, professional priorities, and public concerns that face us now and that are likely to exist for some time to come. In Chapter 13 we address the issue of professional identification, a topic that we have found to be of considerable interest (and concern) among social work students. However, in addition to identifying concerns, we also offer a number of specific strategies designed to enhance professional identification. Finally, Chapter 14 is devoted to a look at the future of social work. Through the medium of a futuristic guest lecture, we get a glimpse of what social work practice might look like in the years ahead, including a look at shifting demographic trends, at evolving technological changes, and at women in leadership.

Supplementary Materials

We realize that text selection is not necessarily based on the availability of an instructor's manual or other supplementary teaching aids. Nonetheless, we have developed the accompanying instructor's manual in the hope that it will be a helpful tool for both new and seasoned educators. Our experience in teaching and talking with students over the years has led us to develop *this* particular text, which represents *our* view of essential content and organization. The instructor's manual has similarly been developed, keeping in mind students' responses to particular kinds of content and to the delivery of that content.

We cannot guarantee that every exercise or discussion question will result in remarkable skill development or in lively debate. Social work education involves too many complex variables that influence both the content and the process of student learning to provide that kind of assurance. We can say that each exercise and discussion question has been used successfully by one or both of us over time, and that we have found them to be helpful adjuncts to student learning. The same is true for the test questions that are included for each chapter. Because many of us would prefer to spend less of our time developing tests, some or all of these items may be of help to you.

ACKNOWLEDGMENTS

No one can ever acknowledge all the persons who in one way or another have contributed to or influenced a creative work. Nonetheless, our thanks to all the students who have passed through our academic lives and through our courses (willingly or otherwise), and in so doing have pushed us to expand our thinking, demanded relevance of learning, and shared their histories and views with us, without whom we would neither have cared to write this book, nor known how. And, in case you're wondering, the students, practitioners, and clients you see throughout the text are, in fact, hypothetical. If they seem "real" to you, then we have done our creative work well.

To our colleagues in the Graduate School of Social Work at the University of Houston: Your comments and critiques (solicited and otherwise), your vision of our profession as a noble one, your patience during our "writing day" absences, and your support and assurance affirmed the need for this work. Ann McFarland typed and retyped numerous manuscript drafts, searched out lost references, and generally maintained a remarkable sense of humor under duress.

We would also like to acknowledge the work of Dr. Holly Van Scoy, whose contributions to the first draft of the manuscript are still apparent to us. We regret that Holly was unable to complete the project with us as her knowledge, skill, and wit were all important parts of our early process.

David Estrin, formerly of Longman Publishing, who had the essential idea for this text before we did, not only believed in but advocated for the explicit inclusion of a feminist framework in the text. He supported, cajoled, and otherwise kept us moving when inertia seemed to be approaching. Without question, this text exists due to David's efforts and insistence that the project needed to be done.

Ginny Blanford and Owen Lancer of Longman ably stepped in to keep everything moving at a most critical time; David Shapiro and Linda Witzling, also of Longman, supported us through the latter stages of completion. We are grateful for your professionalism, perseverance, humor, and, most importantly, your belief in us and in this work.

We would like to thank the following reviewers, whose comments guided us in the process of writing and revising our manuscript:

Margaret Jane Allen, Eastern Kentucky University
Sunny Andrews, University of Nebraska, Omaha
Debra J. DeWitz, University of North Dakota
Claudia Ellano, California State University, Long Beach
Albert C. Holloway, Michigan State University
Jeanne A. Howard, Illinois State University
Howard Karger, Louisiana State University
Pamela S. Landon, Colorado State University
Patricia Lockett, Western Kentucky University
Martha Madison, San Diego State University
Nelson Reid, North Carolina State University
Elizabeth Rompf, University of Kentucky
Joan Rycraft, University of Illinois, Urbana
Edward K. Suh, University of Central Florida

Your suggestions and comments represent the diversity that we have tried to convey in this text, the diversity that we continue to see as a strength in our profession.

We also wish to acknowledge our significant others—our partners and our children—who bore the brunt of our emotional absence as we devoted the many extra hours needed to complete this project. In particular, Karen Haynes would like to thank Jim Mickelson, husband and other coauthor, who intimately understands the excitement of creation and the pain of writer's block, and who has supported this project unfailingly. Many thanks to the Haynes-Mickelson children—Eliot, Kimberly, and David—each of you in your own unique way shared me with this project and provided insights beyond your years. Karen Holmes would like to thank Diana Storms, partner and skillful in-house editor, for her incisive commentaries on the world around us, her support, and above all, her unwavering belief in me. Thanks also to Jonathan, Justin, and Louis, who, in a coparenting sense, are "my three sons": you've taught me more than I realized I needed to know.

Finally, to each other: for having the wisdom to choose coauthors wisely, not only for balance in skills and knowledge, but more importantly, for a shared vision of what is possible.

INVITATION *to* SOCIAL WORK

An Overview and History of Social Welfare

Any introduction to social work must include some description of the long and rich history of social welfare. When did the notion of charity begin? When did it change to the model of social welfare that we know today? What were the underpinnings to what we currently describe as the patchwork of our public and private social services?

Chapter 1 begins where you are today. It begins with a description of several students who find themselves in an introductory social work course. It also provides an overview of the feminist world view that is used throughout the text, as well as selected definitions of *social work*.

Chapter 2 details the old world history and the development of social work through the 1920s. Chapter 3 continues this rich history into the Clinton administration.

CHAPTER 1

Introduction and Overview

The Purpose

Preparation for social work practice typically begins in an introductory social work or social welfare course that exposes students to rich historical traditions and current issues of professional practice. This kind of foundation is particularly important during periods of marked social and economic stress. This book was written during such a period.

Not all students who take the course go on to become social workers; but for the many who do, this initial exposure provides an important knowledge and experiential base on which later course work, field internships, and effective practice can be built. Those who take this course as an elective or those whose career plans eventually focus on other fields of endeavor can gain much from such an introduction as well. Welfare reform, social justice, health care, and the protection of children and others unable to care for themselves are concerns that belong to every thinking, caring member of the human family. These issues have never been and can never be confined to a single profession.

Whether or not you have already decided on your college major or your life's career, we hope that your understanding of complex contemporary social issues will be enhanced by this first course in social work. We also hope that you will leave this course with an appreciation of the efforts of those who have made social work their life's work. Every social worker, whether a nineteenth-century reformer or a contemporary child welfare specialist, probably started with the desire to make this world a better place. Some of you—we hope all of you—share that desire. And, just like you, other students in other parts of the country are beginning their first social work course too. Perhaps that beginning goes something like this.

The Process

The professor stands at the front of the classroom watching with that common mixture of anticipation and anxiety as the students begin to enter the classroom on this first day of "Introduction to Social Work." From experience she knows that they will represent a broad spectrum of interest and background. She knows that this class will include students who have, for a diverse set of reasons, already made the preliminary decision to pursue social work as a career. She hopes that she can feed into their commitment and enthusiasm. Others will have signed up to fill in an elective; because it looks like an easy course; or at the suggestion of a friend. She hopes that she can intrigue a few of these to consider social work as a career. "At least," she thinks, "I hope they will leave this class with a more accurate picture of the social work profession."

She looks at her class list and counts the students. All present. She begins her introductory comments to the new class.

"Good morning. This morning I am not going to spend a lot of time on the course syllabus, assignments, and readings. This morning, I want to talk about the excitement of social work.

"I am a social worker first; an educator second. I know that you come to this class from diverse backgrounds and with different expectations. Whatever your reasons for being here, I hope you will come to share with me the excitement of social work as it enhances people's lives and contributes to social justice in our communities.

"I will presume that some of you are in this class because somehow, somewhere, through personal or professional life experience you saw injustice and wanted to right it; you saw pain and wanted to heal it; you witnessed discrimination and prejudice, selfishness and elitism, and realized that there were alternatives. You may also have seen a world of promise, but also some barriers to the attainment of those promises. Perhaps you saw opportunities, but saw or experienced unequal access to them. You rightly presumed that this class and social work skills might help you to ease the pain, to change the policies.

"Social work is much more than knowledge and skills. It requires passion. I hope that you will come to or continue to care and to care deeply about these problems and issues, because you can make a difference.

"Many people have noted that the quality of human services is a barometer of the social climate in a free society, for these programs

reflect societal concerns and values regarding people who are vulnerable and less powerful. On any given day we can read in the newspapers or view on television graphic identification of increasing problems with insufficient remedies.

"Social work responds to these problems. It exists and persists because people are affected by a host of forces both subtle and brutal. These subtle forces need identification and interpretation; brutal forces need to be cushioned. Social workers humanize what can be an unresponsive and impersonal system.

"Every semester I become reinvigorated because there are people like you who recognize that your own self-interest and the interests of all others are interconnected and interdependent. I maintain my optimism because I continue to see so many social workers who remain impassioned about 'justice and dignity for all.' I am pleased that more and more people are becoming aware of the quality of life for all, not just for themselves.

"Some of you may question whether there will be jobs for social workers when you graduate. Indeed, in no previous time in recent history has our society needed us more. All labor force projections include increased opportunities in diverse fields for social service workers.

"As we proceed throughout this semester you will repeatedly hear that the goal of the social work profession is empowerment to provide needed resources to individuals, families, and communities so that they can pursue their own distinct visions of life. I will charge you to understand what resources are needed; to identify the kinds of strategies that might be used; and to examine your own values as you do so.

"So . . . now you have an idea of what social work and this class are about. Before our next class, I want you to review the syllabus to see if you have any questions and, because it provides a starting point for discussion, I want you to read this editorial. Finally, I would like each of you to write something about yourself and your interest in this course. Please don't write an autobiography, just a page will do, with as much honesty as your trust level will allow."

Several class sessions have come and gone. The professor has put names, faces, and self-descriptions together, but with the large class size, this hasn't been easy. "An interesting group," she thinks to herself, "I wonder what's really going on in their heads about now. . . ."

We'll introduce you to some of these students.

Social Work Month Good Time to Praise Those Who Serve Others

By Karen S. Haynes

With Desert Storm behind us and a returned interest in the nation's domestic agenda, I was suddenly struck with the notion that there is another set of troops who are extremely important, and usually unnoticed, fighting our domestic wars against violence, drug abuse, neglect, physical abuse, mental illness, and family disintegration. And I also realized that this is the perfect time to celebrate those personnel.

You probably did not notice, but March is Social Work Month. I guess it is not surprising that most people in our city are unaware of that. In fact, most years go by without recognition of Social Work Month. Why?

Because among all of the admirable qualities of social workers, publicly praising their own contributions, their skills, their research, has never been one of those

traits. And, unfortunately, the social work profession is also not one usually publicly applauded by others.

A dear and valued colleague suggested that I write this in celebration of all that he and so many other "unsung heroes" have given to clients in this city and to colleagues nationally.

I decided that it was extremely fitting to do so, to celebrate the thousands of social workers in our city whose life work is aimed at helping individuals and families through crisis and to resolve problems, to improve the quality of life in our community, and to continue to be the voice for those who otherwise would have none.

I write this to celebrate the hundreds of social workers in hospitals and other health-care settings in our city who ease the pain for individuals and families traumatized by chronic and often terminal illnesses;

grief-stricken by life's unpredictable catastrophes—those who help provide the adjustment to altered life conditions, the strength to work through grief and the support of death with dignity.

And there are also hundreds of social workers who care for and protect and counsel our most precious resource: our children. The social workers who, daily and with limited resources, are charged with making critical life decisions for children at risk of emotional or physical abuse; the social workers who gain the trust of troubled adolescents and heal the children who have turned to drugs, to crime, to violence. The social workers who with expertise and great sensitivity help to return the confidence and the self-esteem to a child ravaged by family instabilities, community neglect, and society's

Jennifer is a white female from a solidly middle-class family. Her mother is a social worker, and so is her grandmother. They talk frequently about the lavish party they and Jennifer's father will give when Jennifer, who is 20 and a junior, graduates next year. Unfortunately, Jennifer isn't so sure any more about being a social worker, but

policies. The social workers who work in private practice, in outpatient health clinics, and in residential facilities with adults and with children who for sometimes inexplicable reasons have given up their will to live; have lost the ability to function independently; have brought harm to themselves also go unpraised.

I write this in praise of their tireless and selfless work.

And I do not want to overlook the social workers who have devoted their careers to those who once were strong enough and capable enough and young enough to care for themselves and their families: the elderly.

To the social workers who have devoted their talents to directing communities' attention, research, and services to the well elderly, who, with minimal support, can maintain the independent status we all hold so dear; to the social workers who with exquisite balance help loving families through

difficult choices in communities where there are limited resources; to social workers who have had the eminent good sense to discuss and engage corporate leaders about preparing their employees for retirement and to the social workers who devote their days to ensuring a quality of care for our elders.

Additionally, the cadre of professionals who sometimes are not even labeled or viewed as social workers should be celebrated: the social workers in administrative and planning positions who approach those technical tasks with a vision that never loses sight of the goals of dignity and worth, of social justice, and of individuals' right to that kind of treatment. To the social workers who create policies and design programs, and who see it as more than a task to be done and who accomplish it within the principles and values of the profession.

And certainly I would not want to forget the social workers who through their

political activities have lobbied to create policies that are concerned with quality of life and humane issues; those social workers who serve in significant appointed or executive positions who argue continuously for sufficient funding to deliver quality services; social workers in their volunteer efforts who tirelessly work for candidates who have no clear social service agenda.

And, unfortunately, in the wake of Desert Storm, there are those social workers who immediately and for many years in the future will counsel the soldiers and their families through grief and loss; who will work with them to readjust to physical disabilities; and who will help heal them after the brutality of war.

And so, I write this in celebration of all of those social workers who are too concerned with others to celebrate themselves.

source: Houston Post, 27 *March 1991.*

she's hesitant to bring up the possibility of doing something else to her family. What she thinks she'd like to do is work in a kennel, raising show dogs. She worries that her father, an engineer, might see this as impractical and she fears that her mother and grandmother would be disappointed. Jennifer remembers when her older sister, Angela, dropped out of college for a year before completing her BSW. There wasn't a peaceful week the entire 12 months. Jennifer thumbs through her new textbook and thinks that maybe social work might be just fine for her. She hopes so. She certainly is fond of beagles.

Tricia, also a white female, tells everyone that her name is short for Patricia, but she began with a different name altogether. The name on her birth certificate is Constance Marie, but the only people who might remember that now are her biological parents, whom she never knew. Still in her teens when their daughter was born, Tricia's father, an alcohol and cocaine abuser, left just before his daughter was born. Abandoned and unable to care for her infant daughter alone, Tricia's mother relinquished her daughter for adoption. Tricia was placed in a foster home while child welfare workers tried to locate her father. Just after Tricia's third birthday, her father was found when he was arrested in a drug deal; he signed the papers releasing his daughter for adoption. However, because of the father's history of drug and alcohol abuse and because Tricia was no longer an infant, it was another year and a half before she was adopted. Her adoptive parents named her Patricia Lee, but strong-willed even as a child, she preferred Tricia. Now, at the age of 21, herself the mother of a 2-year-old, nothing is going to stop her from becoming a social worker. She attends the university part-time and works part-time at the day care center for developmentally disabled children where her own daughter is enrolled. She's not sure if she wants to focus only on child welfare, but her own experiences as a foster child and as an adopted child have been powerful influences in this direction.

Jahad is a 20-year-old, tall, angular African American majoring in business with a minor in sociology—a minor he just decided on this semester. Jahad once considered medicine as a career, but he did not find his chemistry classes as interesting as his volunteer work with adolescent boys at the neighborhood community center. His volunteer work came out of a sociology class project he did last semester where students were required to explore community needs in targeted low income parts of the city. Jahad discovered that he is especially adept at engaging low income, inner-city youth in wilderness and camping experiences, in spite of his own lack of exposure to tents, campfires, or backpacks before getting involved with the class project. He is considered something of an "expert" by his many young admirers, and he feels a great deal of personal satisfaction in being a role model for the kids with whom he works. Seeing such positive responses from them,

Jahad is convinced that one way to combat much of today's youth crime is to involve these youngsters in positive group activities.

Kimberley is white, and at 18 is one of the youngest students in the class. Her level of enthusiasm is almost contagious. Not yet certain of her career goals, Kimberley spent time in high school as a hospital and nursing home volunteer, as a Girl Scout troop leader, and as a recreational aide at a day care center. Unable to pick a "favorite," she enjoys working with different age groups and in varied kinds of social service settings. With a colorful wardrobe of long skirts and vests adorned with the buttons, ribbons, and slogans of peace and justice causes, Kimberley is especially interested in women's issues and environmental issues. She has read about Jane Addams, the social worker who received the Nobel Peace Prize in 1931, and she sometimes wishes that she had been born earlier so she could have worked with Addams in the settlements of Chicago. Kimberley worries about the public image of social work and wonders why there aren't more movies and television shows with positive portrayals of social workers. In the back of her mind, sometimes she fantasizes about being the one to write, direct, and star in some.

At 29, David knows he is older than many of the other students in the classroom, and with his weathered skin and prematurely graying hair, the difference shows. He is also aware he is one of only a few white males. For a moment, he can't remember what he's doing at a desk He looks out the window at the broad expanse of lawn on the college quadrangle—students hurrying between classes, all of them intent on going somewhere important—and it comes rushing back to him: the social worker who encouraged him to return to school after his life partner Gary died last spring, the dark nights of coming home from work to an empty house. His life had been neatly laid out: a job in which he was successful, a good income, a stable, loving relationship. When Gary got sick, that all fell apart. They had known all too well about Acquired Immune Deficiency Syndrome (AIDS). Together, they had lost many friends and had attended many memorial services. In their five-year relationship, they were careful, never engaging in high risk behavior, never doing drugs; still, Gary got sick and he died. David's life turned upside down. His work no longer brought him satisfaction; it now had little meaning in the whole scheme of things. "Channel your anger and your love with action," the hospice social worker recommended. And that's what brought David back to college and into this classroom. "I'm going to educate people about HIV disease; I'm going to advocate for nondiscriminatory laws for people with AIDS; I'm going to help people with AIDS any way I can," David said firmly; and there was no reason to doubt him.

Lisa, 19, is a white female sophomore. She hasn't decided on her major yet, but is considering premed, social work, or journalism. She knows it won't be a decision that she makes strictly on the basis of facts or information alone, however, because that's not her style. Things have to "feel right" to Lisa; but when they do, watch out. Lisa is known to her three younger brothers as "the dynamo" because she can accomplish so much work all by herself on the family's large midwestern farm. She feels ready to commit herself 100 percent to whatever profession seems most suitable after this semester. Being a doctor and healing people appeals to her, and she has spent many long nights in the barn comforting a sick or injured animal. She thinks that social work might also be a healing profession, but she doesn't feel like she knows very much about what social workers actually do. Lisa has been especially moved lately by the newspaper articles and television coverage of babies in Romanian orphanages, and starving children in families in other foreign countries. Sometimes she thinks that being a journalist and writing about these world problems would be a good thing for her to do, and a way to make people aware of global issues.

LaDonna is a short, solidly built African-American woman whose bearing suggests a no-nonsense approach to higher education. At 47, and after successfully raising six children—four of her own, plus two of her sister's—she has returned to college to complete a degree that she began three decades ago in a small, all-black southern college. LaDonna has experienced first-hand the effects of discrimination and prejudice on African-American children and is anxious to get either a teaching credential or a social work degree. She knows that all children need a good education to be successful, and she feels there are too few role models for African-American children. Even while raising her own children, LaDonna helped provide assistance to those in need through the network of African-American churches. She loved her volunteer work and she believes that a social work degree would enable her to do even more. A widow, LaDonna is taking six courses each semester and going to summer school so she can finish her degree as quickly as possible. "I've already waited too long," she feels, "and I'm afraid of getting too old to make the kind of difference I want to make in this world. And, Lord knows, this world needs all the help it can get!"

Jason, a white male transfer student, is just 19. He's still over-

whelmed by living away from home for the first time. He seldom manages to get his laundry and dishes done in the same week, and if he didn't have a roommate who was slightly more tidy, it is likely that his apartment would be condemned by the public health department as unsafe for human habitation. Jason himself is a little disheveled as well, and extremely disorganized. In trying to sign up for Intro to Sociology with his girlfriend Laura, he mistakenly registered for Intro to Social Work. After he read the course description, however, he decided to stay where he was rather than risk going through Adds and Drops. "No telling what I'd end up with if I tried that," he thinks. Besides, Jason figures maybe he'll get a better understanding of "welfare fraud," which his father, a certified public accountant, has discussed at nearly every mealtime since 1985.

Jennifer, Tricia, Jahad, Kim, David, Lisa, LaDonna, and Jason—these aren't all the students, but merely a glimpse of some of the sorts of students who may be in your class, individuals with a variety of interesting backgrounds, current life situations, and personal and professional goals. Of course, the actual variety in your class and in your world beyond this class is much greater.

In our cast of characters, we've not addressed religious diversity, and for the time being at least, none of our cast is differently abled. Some of your classmates—or you yourself—may be Hispanic or Latino/Latina, Asian American or Native American, Jewish, Protestant, Catholic, Muslim, Buddhist, Hindu, atheist, agnostic, or some ethnicity or religious persuasion we've failed to list. You may be a lesbian woman, a gay man, bisexual, or heterosexual. Within this text, space prohibits elaboration of all the characters we would like to include to reflect all human diversity. However, we would be failing to convey a large part of the message of this text if we did not acknowledge—and welcome—the presence of all these persons in our social work classes, in our profession, in our communities, and in our world.

All of you have registered for a course that will introduce you to the profession of social work. Like the students in our cast of characters, you probably don't really know what to expect from such a course or, more to the point, what to expect from this text.

Perhaps following along with our cast of characters will give you a better idea.

Several weeks later, after a stimulating discussion on the merits and shortcomings of various welfare programs, some of the students moved slowly as the class ended for the day. As they stuffed their note-

books into their backpacks, they appeared unfinished with today's lively—and occasionally rather heated—discussion. Over the course of the semester, a bond had developed among some of them. It began as they shared their reasons for taking the class and discussed the kinds of life experiences that had shaped their interests and their identities. As the time neared for early registration for next semester's classes, some were certain they wanted to take more social work classes, whereas others continued to wonder whether social work was what they really wanted.

Jahad spoke up, "Anybody want to go over to the Student Union for coffee and continue this debate?" Several classmates accepted his invitation and gathered their things for the trek across campus. Those who had another class or other commitments watched them leave, hoping there would be other chances to join in at another time.

A few minutes later, the group of students pulled their chairs up to a big scarred table inside the Union.

Dropping his books to the side of his chair, David spoke up, "That was some discussion! I feel kind of overwhelmed all of a sudden. Making a major career change at my age is looking harder than I thought. It's one thing to decide you want to help people, but it's something else when you think about how to make these systems really work."

"I know what you mean," Tricia broke in. "I've always had the idea that when I was an adult I could just get out there and redo everything so foster care and adoption would work great for everybody. Now I see it's not that simple. . . . I'm going to have to study the history of child welfare and family dynamics and social change theories and who knows what all just to figure out where to start. I'm not sure I can hang in there that long. What about my own daughter? Am I going to have to neglect her to get all this other knowledge and experience? What is a professional anyway? Do I really have to have a degree?"

"Wait a minute," chimed in Lisa. "I think maybe we're all overreacting with this. I don't think that the professor meant to suggest that social work is too hard or complex to learn or that we have to learn it all this semester. This course just introduces us to the range of the profession—from where it started to where it is now. So, naturally it has to cover a lot of ground to do that, but I don't think we should get scared off by all that."

"Lisa's right," said LaDonna forcefully. "This is no time to be getting discouraged and giving up. Some of us have very important

reasons for wanting to become professional social workers. Others of us don't know yet what we want to be, but we may have skills and talents that the field of social work can really use. And all of us need to know about how intolerance, discrimination, hatred, and injustice have affected our families, our communities, and our country. There's not one of us sitting here that doesn't need to know more about that, even if we don't go into social work."

"But it still seems like social workers work mostly with poor people," Jason interjected. "I'm not sure I want to work with just poor people."

Kimberley broke in rapidly, "Social workers don't just work with poor people. Social workers work with all kinds of people in all types of places. Many of them aren't poor at all—that's just sort of an image thing. Remember, our professor said we'd be talking about that more—about how the media portrays social workers unrealistically."

"To tell you the truth, I'm not as worried about image as I am about having a career with a real future," Jahad said. "I love my volunteer work, but people keep saying 'major in business, that's where the money is.' I don't see why you can't have a career you like and have a good future, too. There's got to be a lot of different opportunities out there."

Fittingly, as the students sat in the Union discussing their lives and their concerns, the professor sat in her office reflecting on similar topics.

"I wonder if I've managed to excite any of them about social work?" she mused aloud, directing her comments to the mature twining ivy on the windowsill. "I hope I'm giving them an accurate picture of real issues in practice without creating pessimism about the profession." With a sense of satisfaction, she noted that several of them did seem excited, idealistic, and committed to social work values. A few seemed uncertain of how their values "fit" with those of social work. And some, she already knew, would pursue the profession no further than this initial course. She allowed herself only a moment's pang at this apparent loss, realizing she had the same thoughts each semester she taught this course—ever since her ivy was a mere cutting. And long ago she had come to accept that social work was not a profession for everyone.

She was content that many students from previous years had already gone on to become part of a diverse, committed cadre of professional social workers. She was already certain they would be joined by several of this year's class.

Her reverie took her back to the class 10 years ago. That class had a similar mix of idealism, experiences, and talents. She reflected on where some of those students are now.

Nancy, whose idealism of a decade before was practically legendary, recently became a full-time private practitioner. She is now well-respected in her field and specializes in work with couples and families. Following graduation from the BSW program, she worked for two years in an adoption agency, and then applied to and was admitted into an advanced standing program to earn a master of social work (MSW) degree. After completing her MSW, Nancy accepted a position as a clinical social worker at Catholic Social Services. During her six years in this agency, she took advantage of staff development and continuing education opportunities, and became a certified social worker. She attended numerous workshops and seminars to gain specialized expertise in family therapy, human sexuality, and sexual abuse/incest recovery in particular. Along the way, Nancy became aware that she was a sexual abuse survivor; she got herself into therapy, and worked to resolve her own issues. In a recent conversation, Nancy reflected, "Now I understand my powerful attraction to working with people in emotional pain. I saw myself in them and I wanted to help. And, you know, I really believe I'm a stronger person now, and my own experience—though I wouldn't wish it on anyone else—has made me better able to do this work."

Once-shy Etta had changed over the years. The only African-American student in the class a decade ago, she seemed reserved and unsure of herself. Etta rarely joined in class discussions, although her exams and papers consistently ranked her at the top of the class, and she seemed to feel out of place. But something changed. She reclaimed her African origins, and exuded a sense of confidence that had never been seen in the classroom. Her path took her first into a hospital setting where she worked in the neonatal intensive care unit. Appalled by the number of low birthweight babies, and the increasing number of babies born addicted to crack cocaine, Etta channelled her anger and became an outspoken advocate for these children. She developed innovative proposals for neighborhood-based prenatal health care and drug prevention programs. She organized people in community groups and churches; she talked with them and she listened to them; she enlisted their help and offered to work in partnership with them. She argued rationally and passionately for funding before city and county government officials. She lost some battles, but she feels she has begun to win the war.

Barbara put her BSW degree to work in a different setting. Intrigued with the idea of social workers in corporate settings, she accepted a position in a large manufacturing corporation in its newly developed Employee Assistance Program (EAP). At first she spent most of her time identifying employees' specific needs and locating the appropriate community resources to meet them. Barbara found the information and referral part of her job a challenge, but she became quickly aware of existing gaps in community services that made the job more difficult. In addition, it didn't take long for her to realize that many of the employees coming to the EAP for help with marital or family problems were struggling with alcohol or other substance abuse issues. Crisis intervention became a mainstay of Barbara's skill base, especially when substance abuse was identified. Over the years, the EAP expanded and Barbara moved into a supervisory position. Her responsibilities now include direct supervision of eight social workers, program development designed to enhance employee satisfaction (e.g., on-site child care, wellness programs), and consultation with management and employees to identify emerging concerns that might affect performance and morale. Barbara continues to be excited about her work and enjoys the diversity of responsibilities that comprise her position.

Luz, who identifies herself as Hispanic, recently assumed a position as executive director of a medium-size mental health clinic in a six-county rural area in the Northeast. After receiving her BSW degree, she worked for several years in a child guidance clinic and then returned to school full-time to earn her MSW degree. As a master's student, Luz most enjoyed her second-year field placement, which allowed her to work closely with the executive director of a mental health clinic. She improved her clinical skills in this placement, and had the opportunity to observe and participate in the intricacies of agency operation for the first time. Luz took several administration courses as electives. Even though her immediate goal after graduation was a clinical position, she had her sights set on an agency director's position in a few years. When the director of the mental health clinic (her former field instructor) retired last year, Luz felt she had both the experience and training to apply for the position. She had stiff competition from other applicants, but the board members who hired her were impressed by her careful career planning. They valued her clinical experience in mental health, as well as her educational background that, by her own foresight, had included not only clinical courses, but courses in budgeting, financial management, and program evaluation. Her responsibilities include defining the agency's mission and refining program goals; establishing the agency's annual budget; making quarterly presentations to the agency's board of directors; and the supervision of the four clinical supervisors. Luz feels confident about the future of her agency as well as her role as director.

Carlos is pleased. His career has proceeded in just the way he hoped. He came into the BSW program knowing exactly what he wanted to do. Years ago, introducing himself in class, he told of growing up as a Mexican American in south Texas. "I was poor, but I felt blessed," he began. "My mother, my father, my brothers and sisters, my aunts and uncles . . . we were close. Even as a kid, I knew the hardships we faced weren't much different from those that other Latinos faced, even if they lived far from the valley, in New York, or in California, or in Florida. All of us kids missed a lot of school when the fruits and the vegetables had to be picked. We were cheap labor and we worked hard, but for little money. I want to make life better for my people in the valley. That's why I'm here." Carlos achieved his goal with his present position as a community organizer with Mexican Americans living near the Texas–Mexico border. As soon as he finished his BSW, he went to work at a small community service agency in the town where he grew up. He gained membership on the boards of directors of two agencies that he helped develop through the identification of local citizens' needs. One was a family planning clinic; the other was a neighborhood youth center. Carlos himself seldom travels to the state capitol to lobby, but more frequently and most effectively he organizes hundreds of people in letter-writing campaigns and demonstrations at the state capitol. Carlos is happy in his work, in part because of his very personal commitment to improving life in the Rio Grande Valley.

Ryan, along with many other middle-class white students in the 1970s, was involved with ecological and environmental causes as an undergraduate. As a result, he knew he wanted to attend a graduate school that had opportunities for politically oriented field internships. Not yet able to afford graduate school, Ryan spent three years working in juvenile probation, a position that not only paid reasonably well, but also opened his eyes to some harsh realities. Ryan quickly realized that his parents, though far from affluent, had offered him a stable and comfortable home where all his basic needs were met. In contrast, many of the youth with whom he worked in probation came from low income families where jail or youth camps seemed to be a "step up" in the world. When Ryan started the MSW program, his sights were more clearly set than ever on a political focus. He was interested in change, large-scale social change. He negotiated to do his second-year field placement in a U.S. senator's office, the first MSW student ever to do so. Even before his degree was in hand, Ryan had a firm job offer to join the senator's staff. As his seniority on the staff increased, so did his influence and his abilities in campaign politics. Ryan developed into an excellent public speaker and rarely missed an opportunity to speak out on the issues of poverty, drugs, and juvenile crime. Although he describes his years of experience in the senator's office as invaluable, Ryan is eager to move ahead. He's expected to announce his candidacy for state representative any day now.

Jolted out of her reverie by the annoying "chirp" of the office telephone, the professor still managed a smile and thought, "Not bad, not bad at all."

This text is for students like Jennifer, Tricia, Jahad, Kim, David, LaDonna, Jason, and Lisa. It is also for all the others who don't know much about social work except that they want to know more, and know it in a way that is enjoyable, interactive, and informative. We begin by describing our perspective.

Our Perspective

A *perspective* is a point of view, or a way of looking at things. Many textbook authors do not specify their perspective, perhaps because they are not aware of having been influenced by a particular point of view, or perhaps because they see no need to identify it. We believe it is important to identify our underlying point of view so that you can more clearly evaluate for yourself what you read. We have written this text from a *feminist* perspective. We wouldn't be surprised if some of you cringe at the word *feminist,* but we ask you to stay with us and read on.

We are well aware that the very word can turn off some people and conjure up all kinds of negative images. As we revised this section of the text, the Republican National Convention was being held in our very own city of Houston, Texas. During 48 hours, we heard political leaders (and political leader wannabe's) use the terms *feminist* or *radical feminist agenda* in the most distorted and pejorative ways. We heard, for example, the party chairperson say: "We are America. Those other people are not America."[1] We heard a well-

Social work education in the 1990s attracts a student population as diverse as its client base.

known Republican woman claim that "feminists want to be treated like men. . . . Radical feminists think that children should have the right to sue their parents."[2] We heard one of the keynote speakers proclaim that "radical feminism [includes] abortion on demand, a litmus test for the Supreme Court, homosexual rights, discrimination against religious schools, women in combat."[3] These statements are examples of negative political rhetoric, intended to distort reality and to mislead the listener. These statements emanate from the politics of fear and divisiveness, not the politics of hope and inclusiveness that our view of feminism represents. Like all individuals, including nonfeminists—and like members of any political group, including Republicans, Democrats, or Independents—feminists (both men and women) cannot and should not be stereotyped as clones of one another. Just as nonfeminists hold different views and opinions, those who consider themselves to be feminists support differing views and perspectives.

There is no single, simple definition of *feminism*. A few of the existing feminist perspectives in the social work literature are illustrative of the direction taken in this text. Barbara Collins states that "feminism is both a philosophical perspective or way of visualizing and thinking about situations and an evolving set of theories attempting to explain the various phenomena of women's oppression. Although perceived by many as a loosely connected collection of complaints and issues . . . feminism . . . reaches out beyond such confines. Feminism is philosophical, cultural, and political" (1986, p. 214). Nan Van Den Bergh and Lynn Cooper describe feminism as "a vision, a practice, an ideology. It is a call for transforming the world from competitive, hierarchical, and authoritarian relationships to a world based on gender and racial equality" (1987, pp. 610–611). Ruth Brandwein suggests that feminism is "a radically different thought structure; a different way of seeing the world" (1985, p. 174).

The feminist perspective that shapes this text is an affirming perspective. To affirm, according to *Webster's New Collegiate Dictionary,* is to validate, or to state positively. Our goal is to identify and to affirm what we believe are important connections between feminism and the profession of social work. We have chosen a feminist perspective as the frame of this text for two reasons: First, both of us use a feminist lens as a way of seeing the world around us, and second, a feminist perspective (as we define it here) is highly congruent with the values, ethics, goals, and commitments of the social work profession.

Perhaps it would help to explain what our feminist perspective does *not* represent. As used to shape this text, a feminist world view does not imply that women are inherently superior to men, nor that we intend to engage in "male bashing." (A great relief to Jason, who is already finding his classes and life away from home challenging enough.) A feminist world view is not the exclusive property of women and there are, in fact, men who consider themselves feminist. A feminist world view does not hold only a single goal of equal opportunity in employment or of equal pay for equal work (though it would be nice if these goals could be achieved at some point). The world view we have adopted does not advocate that women act just like men, or that men act like women (particularly because rigid sex role expectations are unhealthy for all persons), nor does it advocate gender separatism, or the annihilation of all existing social institutions (modification of some wouldn't be a bad idea, however). Finally, our feminist world view is not one without humor, though feminists are often stereotyped as having no sense of humor. After all, a sense of humor is one of life's greatest coping mechanisms.

We have shaped this text from the perspective of women. Our feminism brings the contributions of women into clearer focus and it helps us see more clearly the potential of social work to change our society for the better. The realities of gender-based salary inequities, violence and victimization of women, and the "feminization of poverty" are already well documented elsewhere. Although none of these issues has yet been addressed adequately by our social institutions, extensive discussion of them is not our focus here. The feminist world view, as incorporated in this text, extends beyond the mere identification of so-called women's issues. Our feminist lens reflects a global view in which everything is interconnected, and everything and everyone is ultimately interdependent. Our feminist view sees the world as inclusive and whole; it is far more than the mere sum of its parts. Our view is also transformational, suggesting that change can and does occur in people, in structures, and in institutions. Ours is an affirming perspective that envisions potentials and possibilities. Some of the important terms that we integrate in the context of feminism are:

1. holistic, nondichotomous thinking
2. analysis of power
3. relationship
4. reframing and reclaiming
5. the personal as political

Holistic, Nondichotomous Thinking

Holism is a view that suggests that all living things are interacting wholes that are more than the sum of their parts. Holistic thinking encompasses the totality, or the whole of an idea, in contrast to thinking that is characterized by dichotomies, polarities, or so-called opposites. A dichotomy, as defined in *Webster's New Collegiate Dictionary*, is "a division or a process of dividing into two mutually exclusive or contradictory groups." *Nondichotomous* thinking is neither divisive nor exclusive. Rather, it sees the whole as one, and the one as whole. In contrast, our society tends to be characterized by dichotomous thinking as represented in "either-or" statements. You are male or you are female, as if humans are two "mutually exclusive or contradictory groups" with nothing whatsoever in common. Holistic thinking suggests that humans share much in common *and* that there are differences between men and women. As stated by Barbara Collins:

> The social work perspective necessitates movement beyond the limited either/or, psychological/sociological, inner/outer, personal/social dichotomies. . . . [Our] integrated thinking with its ecological view of processes between the individual and the environment is consonant with feminist thought. Both . . . envision the desirable as "transactions between people and their environments" that support individual well-being, dignity, and self-determination. Both reflect a holistic consciousness. (1986, p. 216)

This holistic view values the means *and* the ends, the process *and* the outcome. Social and personal ends (i.e., goals or outcomes) must be connected to their means of achievement (i.e., how we get from "here to there"). For example, our feminist world view supports global peace as an "end," and many would have trouble supporting coercion, killing, and war as a "means" of achieving world peace. When we separate the ends from the means we use to achieve them, we lose sight of the whole (holistic) picture and divide our choices into either-or dichotomous thinking. Feminism, like some eastern philosophies, focuses on connection and relationship as central to life itself—the connectedness of individuals to one another, of humans to the world of nature. Whereas the prevailing world view tends to see nature as something to overcome, harness, or exploit, we suggest the need to be respectful of nature, recognizing that none of us survives if Mother Nature herself does not.

Analysis of Power

To the degree that a society is structured or arranged so that some groups are treated unequally, we suggest the need for an ongoing analysis of inequality and power. Jean Baker Miller recognizes inequality in her conceptualization of a dominant–subordinate matrix of social structure. Miller states that "a dominant group, inevitably, has the greatest influence in determining a culture's overall outlook—its philosophy, morality, social theory, and even its science. The dominant group, thus, legitimizes the unequal relationship and incorporates it into society's guiding concepts. The social outlook, then, obscures the true nature of this relationship—that is, the very existence of inequality" (1986, p. 8). Miller's matrix conceptualizes power and inequality by using the terms *dominant* (those holding power over others) and *subordinate* (those being held in lower positions, "below" the dominants).

Anne Wilson Schaef notes that her book, *Women's Reality*, "expresses a reality of which many women know, but are not always aware—that of being in a culture, but not part of it" (1985, preface to the first edition, n.p.). Although this quote does not make it explicit, Schaef is referring to gender inequality. Women, like other marginalized populations, are born into and live in a culture, but they are not the resource holders, nor the rule-makers, nor the definers of what is deemed truly important. Those who are in, but not of the culture, are marginalized, kept outside the center of resources and power, and remain subordinate to the dominant group. Subordinate groups that have typically been kept out of the center and on the margin include women, people of color, gays and lesbians, the poor, and the homeless.

Feminism reconceptualizes power. Instead of defining power as dominance or control over others, we suggest that the concept be returned "to its original meaning, 'to be able'—from the Latin, *posse*. In this sense, power is derived from the ability to realize potential and to accomplish aspirations and values" (Mary Bricker-Jenkins and Nancy Hooyman, 1986, p. 12). A feminist view reconceptualizes power as empowerment to action and as "a widely distributed energy of influence, strength, effectiveness, and responsibility" (Nancy Van Den Bergh and Lynn Cooper, 1987, p. 612). Dennis Saleebey states that "the empowerment agenda is not based on *returning power* to the people, but on discovering the power within the people (individually and collectively)" (1992, p. 8, emphasis added). To "return" power suggests that someone "owns" or "possesses" this thing called power and that we are charitably "giving" it back. This arrangement actually reinforces the social structure of inequality by distinguishing between "the haves" (dominants) and the "have nots" (subordinates). Describing empowerment in a way that is supportive of and congruent with our feminist perspective, Julian Rappoport suggests that an empowerment agenda "is to be committed to identify, facilitate, or create contexts in which heretofore silent and isolated people, those who are 'outsiders' in various settings, organizations, and communities gain understanding, voice and influence over decisions that affect their lives" (cited in Dennis Saleebey, p. 8). A feminist world view focuses on the empowerment of *all* persons to achieve their fullest human potential or, as stated so clearly by Ruth Brandwein, "Your gain need not be my loss" (1985, p. 176).

Relationship

Feminism sees mutual, reciprocal, empathic relationships as the essential medium for human growth. According to Dennis Saleebey, "Humans can only come into being through a creative and emergent relationship with the external world (with others)" (p. 11). As in the principle of holism, all things are connected, and connection—not separatism—is an essential foundation of relationship. This includes not only being in relationship with people, but also being in relationship with our environment. Relationship is not only the means but also the end, or at least the confirmation, of a healthy culture.

Relationship is fundamentally at the core of our work and at the core of our lives. However, integrating a feminist perspective in this text requires us to acknowledge the different ways in which men and women may experience relationship. Research suggests that men tend to see connection, closeness, or intimacy as threatening, whereas women seek connection and intimacy and see separation as threatening (Carol Gilligan, 1982). Western culture—including the mental health professions—elevates independence and autonomy to the level of revered ways of being. We are taught that we should be strong, independent, and capable of making it on our own. Feminism suggests that this expectation is inherently unhealthy, because it disconnects and separates us from others. Unfortunately, as long as autonomy and independence are culturally defined as desirable, men—who typically aspire to be independent and autonomous—will nonetheless be defined as "healthy," whereas those who seek connection and relationship—typically women—will be defined as less healthy, deficient, and somehow lacking the fortitude to "make it on their own." Just as our feminist view leads us to reconceptualize power, relationship and connection must be reconceptualized in positive, affirming ways.

Renaming and Reclaiming

In the early 1970s, the women's movement encouraged consciousness raising as a way to increase awareness of pervasive sexism in society and its institutions. Consciousness raising became quite the thing to do, and now, some 20 years later, *renaming* and *reclaiming* are included as themes in our feminist perspective. Having learned that history has been, in fact, predominantly his-story, feminists have advocated that history also become her-story.

Just as women and their contributions to the culture have been overlooked, so have the contributions of people of color. Adrienne Rich reminds us that "we make history, or it makes us" (1976, pp. 74–75). Our feminist perspective asks us to review history to rename and reclaim the many contributions of women and people of color. To trace the history of social welfare, for example, is to discover the particular contributions of women throughout history, to identify and name the women who have been significant and influential caretakers, activists, and reformers in the social work profession. Speaking directly to the connection between a feminist view and the status of women in social work, Carolyn Morell states, "We are a male-dominated woman's profession, doing for women what is largely viewed as women's work and generally paid at a women's wage. The project of feminism speaks directly to our experience" (1987, p. 147). The importance of renaming and reclaiming cannot be understated. If, for example, the "work" of caretaking, nurturing, and relationship-building was valued more positively in our society, we would likely see increased salaries among nurses, public school teachers, social workers, and others who choose to make relationship-based caretaking their life's work.

Our feminist perspective also includes a note of caution with respect to renaming and reclaiming. Some would have us believe that by naming our experiences—wife abuse, sexual abuse as a child, sexual assault, sexual harassment, job discrimination, to provide just a few examples—we are creating those problems. It is a frightening twist that when women identify their experiences, they may be accused of having created or caused them. It is important to watch for such distortions because they obscure our reality. We must remember that when we name and claim our reality, we are identifying it, making it visible, and exposing it; we are *not* causing or creating it.

The Personal as Political

"The personal is political," a phrase heard frequently in the consciousness-raising (CR) groups and women's movement of the 1970s, is a way to connect women's "individual" problems with their origins in and their maintenance by the culture. Sociologist C. Wright Mills captures this theme when he distinguishes between "the personal troubles of milieu and the public issues of social structure." According to Mills, trouble is a private matter, a personal problem, whereas "an issue . . . often involves a crisis in institutional arrangements" (1959, pp. 8–9). A feminist world view suggests that women's personal "troubles" are not distinct from, but in fact a reflection of existing structural and institutional arrangements. Thus, the personal *is* political.

In social work, we use a *person-in-environment* perspective as a way of understanding the relationships and transactions that occur between individuals and their life situations. (You'll be hearing much more about this in later chapters.) Some call this a dualistic perspective in that it looks simultaneously in two directions—toward the individuals, and toward their environment. You can more clearly see the similarity as we say looking "toward individuals equals the personal" and looking "toward their environment equals the political." Ann Weick and Susan Vandiver address this connection:

> Social workers understand that the conditions of people's lives are not understood solely in a personal context and that to make an adequate professional assessment, the larger social forces impinging on people's life choices must be taken into account. The constraints imposed by the economic and political structures, by deeply ingrained patterns of prejudice, by narrow role-oriented socialization, and by inflexible institutions conspire to lessen and at times snuff out the faint glimmerings of hope for a better life. The profession's focus is on the personal as well as the political realities of people's lives. (1982, p. xviii)

Defining Social Work

Our next step in getting started is to define what is meant by the term *social work*. We have been tossing this term around for several pages as if we all knew exactly what it meant, and as if we all agreed wholeheartedly. Unfortunately, this apparently easy task isn't all that simple to accomplish. There are many definitions of social work.

Probably the most widely used definition was developed in 1973 by the National Association of Social Workers (NASW), our largest professional organization. This definition states:

> Social work is the professional activity of helping individuals, groups, or communities enhance or restore their capacity for social functioning and creating societal conditions favorable to this goal. (NASW, *Standards for Social Service Manpower*, 1973, p. 4)

A second, and broader way of defining what social workers do is the following:

> Social workers help people live more personally satisfying and socially useful lives. We do this by working in direct practice with clients and/or in indirect practice by working with or through groups, organizations, and communities. In short, social workers seek improvement in the quality of human life. (Wayne Chess and Julia Norlin, 1991, p. 7)

Finally, a third definition of social work is provided by Ruth Smalley:

> The underlying purpose of all social work effort is to release human power in individuals for personal fulfillment and social good, and to release social power for the creation of the kinds of society, social institutions and social policy which make self-realization most possible for all men. (1967, p. 1)

Now, let's change the following words: replace "social work effort" with "feminism," and change "men" to "persons." What you have is a fair approximation of the goals of feminism. Looking at this, we believe that the congruence between a feminist world view and the goals of the social work profession is striking. This congruence sets the foundation of our perspective and our presentation.

Summary

In this chapter we have introduced you to a group of current and former social work students. They are all just as individualistic and interesting as you are, and, like you, they have enrolled in a social work course for a variety of different reasons. We have also introduced you to our feminist perspective and provided you with selected definitions of social work as guides to later chapters. As the course progresses, you will want to begin to develop your own perspectives on the social work profession and to refine your definition of practice.

Jennifer, Tricia, Jahad, Kim, David, Lisa, LaDonna, and Jason? You'll be hearing more about their progress in the course as we go along, too.

Notes

1. Statement by Republican Party chairperson Richard Bond at the Republican National Convention, Houston, Texas, August 1992.
2. Statement by Phyllis Schlafly at the Republican National Convention, Houston, Texas, August 1992.
3. From a keynote address by Patrick Buchanan at the Republican National Convention, Houston, Texas, 17 August 1992.

References

Brandwein, Ruth A. "Feminist Thought-Structure: An Alternative Paradigm of Social Change for Social Justice." In *Toward Social and Economic Justice* 169–181. Edited by David G. Gil and Eva A. Gil. Cambridge, MA: Schenkman Publishing, 1985.

Bricker-Jenkins, Mary, and Nancy R. Hooyman, eds. *Not for Women Only: Social Work Practice for a Feminist Future.* Silver Spring, MD: NASW, 1986.

Chess, Wayne A., and Julia A. Norlin. *Human Behavior in the Social Environment: A Social Systems Model.* Boston: Allyn & Bacon, 1991.

Collins, Barbara G. "Defining Feminist Social Work." *Social Work,* Vol. 31, No. 3 (May–June 1986): 214–219.

Gilligan, Carol. *In a Different Voice: Psychological Theory and Women's Development.* Cambridge: Harvard University Press, 1982.

Miller, Jean Baker. *Toward a New Psychology of Women,* 2nd ed. Boston: Beacon Press, 1986.

Mills, C. Wright. *The Sociological Imagination.* New York: Oxford University Press, 1959.

Morell, Carolyn. "Cause Is Function: Toward a Feminist Model of Integration for Social Work." *Social Service Review,* Vol. 61, No. 1 (March 1987): 144–155.

National Association of Social Workers. *Standards for Social Service Manpower.* Washington, DC: NASW, 1972.

Rich, Adrienne. *Of Woman Born: Motherhood as Experience and Institution.* New York: W. W. Norton, 1976.

Saleebey, Dennis, ed. *The Strengths Perspective in Social Work Practice.* New York: Longman, 1992.

Schaef, Anne Wilson. *Women's Reality: An Emerging Female System in a White Male Society.* Minneapolis, MN: Winston Press, 1981.

Smalley, Ruth. *Theory for Social Work Practice.* New York: Columbia University Press, 1967.

Van Den Bergh, Nan, and Lynn B. Cooper. "Feminist Social Work." In *Encyclopedia of Social Work,* 18th ed., 610–618. Edited by Anne Minahan. Silver Spring, MD: NASW, 1987.

Weick, Ann, and Susan T. Vandiver, eds. *Women, Power and Change.* Silver Spring, MD: NASW, 1982.

CHAPTER 2

Early Social Welfare History

"Wedfare"—Or Welfare?

Mimi Abramovitz and Martha Davis

A recent spate of legislative proposals in states across the country seeks to use welfare programs to control the behavior and family structure of poor women.

Proposed legislation in New Jersey would deny custodial parents, 95 percent of whom are women, minimal need-based benefits increases—$64 per child—if they have additional children while on welfare, and attempts to encourage marriage by allowing certain married-couple households to retain more of their earnings than single-parent families. An initiative by the governor of California, scheduled for statewide referendum in November, would also eliminate incremental benefit increases for welfare families, while requiring that single teen mothers live with their parents or guardians in order to receive benefits. And earlier this year, Wisconsin's governor proposed "wedfare," a plan to eliminate need-based increases to teen mothers with additional children while offering a "marriage bonus" of $73 a month to AFDC families headed by a married couple.

The dual purpose of each of these proposals is to (1) limit births by women on welfare and (2) encourage welfare mothers to marry as a way out of poverty. But both the assumptions underlying these proposals and the strategies they employ are misguided, falling heavily on women of color, and thus promising to fuel the politics of race.

First, the popular perception of a conniving female welfare recipient spurning marriage proposals in order to continue receiving benefits and surrounded by a half-dozen children is a myth, pure and simple. Although by restricting aid to all but a limited group of two-parent families, AFDC forces many couples in need to live apart, solid empirical evidence has demonstrated again and again that the configuration of welfare benefits does not shape childbirth and marriage decisions.

Single-parent families on welfare average only 1.8 children—considerably less than the average national family size. The decisions of poor women to marry and have children are shaped by more potent social and psychological forces than income, just as those of middle class women are.

The "new paternalism" implicit in conditioning public assistance on conformity to traditional wife and mother roles is

Elizabethan Poor Laws establish categories for relief in England.

St. Vincent DePaul organizes "Ladies of Charity" for female volunteers in France.

St. Vincent DePaul establishes "Sisters of Charity" as an order in France.

First "friendly society" forms in the colonies, in Boston, Mass.

1601   **1617**   **1633**   **1642**   **1657**

Plymouth Colony enacts the first colonial Poor Law.

part of a predictable, if unsuccessful cycle. As in the late 1940s and 1950s, when jobs for women became scarce and welfare rolls swelled, the government today resorts to making value-laden distinctions between "deserving" and "undeserving" poor women. These behavior-based distinctions were recognized as illegal during the 1960s, when states' attempts to deny welfare benefits to "illegitimate" children and to restrict unmarried women on welfare from having romantic attachments were squarely disallowed by the federal courts.

If the new welfare proposals will not affect family composition and have failed past legal tests, what will they do? They will deepen the already debilitating poverty of the average AFDC family. No state pays enough AFDC and Food Stamps to keep such a family out of poverty.

By offering higher benefits to married women than single, the new plans imply that marriage is an effective antipoverty strategy for poor women. Yet not only is the institution of marriage changing dramatically in the general population, but despite the presence of two earners, the number of married couples in poverty is on the rise. The "marriage bonus" also suggests that poor women should accept a marriage regardless of its safety and security just to survive.

In addition to creating invidious distinctions between married and unmarried women, these latest welfare "reforms" violate a woman's constitutional rights to equal protection and to make decisions concerning the timing of marriage and childbirth free of governmental interference. All three plans are specifically intended to punish or reward marriage and childbirth decisions of single AFDC parents, more than 95 percent of whom are women. Fathers will be largely exempt from these paternalistic programs.

The "new paternalism" in fact reflects a deep-seated societal distrust of the capacity of poor unmarried mothers to properly socialize their children, especially poor women of color who, while far from a majority, are overrepresented on the welfare rolls.

The popular view that social welfare programs do not work increases support for these new punitive welfare proposals. This view is not supported by studies of how effective less value-laden entitlement programs can be in cushioning poverty.

Recent research shows that based on market income alone, the United States, Canada, Australia, Great Britain, Germany, the Netherlands, France and Sweden have similar overall poverty rates. But the antipoverty impact of income maintenance programs is different. Because of weaker programs in the United

"Settlement Act" passes in England.

1662

"Workhouse Act" is enacted in England.

1697

Ursuline Sisters establish homes for widows and orphans in New Orleans, La.

1729

States, the poverty rate in this country fell only 6.6 percent in the mid-1980s, compared with a 16.5 percent drop in the other nations mentioned. Among children of single parents in the United States, poverty dropped less than 4 percent, while it plummeted nearly 30 percent in the other countries.

The "new paternalism" promises to deepen these international differences, while continuing to blame poverty on poor women rather than adverse economic policies of business and the state.

Mimi Abramovitz is a professor of social welfare policy at Hunter College School of Social Work, City University of New York. Martha Davis is a staff attorney at the NOW Legal Defense and Education Fund.

SOURCE: Washington Post, 4 February 1992.

press that there is sufficient affordable housing. Now, who is right? And whose problem is it? This is just one example of an ongoing debate in the age-old question of when, by whom, and how do private troubles become public issues.

"My intent during these next class sessions is to help you follow the evolution of when and how private caring became institutionalized into formal and structured services and to trace the complex and competing values that framed those decisions. I hope that by doing so, you will finish this course not only with this historical background to present-day issues and services, but with useful perspectives that will help to guide you to answers to tomorrow's questions."

As the class settles in to listen and, for some, to be persuaded that these purposes will be fulfilled, we ask you to remember the definitions of social work provided in Chapter 1. All definitions agree that social work is aimed at enhancement of social functioning and improvement in social conditions. As humans we experience a wide variety of needs. We have physical needs for adequate food, water, shelter, and clothing; we have needs to be physically healthy; we have needs to maintain a careful balance within our planet's environment for such resources as air, water, soil, and plant life.

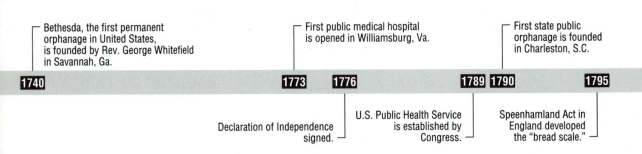

Bethesda, the first permanent orphanage in United States, is founded by Rev. George Whitefield in Savannah, Ga.

First public medical hospital is opened in Williamsburg, Va.

First state public orphanage is founded in Charleston, S.C.

1740　　**1773**　**1776**　　**1789 1790**　　**1795**

Declaration of Independence signed.

U.S. Public Health Service is established by Congress.

Speenhamland Act in England developed the "bread scale."

Our social needs are no less complex. We have needs for family, friendship, love, and for respect and dignity. In the United States, we also have the expectation that needs related to the rights to freedom, privacy, safety, justice, and equality will be met.

Chapter 2 provides an overview of how the complexity of individual needs within highly interdependent societies have been addressed. In this chapter, we trace the early origins of social services in the "Old World" through the Great Depression in the United States. When Americans use the term *social welfare* today, their conceptual and historical frame of reference for the term generally extends no farther back than the social and economic reforms of the New Deal era that followed the 1929 depression. Without question, New Deal reforms had a major effect on the way Americans now approach the provision of assistance for individuals and families in need, effects that will be discussed in Chapter 3. But to more fully understand and appreciate the cyclical nature of the processes shaping today's social welfare philosophies and policies, we need to understand events further out of the past and much farther away than the 1930s United States.

Women's Roles

No one knows who to credit with the first act of social welfare, but there is little doubt that it occurred in prehistoric times—and probably it was performed by a woman. This information may come as a surprise to those who believe that females have only recently begun to play major roles in culture and society. But new understanding of present-day social welfare institutions is provided by examining the whole scope of social welfare history from a perspec-

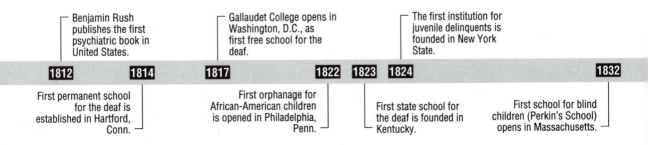

Benjamin Rush publishes the first psychiatric book in United States.

Gallaudet College opens in Washington, D.C., as first free school for the deaf.

The first institution for juvenile delinquents is founded in New York State.

1812   **1814**   **1817**   **1822**   **1823**   **1824**   **1832**

First permanent school for the deaf is established in Hartford, Conn.

First orphanage for African-American children is opened in Philadelphia, Penn.

First state school for the deaf is founded in Kentucky.

First school for blind children (Perkin's School) opens in Massachusetts.

tive informed by knowledge of women's unique and enduring contributions to its development.

It is particularly relevant that the historical and contemporary roles of social welfare in society significantly parallel the original roles of women within their extended families. More than 60 years ago, Robert Briffault (1927), in his comprehensive analysis of social origins entitled *The Mothers,* reported two significant findings: First, the primary unit of primitive societies was not the state or the family, but a group of kinsmen. Second, there was the discovery of important roles played in primitive societies by women, roles that differ markedly from the roles assigned to them by civilized societies.

From this perspective, women "invented" social welfare by the process of introducing into emerging social orders the roles that they had assumed among their kin: those of nurturing children; of providing care for the ill and injured; of developing strategies for feeding, clothing, and sheltering members of their clan; of attending to the prevention of disease and starvation; and, of enlarging the communication of feelings or ideas by speech, song and dance. Anthropologist Mary Rittner Beard notes, "women's success in lifting men out of their way of life nearly resembling that of the beasts, who merely hunted and fished for food, who found shelter where they could in jungles, in trees, and caves, was a civilizing triumph" (1976, p. 285).

Today *social welfare* is the term used to describe the responsibilities within larger societies that women traditionally assumed within their nuclear and extended families: care for those who cannot care for themselves and prevention of the need for such care, as well as the encouragement and support of individual growth and independence.

The value of and the need for welfare as a societal function is attested to by the length of its existence. At the same time, it must be

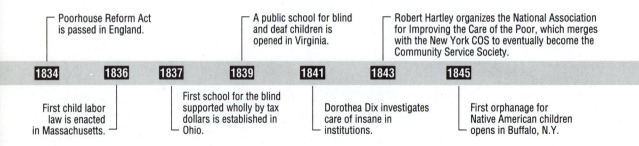

Poorhouse Reform Act is passed in England.

A public school for blind and deaf children is opened in Virginia.

Robert Hartley organizes the National Association for Improving the Care of the Poor, which merges with the New York COS to eventually become the Community Service Society.

1834 **1836** **1837** **1839** **1841** **1843** **1845**

First child labor law is enacted in Massachusetts.

First school for the blind supported wholly by tax dollars is established in Ohio.

Dorothea Dix investigates care of insane in institutions.

First orphanage for Native American children opens in Buffalo, N.Y.

acknowledged that written records of charity and social services reflect a marked ambivalence toward and devaluation of the necessity for social welfare activities, particularly in the United States. There are striking parallels to attitudes toward women during this same historical period. This is probably not a coincidental relationship.

It becomes evident in this and other chapters that professions other than social work trace their historical roots back through the social welfare tradition. Nursing and teaching, for example, have the same long history of association as "women's work," an association that does not arise solely from the gender distributions within each field, but also from a conception of their activities as most appropriately the domain of females. Thus both men and women in these professions are considered to be doing "women's work." This perception has had the effect of creating societal expectations and institutions that are self-perpetuating: expectations and institutions that counsel or guide women into social work, teaching, nursing, or other professions while society simultaneously withholds the status and economic reward afforded the work of males.

The Concept of Charity

Modern social welfare has been principally concerned with the effects of the inequitable distribution of wealth. It has not concerned itself nearly so much with those who have wealth as with those who do not, however much the former may indeed be a part of the problem. The first social welfare approach was *charity.*

Charity already had a long history before it arrived in America

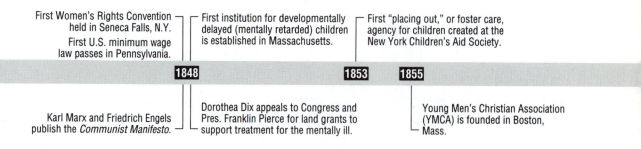

First Women's Rights Convention held in Seneca Falls, N.Y.
First U.S. minimum wage law passes in Pennsylvania.

First institution for developmentally delayed (mentally retarded) children is established in Massachusetts.

First "placing out," or foster care, agency for children created at the New York Children's Aid Society.

1848   1853   1855

Karl Marx and Friedrich Engels publish the *Communist Manifesto.*

Dorothea Dix appeals to Congress and Pres. Franklin Pierce for land grants to support treatment for the mentally ill.

Young Men's Christian Association (YMCA) is founded in Boston, Mass.

with European colonists during the sixteenth and seventeenth centuries. Five thousand years before, the Egyptian Book of the Dead provided among its list of acceptable replies from the deceased to the deity: "I have given bread to the hungry and drink to him who was athirst, apparel to the naked, and a ferry boat to him that had no boat. I have made propitiatory offerings and given cakes to the gods" (Ernest Budge, 1913, p. 587).

King Hammurabi, ruler of Babylon in about 2000 B.C., included as a part of his code of justice the protection of widows, orphans, and the weak against the strong. And Buddhism, founded about 400 B.C., taught that love and charity were superior forms of righteousness (Walter Trattner, 1974, p. 2).

Both the Hebrews and the Christians were exhorted to perform worthwhile deeds of charity in the Old and New Testaments. Much of the philosophy of charity in the United States can be traced as far back as these religious teachings. Later, charity was extolled as a means of personal salvation, designed to help the giver rather than the recipient of alms. As the teachings from the Old and New Testaments became formalized in the development of the Catholic church, charity assumed both a social aspect and an organizational context.

The English Poor Laws

Focusing particularly on the development of charity in Western European thought because of its impact on U.S. history, we can trace the growth and development of the concept during the Middle Ages. As long as feudalism was strong, there was little desire or need for other organized approaches to poverty and destitution. Feudal-

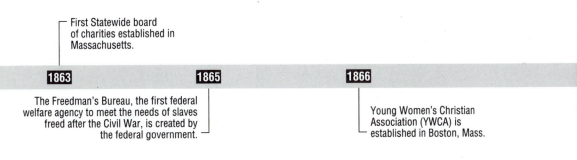

First Statewide board of charities established in Massachusetts.

1863   **1865**   **1866**

The Freedman's Bureau, the first federal welfare agency to meet the needs of slaves freed after the Civil War, is created by the federal government.

Young Women's Christian Association (YWCA) is established in Boston, Mass.

ism was an economic, social, and political system in which the wealthy or connected people (lords) were given oversight and management of governmental land. The land was worked by the poor (serfs) who received shelter, food, and clothing in exchange for their labors. However, when the feudal system was replaced with towns and a free market and economic problems proliferated, the Catholic church gained recognition as the great social agency of Europe, developing an elaborate system of hospitals and monasteries where many human needs were addressed.

The combined systems of feudalism and church might have continued as excellent examples of charity were it not for two unanticipated events. In 1348, the bubonic plague killed nearly one-third of the European population. Therefore, the demand for laborers far exceeded their supply and peasants began to move where they could obtain the highest wages in this new "market economy." However, in 1349, the Statute of Labourers was enacted in England and required peasants to remain in their "home manors" and work for whatever wages the lords wanted to pay them. To further protect the lords, begging and almsgiving were outlawed, except for the aged and feeble.

The second unanticipated change came from the actions of King Henry VIII of England. King Henry VIII's break with the Catholic church in 1531 also included his confiscation of church property, including its more than 450 monasteries. Although this action gave him the church wealth he had sought, he also was faced with the unanticipated problems of the destitute of England whom the monasteries had sheltered and fed. Overnight a king who was seeking an increase in personal freedom and wealth found himself personally responsible for the poor. Without plan or forethought, responsibility for the relief of poverty was transferred from the church to the state (D. L. W. Worcester, 1954, p. 204).

King Henry VIII attempted to meet the challenge with legisla-

National American Woman Suffrage Association founded.

Society for Organizing Charitable Relief and Repressing Mendacity (first Charity Organization Society) is founded in London.

1869   **1870**   **1872**

Visiting services established for all children released from Massachusetts state institutions.

National Prison Association is founded in Cincinnati, Ohio.

Louisa Lee Schyler founds U.S. Sanitary Commission.

Charles Loring Brace publishes *The Dangerous Classes of New York.*

tion designed to protect himself and other property owners from the annoyance and danger of paupers and vagrants who begged from door to door and lingered on every public street. By the act of 1531, only the "impotent paupers," that is, the crippled, the diseased, and the blind, were allowed to beg, and then only in a prescribed area. Begging by the able-bodied was made a crime, but even the severe penalties prescribed for the second and third offenses—for example, having one's ears cut off and public hanging—did not diminish the problem (although hanging certainly did inhibit recidivism).

In 1536, the Act for the Punishment of Sturdy Vagabonds and Beggars was passed, which is sometimes hailed as the first constructive social legislation in history. Under this new law, no one was allowed to openly beg. Each parish of the new Church of England was made responsible for the care of its own poor. Relief funds were collected on a voluntary basis in parish churches, but the expenditure of these funds was under the control of local governments. Private almsgiving was prohibited. Relief of poverty, limited though it was, had become a public responsibility.

Let's return to our classroom for a moment to ponder the significance of these 450-year-old statutes. LaDonna is asking, "How could they call this 'constructive legislation'? It sounds like more of this conservative, controlling, antiwelfare nonsense." Before the professor can respond, Jason jumps in, equally animated. "Well, if people are able to work, you can't just let them lie around and take money. Then, there will never be any incentive for them to work. Some people have to be forced to work or they'd just live off the system. Why my father says. . . ." He is interrupted by the professor's admonition, "O.K., let's look at the issues here.

"The important point about these early laws is to show that our conception of charity, which historically and religiously has meant to care for one's neighbors and to provide goods and services to those in

National Conference of Charities and Corrections convenes its first nationwide conference.

First U.S. charity organization society in U.S. formed in Buffalo, N.Y.

Clara Barton organizes the American Red Cross.

1874　**1875**　**1877**　　**1881**

The "Mary Ellen" case calls attention to the need for child protection laws in the United States.

New York Society for the Prevention of Cruelty to Children incorporates.

Booker T. Washington founds the Tuskegee Normal and Industrial Institute in Alabama.

need, may also have been constructed from self-interest and certainly has been entrenched with debates of who is more in need. Through these examples we also begin to understand the delicate balance between social legislation aimed at social change or at social control.

"As soon as charity becomes institutionalized, then, by definition, it moves beyond the individual charitable act—deciding to whom to give money, services, or goods and how much to give—to a larger communal decision (city, county, state, nation) that requires eligibility criteria, benefit standards, and behavioral compliance by the recipients. When welfare moves from the private sector (the church, the lords) to the public sector (the government) who pays and who profits become public debate."

Soon after Queen Elizabeth I, King Henry's successor, came to the throne, it was determined that the voluntary collection of relief funds was not satisfactory. In 1563, property owners who failed to voluntarily contribute were assessed penalties by the courts. In 1572, the collection of these funds was removed from the church with a national tax, the Parish Poor Rate. Overseers of the poor were hired to register persons in need of public relief. In 1576, public work was mandated for able-bodied individuals who would not or could not find employment as a condition of receiving economic assistance from the government.

In 1601, 70 years after King Henry's first ill-fated attempt at taking care of the needy, these separate laws were brought together in the Welfare and Institutions Code, known more commonly as "the Poor Laws of Elizabeth." This code provided for a classification of the needy into three groups: (1) dependent children; (2) the unemployable (the old and the infirm); and (3) the able-bodied (employable) poor. For each of these categories, different services were provided. The able-bodied were given work by the government in iron foundries and flax, woolen, hemp, or jute mills. The unemployable were placed in almshouses. Dependent children were appren-

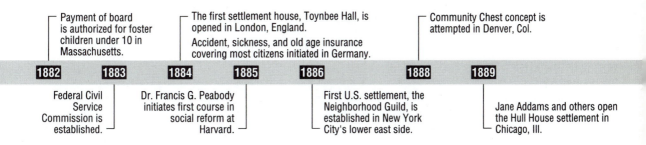

Payment of board is authorized for foster children under 10 in Massachusetts.

The first settlement house, Toynbee Hall, is opened in London, England.

Accident, sickness, and old age insurance covering most citizens initiated in Germany.

Community Chest concept is attempted in Denver, Col.

1882   1883   1884   1885   1886   1888   1889

Federal Civil Service Commission is established.

Dr. Francis G. Peabody initiates first course in social reform at Harvard.

First U.S. settlement, the Neighborhood Guild, is established in New York City's lower east side.

Jane Addams and others open the Hull House settlement in Chicago, Ill.

ticed in private homes, boys until they were 24 and girls until they were married. Parents and grandparents were made legally responsible for their children and grandchildren, thus reducing the incidence of dependency on the state.

In 1630, Charles I appointed a royal commission to achieve uniformity in the administration of the Poor Law. Because the wealth of England was not equitably distributed among parishes, the amount of funds available to support the poor was also inequitably distributed. Soon those who were receiving the public funds, familiarly referred to as a *dole,* began to move from poorer parishes to richer ones in order to receive more money. In 1662 the Settlement, or Residence, Act was passed, restricting the obligation of any parish to those who had legal residence there. Legal residence could be acquired by birth, apprenticeship, or ownership of land. Persons entering a parish could be sent back to their legal residence within 40 days unless they could demonstrate they would not become destitute.

The economic and social effects of this act were significant because they seriously impeded the mobility of the labor force and further crippled the working class. No modifications were made in these regulations until 1795 and no significant changes were made until 1846. In that year the Irremovable Poor Act was passed, which provided that no person would be sent out of a parish who had lived there for five years. Soon the five-year requirement was reduced to one year.

Between 1601 and the mid-nineteenth century, other changes in social welfare evolved, fueled in large part by England's desire to develop a pool of laborers within its own boundaries. The English foresaw that a country's economic status in the evolving industrial marketplace would be dependent at least in part on its ability to utilize its own workers to convert raw materials into products for export. Challenged by intense competition from the Netherlands,

Lillian Wald founds the New York City Nurse's Settlement, which later becomes the Henry Street Settlement.

First U.S. public class for developmentally delayed (mentally retarded) is set up in Providence, R.I.

First training for social workers organized by New York COS held for eight weeks in the summer.

1893 **1894** **1895** **1896** **1897** **1898**

Amos G. Warner publishes *American Charities.*

First federation of Jewish Charities is established in Boston, Mass.

First state hospital for crippled children is founded in Minnesota.

the English had considerable motivation for looking toward the unemployed poor as potential sources for this labor. Thus the concept of *workhouses* was born.

The idea of building places of work for the English poor was accompanied by the expectation that these workhouses would be involved in spinning, knitting, lace work, and in the manufacture of nets and sails. In 1697, the first workhouse was built in Bristol. The workhouse introduced the concept of work rather than money as economic relief, and it soon flourished. Before long, both public and privately owned workhouses were bidding for the labor services of the able-bodied poor, with the lowest bidder receiving parish contracts. Competition was so intense between workhouses that the bidders began to extend their contracts to include individuals formerly considered unemployable, including young children, the aged, and physically and mentally handicapped adults. Whole families were moved into the workhouse, a place where they earned their meager keep by the labor of every member of the family in prison-like conditions.

As the character of England continued to change from agrarian to industrial, more and more families and individuals were displaced from their former positions of self-sufficiency and thrust into the burgeoning lower economic class. It became important at this point to distinguish the "deserving" from the "nondeserving" poor. Laws were passed in 1722 making it legal to withhold relief from those who refused to enter the workhouse. The "workhouse test" (would a family or individual give up freedom and self-esteem by moving into the workhouse in return for scant shelter, food, and clothing?) was an attempt to force all potential workers into the labor force as a condition of receiving public assistance.

Back in the classroom, Lisa's hand is raised. "I'm not sure I understand the difference between almshouses and workhouses," she questions.

First juvenile court is established in Chicago, Ill.

Florence Kelley makes speeches across the United States calling for creation of a centralized, national child welfare agency. Simon Patten coins term *social worker*.

First U.S. analysis of tuberculosis is undertaken by New York social workers, directed by Edward Devine, and leads to the establishment of the National Lung Association.

1899   **1900**   **1903**

"Fighting Mary" McDowell, along with Florence Kelley and Josephine Lowell, organize the National Consumer's League to fight for women's rights in the United States.

Graham Taylor founds the Chicago School of Civics and Philanthropy (now known as the School of Social Service Administration).

The professor smiles, "Yes, that can be confusing. Almshouses were institutions funded by charitable contributions for the 'worthy' poor—the old, sick, feeble-minded. Workhouses were institutions, funded by the sale of the goods made, for the 'unworthy' poor—the able-bodied. Both were 'indoor relief'—or relief provided within institutions, but the conditions of receiving support (shelter, food, and clothes) were directly determined by the value placed on the person's worthiness."

Jahad becomes animated. "You know, one of the boys I worked with last summer told me that his father had to move out of the house years ago and leave the family, so that his mother could receive welfare. But what you just said makes me wonder if that could possibly be true?"

"Yes, Jahad, it's true—maybe we'll understand why a bit later."

During this period, English society struggled to define and differentiate between deserving and nondeserving poor, essentially a distinction between employables and nonemployables. The nonemployable, deserving poor were provided "outdoor" relief, or relief while they remained at home, if they were capable of caring for themselves; "indoor" relief in institutions such as almshouses or poorhouses was provided if they were not. The employable nondeserving poor were sent to workhouses where they became forced participants in England's bid to establish a dominant world economic position. It was not until 1782 that the Gilbert Act abolished the forced confinement of those formerly judged to be undeserving, and permitted economic assistance to be provided to them in their homes. This legislative reform was followed by a series of others, which by 1795 included a system where all worthy families whose incomes were insufficient for maintenance received public subsidies.

There is some evidence that the evolution of this social welfare system in England was at least partially responsible for pre-

Lillian Wald outlines plans for Federal Children's Bureau and enlists the support of Florence Kelley and Edward Devine.

First U.S. medical social worker (Ms. Garnet Pelton) is hired at Massachusetts General Hospital.

1904

1905

New York School of Philanthropy is founded (now Columbia University).

The Charities Publication Committee is formed in Massachusetts.

The Commons (Massachusetts journal of the settlement movement) merges with the New York COS journal *Charities*, resulting in the journal *Charities and the Commons*.

venting a revolt of the English underclass comparable to the French Revolution, a significant event that took place across the English Channel during this same period.

Our students are in heated debate. "See, once the government gets involved, they have to label people and restrict services. The government is always so concerned that somebody is going to get something for free. I just don't understand it," Tricia concludes. "That's not the only reason there are rules and regulations," Jennifer chimes in. "My mother says that rules also protect clients and make sure that everyone gets treated fairly." "Is it fair to label and categorize people based on what you can see or what you assume or what one group thinks is right? That's what stereotyping and discrimination are all about," Jahad comments with emotion.

"I believe you're all getting the picture of just how complicated 'doing good' can be and how differently we perceive problems and their solutions given our unique perspectives. These Elizabethan Poor Laws were simultaneously protective of the elite while still socially responsible for the less fortunate. These laws helped maintain England's success through changing socioeconomic times by restricting the movement of labor. They may have prevented a revolution. They also kept individuals and families from death and crime.

Were they progressive and constructive forces for social change or were they repressive forms of social control? I'll leave you to think about that."

As many historians of the period have suggested, the fundamental assumptions underlying Poor Laws continue to define the arenas for discussion and debate in contemporary society, namely: (1) local government responsibility; (2) financing through taxation; (3) classification of those in need; and (4) provision of different types of relief for individuals and families in different circumstances or categories.

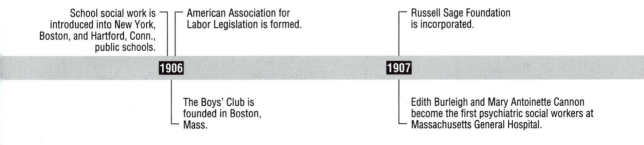

School social work is introduced into New York, Boston, and Hartford, Conn., public schools.

American Association for Labor Legislation is formed.

Russell Sage Foundation is incorporated.

1906

1907

The Boys' Club is founded in Boston, Mass.

Edith Burleigh and Mary Antoinette Cannon become the first psychiatric social workers at Massachusetts General Hospital.

Social Welfare in the United States

Some Disclaimers

Summarizing the development of social welfare in the United States strictly in terms of its relationship to a Western European, principally English tradition, does not provide a complete picture. Such summaries do not place in perspective the systems of social welfare developed by Native American tribes whose existence in the territory called "the New World" and, later "the United States" pre-dated English Poor Laws by centuries. The habit of tracing U.S. history principally through England, no matter how significant that historical relationship was, perpetuates the social myths of English culture and society that have been preserved in the written records conventionally accepted as an accurate representation of real events in England and its colonies. Furthermore, the acceptance of such written records as "complete" inevitably excludes the un-recorded activities and contributions of significant participants.

In particular, little is generally known about the contributions of women or people of color to the English welfare system, because these contributions have gone largely unrecorded. Women remain part of the "anonymous" in history, in much the same way that certain racial, socioeconomic, or ethnic groups have been ignored. Yet in the case of women and social welfare, there is an important distinction, which this historical analysis highlights.

We place great importance on understanding women's role in the history of social welfare precisely because many of its early functions were those already carried out by women in their communities. When these functions were formalized, women continued to perform them. There is, however, one decisive historical fact about women: The areas of their functioning and their status within those

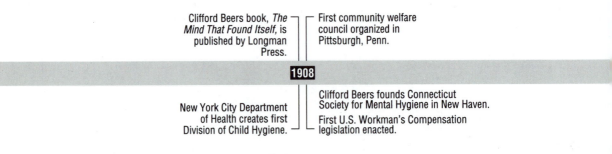

Clifford Beers book, *The Mind That Found Itself*, is published by Longman Press.

First community welfare council organized in Pittsburgh, Penn.

1908

New York City Department of Health creates first Division of Child Hygiene.

Clifford Beers founds Connecticut Society for Mental Hygiene in New Haven.

First U.S. Workman's Compensation legislation enacted.

areas have been determined by men during much of recorded history.

Thus colonial and early nineteenth-century female reformers directed their activities into channels that were typically an extension of their domestic concerns and traditional roles. They taught school, cared for the poor, the sick, the aged. As their consciousness developed, they turned their attention toward the needs of women. Female reformers began to "uplift" prostitutes, organize women for abolition or temperance, and sought to upgrade female education, but only to better equip women for their traditional roles.

Although the social welfare field has traditionally been staffed primarily by female volunteers and professionals, it is difficult, if not impossible, to construct an accurate summary of its development in the United States because so much of women's history remains unrecorded. The effort that follows in this chapter and the next is an attempt to incorporate all currently available information into a history of U.S. social welfare as it was practiced by actual men and women, but to do so with the knowledge that this information remains far from complete.

The U.S. Colonial Period: 1601–1776

This first period of U.S. history, arbitrarily delineated from formal colonization through our country's independence from England, sets the stage for current policies, practices, and debates. Social welfare in the United States during this period was heavily influenced by the English Poor Laws. The principles of local responsibility, family responsibility, and residency were the particular hallmarks of the earliest U.S. statutes and practices. In fact, as late as the 1930s, 13 states retained the use of "pauper" in the legal title of their laws providing for public aid; as late as the 1980s a few states

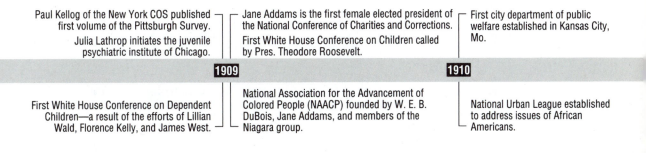

Paul Kellog of the New York COS published first volume of the Pittsburgh Survey.

Julia Lathrop initiates the juvenile psychiatric institute of Chicago.

Jane Addams is the first female elected president of the National Conference of Charities and Corrections.

First White House Conference on Children called by Pres. Theodore Roosevelt.

First city department of public welfare established in Kansas City, Mo.

1909

1910

First White House Conference on Dependent Children—a result of the efforts of Lillian Wald, Florence Kelly, and James West.

National Association for the Advancement of Colored People (NAACP) founded by W. E. B. DuBois, Jane Addams, and members of the Niagara group.

National Urban League established to address issues of African Americans.

retained the use of "overseers of the poor"; and well into the twentieth century more than two-thirds of the states required relatives to provide support for impoverished members of their families.

Along with a common tradition of social welfare philosophies, policies, and practices strongly influenced by the experiences of England, the early development of social welfare in the United States was profoundly affected by the frontier. There was a need for all able-bodied persons to work, and when philanthropy was not enough, responsibility fell to the smallest unit of government. During this period, poverty was not viewed as a major social problem. Society was primarily rural with an abundance of unused fertile land on the frontier, and there was a prevailing attitude that poverty was an individual rather than a social problem; in other words, poor people were lazy, incompetent, no good, or crazy.

In 1642 Plymouth Colony enacted the first poor law in the New World based on the Elizabethan Poor Law of 1601. Many colonies followed suit over time. A second public response during the latter part of this period was the initiation of publicly funded residential facilities. In 1751 the first public general hospital was built in Pennsylvania and later, in 1773, the first public mental hospital in the United States was opened in Williamsburg, Virginia.

Nationalization: 1776–1860

Postindependence through the Civil War represented another definable period of social welfare developments. Although the Declaration of Independence and the Constitution represented an important national and international position about rights, each was equally significant in what it did not protect. Obvious preferential rights were given to white males with property, whereas females, male minorities of color, including Native Americans, were explic-

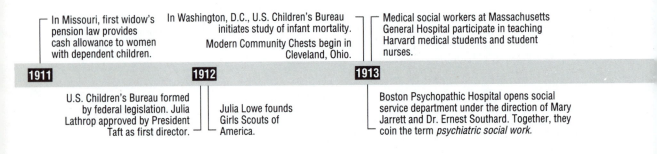

In Missouri, first widow's pension law provides cash allowance to women with dependent children.

In Washington, D.C., U.S. Children's Bureau initiates study of infant mortality.
Modern Community Chests begin in Cleveland, Ohio.

Medical social workers at Massachusetts General Hospital participate in teaching Harvard medical students and student nurses.

1911

1912

1913

U.S. Children's Bureau formed by federal legislation. Julia Lathrop approved by President Taft as first director.

Julia Lowe founds Girls Scouts of America.

Boston Psychopathic Hospital opens social service department under the direction of Mary Jarrett and Dr. Ernest Southard. Together, they coin the term *psychiatric social work.*

itly excluded. Furthermore, rights and responsibilities for social welfare activities were delegated to the states.

Thus, our first federal legislation excluded the majority of our population and awarded responsibility for the "needy" to levels of government least able to afford this responsibility. Because heavy taxation without representation was one of the primary reasons for the pursuit of independence from Britain, and given that taxation was levied in part for poor relief, the rationale behind these policies is self-evident.

In 1790, the first public orphanage began operation in Charleston, South Carolina. The U.S. Congress established the U.S. Public Health Service in 1798; the first permanent school for the deaf opened in Hartford, Connecticut, in 1814; and Gallaudet College, the first public college for the deaf, opened in Washington, D.C., in 1817.

The expansion of the American frontier was further heightened by immigration during this period. In 1790, the year of the first national census, the population of the United States was slightly under 4 million. By 1860, it topped 31 million. Although births and the addition of more states to the union all played a part in this dramatic increase, the most significant factor was immigration, especially in the years between 1830 and 1870.

Immigration and the frontier were very closely related features of economic, social, and political life during the period. Particularly during the mid-nineteenth century, new industries developing along the eastern seaboard needed immigrant women and men for their mills, mines, and factories to replace workers who had sought greater opportunity in the West. Later when the West itself needed workers for the labor-intensive tasks of railroad and highway construction, almost unrestricted immigration was tolerated. The needs of the northern industries also helped support an anti-slavery ideology via "underground railroads" to increase African-

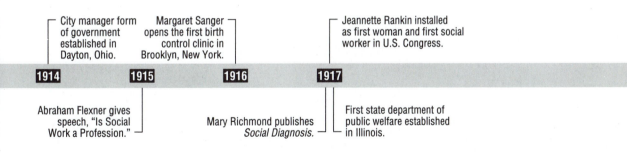

City manager form of government established in Dayton, Ohio.

Margaret Sanger opens the first birth control clinic in Brooklyn, New York.

Jeannette Rankin installed as first woman and first social worker in U.S. Congress.

1914   1915   1916   1917

Abraham Flexner gives speech, "Is Social Work a Profession."

Mary Richmond publishes *Social Diagnosis.*

First state department of public welfare established in Illinois.

American migration from Southern slavery. It was only as the frontier shrank and the need for labor diminished that there was a gradual tightening of immigration laws, first through exclusion of "undesirable" foreigners, then of undesirable individuals, through literacy tests, and finally by national quotas (D. L. W. Worcester, 1954, p. 214).

In the 1840s and 1850s, the vast majority of immigrants came from Ireland, to escape famine, and from Germany, to escape political oppression. Almost all of these immigrants entered the country at seaport cities between Boston and Baltimore and most settled in the cities of the north.

The Irish, who became domestic and construction workers, and the Germans, who turned to labor in industry and commerce, arrived in the United States at a time when the nation was changing dramatically. The shift to an industrial society from an agrarian base brought about what has been described as "violent business fluctuations, depression and . . . poverty and insecurity to many. There has been no other period in American history in which the needs and demands of industry so dominated the nation's political and social life" (Donna Franklin, 1986, pp. 505–506).

It was not coincidental that the high tide of immigration was contemporaneous with significant changes in social welfare and, in fact, with the development of the profession of social work. Throughout the latter part of the nineteenth century and the early part of the twentieth century, social welfare was strongly influenced either by sympathy for the plight of immigrants or by a conscious desire to make them an integral part of the American way of life. In particular, the creation and maintenance of an elaborate system of private charities can be at least partially understood in terms of the active efforts by states to exclude immigrants from eligibility for public relief or assistance. Private charities grew dramatically during this period, due in no small part to the need to rapidly assimilate

In Washington, D.C., Julia Lathrop and Children's Bureau staff draft the Sheppard–Towner legislation in response to information on infant mortality gathered via nationwide survey.

Boston's Smith College creates a permanent graduate school of psychiatric social work based on eight-week training courses developed by Mary Jarrett to meet the needs for psychiatric work during World War I.

Boy Scouts of America and Campfire Girls are founded.

1918

1920

The Commonwealth Fund is organized as a private foundation.

The Nineteenth Amendment providing for women's suffrage is ratified.

into the nation's work force millions of foreigners with a minimum of hardship, cruelty, or strain on the public welfare system.

The necessity for such assimilation became linked not only to economic necessity but to the prevailing intellectual and religious ideologies of the time. Many have asserted that the Christian tradition, particularly Calvinism, was vital to the development of the expansive capitalist spirit that dominated early industrialization.

The Calvinist doctrines that linked success with salvation were supported by the secular liberalism of John Locke, the biology of Charles Darwin, and the philosophy of Herbert Spencer. This Protestant work ethic, as it is more commonly known, is associated with values emphasizing hard work, self-discipline, and deferred gratification, and the belief that such efforts will result in rewards such as money, higher social status, greater freedom, and entry into heaven. From the Lockean perspective, the ideal society was one in which individuals were free to pursue salvation via economic success in a free market economy. Meanwhile, the widely discussed works of Darwin and Spencer seemed to provide evidence that life is indeed a fierce competitive struggle in which only the fittest survive. Industrial strife, poverty, and insecurity were indicators of the immutable laws of evolution, and evolution was not to be restrained (Donna Franklin, 1986, pp. 506–507).

A fourth ideological perspective of the period was the pragmatism of John Dewey, which supported a commitment to rational inquiry, experimentation, and "knowing by doing." Dewey's ideas were translated into a belief that individuals who lived in poverty were not necessarily morally inferior, but were influenced by a social structure that affected their functioning.

Although we are focusing on the U.S. scene, two British laws enacted during this period must be noted for their impact on current U.S. legislation. The first, the Speenhamland Act of 1795, created a "bread scale" in order to subsidize workers when wages were

The Commonwealth Fund establishes 23 demonstration projects in child welfare across the nation.

First homemaker services are provided by the Jewish Welfare Society in Philadelphia.

1921   **1922**   **1923**   **1928**

First child guidance clinic opens in St. Louis, Mo., as a demonstration project by the National Committee for Mental Hygiene.

Milford Conference defines social casework.

too low to survive. This "bread scale" was based on the current price of bread and the number of dependents of the worker.

This rather progressive legislation of "outdoor" relief to the working poor was relatively short-lived. In 1834 the Poor Law Reform established the "Principle of Less Eligibility" so that a recipient of public aid could never receive more than the lowest paid worker. Public assistance was no longer a right and the government was not responsible for the unemployed.

"Why have I jumped to include these two pieces of legislation? Why are they so important 150 years later?"

Jennifer, somewhat hesitantly, answers, "Well, the discussion of welfare payments and the government's responsibility seems to continue in the same way. My mother was saying the other night at dinner that it was criminal that welfare payments were lower than the poverty line in many states and that people still seem to believe that if these benefits were any higher, more people would want to be on welfare."

"Yes," David shook his head, "and the ongoing arguments about whether government is responsible for the unemployed hasn't been solved yet. I don't understand, with all our country's recent economic problems, how some people can continue to believe that others become unemployed by choice. They also don't understand, unless it happens to them, that when you're unemployed, you also have no health coverage. . . . I guess that's a whole different issue."

"Yes," said the professor, "and one we will be talking about more. But you two certainly have made your points that the attitudes and values competing to make or change national policy have remained fairly consistent."

Despite the consistency of some of these public policies, U.S. social welfare underwent substantial changes during this time period. Not only did the field of private charity develop two significant institutional movements via settlement houses and charity organization societies, but states began to enact legislation supporting the funding of an everwidening range of public social welfare programs, most of these providing indoor relief, or assistance to individuals living in specifically designated facilities.

Consider the following examples of such institutions: In 1822, Philadelphia opened the first orphanage for African-American children; in 1824, New York State created the first institution for juvenile delinquents. In Lexington, Kentucky, the first state school for the deaf was established in 1823; and in 1825, the first juvenile detention center was opened in New York City.

In 1832, the first school for blind children was established in Massachusetts. The first orphanage for Native American children was created in Buffalo, New York, in 1845, and the first institution for mentally retarded children, was established in Massachusetts in 1848.

At the midpoint of the nineteenth century, social welfare in the United States was a mixture of public and private charity provided to children, the aged, the mentally and physically ill, and the poor. Public aid continued to be provided primarily for native-born U.S. citizens in institutional settings much like those of England, whereas private charity was provided for immigrants through an unorganized range of philanthropic, private clubs. For example, in 1787 the Philadelphia Free African Society became the earliest black mutual aid society; in 1817 the New York Society for the Prevention of Pauperism was founded; in 1840 the Little Sisters of the Poor was founded to care for the poor elderly.

Public aid was derived principally from revenues raised at the state level, although the federal government had begun to participate minimally through land grants to some state and private institutions as begun in the previous period. Sales of these lands provided funds for building and operating early homes for children, the aged, and the mentally ill. In any event, neither public assistance nor private charity was particularly visible at midcentury. Most people continued to accept the belief that poverty was a matter of personal rather than public responsibility (Walter Trattner, 1974, p. 67).

Dorothea Dix. The prevalence of such beliefs made the efforts of prominent social reformers of the period, such as Dorothea Dix, even more noteworthy. It was Dix who brought the plight of the institutionalized mentally ill to the attention of 17 state legislatures, 2 Canadian provincial governments, the British Home Secretary, the U.S. Congress, and Pope Pius IX. More significantly, Dix was at the forefront of creating a new conception of social reform based not so much on liberal self-interest but on liberal social standards.

Dix was born in 1802 in Hampden, Maine. At age 12, she moved into the impressive Boston mansion of her widowed grandmother. At 19, she opened two schools for young children on the grounds of her grandmother's estate, one for children of the wealthy and one for children of the poor. By 23, she had published an encyclopedia for children, which was the first of many works intended to be both educational and morally uplifting. Like many prominent women of the century, Dix never married, but maintained a lifelong relationship with another woman, which provided personal and professional companionship. She shared with Ann Heath a Unitarian idealism and an avid belief in moral and intellectual improvement that is reflected in their correspondence, in her writings, and in her life's work.

Dix suffered from several periods of ill health early in her career as a teacher and author. We can only speculate about the basis for these illnesses; certainly the activist role she played brought her into conflict with nineteenth-century masculine values. Except for teaching and charity work, there were no established roles in U.S. business or politics to which a well-educated woman might realistically aspire.

Dix's most noted public accomplishments include establishing 32 hospitals for the mentally ill in the United States and others in Canada, Japan, Scotland, the Channel Islands, and Rome. In 1848, she had enough public influence to persuade Congress to set aside more than 10 million acres of federal land to provide for the indigent mentally ill, deaf, and blind; the bill, however, was eventually vetoed by Pres. Franklin Pierce. This veto signified that public aid was still not viewed, for any group, as a national responsibility.

Dix was appointed and served as superintendent of federal nurses during the Civil War and struggled with public health and sanitation issues during and after that conflict. It is also said that she was the only social reformer welcome in the South both before and after the Civil War. As was the case with the social reformer Jane Addams somewhat later, Dorothea Dix was elevated to a status resembling secular sainthood during her lifetime.

Toward the end of this period, many groups were concerned with the rights of the oppressed. The antislavery movements, particularly in the North, combined moral and economic issues. Feminists held a national convention in Seneca Falls, New York, in 1848, which focused on suffrage, equal opportunities in education and employment, and legal rights for women.

National Expansion: 1860–1900

The Civil War left indelible marks on the form and content of social welfare in the United States. One of its effects was highlighting the

Top left:
Jane Addams
(1860–1935). Founder
of Chicago's Hull
House.

Top right:
Ellen Gates Starr
(1859–1940).
Cofounder of Hull
House.

Center left:
Jeanette Rankin. An
early advocate for
women's rights, and
the first woman and
social worker elected to
the U.S. Congress, in
1917.

Center right:
Harriet Tubman
(1820?–1913). Active
in the abolitionist
movement.

Bottom:
Sojourner Truth
(1797?–1883). Born
a slave, an early
abolitionist.

social and economic problems of African Americans, particularly those emancipated from slavery in the South as a result of the Union victory. In March 1865, Congress established the War Department's Bureau of Refugees, Freedmen, and Abandoned Lands, which was the nation's first federal social welfare agency. The bureau was created to administer services to assist freed slaves on a temporary basis during the Civil War and for one year following; however, sentiment in Congress prevailed over the wishes of Pres. Andrew Johnson and the bureau was actually in operation for six years.

The needs of Civil War veterans and their families also had significant social welfare consequences. Combatants on both sides had suffered a high rate of death and serious injury. Veterans and their dependents experienced a great level of need for medical services, housing, and financial support, both during the war and thereafter. There was no stigma associated with social and economic needs incurred through military service, and the needs of veterans were considered apart from the needs of the civilian population as deserving of both state and federal government support. Federal assistance was provided first to soldiers and veterans of the Union and later extended to those of the Confederacy (June Axinn and Herman Levin, 1982, p. 90).

The U.S. Sanitary Commission was established in 1861 as a direct result of the efforts of the Women's Central Relief Association of New York. These women, in part emulating the efforts of Florence Nightingale in Europe during the Crimean War, sought to introduce emerging scientific and medical advances to the diet and hygiene of Union troops, as well as to provide them with financial relief, medical services, and services of a personal nature. The conception of women's appropriate social role in the period is reflected in the all-male composition of the nine-member sanitary commission. Such was the case despite the fact that women's private charity groups were completely funding and implementing its programs and there were many capable and qualified women available for appointment, including Dorothea Dix, who was serving as superintendent of nurses for the Union forces when the commission was created.

Immediately following the war, the Southern states in particular were faced with numerous problems: wounded veterans, widows, and orphans of soldiers; a large number of newly emancipated African Americans; and an economy basically in ruins as a result of the high costs of maintaining a losing military effort for half a decade. Lacking the Northern network of public and private charities to meet social needs, Southern communities and states were forced to piece together a patchwork of poorly funded and often repressive approaches to these needs. In particular, laws harking back to the most unenlightened of the English Poor Laws were enacted to place African Americans in a new kind of economic slavery by leasing them out to reconstruction and industrial enterprises as "apprentices." The solution to African-American dependency and a means for building a slavelike labor force went hand in hand (June Axinn and Herman Levin, 1982, p. 92). Later, the Freedman's Bureau took over the responsibility of organizing the transition between slavery and open employment for those newly freed. It also distributed rations, provided transportation, established orphan homes for children, and established and operated African-American schools. The bureau was also instrumental in the founding of Howard, Atlanta, and Fisk universities; Hampton Institute; and Talladega College.

These unprecedented efforts by an agency of the federal government were not enthusiastically embraced. Although the Freedman's Bureau was able to extend its existence past the original intent of President Johnson, it was unable to survive the tide of popular sentiment that swept it from existence in 1872.

As our class hears some of this from their professor, Kimberley, in her usual animated state interrupts, "Some things don't seem to have changed much—look at who's still running most of our social services—men! Yet we make up most of the workers and volunteers."

LaDonna muses, "Isn't it interesting that the federal program to help African Americans lasted only six years, but veterans' services have expanded." "But don't you think our country owes something to veterans?", asks Lisa. "That's the problem, we can't seem to agree on who we owe what to. . . . ," Tricia adds quietly as the class ends.

As federal efforts such as the bureau waned, private charities once again began to proliferate and extend their influence, particularly in the urban Northeast. What public relief there was still reflected its historical ties to England.

> Nearly every county of every state in the Union had its almshouse, the traditional dumping ground for unsegregated distress. Every city of any size had its heterogeneous collection of private charities. . . .
> Throughout the country there was the British contempt

for the victims of public assistance coupled with profound distrust of outdoor relief. (D. L. W. Worcester, 1954, p. 215)

Social welfare was at this state of development when it was confronted with the worst depression in U.S. history from 1873–1878. From necessity, there was rapid development of public welfare programs in most of the larger cities across the country. As the economic crisis persisted, the administration of public funds to the poor living within communities became a source of widespread political corruption. In Brooklyn in 1878, when economic recovery had finally begun, one-tenth of the city was receiving public relief. When Seth Low was elected mayor on a ticket pledged to end abuses in the welfare system, he abolished all public relief to individuals who were not in institutions. Many other U.S. cities followed Brooklyn's example, dealing public aid a blow from which it took decades to recover.

Charity Organizations. It was within this context that the charity organization societies and the settlement movement appeared on the U.S. scene, both based on models of social welfare that had recently developed in England. There was, indeed, striking similarity between conditions in English urban areas and those of the United States that gave rise to a need for new approaches to social and economic need. The Charity Organization Society (COS) represented the first new model to appear.

> Although the origins of the Charity Organization Society, as one of its early members remarked, is "as undiscoverable as the sources of the Nile" and much controversy has raged around the question of who can claim to be its founders, the conditions which provoked the society into existence in 1869 are beyond dispute. Especially in London, private charities, offering as they did immediate, easy, short-run solutions to the problems of poverty, had spawned to such an extent that many believed the poor had become pauperized as a result. Octavia Hill, whose experiments in housing management and training workers so profoundly influenced succeeding generations of social workers was convinced that this was so. "I am quite awed when I think what our impatient

charity is doing to the poor of London," she told a captive audience at Fulham. (Kathleen Woodroofe, 1962, pp. 25–26)

Conditions were much the same in the United States. With the proliferation of private charities and their inattention to coordinating services among themselves or with relief available from public agencies, there was considerable chaos in the largely male-dominated social welfare system, despite the emergence of state boards of charities whose principal function was to simultaneously protect both the public and the poor. Massachusetts had created the first state board in 1863, followed rapidly by other states throughout the nation.

The National Conference on Charities and Corrections, an organization made up principally of these state boards, was convened in 1874. It made an effort to investigate the common problems of public welfare as well as to encourage the application of scientific inquiry then developing in the biological and physical sciences to the problems of social distress. The first national conference was convened "without a typewriter, telephone, trolley car, taxicab, without a recognized social service technique, for it was not yet born" (Sherman Kingsley, 1928, p. 3). But despite all of its deficiencies, the meeting marked an important milestone in social welfare, the beginning of professional social work in the United States (Edith Abbott, 1931, p. 82).

Even with this hint of progress, the social welfare system of the country still had enormous gaps. There was little or no involvement of the federal government in the social welfare of its citizens, with the exception of services for soldiers and veterans of the Civil War, and some "worthy poor" groups through public institutions. The activities of states remained limited and tied to the patterns of English Poor Laws and were largely directed at native-born citizens, leaving the huge numbers of new immigrants dependent on private charities. In both the public and private sectors of social welfare, males were dominant in policy making and administration.

The dominant ideology of woman's role in Eastern Seaboard cities relegated middle and upper class women to the home, marriage, and motherhood. Biological, psychological, religious, and patriotic arguments defined aspirations to move beyond woman's assigned sphere as a rebellion against God and nature. . . .

Except as matrons in institutions, women were largely absent from public welfare, banned as they were from government and public activity. Woman's special sphere was the moral; by implication, she was not to be concerned with such crass material questions as wages, working conditions, and even the dispensation of relief. As in the family, the special charges of ladies bountiful were other women, children, the aged, and the sick; by implication, they were to avoid the idle, profligate, intemperate, and other immoral poor, particularly if they were men. Woman's special province was the home; fitting service was therefore the creation of small institutions for children and the aged. By implication, women were not to go into prisons, insane asylums, or slums. (Julia Rauch, 1975, pp. 244–245)

Borrowing from the English example begun in 1869, the first American Charity Organization Society (COS) was created in 1877 in Buffalo, New York. By 1882, in spite of considerable opposition from long-established charitable institutions, there were 22 Charity Organization Societies in the country, and 10 others that had adopted aspects of the COS philosophy. Although practices varied according to local conditions, the early work of these societies was based on the principles of investigation, registration, cooperation, and friendly visiting outlined by the London Society.

For the COS, poverty was to be cured not by the distribution of relief but by the personal rehabilitation of the poor. The guiding philosophy was that pauperism could be eliminated through investigating and studying the character of those seeking help and by educating and developing the poor. Case conferences and "friendly visiting" made vivid the problems, the needs for, and the responsibilities of rehabilitation. (Donna Franklin, 1986, p. 508)

The founding of Charity Organization Societies coincided with the expansion of women's participation in the leadership and provision of organized charity services and a weakening of role constraints that limited women's charitable activities. Historical material from the period supports the idea that charity organizations may have flourished particularly because expanding feminist impulses to expand roles and to work coincided with conservative class interests to reduce unnecessary duplication of social services and reduce the number of people on the "dole" (Julia Rauch, 1975, p. 2).

A new concept of virtuous womanhood was emerging in society, one created and sustained substantially by women's involvement in the arena of social welfare. Dorothea Dix had become an American saint, in part, because the activities she undertook were so unusual for a woman. She was an exception, and like many exceptions, her experiences in prisons, jails, and asylums were interpreted by society to prove the "rule" that a woman's place was in the home. At the same time, her activities and those of other women—such as Louisa Lee Chuyler, who had opportunities during the Civil War to assume positions of leadership and visibility left vacant by men engaged in the fighting—provided a new model for expanding role possibilities. Opportunities to be a "friendly visitor" in one of the new Charity Organization Societies gave women the chance to extend their roles as nurturers beyond that of mothers and wives in their own communities.

Even so, there were criticisms directed at the idea of expecting women to assume significant responsibility for the problems of the poor living in the slums. One critic in Philadelphia recoiled from the "ungallant" and "ridiculous" prospect of the "weaker sex" carrying the "onerous burden" of "misery and pauperism" (Julia Rauch, 1975, p. 246). Despite such opinions, the COS movement flourished.

At first, the friendly visitors of the COS were volunteers, but there soon began to develop a cadre of women associated with the COS who looked on social welfare as more than an activity to fill their leisure. They did not reject the notion that women should exude self-sacrifice, purity, and spiritual superiority; rather, they moved these qualities out of the home and into the public world of professional work (Donna Franklin, 1986, p. 512).

Josephine Shaw Lowell and Mary Richmond gave new definition to both social welfare and women's professional roles through the development of the concept of friendly visiting within charity organization societies. Richmond declared in 1890:

> The charitable impulse is a good thing, perhaps the very best thing we have in the world. . . . Acting on this declaration, (the Charity Organization Society) has organized, as a part of its work, and the most important part, as it believes, a system of Volunteer or Friendly Visiting. In districting our city and finding out the condition of the unfortunate in the districts, we have aimed to send to each family that needs an uplifting hand, a patient, persevering, faithful friend, who, by the power of that strongest thing on earth, personal influence, will gradually teach them habits of industry and self-control. (Mary Richmond, 1907, p. 40)

Lowell, an outspoken proponent of social Darwinism with experiences shaped by participation in the activities of the sanitary commission during the Civil War, was instrumental in publicly articulating the moral imperatives that lay beneath even the most mundane activities of friendly visitation. Lowell's design for the COS gave primary importance to virtue, character, and morality.

> To this end, it was women's duty to organize groups of friendly visitors whose first charge was to investigate the moral character of the poor. . . . Visitors were assigned to a special territory, enabling them to become thoroughly familiar with all who live within its limits. Then the COS representative, as one member explained, visited each (of the needy) in her own home, listened to her pitiful story, and gave practical suggestions concerning personal and domestic cleanliness and order which effected a marked improvement and created in sluggish minds a real ambition to make a home. Lowell and the supporters of the COS . . . were certain that face-to-face contacts and one-to-one relationships would promote reform. (David & Sheila Rothman, 1972, p. 74)

The Settlement Movement. A markedly different approach to social welfare was taken by those who brought the English experiment with settlements into the hearts of U.S. cities. Toynbee Hall opened its doors in the London East End slums in January 1885. Like many of the northern industrial cities of the United States, London had become a city plagued with problems of labor exploitation and slums. In the minds of many college-educated, middle-

Meeting of the National Federation of Settlements, September 1920, at East Aurora, NY. Seated, *left to right:* Charles C. Cooper (Kingsley House, Pittsburgh); Graham Taylor (Chicago Commons); Jane Addams (Hull House, Chicago); Harriet E. Vittum (Northwestern University Settlement). Standing, *left to right:* Lillian Wald (Henry Street Settlement House, New York); John Elliott (Hudson Guild, New York); Dame Henrietta Barnett (Toynbee Hall, London); Mary E. McDowell (University of Chicago Settlement House).

class London Christians like Beatrice Webb, "the industrial organization, which yielded rent, interest and profits on a stupendous scale had failed to provide a decent living and tolerable conditions for a majority of the inhabitants of Great Britain" (Sydney & Beatrice Webb, 1927, p. 193).

As a solution to these devastating effects of urbanization and industrialization on the working class, a group of students from Oxford and Cambridge universities influenced by Prof. Arnold Toynbee and directed by Canon Samuel Barnett and his wife created the University Settlement, a residence where students were to live among and participate in the daily life of the poorer classes. In its English conception, the settlement had much in common with the Salvation Army, the COS, and other British social welfare efforts.

Barnett's experiment in England had the most far-reaching effects in the United States, where the idea was introduced by Americans who had visited Toynbee Hall—among them Stanton Coit, Jane Addams, Robert A. Woods, and Vida Scudder. All of the earliest U.S. settlements were patterned after Toynbee Hall. Coit returned from London and founded the Neighborhood Guild of New York in 1887 with Charles B. Stover. Addams visited Toynbee Hall three times before establishing Chicago's Hull House in 1889 with her companion Ellen Gates Starr. Canon Barnett was so impressed with Addams's "Toynbee Hall experiment," as she called it, that he paid her what was (in its time) the ultimate compliment, calling her "the greatest man in America."

Scudder spent several months in England and wrote articles of praise for the settlement concept in the Christian Union. She proposed something like Toynbee Hall for women; they would live together, teach the poor skills, and instill in them the "spiritual and hidden wealth of a sensitive nature attuned to beauty"; the residents would develop a "hearty, mutual comprehension and friendship between the classes" and "avert our social dangers." Scudder, with graduates from the women's colleges of Wellesley, Vassar, Bryn Mawr, Radcliffe, and Smith, founded the College Settlement in New York in 1889. Within a year, young women from other eastern schools established settlements in Boston and Philadelphia. Woods and William Jewett Tucker established Andover House in Boston in 1891. By 1895, more than 50 settlements had been established in this country, and by 1900 their numbers exceeded 100, including several in the rural South.

These U.S. settlements, although all inspired by Toynbee Hall, rapidly began to differ from English settlements. Small group activities and clubs received more attention in the United States; women were far more dominant in the movement; and, perhaps as a result, there was greater emphasis on the problems of children, youth, and health. All of the settlements enjoyed a certain amount of popularity, but the activities at Hull House came to be practically synonymous with settlement work in the United States.

Jane Addams and Hull House. Hull House, largely through the efforts of Addams, became a model for settlement houses everywhere, providing an almost endless array of services and activities in one of Chicago's poorest neighborhoods.

As her reputation as a settlement worker expanded, Addams traveled across this country and Europe, lending her energies and name to a wide range of emerging social welfare causes and organizations, including the American Civil Liberties Union, the National Association for the Advancement of Colored People, the Juvenile Protection Association, the U.S. Children's Bureau, and a women's trade union league. She mediated strikes, wrote prodigiously on social reform, and worked tirelessly for women's suffrage and world peace. Addams and Nicholas Murray Butler, president of Columbia University, were jointly awarded the Nobel Peace Prize in 1931.

The Progressive Era: 1900–1929

This period is best described as one of continued population growth and corporate wealth. The population grew from 76 million in 1900 to 123 million 30 years later. Additionally, through corporate monopolies, wealth became highly concentrated, supported by governmental protective tariffs.

The influence of Addams and the settlements continued to be extended into virtually every area of social welfare by the strong-willed group of women and men who passed through Hull House en route to positions of significance in public life. Julia Lathrop became the first head of the U.S. Children's Bureau in 1912; Florence Kelley assumed a position of leadership in the National Consumer's League; Sophonisba Breckenridge, the first woman to be admitted to the Kentucky bar served as a noted professor at the University of Chicago School of Social Service Administration; the Abbott sisters, Grace and Edith, both became major contributors to social work practice and education following their days at Hull House; Harry Hopkins moved on to become a principal force in New Deal social reform; and Herbert Lehman became a governor, then U.S. senator from New York.

The settlement movement that emanated from the Hull House model was distinctive in that it looked beyond the individual to economic, political, and social conditions as an explanation for personal problems, including poverty; it utilized a pragmatic, experimental approach to acquiring knowledge of individuals and society; and it concentrated on the totality of problems in a single geographic area. It did not lose sight of the economic and social needs of individuals, but the central focus was on the experiences, thinking, and actions of local populations that could effect broad social and economic reform (Donna Franklin, 1986, p. 508).

The Progressive Era attacked political, economic, and social conditions. It was not a focused movement, but included a variety of antimonopoly, city beautification, civil service, governmental, and social reforms. In 1909 the National Association for the Advancement of Colored People (NAACP) was founded with two social workers, Mary White Ovington and Henry Moskowitz, among its organizers.

Progressives advocated prohibition, laws to outlaw prostitution, efforts to limit immigration, policies to limit child labor, and legislation to correct unsafe conditions in the workplace and to establish unemployment insurance. Traditional reformers were joined by journalists known as "muckrakers" in exposing the social problems of the time.

Progressive reformers' concern for children led President Roosevelt to convene the First White House Conference on Children in 1909. With settlement workers such as Lillian Wald of the Henry Street Settlement in the lead, campaigns for specialized health care for children culminated in the establishment of the New York City Bureau of Child Hygiene. In 1912, the federal government, in response to the intensive lobbying of women like settlement workers Lillian Wald and Florence Kelley, established the U.S. Children's Bureau to promote the health and welfare of the nation's children. Julia Lathrop, a resident of Hull House for two decades, became the bureau's first director.

It was also during the Progressive Era that women entered the political arena. In fact, in 1917, Jeannette Rankin, the first woman and the first social worker, was installed in the U.S. Congress. Then, in 1920, women finally achieved the right to vote with passage of the Nineteenth Amendment to the Constitution. The accomplishment of woman's suffrage, after almost three-quarters of a century of effort, was the result of a coming together of women across all class boundaries. Again, the efforts of settlement workers such as Florence Kelley and Jane Addams were instrumental in the final accomplishment of this social and political reform.

In 1921, Congress enacted the Sheppard–Towner Act, the first national health care program in the country's history. Most women saw its passage as a direct consequence of their new enfranchisement as voters. Its mandate was clear: to reduce the infant and maternal mortality rate. So was its strategy: to provide states with matching federal funds to establish prenatal and child health cen-

Introduction

"I just can't believe, with all the things to learn about being a social worker, that we're really going to spend all this time reading history. I'm in this class because I want to do something, not just memorize a bunch of dates," Tricia complained to Kimberley, who was sitting next to her. "I'm really not looking forward to the next two weeks." "Well, I don't want to memorize dates either, but some of those early women like Jane Addams are fascinating. I hope we get to learn more about them."

At this moment, the professor begins the day's lecture. "I suppose some of you may not be looking forward to this section of the class on the history of social work and social welfare. I know that you want to get on with learning about what social work is today and what social workers do today and will be doing in the future. But I think you'll find that the history, even the 650-year-old history of England, is very much present in our 'modern' social welfare legislation and our 'current' social welfare services.

"For example, let's take some articles from this week's newspapers to illustrate this point. How many of you saw the article in the Chronicle *entitled 'City Council Outlaws Panhandling on Downtown Streets'? Well, maybe the city council thinks this is a new problem and that theirs is a novel solution. However, England passed a similar law in 1536, more than 450 years ago.*

"As the workfare/welfare debate continues on the national scene, how many of you have thought about the connections to Charles Dickens's workhouses? The basic concepts and values remain unchanged throughout these centuries: The 'worthy' poor are taken care of; the 'unworthy' are treated as such.

"In last Sunday's edition of the Telegraph, *there was a big story with a lot of pictures about the charity golf tournament to aid the Homeless Coalition. Meanwhile, our mayor has repeatedly told the*

ters (David & Sheila Rothman, 1972, p. 136). To qualify for federal funds, states were required to set up separate units within their state departments of health that would coordinate state health programs with the Children's Bureau. Furthermore, the state agency had to create county agencies to administer the funds. All of this was intended to create a powerful and pervasive network of governmental bodies whose exclusive concern was child welfare. For all of the enthusiasm, successes and political influence of its supporters, Sheppard–Towner was not destined to be the model under which generations would receive health services. By 1929, the male-dominated medical establishment had mounted a campaign that eliminated it. Its defeat marked the end of female expertise in the field of health care and, at the same time, shifted responsibility for the provision of preventive health services from the public to the private sector. Women trained in hygiene working in state-supported, federally funded clinics were replaced by (generally male) physicians in private practice.

Other Progressive social reforms had greater longevity. These included the establishment of workmen's compensation, mothers pensions, juvenile courts, and child labor laws principally enacted in the period by local governments. Local reforms were needed, of course, but the nation desperately required programs with a wider scope. Most Americans of the period, however, even including some reformers, believed that social welfare issues belonged to local governments under the Constitution and by the precedent of the poor laws. This perception was reinforced by rulings of the U.S. Supreme Court restricting the federal government to activities that were specified by name in the Constitution. Progressive social reformers struggled to achieve fundamental changes in a society dominated by an emphasis on rugged individualism and survival of the fittest. Dependent on private contributions from the wealthy, they were challenged to fashion their attacks on poverty and social injustice from the ground up.

With the advent of World War I, these efforts stalled, in part because of widespread mistrust of liberal social philosophies, including socialism and anarchism, and in part because Sigmund Freud's theories of personality development gained popularity in the United States and diverted attention from social conditions to the diagnosis and treatment of individuals' psychiatric ills instead. Not coincidentally, it was during this period that social work be-

We Say So Much, Do So Little to Help Children

By James S. Mickelson

There exists in this nation a mythological belief that children and youth are valued. Almost anyone would acknowledge that children are the future and are important. Yet, as in so many spheres of American life, what we say about children and what we do about them are not always the same. Failing to recognize the discrepancy between our words and our actions, we delude ourselves into thinking that reality is what we say it is; that children are important to us.

Now we have the Cadillac of reports, a bipartisan, 519-page document from the national Commission on Children, released Monday. The title is *Beyond Rhetoric.* We at Children at Risk, a child-advocacy group in Houston, are skeptical of yet another report without action.

There is no dearth of statistical horrors documenting the plight of our children. Our publication released last fall, *Children at Risk,* is among those abundant with shocking statistics: One in five children lives in poverty; 2.5 million cases of child abuse occur annually; America's infant mortality rate is higher than such nations as Spain, Singapore and Hong Kong; every night, 100,000 American children go to sleep homeless.

It is unlikely that yet another report, even that by the National Commission on Children, will have any effect because we as a society cannot get beyond the rhetoric. What we say about children and what we do about them are not consistent. Even with this new, bigger and better report, we will fail to

came interested in issues of professionalism, including professional education and scientific methodology. Chapter 11 will describe these efforts and issues in more detail. Not until the depression of 1929 were Americans forced to recognize that significant social problems continued to exist in our society and that some social problems were not because of individual's faults.

Let's return one last time to our students. Lisa is asking, "I don't understand how children's issues are still such a national issue. We still have a lot of low weight babies and very little prenatal care. I didn't know that the federal government had established a children's bureau in 1912. Why recently in my home town there's been a lot of media attention to children's issues and some very sharp criticism about what we aren't doing." The professor walks to a pile of manilla folders and says, "Here it is. A recent editorial that might help answer your question, Lisa." She distributes this to the class.

perceive the dimensions of problems faced by our children and ultimately fail to take action. I have seen too many reports that failed to spur us to action. The facts appear to be we have a secret in this country: We hate kids.

Where are the Bush administration's priorities? Last year, the White House acknowledged that a major new investment in children would have a "big payoff" for American society in the long run, but it shelved the idea because it was not likely to show an immediate reward. It seems that we have $200 billion to throw at the savings and loan bailout; we throw billions at the HUD-FHA scandals; last year, we gave $8 billion in military aid to countries that our undereducated children can't even find on a map. Yet when it comes to children's needs, we are told, "You can't solve problems by throwing money at them."

But, just as economic investment is essential to the preservation and growth of a nation's economic capital, so is investment in a nation's children essential to the preservation and growth of its human capital. Children are, of course, more than simply raw human capital. They are our flesh and blood, the society of the future. The manner in which they are treated is a reliable indicator of how humane is the society to which they belong.

Politicians are always kissing babies. It makes for a good photo, but it is in reality the kiss of death.

For the sake of the children, the Children at Risk committee calls upon the U.S. Congress, the Texas Legislature, Harris County Commissioners Court and the Houston City Council to respond. We must respond quickly and cohesively to the cries of the children, much in the same way our country did for Kuwait. As the armed service personnel faced danger and death in the Persian Gulf, our children continue to face danger and death in our own back yard. Now is the time for our elected officials to act on what nonvoters need, not just cater to what voters want. We must go beyond the rhetoric.

Mickelson is chair of the Children at Risk committee, an advocacy group for children in the Houston area.

SOURCE: Houston Chronicle, 27 June 1991.

"Jahad, you look puzzled," the professor notes. "Well, I've been hearing a lot in my business classes about the mismanagement of not-for-profit social agencies. Didn't the Charity Organization Societies achieve any coordination or efficiency?"

"I think that will be answered in our next class session."

Summary

We hope that it is evident that social welfare is not a new concern of humans. Even before recorded history it is likely that some members of every clan or tribe assumed responsibility for orphaned children, widows, the aged, and sick, and injured members in their midst. As societies became larger and more complex, these roles gradually evolved from informal neighborliness and charity into what we know as the social welfare system.

In the United States it is traditional to trace the development of the social welfare system as evolving out of Western European, principally English, roots. Using this framework, the influence of many English social welfare practices is evident, particularly the Elizabethan Poor Laws, the Settlement House Movement, and the Charity Organization Societies.

One unifying theme for most of this period in both England and the United States was that the role of women in social welfare was largely invisible and undervalued. Despite the prominence of a few notables, most women who provided social welfare services did so with little fanfare, and, in some cases, in the face of social disapproval.

Competing values created a patchwork of federal, state, local, and private services. Ideological compromises, changing political and economic times, and improvements in scientific methodology continued to change the nature of services and the shape of the guiding policies.

References

Abbott, Edith. *Social Welfare and Professional Education.* Chicago: University of Chicago Press, 1931.

Axinn, June, and Levin, Herman. *Social Welfare: A History of the American Response to the Need,* 2nd ed. New York: Harper & Row, 1982.

Beard, Mary Rittner. *Women as a Force in History: A Study in Traditions and Realities.* New York: Octagon Books, 1976.

Briffault, Robert. *The Mothers,* vol. 1. New York: MacMillan, 1927.

Budge, Ernest Alfred Wallis. *The Papyrus of Ani.* New York: W. W. Norton, 1913.

Franklin, Donna. Mary Richmond and Jane Addams: From Moral Certainty to Rational Inquiry in Social Work. *Social Work Review,* Vol. *60* (Dec. 1986): 504–525.

Kingsley, Sherman C. "Who Needs Social Services." Presidential Address. *Proceedings of the National Conference of Social Work 1928,* 3–13. Chicago: University of Chicago Press, 1928.

Rauch, Julia. "Women in Social Work: Friendly Visitors Among the Poor." *Social Service Review,* Vol. 49, No. 2 (June 1975): 241–259.

Richmond, Mary. *The Good Neighbor in the Modern City.* Philadelphia: Lippincott, 1907.

Rothman, David, and Sheila Rothman, eds. *On Their Own: The Poor in Modern America.* Reading, MA: Addison-Wesley, 1972.

Trattner, Walter I. *From Poor Law to Welfare State: A History of Social Welfare in America.* New York: Free Press, 1974.

Webb, Sydney, and Beatrice Webb. *English Local Government: English Poor Laws History.* New York: Longmans, Green, 1927.

Woodroofe, Kathleen. *From Charity to Social Work in England and America.* Toronto: University of Toronto Press, 1962.

Worcester, D. L. W. *Grim the Battle.* New York: Exposition Press, 1954.

CHAPTER 3

Contemporary Social Welfare

Introduction

Jahad leans toward Kimberley, "I hope we get to the current stuff soon. Some of the students in my business class just keep talking about how much this country is spending on 'entitlement' programs, whatever they are, and saying that if there were fewer 'bleeding hearts' and more business-minded people involved, these programs wouldn't be costing so much and doing so little."

"I know," responds Kimberley. "Social workers and social programs keep getting a bad rap. All this negative image stuff will keep people from choosing this as a career. Somehow it's like social workers are to blame for the problems and are also responsible for all the solutions. It just doesn't seem fair."

The professor interrupts their discussion by saying, "As we begin the discussion of our more current welfare system, I thought that it would be interesting to hear from some people who were present and involved during some of these significant time periods.

"Our four guest speakers are Jennifer's grandmother, Ms. Grace Lloyd; Ryan, the senior aid to our state senator; Bob Chandler, current executive director of our local Neighborhood Center; and Dennis Richards, state commissioner of Human Services."

We have now traced the beginnings of formalized and structured social services and their development from private, voluntary, often religious or ethnic roots, to more developed organizations with some professional staff. However, throughout most of the 1920s, it should be evident that the federal government did not see a role for itself in either the funding or the delivery of social services, except for highly targeted and specialized populations such as veterans, the deaf, or the blind.

This chapter will describe the birth and growth of the U.S. "welfare state." Ideologically, the term *welfare state* refers to a belief that government is the only institution capable of bringing some measure of social justice to its citizens. The birth begins with the initiation of the Social Security Act in 1935 and develops through the creation of an entire federal bureaucracy with the enactment of the Equal Opportunity Act in 1964. The expansion of public funds and publicly supported services continued via the Title XX Amendments to the Social Security Act in 1974. The last part of this chapter will describe the restructuring and refinancing of these public programs via the Omnibus Budget Reconciliation Act of 1981 and the Gramm–Hollis–Rudman Act of 1985 under the New Federalism of presidents Reagan and Bush.

The Social Security Act of 1935

It is something of an understatement to suggest that World War I interrupted the Progressive Era. In almost every sense of the word, this war effectively brought social reform efforts to an end. The U.S. victory in the conflict, moreover, was taken to indicate the essential validity of the established U.S. social, economic, and political order. It would take another equally catastrophic event to change the widely held view of overall U.S. superiority.

That catastrophe was the Great Depression of 1929 and the aftermath of bankruptcies, suicides, stock market collapse, and deflated prices on practically everything. New responses to these events were somewhat slow in developing, despite the gravity of the economic conditions. Americans had weathered several significant depressions in the not-so-distant past, most notably in 1873 and 1893. The country had survived these without resorting to massive reform of its fundamental assumptions about relief; the initial expectation was that the depression of 1929 would be essentially the same.

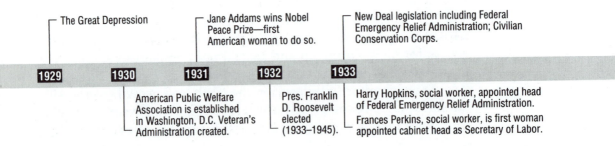

The Great Depression

Jane Addams wins Nobel Peace Prize—first American woman to do so.

New Deal legislation including Federal Emergency Relief Administration; Civilian Conservation Corps.

| 1929 | 1930 | 1931 | 1932 | 1933 |

American Public Welfare Association is established in Washington, D.C. Veteran's Administration created.

Pres. Franklin D. Roosevelt elected (1933–1945).

Harry Hopkins, social worker, appointed head of Federal Emergency Relief Administration.
Frances Perkins, social worker, is first woman appointed cabinet head as Secretary of Labor.

Pres. Herbert Hoover, a civil engineer by profession, had faith in the ability of the existing social welfare system—comprised mostly of voluntary private charities, such as the Red Cross and family service agencies—to rise to the occasion, as it had in the previous depressions. In this, he overestimated the resources of private charities and the precarious financial status of local and state governments, which themselves were very nearly insolvent. By 1932, 20 million people (of 123 million) were on the relief rolls. In many cities, more than 50 percent of the workers were unemployed (Nathan Cohen, 1958, p. 162).

The nation's confidence in Hoover and his social Darwinist faith in survival of the fittest wavered and finally expired in 1932. The Democrat Franklin D. Roosevelt was ushered into the White House amid hopes that he could put a stop to the nation's downward economic slide and restore the United States to the relative prosperity of the 1920s. Roosevelt's whole plan of action, which has come to be known collectively as the New Deal, brought important changes in almost every area of American life—not the least of which was in the social welfare arena. And, among the leadership he chose to construct and implement his New Deal programs were social worker Harry Hopkins, who directed the Federal Emergency Relief Administration, and social worker Frances Perkins, who was the first woman to head a cabinet department, the U.S. Department of Labor.

Social Reforms of the New Deal

Among the major reforms of the New Deal were those that emanated from the Social Security Act and became law in 1935. The act marked the shift from private and local social welfare to public

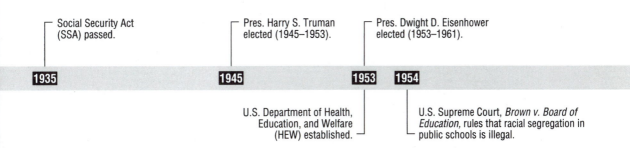

Social Security Act (SSA) passed.

Pres. Harry S. Truman elected (1945–1953).

Pres. Dwight D. Eisenhower elected (1953–1961).

1935   1945   1953   1954

U.S. Department of Health, Education, and Welfare (HEW) established.

U.S. Supreme Court, *Brown v. Board of Education,* rules that racial segregation in public schools is illegal.

social policies with an emphasis on tax support and federal leadership. Hopkins was also a member of the Committee on Economic Security. He outlined the central features of the Social Security Act in his remarks to the annual meeting of the American Public Welfare Association and National Conference of Social Work in May 1934:

> I cannot envisage any plan, or any scheme, or any legislation, that will eliminate the need for outdoor relief. I may be wrong about that, but I personally cannot envisage a plan that will eliminate the necessity for relief on an individualized family basis for a great many people. Therefore, in all these welfare departments there will be a section whose business it is to take care of people in emergencies, to give them outdoor relief. But there are very large groups in all cities and all counties in America, very large groups whose benefits should come to them in an orderly fashion. (Harry Hopkins, 1934, p. 398)

In his speech, Hopkins discussed the needs of the elderly, widows, and the totally unemployable. He also addressed issues in the field of public health, particularly national health insurance, unemployment insurance, and public housing.

The passage of the Social Security Act (SSA) in 1935, although intended as a temporary measure, was indeed the beginning of the U.S. public welfare state. It was federal legislation when previous social welfare legislation had been predominantly state and local and, at least for part of the legislation, it used taxes as the source of revenue.

The Social Security Act, much like its early Elizabethan predecessors, publicly defined and differentiated between the worthy and the unworthy poor. One group of worthy poor were those

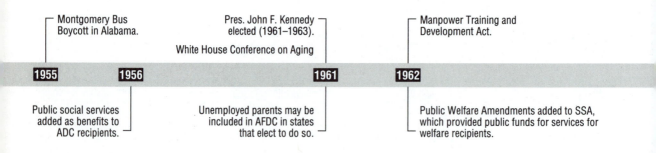

Montgomery Bus Boycott in Alabama.

Pres. John F. Kennedy elected (1961–1963).

White House Conference on Aging

Manpower Training and Development Act.

1955　　**1956**　　　　　　　**1961**　　**1962**

Public social services added as benefits to ADC recipients.

Unemployed parents may be included in AFDC in states that elect to do so.

Public Welfare Amendments added to SSA, which provided public funds for services for welfare recipients.

who had worked continuously and become poor through no fault of their own. The Great Depression, more clearly than ever before, demonstrated to the nation that people who had worked hard their entire lives could become poor overnight through no fault of their own. That is, people realized that U.S. workers had not (and likely would not) voluntarily saved enough to prevent poverty at the time of retirement or unexpected unemployment. Thus, the federal social insurance portion of the SSA was instituted to protect the working class by forcing savings.

The public assistance side employed a "needs test" and used public revenues (tax dollars). On the other hand, the social insurance side viewed these benefits as a "right" and used private revenue sources—that is, contributions made by the employer and the employee.

A predecessor to this program was the Federal Employees Retirement Program, which was begun in 1921. By 1931, 17 states had enacted their own old-age assistance programs. The initial portions of the Old Age and Survivors Act (OAS) afforded retirement and survivors benefits. In 1956, disability insurance was added, and in 1966, health insurance (Medicare). The act is now known as Old Age, Survivors, Disability, and Health Insurance (OASDHI).

Also for this group, the act created federal unemployment insurance, financed entirely by taxes on payrolls, to protect workers who became involuntarily unemployed. Incentives were provided to encourage states to become partners in the system. All states complied very shortly after the act was passed.

Other worthy groups were the blind, the disabled, children, and those elderly who had not been in the labor force. The public assistance portion of this act, not surprisingly, created categories of public aid that coincided with these groups: (1) Aid to the Blind (AB); (2) Aid to the Permanently and Totally Disabled (APTD); (3)

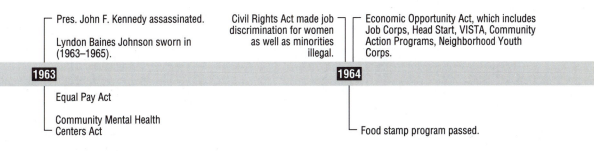

Pres. John F. Kennedy assassinated.

Lyndon Baines Johnson sworn in (1963–1965).

Civil Rights Act made job discrimination for women as well as minorities illegal.

Economic Opportunity Act, which includes Job Corps, Head Start, VISTA, Community Action Programs, Neighborhood Youth Corps.

1963

1964

Equal Pay Act

Community Mental Health Centers Act

Food stamp program passed.

Old Age Assistance (OAA); and (4) Aid to Dependent Children (ADC). Although these groups were deemed worthy of public aid, it was not seen as a right; recipients had to prove their need.

The mechanisms established required initial and continual eligibility determination to prove this need. This legislation also recreated the funding formulas of the federal–state match originated in 1921 with the Sheppard Towner Act. It was also significant that the passage of this act reversed the pattern laid by President Pierce's veto in 1848, which established state, not federal, responsibility in the welfare arena.

Finally, the public aid portion of this act set the pattern, through the present time, for federal mandates to states in the public welfare arena. States were required to follow the federal guidelines for the implementation and delivery of these four programs; states had to have all four programs; and these programs had to be administered under one centralized state agency: the Department of Public Welfare.

A fifth categorical program, called General Assistance, was established by this federal legislation for the unworthy poor. It covered those cases of economic hardship that did not fall into the aforementioned categories. However, states were not mandated to have this program, nor were any federal dollars provided. This gave the message that recipients of General Assistance were even less worthy than those in the previous four categories; not surprisingly, many states chose not to adopt this program.

Two important points should be highlighted: (1) There is a similarity in shape and intent between the 1935 SSA and the 1601 Elizabethan Poor Law; and (2) this 1935 act laid the foundation in structure and funding for U.S. public welfare until present times. The eligibility requirements, continual eligibility determinations, and the establishment of a public agency to provide this oversight, are not so far removed from their 300-year-old predecessors. The

Older Americans Act passed.

Pres. Lyndon Baines Johnson elected (1965–1969).
Wilbur Cohen, social worker, appointed Secretary of HEW.

National Organization for Women founded.

Work Incentive Program amendment to SSA.
Public Welfare amendments, which separated the social services delivery from financial eligibility determination.

1965　　**1966**　　**1967**

Medicare added to social insurance program of SSA.

Medicaid added to public assistance program of SSA.

"Feminization of Poverty" used to denote increased number of female-headed poor households.

fact that we are still debating the structure, function, and funding of the U.S. public welfare system attests to its staying power.

"I believe that Ms. Lloyd might want to provide some personal commentary here," the professor says.

"One of the advantages of being over 80 years old is being able to talk about this historic time in our history. Although my granddaughter sometimes groans when I start some of these stories, I, like many of you, thought that I could change the world, and, while I was still in school, I watched social workers do just that. I can remember some of the debates before the passage of the Social Security Act. Many of you probably have grandparents who talk about living through the depression, but I was in school studying social work in 1935. The New York School of Applied Philanthropy (now Columbia University) actively followed the issues and the debates. We read some of the reports of the Unemployment Committee of the National Federation of Settlements published in 1931. Helen Hall, who chaired that committee, was well known for her long service in the Henry Street Settlement in New York and was invited to our class to talk about that report. This was the first study about the effects of unemployment on the family (Marion Elderton, 1931).

"Indeed, one of our faculty traveled to hear her friend, Dorothy Kahn, executive director of the Jewish Welfare Society of Philadelphia, testify before the Senate Subcommittee on Manufacturers about unemployment. Ms. Kahn, it was reported, spoke personally and effectively from her perspective as a family social worker. She described the tragic results of unemployment, such as evictions, poor health, and strains on families. She presented figures that said that the amount of public relief available was less than one-fourth of the estimated need.

"I can tell you that it was very empowering at that time to know that social workers and some socially minded senators created the Federal Emergency Relief Administration in 1933 and the Social Security Act in 1935. I had gone into social work because I wanted

| Pres. Richard M. Nixon elected (1969–1974). | Equal Rights Amendment approved by Congress, sent to states for ratification. | U.S. Supreme Court in *Roe v. Wade* repeals abortion laws.

Child Abuse Prevention Act | Gerald Ford assumes presidency (1974–1977).

Comprehensive Employment and Training Act (CETA) passed. |
|---|---|---|---|
| **1969** | **1972** | **1973** | **1974** |
| President Nixon proposes the Family Assistance Plan and national health insurance. | Supplemental Security Income Programs (SSI) combine previous separate categorical forms of public assistance for adult poor, aged, blind, and disabled. | | Title XX Amendments to SSA fund personal social services to the near poor, not just current welfare recipients. |

to change the world and I got an early opportunity to watch social workers, women especially, do just that. Of course, I didn't realize at that time just how long-lasting the effects of these New Deal policies would be."

Legislative initiatives during the four-term presidency of Franklin D. Roosevelt made striking efforts to effect change in most of these areas, breaking much new ground in the territory of social welfare. Other aspects of the New Deal included public housing and public health measures.

As far-reaching and innovative as New Deal reforms were, however, they did not address the needs of many minorities and women. Racial discrimination against African Americans remained strong throughout the country. African Americans were forced to live in segregated neighborhoods, attend segregated schools, use different public facilities, and sit at the rear of public transportation. The economic conditions bolstered racial tensions, which grew out of competition for scarce jobs between individuals of color and whites. African Americans were often the first to be laid off in factories or on the farm, and were further victimized by poll taxes—such as fees for voter registration—literacy tests, and by discriminatory marketing practices in housing.

Hispanics constituted the majority of agricultural workers in the Southwest by 1930. Farm workers were not covered by New Deal labor legislation, and therefore were denied collective bargaining rights that were otherwise enforced by the federal government. Agricultural wages were depressed greatly by the illegal immigration of Mexicans into the United States along the borders of Texas, Arizona, and California. Many Spanish-speaking individuals were deported to Mexico during the years following the depression in an effort to control welfare expenditures.

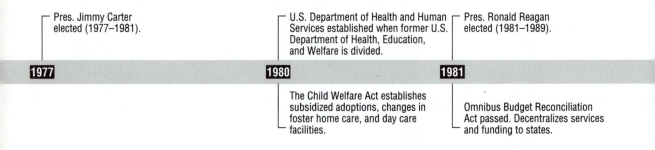

Pres. Jimmy Carter elected (1977–1981).

U.S. Department of Health and Human Services established when former U.S. Department of Health, Education, and Welfare is divided.

Pres. Ronald Reagan elected (1981–1989).

1977   **1980**   **1981**

The Child Welfare Act establishes subsidized adoptions, changes in foster home care, and day care facilities.

Omnibus Budget Reconciliation Act passed. Decentralizes services and funding to states.

Women were unable to capitalize on their newly won right to vote during the New Deal era, because they failed to reach consensus on a legislative agenda representing their collective social interests. Some women, including Eleanor Roosevelt, favored legislation to protect women; others supported the passage of an equal rights amendment to the Constitution to promote equal opportunity. Few social measures passed during this period had positive consequences for women. However, many more women joined the work force out of economic necessity, which resulted in a substantially expanded perception of "women's work."

Although birth control clinics remained illegal in many states in the 1930s, the majority of married and middle-class women secured family planning information from their private physicians. Abortions were illegal in every state, but illegal abortions were almost universally available to those who could afford them, albeit sometimes at the risk of a woman's life. Women remained discriminated against in both obvious and subtle ways across the whole social order. For women of color, the discrimination was doubly oppressive.

Despite these shortcomings, the development of social legislation during the New Deal brought changes in the lives of many U.S. citizens. From the vantage point of history it is comparatively easy to highlight its deficiencies, but, on balance, the New Deal is more remarkable for what it did accomplish than for what it did not. The New Deal created a national welfare state that took the place of, added to, or probably as accurately, introduced local programs. It also created social programs rather than focusing solely on regulation of the poor. By going beyond the legalistic approach of the Progressives, Roosevelt drastically altered the scope of U.S. public welfare (Bruce Jansson, 1988, p. 150).

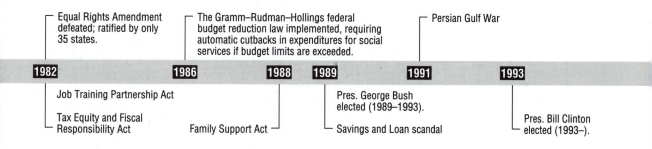

Equal Rights Amendment defeated; ratified by only 35 states.

The Gramm–Rudman–Hollings federal budget reduction law implemented, requiring automatic cutbacks in expenditures for social services if budget limits are exceeded.

Persian Gulf War

1982 **1986** **1988** **1989** **1991** **1993**

Job Training Partnership Act

Tax Equity and Fiscal Responsibility Act

Family Support Act

Pres. George Bush elected (1989–1993).

Savings and Loan scandal

Pres. Bill Clinton elected (1993–).

Postwar Welfare Reform: The 1940s and 1950s

Immediately following the New Deal, and during the years following World War II, there was a period of economic growth and relative quiescence in the field of social welfare, particularly welfare reform. The war decreased unemployment and expanded the numbers of women, retirees, and minorities in the labor force. There was some income redistribution favoring low income groups and there was an increase in personal savings due to the restrictions on the availability of goods combined with generally higher incomes. During this time there were also some improvements in public health measures, primarily because health exams required during the draft illuminated many health problems.

Following the war, conservatives were unable to dismantle the New Deal programs as they had hoped, but liberals were also unable to muster support for new social agendas as they had dreamed. The principal contribution of the Republican administration of Pres. Dwight Eisenhower (1952–1960) was the creation of the Department of Health, Education, and Welfare as a cabinet-level post in 1953. The 1950s were notable primarily for significant migration of African Americans from the cities and farms of the South to the North and for the beginnings of the civil rights movement. Promises of increased access to the political system and reduced barriers to education, employment, and housing maintained relatively quiet race relations until 1954. In that year, the Supreme Court decision, *Brown v. Board of Education*, ruled that "separate but equal" facilities in education were not, in fact, equal. Then in 1955, there was the Montgomery Bus Boycott in Alabama.

The initiation of public social services, not just public assistance, also began during this period. The demographics of recipients of these social welfare programs changed: There were fewer elderly recipients of Old Age Assistance (OAA) and more of Aid to Dependent Children (ADC). In 1956 the provision of social services was added to ADC programs, permitting publicly funded services, such as counseling, to be delivered to the beneficiaries of the financial program. In 1962 the ADC program was changed to aid caretaker parents and the name was changed to Aid to Families with Dependent Children (AFDC). However, the 1950s brought in the threat of communism and the perception, now that the effects of the depression were fading, that the newly created public programs were the initial step toward a Communist state. The role of "witch hunts" in attempting to find the so-called Communists in Congress also led to the infamous "midnight raids" on the homes of welfare recipients, primarily the recipients of AFDC. These raids were to assure that there were no able-bodied men in the household of women receiving this aid.

During this period poverty was rediscovered in America (John K. Galbraith, 1958; Michael Harrington, 1962) and there was renewed criticism of the public programs. There were concerns that these public programs were not working: That is, they had not eradicated poverty and reduced the welfare rolls. The economic recessions of 1948, 1953, 1957, and 1961, and rising unemployment only strengthened these concerns.

The Great Society: The 1960s

In 1960, Democrat John Kennedy became president at a time when the nation was becoming increasingly aware of its minorities and the underprivileged. Various explanations for their problems were advanced, and some of these "new" structural and cultural theories bore striking resemblance to the explanations of poverty popularized by workers in the early private charities. In any event, theoretical explanations were accompanied by a social welfare legislative and action agenda that emphasized reform of individuals rather than reform of the social order.

Kennedy attempted to walk a tightrope in handling mounting pressures by racial minorities, particularly African Americans, to achieve fundamental social change. Adopting the tactic of nonviolent protest, the civil rights movement had effectively made the concerns of citizens of color increasingly visible and valid. The activities of white extremists in the period were more often portrayed with accuracy in the media, and public support for minority concerns in general and civil rights in particular rose accordingly. In the early 1960s, efforts to bring about change focused on registering African-American voters in Southern states. This was an effort joined by thousands of middle-class white college students, further attesting to the growing acceptance of an egalitarian social and political order.

Voter registration activities and nonviolent protests in the South were often challenged by violence. In some cases the violence appeared to be sanctioned by elected or appointed officials, including governors, mayors, state legislators, members of Congress, public school superintendents, and university presidents. Kennedy finally took action to create federal protection for the civil rights of all citizens, but his proposed legislation did not pass Congress before his assassination in November 1963.

During this same time, women's family and employment patterns, which had slowly begun to change during the post–World War II era, reflected clearer trends. Declining birthrates, liberalized sexual norms, the growing number of female-headed households, and most importantly, the entry of women into the labor force in unprecedented numbers exposed gender discrimination and inequality (Mimi Abramovitz, 1992, p. 98).

Kennedy had established the Commission on the Status of Women in 1961, and although the commission's 1963 report documented gender inequality, it nevertheless opposed the Equal Rights Amendment (ERA), remained silent on the issue of birth control, and did not refute the notion that "a woman's place is in the home." On the other hand, the passage of the Equal Pay Act in 1963 signaled a federal commitment to eliminating gender-based discrimination (Leila Rupp and Verta Taylor, 1987).

During his brief tenure in office, Kennedy was unable to fulfill campaign promises to secure federal aid to education or medical insurance for the elderly; these were two measures that he favored strongly. However, his Manpower Development and Training Act of 1962 was signed into law, as was legislation in 1961 creating the Area Redevelopment Agency. He also supported the 1963 Community Mental Health Centers Act, which further expanded the public role and responsibility in the area of mental health by focusing on outpatient services, by mandating services, and by establishing geographic and population based "catchment areas."

Kennedy's welfare advisors also formulated and passed the 1962 public welfare amendments. This was an ill-fated "services strategy" for recipients of Aid to Families with Dependent Children (AFDC), most of whom were female. The strategy involved a substantial match of federal funds for local dollars to support the provision of social services in an effort to help women get off welfare and

eliminate welfare "abuse." Unwittingly perhaps, Kennedy also contributed to the creation of new social and political schisms in the
United States by launching the fastest buildup of the military during any period of peace and by introducing military advisors to
South Vietnam.

When Vice-President Lyndon B. Johnson assumed leadership
of the Democratic party and the nation in a military jet somewhere
between Dallas, Texas, and Washington, D.C., on 22 November
1963, few Americans—least of all those involved in social welfare—
could guess the impact of an assassin's bullet on the future course
of history. Johnson was able to achieve a level of success in social
welfare that nearly approached that of his former mentor, Franklin
Roosevelt. Federal legislation emerged from Johnson's conception
of the Great Society: legal aid for the poor, medical insurance for
the elderly, federal assistance for public schools, health care for the
poor, job training for disadvantaged youths, enforcement of civil
rights for members of minority groups, nutritional and health programs for women and young children, community development
programs, and health care for migrant workers.

Johnson pushed the concept of federal responsibility into
every corner of U.S. life with consummate political skills honed by
a lifetime of legislative experience in state and federal elected offices. Johnson took a strong stand on civil rights and his position
resulted in the passage of the Civil Rights Act of 1964, a landmark
piece of legislation that protected voting rights, required the desegregation of public facilities, and mandated nondiscrimination on
the basis of gender and race in the employment practices of any
business or institution receiving any type of federal funds.

Furthermore, the Food Stamp Program was created in 1964
under the direction of the U.S. Department of Agriculture. One innovation of the program made food coupons available not only to
families on welfare, but to families of the working poor whose income fell below a level established statistically by the federal government—euphemistically called "the poverty line." Once again, it
is not difficult to see the relationship between the philosophy of the
Elizabethan bread scale and our modern version of the poverty line.

Both Medicaid and Medicare legislation were passed a year
later as amendments to the Social Security Act (Titles XVIII and
XIX). Medicare vested the federal government with primary responsibility for its implementation, but Medicaid was created as a
matching grant program, with the federal government providing

the monies and state governments assuming policy and administrative roles in determining how and for whom the funds would be used. As noted earlier in this chapter, Medicare was added as the health insurance benefits to the social insurance program of the SSA, whereas Medicaid was added to the public assistance portion.

The War on Poverty

Johnson next attacked the problems of the economically distressed head-on, actually declaring a "War on Poverty" along several fronts. Whereas the Social Security Act had focused on money, the War on Poverty focused on opportunity. Within the rediscovery of poverty, definitions of cultural deprivation, and geographically defined pockets of poverty were described. Resultant programs were aimed at improving opportunities and were targeted at youth, rural poverty, employment and training, and education. Specific programs included the Job Corps, the Neighborhood Youth Corps, Work Incentive Program (WIN), Volunteers in Service to America (VISTA), and Community Action Programs (CAP). CAPs further included programs such as Head Start, Legal Aid, Upward Bound, and Planned Parenthood.

The programs, which included training, public health, food distribution, and rent subsidies, were so diverse that no fewer than six federal departments wanted the control of these new and substantial dollars. To avoid the obvious political dilemma, once again the federal government created a new bureaucracy, the Office of Economic Opportunity (OEO), to deliver these programs. A few programs were parceled out to other departments, but the largest number remained under the OEO.

However, this time there was a new twist in the flow of funds. There was no state administrative structure required because these programs were to be planned, delivered, and administered at the local level. "Maximum feasible citizen participation" became a goal, and *grantsmanship*—the ability to write appealing proposals—became the funding mechanism rather than money allocated on the basis of population size.

Another innovative aspect of this "opportunity" approach allowed nonprofit and nongovernmental organizations to provide these public services via contracting mechanisms. However, these innovative aspects also caused the greatest issues. Bypassing state and city governments meant threatening these governmental enti-

The signing ceremony on 6 August for the Voting Rights Act of 1965. President Lyndon Baines Johnson greets civil rights leaders, the Reverends Ralph David Abernethy and Martin Luther King, Jr., both of the Southern Christian Leadership Conference.

ties because they had no control. For example, the establishment of public legal services at local levels created organizations that could sue the very governmental entities that had no programmatic control over them. Although competitive grantsmanship was viewed as innovative (as was opening this up to nonprofits), it did not always succeed. The greatest dollars were not always channeled to the neighborhood "pockets of poverty" with the greatest need, and often went to those agencies with the greatest sophistication at grant writing.

Mounting public concern over the increasing size of AFDC rolls was countered by the welfare amendments of 1967, a confusing mixture of incompatible policies that ultimately satisfied no one (Bruce Jansson, 1988, p. 171). Before 1967, all services provided to AFDC recipients were delivered by one worker who was responsible for financial as well as social services. These amendments limited caseload size and separated the financial from the social service function.

The term *feminization of poverty* was coined to describe the fact that the number of female-headed households had significantly increased and led ultimately to a high dependence of women on the welfare system. The reasons were complex, but certainly among them were death, divorce, and desertion. These circumstances left unskilled women with a choice between a low paying job or welfare. The absence of day care became a substantial barrier to female employment as well as a continuing public issue; other obstacles included allowable child care costs, the unemployed parent clause, and the ineligibility of pregnant women with no other children. The Work Incentive Now (WIN) program, which funded job training programs for women and day care, was a partial solution to these issues.

Women were encouraged by the successes of minority and civil rights groups and pushed for inclusion in civil rights statutes. Betty Friedan gave a new sense of urgency to women's issues with the publication of *The Feminine Mystique* in 1963 and its emphasis on "real" equality with men. Congress responded more readily than usual with passage of an Equal Pay Act that same year and inclusion of gender discrimination in Title VII of the Civil Rights Act of 1964.

> Despite these changes, the women's movement was soon issuing far more radical proposals. Amazing as it may seem . . . , the organizers of the National Organization for Women (NOW) in 1966 believed that ending sexual discrimination in the work place and establishing a network of day care centers would immediately accomplish the social and economic equality of women. (Jack Rothman, Joseph Teresa, and John Erlich, 1978, p. 243)

In 1967, one year after its creation, NOW turned its attention from securing enforcement of the 1964 Title VII Amendments to the Civil Rights Act to the passage of an equal rights amendment to the U.S. Constitution.

President Johnson's ability to further develop his program of social legislation in a second elected term of office was rendered impossible by his military agenda in Vietnam. As the war effort escalated and claimed the lives of increasing numbers of young Americans, Johnson's popularity with the electorate plunged. In the end, his political ambitions were another casualty of the most unpopular war in U.S. history.

"The sixties were another period of time I wish I had been part of," says Kimberley wistfully, looking, especially today, much like a flower child herself. *"People were angry; they marched; they got things accomplished. Where did that activism go?"*

"Let's hear about that activism from our second guest, Bob Chandler."

"While I was listening to Ms. Lloyd, I couldn't help feeling the same excitement that I remember as a community organization student when I was in graduate school in the 1960s. Despite my father's disappointment, I went into social work instead of law. And, I think you'll be interested to hear, I never regretted that decision.

"I remember it as a frightening time as well as one when change seemed possible. I also remember thinking that it surely couldn't be too hard to figure out how to give people more access to programs that would keep them out of poverty. Lately, though, I wonder whether we've made much progress."

Lisa asks, "It seems like there were so many good ideas and that the country really wanted to win the War on Poverty. What went wrong?"

"I guess that I've come to realize that, first of all, it isn't simple to identify what went wrong. Some of the initiatives of the War on Poverty are still around, still working—like Head Start; like my own agency, which was created from the Community Action funds; like community health clinics; legal aid. Another thing to realize is that in the enthusiasm, people also believed in 'quick fixes.' Poverty, the kind due to lack of education, unequal job opportunities, lack of positive role models, isn't fixed in a year, or even a couple of years. Investment in helping people have better lives is a long-term investment—we still can't seem to figure that out.

"Looking back, another extremely important and obvious lesson is that social programs cost money and if the solution doesn't seem immediate, people feel the funds that come from their tax dollars have probably been misused. So, the normal response, which we have now seen in the 1970s and the 1980s, is to ask for more accountability of the dollars and cut back total expenditures. This is probably a good place to return to that next time period."

The Era of Accountability: The 1970s

The presidency changed both hands and parties with the 1968 election of Richard Nixon. One social welfare historian termed the following 12 years "the paradoxical era" (Bruce Jansson, 1988, p. 179) because Nixon and his successors—Republican Gerald Ford

(1974–1976) and Democrat Jimmy Carter (1976–1980)—were relatively conservative presidents who had little outward interest in social reform. But despite this apparent lack of interest, federal spending on social programs increased dramatically. As we shall see, concerns to reduce poverty and get people off the welfare rolls and to assure that only the worthy received benefits may have been the conservative goals; but the operationalization of these programs cost increasing tax dollars.

Social welfare reforms enacted in Nixon's first term included the Supplemental Security Income (SSI) Program, significant revisions in the food stamp program, revenue sharing, the addition of Title XX to the Social Security Act, consolidation of social services, the addition of family planning initiatives to the Public Health Act, establishment of the Occupational Safety and Health Administration (OSHA), indexing the Social Security Program to changes in costs of living, and the establishment of federal policies that resulted in the desegregation of Southern schools.

Two of Nixon's first-term proposals, the Family Assistance Program and national health insurance, were not passed by Congress. Other legislation, initiated during his presidency, was passed after his resignation from office, including the Comprehensive Employment and Training Act (CETA) of 1974, the Community Development Block Grant Program (Title XX) of 1974, the Rehabilitation Act of 1973, and the Child Abuse Prevention Act of 1973.

These programs significantly increased the responsibility of the public for "private troubles." Public monies—federal, state, and local—expanded to cover these new programs. Federal and state guidelines for program structure and client eligibility became normative, as did the required match in the funding formulas.

Supplemental Security Income (SSI) was less a new program than a restructuring of the categorical programs from the public assistance portion of the SSA. The SSI further delineated the worthy from unworthy poor by grouping the Aid to the Permanently and Totally Disabled (APTD), Aid to the Blind (AB), and Old Age Assistance (OAA) under this program and changing it from state to federal administration. This separation left the AFDC as the only federally aided "welfare" program, which made it an easier target for attention and criticism. To be fair, the rationale was not entirely for that purpose. These programs, unlike the AFDC, could have only one determination of eligibility instead of repeated ones; they were not "needs tested" programs and could be federally administered through the Social Security Administration.

Once again the country's concern was that the War on Poverty had not been won through the opportunity strategy. Consequently, the backbone of the Title XX amendments to the SSA passed in 1974 were support services and prevention. For the first time, federal dollars were able to be used to "prevent economic dependency," and programs such as planned parenthood, information and referral, and day care were included. With the precedent of the Economic Opportunity Act (EOA), these services could be provided by non-profit, nongovernmental agencies on a contractual basis.

These accomplishments are paradoxical because they were accompanied by a steady stream of critical rhetoric from President Nixon: Nixon tried to discredit Lyndon Johnson's domestic welfare record by criticizing federal involvement in social welfare, exaggerating welfare fraud, and attacking liberalism in general. Nixon incurred the wrath of the social welfare field with verbal attacks on social workers, child development staff, psychologists, psychiatrists, and community activists. However, he reflected the sentiments of many conservative citizens who by the election in 1972 had become preoccupied with issues of crime, inflation, and government spending.

Once again the public was dismayed at the growth in the welfare state without seeing any accompanying reduction in poverty. Many of the measures enacted were managerial and/or structural rather than substantive programmatic mechanisms. In fact, although Title XX poured new federal dollars into public social services and into expanding the targeted beneficiaries, it also included increased mechanisms of accountability.

Although the funding was once again expanded for public social services, the overarching goal of this legislation was "to keep people off welfare." The country was tired of "do gooders" who had not alleviated poverty. Accountability measures were introduced here, and the language of evaluation, like cost/benefit analysis and determining and comparing unit cost of service, was developed.

"Well, what's wrong with that?" Jason asks. "Shouldn't we be able to ask where our tax money goes and whether it's doing any good?"

"Yes," Dennis Richards responds, "but when the questions aren't the right ones to answer and when the tasks of accountability

become more time consuming than service delivery, we've probably gone too far in the other direction. Unfortunately, it took us too long to recognize and counter the shift.

"I was a program director at a family service agency when the Title XX amendments passed. Our executive director called a management meeting to explain how this would change who we could serve, how we would get funded, and how we would have to keep records of these monies differently from all other funds. But we were excited anyway. We would finally be able to provide services not just to those already on welfare but to low income people so that we could prevent them from going on welfare.

"Our agency budget grew and so did our client population. But because the requirements of this new money also mandated that at least 50 percent of clients in any service funded had to be welfare recipients, in order to serve the near poor, we had to find and serve the already poor. In our state and in many others, the unintended consequence of this program was increasing welfare rolls.

"Another headache, for some agencies so great that they finally stopped applying for these funds, was that they were on a reimbursable basis and the federal government did not quickly reimburse. The paperwork was incredible and the cash flow for many agencies became too difficult to balance."

"Why didn't anybody realize that as they were proposing the legislation?" LaDonna pondered out loud.

During the same time as the initiation of some of this social service legislation, many African Americans espoused black separatism and black power. Prominent sports figures such as Cassius Clay (Muhammad Ali) and Lew Alcindor (Kareem Abdul Jabbar) changed their names to more accurately reflect their African "roots." Militant gays and lesbians organized and demanded that their sisters and brothers come out of the closet and into the mainstream of U.S. social life. Native Americans staged protests, recapturing tribal lands and demanding the enforcement of treaties that had been ignored for centuries. Hispanics in California fields staged strikes and engaged the support of liberals and moderates for boycotts of agricultural products such as lettuce and grapes. And handicapped and aging Americans began to advocate for an end to their treatment as second-class citizens.

Radical feminists advocated for the solidarity of all women. In 1972, Congress passed the ERA although it was ultimately defeated. However, its near victory and the 1973 Supreme Court decision, *Roe v. Wade*, to legalize abortion, signaled a strengthening and coalescing of the fight against male domination, on-the-job sexual harassment, and domestic violence.

However, efforts to mobilize these disparate groups with little in common except the common experiences of being ignored, oppressed, or both, alienated many Americans. Nixon turned this alienation to his political advantage in the 1972 election, accomplishing a further polarizing of national interests in his campaign against the considerably more liberal Democratic candidate George McGovern.

In his scandal-plagued second term, Nixon used the overwhelming support of the electorate as a mandate to wage war against any element of the federal government he perceived as liberal. This war was brought to an early end by Nixon's resignation in the aftermath of the Watergate scandal.

For a brief time, the nation's life was permeated by an atmosphere of anxiety. Gerald Ford, who had become vice-president with the resignation of Spiro Agnew in the wake of an earlier Nixon administration scandal, took office. For the first time in U.S. history, a president who had not been elected by the people as either president or vice-president assumed leadership.

Ford turned out to have no particular national domestic agenda, especially in the area of social welfare. The Democratic majorities in the House and Senate were able to increase funding for school lunches, education, health care, and the unemployed. Ford's two years in office can be best characterized as a continuing standoff between conservatives and liberals over the size of social spending (Bruce Jansson, 1988, p. 191).

Following the political excesses of Watergate, the U.S. public installed the closest thing to a nonpolitician in the Oval Office. Jimmy Carter, a relatively obscure former governor of Georgia, made a name for himself on the campaign trail by attacking the federal bureaucracy, particularly its assumption of responsibility for so many aspects of U.S. life. Whereas his attacks on Washington excesses and support for human rights gained him the support of some liberals, his moral values brought him the support of some conservatives. Moderates were attracted by his emphasis on big business, internationalism, and his interest in efficiency and honesty in government. Together these disparate elements provided him with enough votes to slip past Ford into the presidency.

In 1977, Carter introduced a plan for the reformation of the

In *Roe vs. Wade* (February, 1973), attorney Sarah Weddington successfully argued before the United States Supreme Court that women should be permitted the right to legal abortion.

U.S. public welfare system, but the plan was rejected by Congress. In 1979, he introduced a national health care plan, which met a similar fate. To the dismay of feminists, Carter was an outspoken critic of abortion and supported a constitutional amendment to overrule the 1973 U.S. Supreme Court decision of *Roe v. Wade*, which had rendered most state prohibitions on abortion unconstitutional. He supported legislation that severely limited the ability of poor women to secure abortions, even though they were legal, by prohibiting the use of Medicaid funds for such procedures.

By 1979, Carter's popular support had eroded significantly.

Gasoline prices were at a record high, the economy was faltering, Americans were being held hostage in Iran, and Carter was unable to mobilize the government to significantly improve any of these conditions. Actor-turned-politician Ronald Reagan landed the role of a lifetime when he was swept into office by a landslide in 1980. By the time he turned the presidency over to his vice-president, George Bush, in 1989, Reagan had turned in a performance certain to be remembered among social welfare advocates.

The New Federalism: The 1980s

Reagan's presidency was marked by the 1981 passage of the Omnibus Budget Reconciliation Act (OBRA), which resulted in significant and systematic funding reductions to social programs. The creation of the Presidential Task Force on Regulatory Relief further spawned the 1982 passage of the Job Training Partnership Act (JTPA), which replaced many CETA public service job training programs by "private sector initiatives." The 1982 Tax Equity and Fiscal Responsibility Act (TEFRA) raised corporate taxes and reduced federal spending on social programs simultaneously. Additional amendments to the Social Security Act increased the retirement age, reduced some benefits, and taxed some pension benefits.

OBRA's budget cuts resulted in a 11.7 percent reduction in AFDC funding, stiffer eligibility requirements, and a 19 percent reduction in food stamp funding. The poverty rate in 1984 rose to 15.3 percent, higher than any year since the early 1960s (Howard Karger, 1992, p. 6). These measures were furthered during his second term by the 1986 passage of the Gramm–Rudman–Hollings Act, also known as the Balanced Budget and Emergency Deficit Control Act.

Economist Robert Lekachman (1982) wrote an exposition on Reagan's economic and social policies:

> Ronald Reagan must be the nicest president who ever destroyed a union, tried to cut school lunch milk rations from six to four ounces, and compelled families in need of public help to first dispose of household goods in excess of $1,000.
>
> This amiable gentleman's administration has been engaged in a massive redistribution of wealth and power

for which the closest precedent is Franklin Roosevelt's New Deal, with the trifling difference that FDR sought to alleviate poverty and Ronald Reagan enthusiastically enriches further the already obscenely rich. (p. 3)

Many of these economic changes grew out of a perspective known as supply-side economics. In theory, the supply-side point of view holds that tax cuts to the very wealthy and big corporations will eventually translate into, or "trickle down" to, more jobs for the employable and more philanthropic activities to assist those in need. Supply-side economics contributed to the continuing decline of U.S. social welfare, adding to ground already lost in the previous three decades.

As the United States entered the 1990s, our federal social welfare system was in a state of collapse. Federal policies and practices were directed toward returning responsibility for public relief and other social programs to the states. The growth of private charities was encouraged and the value of volunteers in the provision of social services repeatedly stressed. However, the notion that these reductions in public dollars would be matched by increases in charity and benevolent support proved to be entirely theoretical.

With the twenty-first century on the horizon, it was impossible to determine how far back our social welfare system would have to retreat to look for old solutions to meet both new and worsening social problems, including:

Acquired Immune Deficiency Syndrome (AIDS)
pervasive abuse of illegal substances
a sharp increase in serious crime
steep adolescent pregnancy rates
high infant and maternal mortality rates
increased incidence of Fetal Alcohol Syndrome
high rates of child physical and sexual abuse
spiraling school drop out rates
significantly decreasing school achievement
a rising tide of homeless individuals
significant increases in domestic violence

These complex and interconnected social problems needed attention. Also there was continuing pressure from members of marginalized populations such as lesbians and gays, African Americans, Hispanics, Southeast Asian immigrants, the handicapped, and women to secure equal protection under the law. At the same time, society as a whole was attempting to adjust expectations and standards of living to a society based on technology rather than industry, and the result was more factions warring over fewer dollars.

The central thrust of the Reagan presidential agenda was to return to the former model of social services as charity, delivered by well-meaning volunteers, to the worthy poor. Because the enormity of the federal deficit had to be acknowledged and solutions offered, President Reagan chose to slash domestic social services and return decision making to local units. Thus, President Reagan was "the first president since Franklin D. Roosevelt to challenge the federal ideology of his time. His alternative vision of federalism can be summarized in three phrases: 'separation of powers,' 'devolution of responsibilities to governments that are closer to the people,' and 'less spending by all levels of government.' " Each of these had powerful antecedents in conservative thought (George Peterson, 1984, p. 223).

The deficit was explained by focusing not on escalating military expenditures but on public social service costs. Social welfare programs—and social workers—had not cured poverty despite huge investments of federal funds. Once again, welfare reform focused on overhauling the traditional systems rather than on developing new ways of responding to emerging problems like illiteracy, high school dropouts, teen pregnancies, homelessness, and unemployment (Karen Haynes and James Mickelson, 1992, p. 170).

The rhetoric in the early 1980s emphasized the "safety net" for the worthy poor. But the passage of the Gramm–Rudman Balanced Budget and Emergency Deficit Control Act of 1986 signaled that the definition of safety net meant benefit cuts and other reductions in virtually every low income entitlement program. Federal assurance continued that state and local governments and philanthropic associations would replace the lost federal dollars and that waste and fraud would be reduced.

"But the government had to cut spending. People were angry that they were just paying more in taxes while some people just lived off society—at least that's what I remember hearing," Jason states in a confused voice.

The professor asks, "Did any of you see the recent editorial on Social Security in the paper last week? If not, I'll pass it out."

"Can I answer that?" Ryan asks. "I was helping run the sena-

Washington's Shell Game with Social Security

By Martin L. Gross

The great unresolved government scandal of our time is the abuse of Social Security taxes—plus the misuse of that money over the years—by the Congress and the president.

Today, the abuse has become endemic. In 1992, the government will "borrow"—a euphemism for "steal"—$50 billion from the Social Security fund and use it to pay the general bills of its bloated bureaucracy.

That's not a one-year aberration. It's been going on for some time, and the Social Security fund now has government IOUs for $330 *billion.* In no time, the government will have taken $1 trillion from the aged, money that could and should be used to increase benefits or lower Social Security taxes.

The problem started in 1935 when FDR put through the Federal Old Age Insurance and Survivors Act, which set up the system. It was called the Social Security Trust Fund, but that's only rhetoric. The money was never really segregated, or in trust, and the government constantly borrowed from it.

Where did all this recent surplus money come from? In 1983, Congress and the president, seeking to "save" the system, raised Social Security taxes, creating an enormous pool of money. It's estimated that there will be a $6 *trillion* surplus by the year 2030. But will the money really be there? Not if the profligate federal government continues to take it, as it is now doing.

Washington is playing a nasty shell game with aged citizens' money. By using this surplus as part of the general fund instead of borrowing money on the outside, they can pretend that the deficit is smaller than it really is. A true accounting in 1992 would show a $450 billion deficit instead of the $400 billion claimed.

If the government didn't cheat its aged, Social Security taxes, which are too high, could be lowered considerably without affecting benefits. Or, the surplus could be invested in such guaranteed bonds as Fannie Maes, starting the Social Security fund on a growth pattern like other pension plans.

If we had done that 60 years ago, our senior citizens would now be comfortable retirees.

But the least we can do today is to stop cheating our aged.

The High Status Skies

The United States government owns and operates 1,200 airplanes, with pilots, airfields, mechanics, and all that's needed to keep them aloft.

So? Every country needs an air force to protect itself, doesn't it? Since when are military aircraft a novelty?

But these are not military planes. These are civilian aircraft of 100 different varieties owned and operated by *civilian* government agencies like the Departments of Energy and Transportation. Their purpose? Mainly to fly their executives and employees around the country without their having to suffer the inconvenience of mixing with the sweaty, taxpaying public.

Piloted private planes

have become an exalted status symbol among Washington bureaucrats. They're also a great waste of money. Even usually understated government auditors are aghast: "Federal ownership of planes is inefficient and wasteful," says a General Accounting Office report.

But typically, nothing has been done to halt this near-secret boondoggle. Bureaucrats continue to slide Cessnas and Gulfstreams into their budgets by falsely claiming that the plane is needed for a technical "mission."

Say the auditors: "Some agencies classify certain aircraft as mission-related even though the aircraft are used primarily to provide transportation or to keep their pilots qualified."

In reality, federal executives use the aircraft not only to fly themselves and employees on business, but also to transport their parties to convention resorts and other desirable destinations.

Checking on two Department of Transportation planes, the auditors found that their use for routine transportation was not justified: Commercial travel would have been cheaper; flights were made with only a few passengers on board; and the planes were used to fly

high-ranking bureaucrats and Coast Guard officials—often with their spouses and guests—on trips in the United States and even overseas.

Can this misuse of taxpayer money be halted? First, that requires that someone actually be in charge of the government, which as we shall see is not the case. In Washington, everyone fends and plots for himself. For example, when the inspector general of the Department of Energy advised the Bonneville Power Authority that buying a new aircraft would violate government guidelines, the BPA went ahead and bought the plane anyway.

How expensive is this craving for the bureaucrat's ultimate status symbol?

Very. The cost of the aircraft has been estimated at $2 billion. The depreciation runs at least $200 million a year. The annual upkeep costs another $800 million. There's also the added cost of civilian airports and military bases that accommodate the planes. And if that's not enough, government agencies *lease* still another 5,000 private planes each year at a cost of $100 million.

Because the planes are not standardized, each different model—from more than 25 different manufacturers—requires its

own specially trained pilot, mechanics, and individual spare parts, raising the cost even further.

The tariff runs the taxpayer well over a billion dollars a year, a figure that will grow considerably as the old planes are replaced by new ones.

Decorating and furniture
How much could the federal government possibly spend on decorating?

Much more than you, or I, or any reasonable person could imagine.

When we think of government furniture, we conjure up images of chipped metal desks and 1950s vinyl-covered chairs in Post Offices or Social Security bureaus.

Think again. That's a smoke screen so we won't think about the expensively decorated federal offices—complete with Herman Miller desks, rugs, and the latest built-in wall systems—that have been refurbished at some bureaucrat's whim. It is a scandal waiting to be born.

Are there any controls on such spending? The answer is simply "No." Then who's to stop a ranking bureaucrat from spending $100,000 redoing his already resplendent office? No one. The decision to buy furniture is made by individual agencies, not any central group. They can refurnish all or part of their offices—whether they're moving or staying put—without a decision from the White House or even the General Services Administration, which some government people mistakenly believe is in charge.

How much does the government actually spend on furniture and decorating each year?

"No one in the government really knows," says a top GSA spokesman. "We know how much the agencies spend when they use our contract system. But that doesn't include the Department of Defense, who mainly do their own buying, and even agencies who don't like what's available from our suppliers. All I can find out for you is how much money went through our contract system."

I asked him to find out his end, and after a computer run, he did. The figure turned out to be $676 million just in fiscal 1991! He agreed that estimating that to be half the true total would be conservative. More liberally, it would be three times as much.

Does that mean $1.35 billion to $2 billion a year on new furniture and decorating?

That's right, and there's no cutback or stopping points in sight. Where does that show in the federal budget? Nowhere. There's no such listing as "Furniture" or "Decorating" in the hefty document. Budget items are not clearly stated, on purpose. The government plays cat and mouse with the taxpayer whenever it can.

Did they say almost $2 billion for furnishings in one year? That's more than the entire budget of the state of North Dakota.

SOURCE: *Martin L. Gross, "Washington's Shell Game with Social Security." In Martin L. Gross,* The Government Racket: Washington Waste from A to Z *(Bantam Books, 1992), pp. 208–210.*

tor's reelection campaign in 1984 and that's the kind of question we got everyday. First, we would quickly point out that the large majority of people on welfare are women with small children. We would also note that there were several alternatives: We could tax the wealthy more; we could decrease spending in other areas like the military; we could prioritize human need and pay a bit more taxes to take better care of our future. 'Pay now or pay later' the senator used to say. If we don't put money into our children today, into education, pregnancy prevention, delinquency prevention, drug awareness, we will be putting money into more prisons in the future."

Perhaps the most telling illustration of Reagan's accomplishments is the adoption of the Family Support Act of 1988. This act, aimed at establishing education and job training programs for AFDC recipients, has been described as "a triumph of style over substance" (Howard Karger, 1992, p. 13). The bill assumes that the economy is able to produce large numbers of well paying jobs, includes punitive measures for noncompliance, and does not tackle the important issue—the absence of a federal AFDC benefit standard.

Private, not-for-profit social services, although not directly targeted, were hit with higher caseloads. New problems emerged for which programs were neither in place nor planned. Fewer dollars were available because the private mechanisms of the United Way campaigns, annual donor drives, private foundations, and public demonstration and training grants were also affected by the recession. Consequently, these not-for-profit and public agencies experienced the same reductions in funding simultaneously with increases in caseloads.

Reinstituting the Charity Model

Perhaps without conscious recognition, social work was presented with the dilemma of either being an agent of social control or an agent of social change and chose the former role. In order to cope with these reductions in funds and increases in service demands, not-for-profit agencies did not turn clients away nor did they encourage clients to demonstrate actively against the government, which would have represented a social change model. Instead, agencies utilized social control solutions that did not increase service delivery budgets: higher caseloads, increased use of volunteers, consumers as deliverers of service, or increased fees for services.

There are several explanations for the acceptance of a social control model and the utilization of privatization as a solution (Karen Haynes and James Mickelson, 1992, p. 172). First, there was the emergence of the New Right, which represented a combination of economic libertarianism and social traditionalism. This paradoxical combination invoked different themes with regard to its different areas of concern. The New Right spoke of "freedom and individualism on economic matters, restraint and community on social matters, and total mobilization on national security matters" (Jerome Himmelstein, 1983, p. 17).

Although it may seem inconsistent with our professional history, threads of the New Right philosophy became imbedded in our social welfare practices. For example, with the renewed emergence of hunger and homelessness, social workers and the private sector were quick to mount food drives and create temporary shelters rather than to mount large-scale campaigns to expand AFDC benefits, food stamp eligibility, or the public housing supply. The public became uncomfortable as people began to beg in the streets, an uncommon sight previously. Social workers and social agencies responded with meal tickets that the public could purchase and give to the beggars to use in the agency soup kitchens. Such a response was cited as a creative approach to addressing the needs of the new street people as well as to developing revenue for the agency. This creative approach accepted begging rather than questioning hunger in this wealthy nation. It was creative only in its ability to relieve the public's guilt.

The expanding problems related to the increase in AIDS or domestic violence resulted in similar creative mechanisms: the increased use of self-help groups and reliance on volunteers, rather than the demand for increased professionals; for adequate programs such as hospices and shelters; and for increased funding for research on effective methodologies or preventive strategies.

Traditional social service agencies were quick to call these solutions creative and proactive. Professional social workers began to defend if not promote them in professional circles as acceptable solutions rather than "Band-Aids."

In the early 1980s political rhetoric added to the problem. President Reagan held up a newspaper want-ad page on television, and said that with all these jobs, anyone can work, which left in the minds of the public a nagging doubt about the unemployed. Similar rhetoric toward civil rights, poverty, and women's roles, led to a resurgence of previous stereotypical attitudes.

Canned food donated to the poor became an acceptable method of feeding the hungry, and, as homelessness increased to such a degree that it became a major national issue, specialized day care service for homeless children, classes, meals, or mail delivery emerged. We did not increase the supply of public low income housing. Instead of mounting proactive campaigns, the social work profession attempted to hold off further reductions. Strategies in our repertoire that were consistent with the privatization model were utilized.

Although undoubtedly this era had a devastating effect on public social services and created new obstacles to professional social workers who wanted to enter or move up in the public social services, it may finally have had a positive, although unintended, effect on the profession of social work. The managerial and bureaucratic language of the 1970s began to be replaced in the classroom with the language of advocacy.

The reduction of governmental supports coupled with the recession brought many social problems closer to home and made them more publicly visible. In addition, an unanticipated consequence of the new philanthropy through the use of affluent volunteers and consumers as service deliverers was to broaden the base of support for services; to increase the understanding of human suffering; to enlighten more people about the cause of that suffering; and to value the need for professional, systematic, and institutionalized responses to that suffering (Karen Haynes and James Mickelson, 1992, p. 173).

Coalitions like Generations United, composed of an assortment of sometimes disparate groups, were constructed to combat further reductions. An additional by-product of these coalitions was that other professional and volunteer groups became more educated about and supportive of professional social workers' roles and skills and of the need to form coalitions for increased advocacy.

With the increased pressure on the nonprofit human service organizations, executive directors increased their political activities to advocate for clients to receive governmental social services that the agencies had relied on to supplement their clients' needs. Although directors faced conflicting expectations and demands from different constituencies about political activities, research indicates that they were advocating on different levels (Edward Pawlak and John Flynn, 1990, p. 309).

Social workers learned advocacy techniques from the Reagan administration as well. Social work advocates, who had always struggled with the question posed by policymakers about where the additional money for a new program or to maintain current ones was going to come from, found the answer from Secretary of Defense Caspar Weinberger, who gave the following response to Congress when he proposed a tremendous increase in the defense budget: "That's not my problem. I'm here to tell you what needs to be done."

The 1990s and Beyond

The Reagan administration did not achieve all its objectives and the welfare state, despite systematic attempts to dismantle it, remains. Its progress has been impeded, however, and its structure fragmented.

What's Good for Private-Sector Goose Not for Nonprofit Gander?

By Karen S. Haynes

Once again, America's double standard is raised to national attention, yet few will recognize it and fewer still, acknowledge it. In watching national news recently, I have connected two issues that have not been connected by the media or the general public. But, as each story unfolded, I couldn't help the feeling of an increasing awareness of seeing, once again, the American double standard.

What issues are these? One is the announcement of General Motors' 12 plant closings laying off 16,300 workers immediately, with 9 more plant closings and 58,000 more layoffs by 1995, followed by the new plant opening in Poland. The other was the announcement of the financial audit of the president of the National United Way of America and his subsequent retirement.

The American double standard is that it is acceptable for a corporate CEO to be paid extremely well, have a large fringe benefit package and a large expense account in an organization whose goal is to maintain a profit that even if the salary and expense account is maintained at the expense of the company's employees. However, it is clearly unacceptable to have a large salary, benefit package, and expense account (even though much smaller than the corporate CEO's) when the goal of the organization is to raise money in order to help people.

Although when the story first broke about William Aramony's salary, fringes and expenses, I felt a sense of, well, certainly, surprise and then concern that this, indeed, seemed excessive for an organization that raises money to help other organizations. And if the story had not occurred at a time when General Motors was also making headlines for the difficult and painful decisions of closing plants and laying off long-term employees, perhaps I would not have felt such outrage at this double standard.

But the more I think about it, the more I read, and the more I watch the indignation of the public at United Way's excesses, the more outraged I become that that same public is remaining relatively silent and, indeed, accepting of the inevitability of plant closings in order to maintain the excesses of administrative salaries and profit. Robert Stempel, chairman of General Motors, has said that GM's situation is critical. A $2 billion loss in 1990, followed by a $4.5 billion loss in

While the Reagan administration did not succeed in bringing about a political realignment in electoral politics, it successfully weakened the liberal consensus. . . . The hardening of public opinion as well as the deliberate weakening of the trade unions has exacerbated the problems facing the Democratic party and its traditional

1991, supports that statement. But has he resigned? Has the public demanded he reduce his multimillion-dollar annual salary and fringes?

When I think that the same public does not blink an eye at the multimillion-dollar contracts of entertainers or athletes I am not only outraged, but I become baffled at the strange prioritization of our values.

The message is clear to me: It is acceptable and, probably even more than that, it is desirable, to earn an incredible amount of income if one receives that income by entertaining others or selling others goods. It is unacceptable to attain a high salary by helping people improve their quality of life, deal with individual family crisis and pain, or help people to achieve the self-esteem, education, or skill essential to be productive, functioning adults at home and in the workplace tomorrow.

Clearly, I don't believe that people whose job it is to help other people deserve poverty wages. Indeed, if those individuals were paid what they save taxpayers, they might be part of the *nouveau riche*. I am not defending what do appear to be excessive salaries, fringes, and expenses for the National United Way president. I am questioning the root of outrage at that and not at other salaries.

Indeed, most United Ways spend less than 10 percent of their contributions on administration, which must certainly be less than a corporation such as GM with 14 layers of management.

Certainly corporate and industrial management today and, even more important, in the future, need to be extremely talented. They need to be able to have the long-range vision to see the big picture of how their product or service fits no longer in just a local market but in a global one. They need adept fiscal managers and increasingly they need politicians. They must have skills to communicate with a culturally diverse labor force. That combination of skills comes with education, experience, and a great deal of hard work and ought to be well-compensated. But those managerial skills are not less necessary in the not-for-profit world than in for-profit organizations.

In fact, some would argue that those skills must be even more finely tuned in organizations where goal achievements may be more elusive, where tangible rewards are fewer and where societies' praise and acknowledgements are far less.

Let's put this in perspective. One president of one human-service organization was paid extremely well to orchestrate a national campaign through which millions of Americans are helped while many CEOs are paid well for designing plans that impoverish thousands so their own profits can be made.

Isn't that a double standard?

SOURCE: Houston Post, 27 March 1991.

welfarist allies. While welfarists within the party search for ways of presenting their ideals in ways that are electorally realistic, many have turned away from the party's historic commitment to welfare. (James Midgley, 1992, p. 22)

Unfortunately, by the time of President George Bush's inauguration in January 1989, "the triumph of Upper America was both complete and precarious—precarious because its success was becoming so obvious" (Kevin Phillips, 1990, p. 211). Despite attempts at some down-home images, the United States that President Bush came from and represented was one of old family wealth.

His "kinder and gentler" campaign platform and the notion that volunteers, those "thousand points of light," could help achieve this domestic agenda, continued both the privatization and volunteerism and suggested little ideological or philosophical redirection during his presidency. However, the early months of the Bush administration were plagued with the Savings and Loan scandal and increasing reminders that the rich were indeed better off, while the working and middle classes were not.

Bush's international agenda turned the focus away from the domestic and became more central during the buildup and conflict of the Persian Gulf War in early 1991. Although it began to appear that the 1990s would be a time to redress these excesses and change the ideology from a singularly economic one to a redistributive one again, the double standard remained strong.

For social work, the points of optimism that arose from these conservative strategies and philosophic attacks included a rising tide of advocacy, coalition building, and national social welfare agenda setting (Linda Reeser and Irwin Epstein, 1990, p. 15). Increased legislative activity by associations like the Child Welfare League of America and the Children's Defense Fund, and coalitions like Generations United are developing proactive strategies to begin to redress the devastating effects of the past decade.

Finally, the brightest spot of optimism occurred with the presidential election of 1992. Although "family values" were the early buzzwords of the campaigns, postelection analysis concluded that the domestic economy was the deciding issue and that specific plans rather than unfocused pledges won out at the polls.

It was assumed early on that the incumbent, George Bush, had an easy lead and that the Democratic party did not have a strong contender. However, schisms in the Republican party cropped up when the rhetoric of family values contrasted against the veto of the Family Leave bill and Vice-President Dan Quayle's attack on Murphy Brown (single mothers), and, in particular, with the Republican convention platform, which stretched to the far religious right (strong and rigid antiabortion laws).

Meanwhile, independent candidate Ross Perot, Texas oil billionaire, entered, withdrew, and reentered the race creating yet another choice and helping to maintain a focus on the domestic economy. The Democratic candidate, Arkansas Governor Bill Clinton, focused on specific plans related to the economy and health care and relied on town meetings and bus tours to get out and talk with the people.

This election not only represents a change in political parties and ideologies after 24 years (since the election of Lyndon Baines Johnson in 1965, with the exception of the four-year term of Jimmy Carter, 1977–1981), but the first election of a president and vice-president born after World War II (part of the baby boomers). From a perspective of social welfare history, this election clearly represented optimism for more progressive and inclusive policies, for greater representation of minorities and women in policy-making positions, and for progressive reform in health care and welfare. Obviously, only time will show the validity of this optimism.

Summary

This chapter has traced the initiation and growth of the public social welfare system in the United States. Since the enactment of the Social Security Act in 1935, we have acknowledged that structural and societal problems can create inequalities in opportunities and that private troubles may need public solutions.

Although the expansion of public social services eventually entailed greater accountability, the large welfare structure had neither eliminated welfare dependency and unemployment, nor provided sufficient opportunities for educational advancement of special groups such as racial and ethnic minorities, women, or the handicapped.

The attempted dismantling of the welfare state by President Reagan was supported by a strong ideological effort by the Moral Majority, which placed social workers and liberals in "anti" family positions. The unintended consequence of this conservative agenda has been the repoliticalization of the social work profession and the coalescing of heretofore disparate groups.

References

Abramovitz, Mimi. "The Reagan Legacy: Undoing the Class, Race and Gender Accords." *Journal of Sociology and Social Welfare,* Vol. 19, No. 1 (1992): 91–110.

Cohen, Nathan. *Social Work in the American Tradition.* New York: Dryden Press, 1958.

Elderton, Marion, ed. *Case Studies of Unemployment.* Philadelphia: University of Pennsylvania Press, 1931.

Friedan, Betty. *The Feminine Mystique.* New York: Dell Publishing, 1963.

Galbraith, John K. *The Affluent Society.* Boston: Houghton Mifflin, 1958.

Harrington, Michael. *The Other America.* New York: MacMillan, 1962.

Haynes, Karen S., and James S. Mickelson. *Affecting Change: Social Workers in the Political Arena.* New York: Longman, 1991.

———. "Social Work and the Reagan Era: Challenges to the Profession." *Journal of Sociology and Social Welfare,* Vol. 19, No. 1 (March 1992): 169–183.

Himmelstein, Jerome. "The New Right." In *The New Christian Right.* Edited by Robert C. Liebman and Robert Wuthnow, 13–30. New York: Aldine Publishing, 1983.

Hopkins, Harry. "Editorial." *Social Service Review,* Vol. 8, No. 3 (Sept. 1934).

Jansson, Bruce S. *The Reluctant Welfare State: A History of American Social Welfare Policies.* Belmont, CA: Wadsworth, 1988.

Karger, Howard. "Income Maintenance Programs and the Reagan Domestic Agenda." *Journal of Sociology and Social Welfare,* Vol. 19, No. 1 (March 1992): 45–63.

Lekachman, Robert. *Greed is Not Enough: Reaganomics.* New York: Pantheon, 1982.

Midgley, James. "Society, Social Policy and the Ideology of Reaganism." *Journal of Sociology and Social Welfare,* Vol. 19, No. 1 (March 1992): 13–29.

Pawlak, Edward J., and John P. Flynn. "Executive Directors' Political Activities." *Social Work,* Vol. 35, No. 4 (July 1990): 307–312.

Peterson, George. "Federalism and the States." In *The Reagan Record.* Edited by John L. Palmer and Isabel V. Sawhill, 217–259. Cambridge, MA: Ballinger Publishing, 1984.

Phillips, Kevin. *The Politics of Rich and Poor Wealth and the American Electorate in the Reagan Aftermath.* New York: Random House, 1990.

Reeser, Linda Cherry, and Irwin Epstein. *Professionalization and Activism in Social Work: The Sixties, the Eighties, and the Future.* New York: Columbia University Press, 1990.

Rothman, Jack, Joseph G. Teresa, and John L. Erlich. *Fostering Participation and Promoting Innovation: Handbook for Human Service Managers.* Itasca, IL: F. E. Peacock, 1978.

Rupp, Leila J., and Verta Taylor. *Survival in the Doldrums: The American Women's Rights Movement, 1945 to the 1960s.* New York: Oxford University Press, 1987.

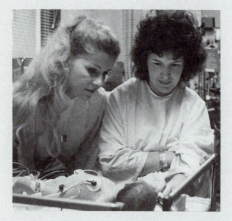

Social Work Practice: Opportunities and Populations

An understanding of the notion of basic human needs and their relationship to the origins of organized social welfare provides the foundation for examining social work practice. Where do social workers find jobs? With whom do they work? What kinds of knowledge does one need to practice social work? What are the value and ethical guidelines used by social workers? The four chapters that make up this unit provide information in relation to these questions. In Chapter 4 a matrix approach is outlined to show where, with whom, and how the practice of social work occurs. Chapter 5 discusses the challenges represented by diversity, focusing especially on an appreciation of diversity itself. In Chapter 6, we identify and discuss social work values and ethics, including case studies that bring to life the complexities of values and ethics in practice. Finally, Chapter 7 gives form and shape to the knowledge base of professional social work practice.

CHAPTER 4

Social Work Practice Opportunities

Introduction

Some students enroll in their first social work class knowing exactly what they want to do when they graduate. They know in what specific area, and with what kinds of people, they would like to work. They may even be preparing for a certain job in a particular social service agency. Other students have less clearly defined ideas of their futures as professional social workers. They may have only very general thoughts, for example, that they would like to work with people. Some are drawn to working with certain kinds of individuals such as older persons or children. Others are attracted to working in certain settings such as hospitals, adoption agencies, or public schools, and some are concerned with having an impact on major social problems such as substance abuse, poverty, mental illness, or homelessness. Some students take an introductory class in social work just to learn more about social workers and what they actually do. We recognize that many students in an introductory course may be "shopping," looking for the major that really seems to fit their interests and their life philosophies.

No matter which kind of student you are—one who knows what social work job you want, one who has a general idea and wants to work with people, or one who is searching for the right career—this chapter will provide you with an overview of at least some of the wide range of practice opportunities available to individuals with social work training. For those of you searching for the right career, we hope you will find the array of social work practice opportunities intriguing enough to make social work your choice. For those with a general notion of wanting to work with particular client groups, in specific settings, or with selected social problems, we hope that our examples help to clarify your choices. Finally, for those of you who have already decided on your focus as a social worker, we trust that our discussion of the many practice opportunities available to you will validate your choice.

We have attempted in our discussion to highlight practice opportunities open to BSW practitioners. There are many variables that can effect whether a particular position requires a Bachelor of Social Work (BSW) or a Master of Social Work (MSW) degree, or whether any social work degree is required. Licensing or accrediting standards of an agency or setting, the insurance or legal regulation requirements in a given state, and the particular level of skill and specialization can all influence job requirements. Most of the practice opportunities discussed here, however, are available to graduates of accredited BSW programs.

Social Work Practice

Previous chapters have taught you that social work practice, past and present, is extremely diverse. There is both a richness as well as a confusion in this diversity. As we address the questions of what social workers do and where they do it, the answers are neither as simple nor as straightforward as you might like. Social workers, BSWs and MSWs, are engaged in interventions with individuals, families, small groups, communities, organizations, and associations. Social workers use skills that range from the most general— such as interviewing and assessing, linking clients to appropriate services, providing information and referral, and advocating—to those that are more specialized—psychotherapy, program planning and administration, program evaluation, and policy analysis.

However, regardless of the target of intervention or the technique, social work is unique because social work practice always includes a focus on "person in environment." This means that social workers, unlike other helping professionals, are *always* aware of the interconnectedness of specific clients and their problem with larger systems or other individuals. An abused child may be the "target of intervention," but social workers recognize that the family, the school, the church, and friends may be part of the problem as well as part of the solution. An alcoholic employee may be the "target of intervention," but family, co-workers, and friends are affected by the problem and they are part of the solution. The larger social system—law, government, media (television, radio, newspapers, books, and magazines)—with its values, assumptions, and methods will also be considered by social workers as part of what is impacting any given individual, family, or group.

Social work practice occurs in a wide variety of practice settings, and, social workers may be more visible in some settings than others. Employees in some settings are referred to as social workers even though they do not have professional social work education or training. For example, you may associate social work with "public social services" such as financial aid or food stamp programs. Public assistance programs like these are traditional social work practice environments. In these settings, the general social welfare of clients is the primary focus of the agency. The presence of social workers is likely to be more obvious in such traditional settings where social welfare is the framework, as opposed to a "host" setting where social work services are secondary to that setting's primary function.

Examples of host settings for social workers include hospitals, nursing homes, correctional facilities or probation offices, and the schools. In hospitals, health care and medical treatment are primary functions; in nursing homes, long-term health care and maintenance are primary; in prisons or in probation, protection of the public and rehabilitation of offenders (to varying degrees) are primary; in the schools, education is the primary function. Thus, even though clients in each of these settings can and do benefit from the services provided by social workers, these services are viewed as secondary to the primary goal of the host setting. Many social workers are employed in host settings, and many persons who are employed in both public and private social services are not professionally educated (BSW or MSW) social workers.

Approaches to Conceptualizing Opportunities

You can begin to see how this professional diversity can be confusing, but this same diversity is also the profession's strength. Social work plays such a vital professional role in so many practice settings that any discussion of practice opportunities requires a somewhat artificial delineation. Over time many different models have been used to describe and define social work practice opportunities; the following four are the most common:

1. a field of practice model, where the focus is on the setting, such as physical health care, mental health, or corrections;

2. a target population model, where the focus is on the identified client group, such as children, adolescents, or older people;

3. a social problems model, where the focus in on a identifiable problem, for example, substance abuse, teen pregnancy, or sexual abuse/incest;

4. a methods model, where the focus is on the particular skills being utilized, such as individual counseling, group work, administration, or community organizing.

There is really no one best or right model. Each has merit as a way of looking at and understanding practice opportunities.

Field of Practice Model

This model describes practice opportunities in terms of the specific settings (i.e., *fields*) in which social workers provide services. When we use the fields of practice model our focus is on *where* practice opportunities exist. To examine social work practice opportunities in the field of health, we would list the settings in which health care is provided: for example, acute care hospitals, outpatient public health clinics, home health care agencies, nursing homes, and hospices. Other examples are mental health (psychiatric hospitals and mental health clinics); corrections (prisons, probation, and parole departments); schools (junior and senior highs, college or university counseling centers); and, increasingly, corporations and large businesses (employee assistance programs).

The field of practice model is valuable because it focuses on the commonalities within each field with respect to various aspects of practice, such as funding, staffing practices, and structure of service delivery. For example, we have already listed the settings in which health care practice occurs. We can now examine how health services are funded through public and private sources, usually on a reimbursement for service basis. Medicare, Medicaid, private insurance, and co-payments are common financing mechanisms in health care. Using this delivery system or setting model, we would include information about the regulations for social work practice

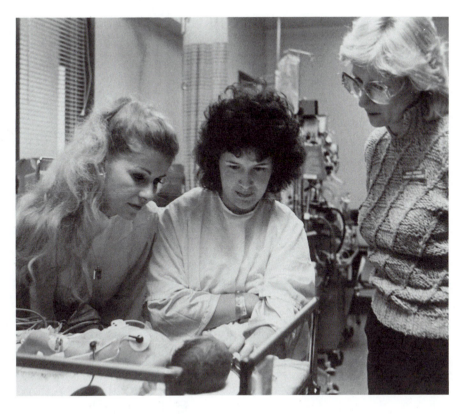

Neonatal care is one of the many practice opportunities for social workers in health care settings.

in health care. Hospitals have "protocols" for client or patient service and are *accredited,* which means they must meet national standards for service delivery. Nursing homes are regulated by state statutes, which usually dictate explicit staffing ratios and minimum staff qualifications.

If there is a national service delivery system, as there is (at least in part) for public child welfare, the advantage of this model is that it provides for a structural picture of the linkages between the levels of service delivery. That is, one can see the linkages between the local public child welfare agency, through a state agency, to the federal Department of Health and Human Services (HHS), which mandates certain conditions for service delivery if federal dollars are used.

We will look again at fields of practice or settings when we examine "Professionalization" in Unit IV, particularly in Chapter 13.

Target Population Model

Another approach to understanding practice opportunities is to focus on populations served. This approach focuses primarily on *who* is served and may include either (1) certain oppressed, marginalized, or disenfranchised populations—such as the handicapped; ethnic, racial, and linguistic minorities; women; gay men; and lesbian/gay women—or (2) specific age groups within the life span, such as children, adolescents, adults, or older persons.

The benefit of using this model is the assumption that there are commonalities among persons in each group that we can learn and use in practice to better understand that target population. Focusing on a specific target population allows us to become somewhat specialized in our knowledge base, not only by learning about, but also by learning from our clients. This model frequently allows us to build on knowledge of what it means to be part of a marginalized group. This knowledge helps the social worker explore the extent to which general information about a particular group fits the specifics of a particular client.

If the target population is an age group, then knowledge of life span concepts and developmental stages is important. For example, it is essential that a social worker whose primary target population group is adolescents understand the general adolescent need for independence and peer acceptance—and be able to differentiate behaviors associated with these needs from abnormal acting out, aggression, or destructive conformity.

We will explore the nature of the social work client population more widely in Chapter 5.

Social Problems Model

A third model of understanding social work practice opportunities utilizes the social problem perspective and focuses on the *causes* and conditions of the social problem rather than the settings of service delivery or the characteristics of the target population.

This focus requires that practice be viewed in terms of the primary *presenting problem:* such as poverty, homelessness, hunger, HIV/AIDS, developmental disabilities, or pregnancy. In this

Our practice efforts
with children are often
warmly rewarded.

model, the social worker would need (1) knowledge and theory pertaining to the causes, both societal and individual, of a particular problem; (2) awareness of community resources that might be brought to bear on this problem; and (3) the ability to identify and help prioritize the most appropriate solution(s), both immediate and long term.

Here, we can observe the applicability of the *systems perspective,* which will be discussed in more detail in Chapter 8. The systems perspective, in short, means that social workers must be able to include in their assessment of a presenting problem the larger, systemic issues. For example, hunger may be temporarily satisfied by giving people food directly through food pantries or soup kitchens. This is an appropriate, immediate short-term intervention. However, in a broader systemic view, hunger in our world must be seen as linked to poverty, illiteracy, lack of training and education, illegal immigrant status, illness, discrimination and oppression, unemployment, substance abuse, politics, war, geographic and climactic conditions, and so forth. Ultimately, the existence of hunger is a reflection of the degree to which human life, as well as the health of the planet, are valued.

Methods/Skills Model

The final model that we have used to conceptualize social work practice opportunities focuses on the skills utilized. Services or agencies have sometimes been grouped by how social workers practiced or by which of the methods (skills) was predominantly used in that setting. Agencies were identified, for example, as casework, groupwork, community organizing, planning, or administration.

The primary knowledge base for this approach comes from the theories underlying the skills. Chapter 7 will discuss in greater detail psychosocial theories (psychoanalytic, psychodynamic, behavioral) that were and are utilized for casework or direct practice. Theories of groupwork, leadership, and social norm development are used in working with small groups. Theories of community, social action, and empowerment are relevant to community organization skills. Administration and management require some grounding in employee motivational theories and theories of organizational behavior.

The Synthesis of Practice Opportunities

Although all of these approaches to conceptualizing social work practice are valuable and ultimately provide students with information about essentially the same opportunities, none of these alone accurately portrays the dynamic and complex nature of social work practice as it has evolved to date and as it continues to evolve in the 1990s. One way to convey this dynamism and complexity is to consider the range of social work practice opportunities in terms of a multidimensional matrix, which includes attention not only to specific populations and practice settings, but also to the enormous variety of social problems with which our society must constantly deal. An example of this kind of matrix is shown in Figure 4.1.

One dimension of this matrix—shown vertically on Figure 4.1 and noted by Roman numerals (I–VI)—provides a way of thinking about social work in terms of the targeted population through the developmental life span stages of those served, ranging from work with unborn infants to work with the very elderly. As noted earlier, even age categories are somewhat arbitrary and change with new knowledge. For example, only recently have we come to acknowledge that the "elderly" population includes subpopulations reflective of health status, retirement status, and longevity—such as the very elderly and the frail elderly.

The second dimension—shown horizontally on Figure 4.1 and noted by letters (A–E)—provides attention to some of the many fields of practice or delivery systems within which social workers currently provide services. The systems listed on this dimension are also modified to meet growing and changing social needs. As was noted in Chapters 2 and 3, systems to meet social welfare needs have grown slowly and in piecemeal fashion over the past 200 years in the United States. Although most of these systems have achieved the appearance of stability, many actually are in a state of disequilibrium, and as a result may be subject to significant changes in the next several years.

The health care system, including health insurance and private medical care, for example, is stressed very nearly to its limits and is barely functioning for many Americans, especially the economically disadvantaged. Adoption of long proposed uniform national health insurance may bring about significant changes and

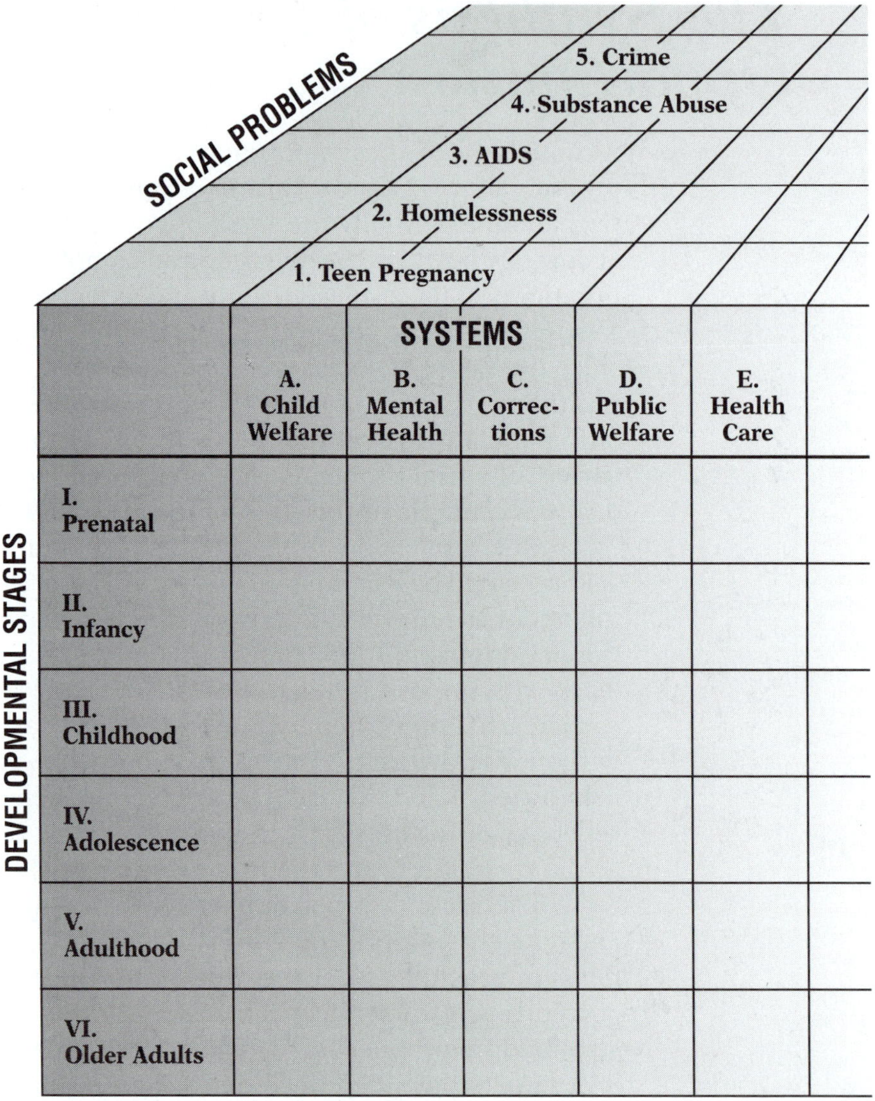

FIGURE 4.1 A Model for Social Work Practice Opportunities

would certainly impact the delivery of social services within the health care system, including the kind and number of available social work opportunities. The same is true for the federal and most state correctional systems, the public school system in many communities, and the public welfare system. In all of these systems you will find many social workers currently providing significant amounts of service.

The third dimension of the matrix—depicted from front to

back and noted with Arabic numerals (1–5) on Figure 4.1—reflects some of the current social problems with which society is presently struggling. Unlike delivery systems, which have evolved over relatively lengthy periods of time and may have established structures and funding mechanisms, social problems often emerge, and at times disappear, much more quickly. For example, as you learned in Chapter 2, begging was considered a social problem in England during the 1600s and then "disappeared," only to reappear from time to time through history. AIDS, on the other hand, was not even diagnosed in a human being in the United States until 1981, and yet has become an enormous international social problem in the subsequent years.

Finally, in any one of the blocks represented on the matrix, the specific skills that a social worker uses can provide another model for examining social work practice. *None* of these models alone (including our matrix) describes the totality of what social workers do.

Case

CARA

Cara is a 39-year-old African-American mother of three who has had 13 years of experience working with unwed mothers in an institutional setting. Most of her work takes place within the cell on the matrix we would identify as IA5: Prenatal, Child welfare, Teen pregnancy. The social work skills she uses in performing her job include assessment, group counseling or therapy, individual counseling or therapy, resource referral and linking, education, and advocacy. Most of Cara's clients are adolescents who come to the maternity home where Cara is employed to live for the last three to six months of their pregnancy. In about half of the cases, these young girls relinquish their infants for adoption; the other half keep their babies and return home after delivery.

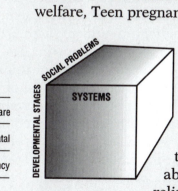

Child Welfare

Prenatal

Teen Pregnancy

Cara has noticed that over the past five years, the population she works with has been gradually changing, with new concerns emerging as practice issues. For example, she must now consider issues related to HIV infection in her adolescent and pediatric clients; she has become aware of many more run-away, "throwaway," or homeless young women; and she is acutely aware of substance abuse and its impact on pregnancy, par-ticularly crack cocaine, nicotine, and alcohol. Cara has also seen an alarming increase in cases of pregnancy resulting from incest or other sexual abuse.

Cara finds herself working with many service delivery systems: general health care, mental health, public health, and corrections. Furthermore, she works with individuals of many different ages—from the pregnant adolescent's family and from the adoptive family.

"On your matrix, my job would appear best described as assessment, treatment, and referral within cell IA5," says Cara. "But on any one day, at any one time, I might be spending most of my time and energy at any point on the matrix, depending on a particular client's needs."

Almost all social problems have an impact on many, if not all, social service delivery systems simultaneously, although their effect is seldom uniform across all systems. A problem such as HIV infec-tion, the infection that leads to Acquired Immune Deficiency Syn-drome (AIDS), for example, has affected almost every social service delivery system. The health care system has felt the most immediate and severe impact. Outpatient treatment with azidothymidine (AZT), a drug that has shown promise in slowing down the onset of full-blown AIDS, is extremely expensive, often running into thou-sands of dollars over a matter of months. The cost of inpatient hos-pital care for those with AIDS has become astronomic whether the hospital is private or public. Health insurance premiums of all per-sons reflect these growing costs, and insurance companies are in-creasingly insuring only the most healthy. Other systems—such as corrections, child welfare, education, and public welfare—have ex-perienced the effects of AIDS somewhat later and less intensely.

The social problem dimension also provides a way of looking at the kinds of issues to which social workers might direct attention not only as individual practitioners, but also as collective advocates for social change, through legislative advocacy, membership in pro-fessional organizations, and political activism.

Similarly, by using the field of practice model, you can focus on the types of service and the auspices of that service, but it does not necessarily limit the client group by age or by problem. The mental health delivery system treats all age groups, perhaps with the exception of the unborn child. It deals with an array of problems, including interpersonal relations; many of these interpersonal problems (parent–child conflicts; spouse/partner relationship conflict) are related to or exacerbated by larger social problems, such as substance abuse or poverty.

Social Work Practice Opportunities: The Life Span Model

The field of social work is so immense and enormously varied that entire books are devoted to detailing all the current opportunities for social work practice—and before these books are in print, new opportunities will have evolved. Instead of using the more traditional fields of practice model in defining social work opportunities, we find it more useful to align opportunities along a spectrum of human development. The life span model provides a basis for exploring the profession of social work; building on it, you can create and add to your own knowledge as you learn of new social problems and changes in social service delivery systems, or as you gain greater appreciation for the complexities of human development.

It is not uncommon for individuals to be drawn to social work because of a special interest in individuals of a particular age. "I'm going into the field because I am concerned about children," a student such as Tricia states emphatically. "I really enjoy older people," says one like Kimberley with no less enthusiasm. Others chime in the discussion to describe their interests in young adults, adolescents, or school-age children. Many individuals express a preference for work with individuals, groups, or families in a certain developmental stage. This exploration of career opportunities will use the developmental dimension as the principal organizing focus.

Prenatal

Individuals interested in providing prenatal social services immediately find themselves providing services to parents, siblings, extended families, and communities as well, including advocacy activities at the state and national level. There are opportunities within almost every system for social work practice focused on prenatal services.

In the health care system, for example, social workers may provide genetic counseling, pregnancy or infertility counseling, artificial insemination counseling (to heterosexual couples and singles; to lesbian couples and singles), counseling around abortion (including sexual assault, sexual abuse, and incest counseling), and therapeutic services related to prenatal care where birth defects have been identified. Social workers may work in settings such as Planned Parenthood clinics, hospitals, abortion clinics, adoption agencies, women's health centers, artificial insemination settings, homes for unmarried mothers, or in child welfare or public welfare settings where prevention services are provided.

You will recall from the previous chapter that a federal program administered by the states known as Women, Infants, and Children (WIC) also provides counseling and nutritional services to this population. Social workers with an interest in macrolevel practice may find opportunities lobbying for legislative change for special interest groups with an agenda stressing services concerning the unborn. Examples include pro-choice and anti-abortion organizations, organizations focused on prevention of birth defects such as March of Dimes, organizations focused on advocacy for individuals with genetic disorders or other neonatal problems. Still other opportunities are found in efforts to change laws relating to adoption, foster care, or child abuse. For example, our laws reflect our judgments concerning who is a "fit" parent. Singles as well as gay and lesbian persons are often barred from adopting.

Social workers who work with prenatal services must also deal with a wide range of social problems, including substance abuse, HIV/AIDS, adolescent pregnancy, incest and sexual abuse, sexual assault, poverty, absent fathers, and discrimination. Social problems such as fetal alcohol syndrome, cocaine use, malnourishment, and lack of prenatal care—not to mention inadequate medical resources, educational system dropouts, and incarceration of pregnant females—require the attention of the social worker interested in providing multifaceted services to a variety of clients.

Infancy and Early Childhood

No less complexity is found in the provision of social work services to newborns, infants, and young children. Social workers attracted to this developmental stage have opportunities in health care settings, public and private schools, day-care licensing and development, child welfare agencies (including adoption and foster care agencies), mental health agencies, the criminal and civil justice system (including services involving physically and sexually abused children, neglected children, and custody cases), along with opportunities for advocacy around issues of significance to young children.

Certain lifelong problems of individuals often become evident in infancy and early childhood, including pervasive developmental disorders such as autism, and disabilities such as cerebral palsy, epilepsy, and mental retardation. Social workers deal with families, communities, and service delivery systems around the needs of these individuals for specialized resources and support.

Social workers with an interest in infants and young children most often work with the children's parents, members of their extended families, and with organizations that serve the young child as well. Much of the work of public welfare professionals, including public assistance workers and protective service workers, revolves around the economic, social, health, and educational needs of children in families served by these agencies.

Those who work with individuals at this developmental stage and their parents confront many of the same social issues as those who provide prenatal services, except that the effects of poverty, discrimination, genetic disorders, substance abuse, AIDS, and other medical disorders are often already evident. Students interested in social work opportunities with infants and children must develop specialized knowledge and expertise in many areas, including a concern for environmental issues—for example, lead paint poisoning, asbestos in homes and schools, the effects of pollution and pesticides on child growth and development—and for the provision of a generally safe environment for young children—including issues such as gun control, poison control, and the use of safety belts and infant car seats.

School-Age Children

Social work opportunities in the provision of services to children in elementary school require mastery of a similar range of knowledge, attitudes, skills, and service modalities. By school age, a child typically has become formally involved in several service delivery systems, but most centrally a public or private school system. Children at this stage also may have had considerable involvement with the health care system, particularly if they or members of their family have any chronic illnesses, mental or physical disabilities, or serious physical injuries from accidental trauma. Social workers provide services in public and private health care settings as medical social workers; in educational settings as school social workers; in child welfare settings as caseworkers for child placement, child custody, and facility licensing workers; in juvenile justice systems as caseworkers and casemanagers for youthful offenders; and in mental health and private practice settings for individual, group, and family treatment with children and families.

Among the social problems with a particular impact on school-age children are substance abuse, including parental and personal abuse of alcohol, crack cocaine, and marijuana; physical and sexual abuse of children; truancy and absenteeism; and the abduction of children from a custodial parent. Additional issues for workers with individuals at this developmental stage include the rights of grandparents and other co-parental persons, child exploitation and pornography concerns, day care for working parents, and pediatric AIDS.

Adolescence

Problems that emerge in childhood often become even more complex for adolescents, and those with an interest in working with individuals in this developmental stage will find an increasing range of social work opportunities. The juvenile justice system, for example, which begins to work with youngsters about the age of 10, becomes more highly elaborated for older youth offenders. Correctional facilities for adolescents, which may take the form of work camps, farms, or other specialized out-of-home rehabilitative approaches, provide settings for social work services, as do juvenile probation and juvenile court.

In the health care setting, adolescents require social work in-

Today's adolescents and young adults need a wide variety of social work services.

terventions around emergency room services for accidental injuries and gang violence, around the provision of sex education (particularly HIV/AIDS prevention) and pregnancy prevention services, in the area of teen pregnancy and teen parenting, and around general nutritional and health awareness. Specialized treatment facilities for substance abuse or eating disorders also provide services to this age group; suicide is another significant concern.

Mental health services of all kinds, some of them targeted particularly to youth—including teen hotlines, sexual assault services, resources for runaway or throwaway youth, homeless shelters, and outreach services—utilize social workers to provide the majority of their services. School systems also make considerable use of social workers in work with junior and senior high school students. These services may be provided to individuals or to groups and often have a family or community component as well.

It is also worth noting that some services provided to younger individuals are less available to adolescents. Adoption workers, for example, work less frequently with adolescents than with younger children; however, foster care and residential placement of adolescents continue to be options, particularly through ages 16 to 17.

Social workers who work with adolescents must also address larger social issues: poverty, discrimination (for example, homophobia resulting in significant numbers of youth suicides and suicide attempts), adolescent HIV/AIDS, youth gangs and violence, increases in the school dropout rate, and underemployment and unemployment of youth. Here, as is the case with every other developmental stage, social workers have many opportunities. They may intervene with individuals and with families, at the community or the legislative level, or with state or federal government processes. There are as many opportunities to influence social legislation for adolescent concerns as there are to influence individual adolescents' lives.

Young Adulthood

Social workers drawn to the concerns of young adults have many of the same career opportunities in social work as those who work with adolescents, but there are a number of other options as well. During this life phase, most individuals enter into significant personal relationships, make decisions about residing independently from their parents, enter the work force, and make decisions about marriage and parenthood. Any of these significant life decisions can become problematic and suggest the need for social services. Substance abuse, mental health problems, infertility, economic problems, homelessness, sexual assaults, and issues related to the care of young children, aging parents, or both are among the problems experienced by young adults. Systems providing services include public welfare, public and private health care systems, the mental health system, and specialized resources for homelessness, sexual assaults, and parenting. Social work services are provided in all of these systems, as well as through private providers and employers. A relatively new resource for employed adults is the Employee Assistance Program (EAP). As you will recall from the experience of our former student Barbara, social workers in EAPs are involved in assessment, referral, and direct service provision in the individual's workplace setting.

This age group is not immune to the effects of larger social issues, including many of those previously noted. They are particularly affected by issues such as discrimination (including sexism, racism, heterosexism, and handicap status); sexually transmitted diseases (including AIDS); underemployment and unemployment; availability of affordable, safe housing; and reproductive rights. Because many young adults are involved in parenting for the first time, there is natural collaboration between social workers who provide prenatal and neonatal services and those who work in settings with young parents.

There is also a preponderance of young adults in the criminal justice system, including those incarcerated in correctional facilities. Individuals who want to work with this age group can find many opportunities in the jails, prisons, and parole and probation systems across the country. In the child welfare system, there is also considerable contact with young adults—in terms of certifying adoptive and foster families to provide care, in terms of working with young parents relinquishing their children (voluntarily or involuntarily) for placement, and in family preservation programs.

In health care settings, work with young adults often centers more around the provision of services due to accidental injury than to services due to chronic illness. Rehabilitation facilities for the treatment of injuries, for example, are providing increasing opportunities for social work services to young adults injured in automobile or motorcycle accidents, sports accidents, and, too often, to those injured by guns, knives, and beatings, a reality unfortunately too common among minority youth (particularly males).

Middle Age

By middle age the concerns of young adulthood have abated somewhat, and they are replaced by a new set of concerns, including issues around physical health and economic security. Acute mental health problems around life events—for example, changes in residence, unemployment, divorce, death of parents or a spouse, and growing independence of children—are common themes to which social workers address interventions. Mid-life adults may be relatively more affected by economic conditions, and may also be dealing with the advent of certain chronic physical disabilities such as arthritis, cardiac or respiratory disorders, or cancer. In health care or rehabilitation settings, social workers frequently have opportunities to provide services to these clients, stressing adaptive functioning and modifications of certain life-style behaviors such as smoking, eating, and exercise.

In the correctional system, middle-age adults who are habitual offenders are served, along with a smaller number of individuals who have committed serious crimes. The emphasis for middle-age adults is often less on rehabilitation than on punishment and long-term incarceration.

In mental health settings, affective disorders such as depression are diagnosed more often for the first time in middle-age adults. Interestingly, however, patients with chronic mental illness, such as schizophrenia, may experience a leveling off of active symptomatology during this life stage. Mental health treatment of individuals at this stage most often involves individual, group, or family therapy for acute conditions and life situations, and case management services for chronic disorders.

Case

TRAN NYEN

As an Asian immigrant to the United States in his youth, Tran Nyen was especially eager to work with the Asian population as a social worker. His first job had been in the county correctional system (at VC1 on the matrix), but he had recently accepted a position as an emergency room (ER) social worker in a large, metropolitan public hospital (this position addresses several points on the matrix: I–IV, all developmental stages; A, child welfare; B, mental health; D, public welfare; E, health; 1–5, all the social problems noted).

Health Care

All Ages

Crime/
Cultural Discrimination/
Substance Abuse

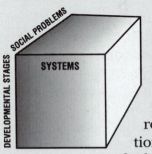

Tran Nyen dealt with many crisis situations in the ER. Increasing numbers of Asian teens were brought to the ER suffering from knife or gunshot wounds, victims of escalating gang violence in the surrounding urban area. Tran Nyen recognized that gang rivalry rooted in ethnic and cultural discrimination, as well as increasing substance abuse, laid the foundation for much of this violence. He was becoming acquainted all too quickly with the aftermath of drive-by shootings or drug overdoses as he talked with grieving parents struggling to understand how their child could have been injured or killed.

Tran Nyen had retained his ability to speak several Asian languages as well as French and English. He found his presence in the ER especially beneficial to other Asians, especially because some were hesitant to speak freely with strangers and many had difficulty with English, particularly in such stressful situations. From his own experience he could understand and appreciate the struggle to "fit" in a different culture, in particular for adolescents born in this country with parents who held more strongly to their native customs. Although saddened by the human tragedies he so often saw, Tran Nyen was challenged by his work and he felt great satisfaction from helping people in crisis.

With the baby boom generation now reaching middle age, we are likely to see more programs and services being geared to the needs of our aging population. Educational systems, particularly higher education, have recently begun to examine the provision of services to older adults, particularly those in a midlife career crisis. Social workers can be useful resources in assisting individuals through such crises and into productive, satisfying second or third careers or personal relationships.

Divorce and remarriage transitions also provide social work practice opportunities. Divorced persons with children who marry another person with children combine to create "blended" families, and the transitional adjustments of a blended family can take several years. Midlife women also may find themselves in dual or multiple caretaker roles of spouse, of mother, and of daughter who cares for one or more aging parents. As people live longer, the life span of caretaking extends. As a result, many midlife persons, especially women, find themselves in the "sandwich generation," attempting to care for children and aging parents while maintaining their intimate partnership/marriage and, frequently, their job outside the home.

Substance abuse, including alcohol and drugs, is an increasing problem for individuals at middle age as well. Health insurance issues, particularly with loss of employment benefits, also figure significantly into the concerns of middle-age adults.

Older Adults

In general, older persons have many of the same concerns as middle-age adults, but must contend more often with major losses. They face chronic and acute physical illnesses, economic instability, retirement, the death of a life partner, inadequate residential resources, and diminished physical and, perhaps, mental capabilities.

Conditions such as Alzheimer's disease, other dementias, stroke, and cardiac problems affect disproportionately more older adults than other age groups. Specialized settings for the elderly include adult foster homes, day-care programs, nursing home facilities, and retirement communities.

Discrimination based on ageism or handicapped status is often of more significance than other forms of discrimination at this stage, although all types of discrimination continue to have effects. Older individuals are found among the mentally ill, the homeless population, substance abusers, and the neglected and exploited. Elder abuse—the abuse of a parent by an adult child—is a growing concern. Social workers provide services to elderly adults around these issues in hospitals, nursing homes, public health clinics, adult protective services, and in a variety of mental health settings. Other growing services to the aging population include in-home services to continue independent living, public guardianship, and the vast array of social services provided through senior citizen organizations.

Social workers in the criminal justice system deal less frequently with the elderly because their infirmities often preclude their incarceration or active need for probation or parole interventions. Nevertheless, the prison population in the United States is aging right along with the general population.

In all service settings, and with all age groups, issues of loss are prominent themes of social work intervention, but they are more pronounced with older persons. Coming to terms with deteriorating health, declining financial resources, losing loved ones, and facing one's own death are all part of working with older persons.

Social Work Careers

Like all career decisions, deciding to become a social worker is a major choice. Whether you are still in the process of deciding what you want to do, or whether you know you want a social work career, here are some points to consider.

You may or may not have an idea right now about the population with whom you would prefer to work, or the kind of client problem, or even whether you want to work with individuals or with community associations. You may or may not know whether you like advocacy or counseling. Nevertheless, it is very likely that during your career as a social worker you will, by choice or by circumstance, work with a variety of client population groups, with different problems and in different systems. Few social workers remain forever in the same setting or with the same client population.

Social work careers, more frequently than not, require work with many different age groups. Although the client may be a teen, treatment may involve parents, peers, or siblings. Social workers may be employed in a substance abuse setting with their work focused principally on the problems associated with substance abuse; however, because problems seldom occur singly, recognizing and treating problems related to domestic violence and work or school absenteeism are necessary adjuncts in substance abuse work.

Social workers are sometimes attracted by lateral career moves, across "fields of practice." You may start employment in a hospital setting (health care) and find a more interesting employment site is a community mental health center or private psychiatric hospital (mental health), or a family service agency (child and family). Some social work careers are changed or redirected by people who move from direct practice with clients into supervision and administration.

Case

BRENDA

*B*renda had worked in the intake unit of a public outpatient mental health agency for three years when her supervisor began to encourage her to consider returning to graduate school. The supervisor indicated the availability of a small agency stipend to help pay her tuition, in return for which Brenda would come back and work for the agency at least three more years. The only problem for Brenda was knowing that when she returned (MSW in hand) most of her responsibilities would shift to staff supervision with little to no direct client contact.

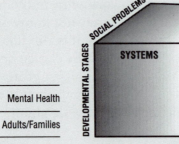

In her three years at the agency, Brenda had really enjoyed doing client intakes. As the first person to see the individual client or family when they came for service, she found her work very exciting and she liked the variety of working with people of all ages and backgrounds. Brenda knew she had good skills in helping people define their problem, in gathering relevant information for social histories, and in developing client assessments. Her role as intake worker was short term and she felt confident about her ability to match clients with ongoing service providers in the agency.

Looking ahead to less direct client contact and more staff supervision made Brenda feel a bit uneasy as she had little experience with longer term or ongoing work with people. On the other hand, she could not envision herself always doing the same job from now through retirement. She thought she would approach her supervisor about the possibility of creating a blended position, a position where she could still do intakes part of the time and do staff supervision as well. That way she felt she could keep her clinical skills sharp, provide for career mobility, and have the kind of flexibility that appealed to her. For Brenda, this sounded like the best of all possible avenues.

Summary

Where do social workers provide services? And to whom are these services provided? And what kinds of services are provided?

As the previous discussion has indicated, social workers provide services within every human service system of our society. They provide services in the educational system, in the health care system, in the criminal justice system, and in the mental health system. They also provide services in the private sector, including private practice and corporate settings.

They provide services to individuals of all ages and with all kinds of problems, including physical and mental illnesses, economic and employment issues, developmental disabilities, phase of life adjustments, substance abuse, eating disorders, educational disadvantages, and problems in social functioning. Social workers work with individuals who are discriminated against, marginalized and oppressed, including members of ethnic and racial minority groups, lesbians and gays, women, the poor, and the handicapped. They provide assistance with concerns such as infertility, genetic disorders, death and dying, relationship endings, and family functioning.

Social workers may choose to work with individuals, families, communities, or all three. Some social workers may opt to focus their interventions at the societal level advocating for changes in laws, policies, and procedures, whereas others manage the organizations in which social workers and other professionals are employed.

A social worker may be called a counselor, a therapist, a caseworker, a casemanager, a rehabilitation specialist, a planner, an administrator, an advocate, a policymaker, or a politician. Whatever the title, all bring to their work the social work perspective of person-in-environment, as well as the expertise that specialized training in social work affords them for the resolution of significant social problems.

In this chapter, we have attempted to convey the richness and breadth of this splendid profession rather than add to your confusion. Social work practice is what social workers do. The possibilities are endless and the future challenging.

CHAPTER 5

Diversity

Introduction

The dictionary defines *diversity* as "a point of difference," but the concept is infinitely more complex than that for social workers. Diversity is one of the features of social work that undergirds both the profession's values as well as the daily activities of practitioners. It is hard to accomplish any social work activity, however small, without encountering diversity. There may be diverse populations and settings such as those described in Chapter 4; diverse approaches to social change, group processes, or individual treatment represented by varied theories or schools of thought; or diverse options for the support of social programs by society. In this chapter, brief scenarios and case illustrations are interspersed with selected definitions and projections of the new demographics of diversity. Our purpose is to explore some of the aspects of diversity that beginning social workers are most likely to encounter as they start their professional careers.

Why Do We Need to Discuss Diversity Anyway?

Many social work texts, especially those intended to introduce students to the profession, include separate chapters on selected groups. Some include units on "Special Populations," with specific chapters devoted to women, lesbians and gays, the elderly, Native Americans, Asian Americans, Mexican Americans, or African Americans (Armando Morales and Bradford Sheafor, 1992); or "Special Populations and Issues," with chapters on ethnicity, gender, age, violence, human sexuality, and so forth (Martin Bloom, 1990). Some include discrete chapters titled "Racism, Ethnocentrism, and Strategies for Achieving Equal Rights" (Charles Zastrow, 1993) or units on "Special Issues and Populations" (Diana DiNitto and C. Aaron McNeece, 1990), again including content in the afore-mentioned areas.

As you'll soon see, our approach in this text is different. First, we are not really convinced that teaching about or writing about so-called special groups will substantially enhance an understanding of those groups. Given who *we* are, it seems presumptuous for us to try to explain the experience of people who are, in fact, different from us. Although we can offer some informed observations, we cannot truly speak for groups of people whose experiences we may not have shared ourselves. Second, we doubt that it is really possible to provide enough textbook information to help students feel secure in working with persons who are different from themselves. Finally, no matter how much eloquent information is given about special populations, it will not likely be "heard" unless people understand that difference—diversity—can be a positive force in our society and in our own lives. These are our reasons for approaching this issue from a different perspective. Let's begin with some exercises to stimulate your thinking about the meanings of value and diversity:

1. Look around the classroom where you are now sitting and note the differences represented by the individuals in a single room. Multiply that number of differences by 250 million, the approximate U.S. population in the 1990 census. Consider the possible combinations of gender, ethnicity, age, sexual orientation, physical capabilities, religious preference, abilities, interests, and life experiences represented by 250 million lives.

2. Discuss with someone you do not know very well the celebration of holidays; for example, those near the end of the year at Christmas, Hanukkah, or the Winter Solstice. Even if you discover a religious or spiritual orientation in common, you will probably find that there are many differences in the ways each of you celebrates the holiday. Such differences—even seemingly minor ones—often can be the source of considerable friction in interpersonal relationships; on a larger scale, they can underlie major confrontations between subgroups in our society.

As you will notice in discussing your own family's holiday customs, it is difficult not to feel that these represent the right way, the best way, or even the only way to celebrate. You might even have some feeling that other, different ways of celebrating are strange, misguided, or wrong. If so, your beliefs and feelings could be described as *ethnocentric*—a tendency to negatively evaluate or judge other cultures by the standards or norms of our own. Most social workers, if we are honest with ourselves, know that we cannot escape being somewhat ethnocentric. Our best hope is to recognize the characteristics we ourselves bring to the work we do and learn to use these productively, especially in situations where they may not be shared or even particularly appreciated or valued by our clients.

 Case

BARBARA AND JOHN GOODTREE

Corporate Human Resources

Adults

Alcoholism/Cultural Diversity

*B*arbara sat at her desk in the Employee Assistance Division, reviewing her case notes on John Goodtree. John was a 50-year-old Native American welder and longtime employee of the Martin Company who had once served as supervisor on the assembly line. He had only recently returned to work after six weeks at the chemical dependency treatment facility to which Barbara had referred him; he had returned appearing sullen and withdrawn. John's supervisor feared he was already beginning to fall back into his former pattern of alcohol abuse and had discussed John with Barbara twice in the past week. Barbara wondered what she could say to John that would assist him in staying sober and on the job. She wondered, too, how much difference it made to their relationship that she was female, white, and some 15 years younger than he? Should the effect of these differences in age and backgrounds be confronted directly, indirectly, or not at all in their sessions?

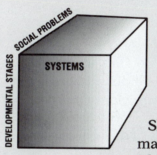

Case

CARLOS AND VENEESE

*C*arlos found himself wondering something of the same thing as he looked around the round table in the small board room of the Santo Cristo Family Planning Clinic in south Texas. Two other members of the board were Hispanic, although one preferred to be called Mexican American. The newly elected chairperson was an African-American woman with whom Carlos felt he had less and less in common each time the board met. He and Veneese were constantly at odds, each appearing to have a different vision for the next phase of clinic development. Despite his role as one of the founders of the organization, Carlos was considering resigning his position on the board to defuse the anger he could feel beginning to build in himself at every board meeting. He wished for the hundredth time that he could better understand what Veneese meant by a "woman's point of view" or "the distinct needs of people of color." "What am I, if not a person of color?" Carlos mused silently. "I think I have more in common with Veneese than we have differences. Or is that just part of my male point of view?"

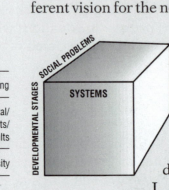

Family Planning

Prenatal/
Adolescents/
Adults

Cultural Diversity

Case

LUZ

*L*uz did her thinking aloud as she addressed the student interviewing for the field placement vacancy at her agency. "I don't know if I'm getting old, or maybe I was always more conservative than necessary, I need to tell you I'm kind of shocked. We have certain standards of dress in our agency that your present, ah, ensemble does not conform to," she said, looking in amazement at the angular young man with the partially shaved head, oversized shirt, and baggy jeans who had been referred by the local university with fine recommendations. When he got up with a shrug and left her office without a backward glance, she wondered—and not for the first time—if she'd been too quick to judge; if she hadn't perhaps missed a "diamond in the rough" by expecting all social work students to look and act just as she and her friends looked and acted years ago. "Am I guilty of expecting everyone else to think

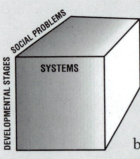

Public Welfare

Adolescents/Adults

Cultural Diversity

and act as I do?" she asked herself. "Was it his hair or clothes I really found objectionable? Or am I finding it hard to adjust to the notion of social work professionals being so much younger than I am, yet qualified to work in this setting?"

One of the pieces of practice wisdom that has been handed down through the years in both social work practice and in education is the admonition to "start where the client is." This means that each of us, as practitioners, need to be sure that we are *with* the client, rather than making assumptions about where the client is. In the scenarios you have just read, Barbara, Carlos, and Luz would all benefit from remembering that bit of advice.

Barbara, for example, would do well to ask her client if *he* sees any difficulty in their gender, age, and ethnic differences. While Barbara sits and wonders (and, therefore, may be distracted in the interview), it is very possible that these issues are the least of John Goodtree's concerns. Carlos, struggling in silence with his anger, may decide to resign from the board without ever having asked Veneese to help him understand what she means by "a woman's point of view" or the "distinct needs of people of color." Whereas Carlos considers himself a person of color, Veneese may be suggesting that the needs of African Americans are not the same as those of Mexican Americans. Although persons of color may share some common experiences—such as discrimination—there are still significant differences between, among, and within groups. Finally, in the case of Luz, she may have lost the opportunity to work with an excellent intern, albeit a young man who may need some "polishing" as a "diamond in the rough."

In each case, if Barbara, Carlos, and Luz had been able to start where the other person was by exploring with them and asking for more information, it is likely that a stronger working relationship would have been established. "Starting where the student is" is also necessary in the process of social work education. As new ideas are presented, some of these will not always be congruent with established beliefs. As educators we need to be sensitive to where students are starting, or we risk not establishing a working relationship and, as a result, we will likely not even hear one another.

Social workers see diversity nearly every day of their working lives. The clients, patients, or public interest groups with which they deal span wide ranges in ethnic composition, age, sexual orientation, social class, religion, and physical and mental abilities. They are strikingly different from one another as well as different from the social workers providing service to them. Dealing with this diversity positively and productively can be a particular challenge for professionals in any setting or with any population.

A Few Definitions

Many terms are used in discussions of diversity, but not all of them have meanings that are useful for a discussion such as ours. Words such as "race," "culture," "minority," "ethnicity," and "class," which we have already used, for example, can be defined variously, depending on their contexts and on who is using them. The term *race*, for instance, is used widely in discussions of human differences, but it is very difficult to define, and—as it turns out—it is not very accurate in describing differences between people or groups of people.

Race

From one perspective, in fact, "races" exist only to the degree that genetic characteristics of individuals—such as skin color, eye shape, or hair form—are given prominence as criteria for allocating or withholding social and economic benefits. From this point of view—which may be a particularly helpful one for social work practice—race is a social concept, not a biological one, and racial distinctions serve no purpose other than to make and justify divisions between groups of people (James Green, 1982). Moreover, the validity of race as the sole explanation of an individual's behavior has been effectively challenged time and again. Overwhelming evidence exists of at least as much difference within so-called racial groups as between them, findings that underscore the greater significance of cultural and ethnic group diversity in U.S. society (Barbara Solomon, 1987).

This is not to suggest that the concept of race is not alive and well in this country and in others; or that individuals with certain genetic characteristics do not meet with significant discrimination, oppression, or injustice. Racism is, in fact, a major social problem today, just as it has been since the beginning of recorded history. Racism still refers accurately to beliefs that assert the inherent superiority of particular racial or ethnic groups over other groups. The racist—the name for an individual who practices racism—often goes so far as developing a form of ethnocentrism that perceives nationality, language, and religion as indicators of race, ascribing to diverse individuals innately inferior physical and cultural attributes as well.

In the United States during various periods of time (and up until the present), many groups of individuals have been considered to be racially different: African Americans, Asians, Latinos, and Native Americans. You will note that none of these so-called racial groups originated in Europe, underscoring the fact that in Western societies such as the United States there is a preference for groups and cultural patterns that are Western European in origin over those with other heritages.

Ethnicity

As a general rule, the term *race* was historically used to designate oppressed people of color, whereas the less pejorative term *ethnic* was used to describe people of European origin. This has been interpreted by some as an acceptance of the cultural diversity of more favored groups and a denial of the ethnic and cultural validity of persons of color (Harriet McAdoo, 1987). Given that the historical use of the term race has probably contributed to exacerbating rather than improving social conditions for oppressed, non-Europeans in the United States, the use of the term ethnic would appear to now be more inclusive, more positive, and more accurate for all of the different subgroups of the U.S. population. From this perspective, for example, certain subgroups of African Americans or blacks would be identified as ethnic groups of color, one of the many oppressed populations that remain in the United States in the 1990s.

Minority-Subordinate Status

There may be some who feel the need to incorporate the term *minority* in discussions of ethnically diverse populations. However, we must be careful to keep in mind that, strictly speaking, minority status has less to do with ethnicity than it does with power and social control (or, more accurately, lack of such control). Minority groups do not necessarily have to be ethnically distinct (although they quite possibly might be and often are). It is not even necessary for members of a minority group to be in a numerical minority, as is evident in the consideration of women—who constitute more than half of the U.S. population—as a minority group. Minority standing refers to disadvantaged status with respect to power, not numbers, and the degree to which the individuals who are identified with one group may be denied access to privileges and opportunities available to others.

The example of South Africa's prior politics and social life until late 1991 demonstrates, in fact, how oppression was effectively accomplished through the mere use of the concept "minority." During most of the twentieth century in South Africa, the 80 percent of the population that was black was divided into 10 distinct minorities as a way to dilute their political effectiveness and power. The white supporters of apartheid, or racial segregation, were thus able to effectively slow the formation of a national political response to oppression by blacks for many decades (Harriet McAdoo, 1987).

Another way in which the concept of minority status has been framed is the dominant–subordinate matrix discussed by Jean Baker Miller (1986):

> Dominant groups usually define one or more acceptable
> roles for the subordinate. Acceptable roles typically
> involve providing services that no dominant group wants
> to perform for itself (for example, cleaning up the
> dominant's waste products). Functions that a dominant
> group prefers to perform . . . are carefully guarded and
> closed to subordinates. Out of the total range of human
> possibilities, the activities most highly valued in any
> particular culture will tend to be enclosed within the
> domain of the dominant group; less valued functions are
> relegated to the subordinates. (pp. 6–7)

Who might this description of dominant–subordinate roles refer to in the 1990s? Miller is actually describing male–female roles. As you considered who Miller might be describing, you no doubt noticed that the dominant–subordinate matrix can be applied to any number of groups that are disadvantaged with respect to power and control.

Traditionally, people of color such as African Americans, Native Americans, and Hispanics (particularly Mexican Americans and Puerto Rican Americans), women (especially low income women), and persons with physical or mental disabilities have been disadvantaged with respect to power and control. Some might note that children are persons without power and control as well, yet childhood is a temporary state out of which individuals move into increasing degrees of power and control—unless you are a member of one of the previous groups, in which case you may still, as an adult, encounter barriers to your achievement of power. Others might note that older persons are increasingly seen as a disadvantaged group because they move out of their "prime" into relatively less powerful positions following retirement—unless they happen to be wealthy, which invariably helps to maintain power and control.

Most of these traditionally disadvantaged groups share a variable: their visibility. A person of color is quite visibly a different color. A woman is identifiable as female. A person with a physical handicap is noted as differently abled. However, gay men and lesbian women are not necessarily visible; despite widespread stereotypes, the vast majority of gay men and lesbian women can, if they choose, "pass" as heterosexual. This results in a double disadvantage because if they cannot be seen, neither can their oppression.

Miller (1986) makes another important point in considering difference when she states that "it is not always clear that in most instances of difference there is also a factor of inequality—inequality of many kinds of resources, but fundamentally of status and power" (p. 3). Status and power are easily translated into economics when comparing dominants and subordinates. On the average, people of color earn less than white people even when their education levels are identical. Women earn less than men with the same level of education. With the 1992 Americans with Disabilities Act (ADA) now in effect, persons with disabilities are protected from job discrimination and are entitled to barrier-free access, which should move them into a competitive position in terms of income opportunities. In contrast, few cities in the nation have enacted nondiscrimination policies for gays and lesbians. Still, because of their invisibility, there are no data that would tell us how their economic status compares with other groups.

In the fall of 1990, *Time* magazine's editors wrote the following about women, the largest nonethnic minority group in the United States:

> A generation from now, if all the dreams of reformers have come true, a special issue devoted to women will seem about as appropriate as a special issue on tall people. This is not to say that by then men and women will have become indistinguishable, their quirks, cares and concerns interchangeable. Rather, the struggles of the last decades of the 20th century will have brought about the freedom and flexibility that have always been the goals of social reform. Issues like equal pay, child care, abortion, rape, and domestic violence will no longer be cast as "women's issues." They will be viewed as economic issues, family issues, ethical issues, of equal resonance to men and women. (*Time*, 1990, p. 12)

The statement suggests, but does not make explicit, that "ownership" of particular issues—women's issues, gay and lesbian issues, or minority issues—is a reflection of a group's relative inequality within society. Otherwise, all issues would be equally important to all persons and it would no longer be necessary for certain groups to claim special issues or interests.

Congruent with a special interest approach, Jerry Weaver (1976) called minorities "communities of interest," or communities made up of those who share a similar set of values, life-styles, and expectations, but with the common and definitive characteristic that they are exposed to a similar set of limiting political and economic circumstances. In this sense, minority refers to social, political, and economic disability, not to cultural or ethnic differences. Thus women in the 1990s clearly retain their minority/subordinate status, as do many ethnic groups, lesbian women and gay men, physically and mentally handicapped citizens, the homeless, and the poor.

Cultural Diversity and Minority Status

Diversity must begin with some essential sense of difference, thus the massive immigration of the late nineteenth and early twentieth centuries in the United States provides an historical look at what developed into models of minority-dominant group relations in the United States.

Between 1860 and 1900, some fourteen million immigrants came to America, and about another nine million, mainly from southern and eastern Europe—Austrians, Hungarians, Bohemians, Poles, Serbs, Italians, Russians, and so on—arrived between 1900 and 1910. (Walter Trattner, 1989, p. 148)

In search of political freedom and economic opportunity, but without the skills needed for many industrialized jobs, the new immigrants flooded the cities' factories as unskilled laborers. Arriving together and remaining together in the same neighborhood tenement housing, they were able to maintain their distinctive cultural traits, such as native language and customs. Within the dominant culture, there was, however, a tremendous push for the immigrant groups to assimilate, that is, to blend in and to become "American."

Some immigration officials, unable to spell or pronounce the immigrants' names, encouraged the newcomers to change their names to sound more American—Bartowski might become Barton,

Tens of thousands of immigrants, primarily from Europe, passed through the Great Hall at Ellis Island, in New York harbor, in the late nineteenth and early twentieth centuries.

Schmidt might become Smith. As a result, immigrants often lived two lives: one within their neighborhoods where their cultural identity was maintained; and another outside the bounds of the neighborhood where they interacted with members of the dominant culture, and their cultural identity was hidden or given up entirely.

To some extent, workers in the settlement houses participated in this model of cultural assimilation by trying to help the new immigrants learn the ways of the dominant culture. Some critics of the settlement house movement have gone much farther in calling most settlements "religious missions" that "reflected, acted upon, and transmitted the values and attitudes of the larger society; beyond their proselytizing activities, they adopted a derogatory view of ethnic traditions and assumed that their proper role was that of Americanizing the immigrant with all possible speed" (Raymond Mohl and Neil Betten in Trattner, 1989, p. 151). Within this historical period, cultural sameness—homogeneity—was clearly valued over cultural diversity. The concept of the American melting pot was born, wherein ethnic groups' cultural heritage and diversity would eventually "melt" into the singular entity of being an American. Of course, this was possible only for white ethnics. Because of their skin color, nonwhite ethnics have never, for the most part, been able to melt into the dominant culture.

Perhaps the concept of the melting pot may not be as appealing as once thought.

David and Jennifer walked together toward the library after class. They were each trying to piece together their family histories, trying to recall if they had been told of any relatives who might have immigrated here in the early 1900s. Jennifer knew that her grandmother could probably tell her, and she made a mental note to ask her.

When she talked with her grandmother later that week, Jennifer got a new perspective on the melting pot theory. "Well, I always like to think about it this way," Grandmother Lloyd said, smiling just a bit. "You like salad, right Jennifer?" Intrigued as usual with her grandmother's backward way of making a point, Jennifer said, "You know I do! What's that got to do with the melting pot theory?" "So you like iceberg lettuce, romaine lettuce, tomatoes, peppers, spinach, and all the things that go into a salad?" Grandmother Lloyd continued, unperturbed by Jennifer's impatience. "Of course I like all those things," Jennifer sighed. "Well then, how about if you put all those things in the blender and have yourself a nice salad?" Feeling queasy at the thought of a "blender salad," because the salad would lose so much in this blending process, Jennifer was powerfully struck with the analogous implications of a melting pot society. All the different colors, textures, and flavors of the unique individual ingredients would be gone; she would be left with a thin, bland, unpalatable, and murky mess.

Walking into class later that week, Jennifer told David about her grandmother's salad metaphor, and found that David had come up with a metaphor of his own. David had pictured a huge tapestry like the AIDS memorial quilt. "Instead of trying to melt or blend away differences," he said, "we could picture society like a huge tapestry or weaving. Every group, every color and nationality, could have their own panel that represents their uniqueness. Everyone could be included, side by side, and it could all be surrounded by a border that binds us together through our shared humanity. Each part maintains its integrity and uniqueness while at the same time enhancing the larger whole. Think what the quilt would lose in impact if all the individual panels were unwoven until they were merely thread and then woven into one large quilt with no distinguishable individual panels."

As Jennifer and David shared their metaphors in class, the discussion led them all to see how the individual parts are enhanced when combined with and connected to other parts, and how the whole is enhanced by maintaining the individual parts.

By the 1960s, the civil rights movement, led by Dr. Martin Luther King, Jr., was drawing attention to racial inequality and the plight of black Americans who were seeking social, economic, and political equality with their white counterparts. As a group, blacks remained far out of the mainstream of opportunities that were afforded to white ethnics. Other black leaders emerged with different visions. Stokely Carmichael emphasized the validity of black culture and advocated black pride, proclaiming, "Black is Beautiful." The Black Power movement sought cultural pluralism rather than cultural assimilation. In cultural pluralism, members of racial or ethnic groups maintain their heritage and cultural identity while living within the dominant culture. Cultural pluralism stands in opposition to the grand melting pot approach that prevailed for many years.

Cultural pluralism, at the extreme, can become separatism, a total movement away from and out of the dominant culture. Malcolm X, a black Muslim, founded the Black Nationalist movement in 1964. Although some black Americans supported black separatism, most did not. However, what is most relevant in this brief historical review are the notable shifts in prevailing views about diversity as represented by minority-dominant relations. For white ethnics, assimilation was the norm. For ethnic groups of color, such as African Americans, there are variations represented by support for equal rights, by support for cultural pluralism, or by support for cultural separatism. It is also worth noting that these variations are themselves suggestive of diversity *within* a group. That is, no one can claim to speak for all African Americans, or for all white ethnics, or for all members of any group. Just as there are individual differences—physical, social, political, and economic—among members of the dominant culture, likewise there will be diversities among members of minority groups. As we engage in our work with clients, this is an important point to remember.

Rather than succumbing to ethnocentric views of judging those different from ourselves negatively, social workers must recognize, respect, and value diversity. We strive to emphatically connect with the experience and perspective of others. To the extent that we are successful at this stretching and bridging, we may be helpful. To the extent we are unable to enter and appreciate another's experience and reality, we will not only fail to help, but may in fact do considerable harm.

Sexual Orientation and Minority Status

In the United States, as we have already noted, people of color and women are not the only groups subject to victimization by the labeling and oppression associated with minority status. Juan Palomo's 9 July 1991 *Houston Post* article (see pages 154 and 155) reminds us that "silence does equal death" when hatred and intolerance of diversity are left unchallenged.

Lesbian women and gay men make up approximately 10 percent of the population, but for social workers this proportion is much less important than their need to receive social work services in nonjudgmental, accepting settings. A deeply ingrained hatred of homosexuals continues in the American consciousness. As *Newsweek* noted in 1990,

There is no way to explain away the prejudice in this
country against gays. People lose jobs, promotions, homes
and friends because of it. Incidents of violence against
gays are up across the country. Hundreds of anti-sodomy
laws remain on the books, and gays are shamelessly
discriminated against in insurance and inheritance. The
fact is that a lot of people are pigheaded enough to judge a
person entirely on the basis of his or her sexuality.
(Jonathan Alter, 1990, p. 27)

*As David nears 30, he continues to wonder if he'll beat the odds
and remain HIV negative. When his partner Gary died last spring,
David became even more fearful of testing positive for HIV, but so far,
he has continued to test negative. As a gay man, David is all too aware
that being a member of a minority group is not easy. He has been
"bashed" more than once as he walked innocently down the streets;
he's been spit on, and called names repeatedly. He has seen friends
evicted by a landlord who didn't want any "homos" in his duplexes.
David could not get spousal health insurance coverage for Gary, despite their long-term, monogamous relationship. In spite of the adver-
sity he has experienced as a result of being open about his sexual
preference, David is comfortable with himself. He is also proud of his
fellow gays and lesbians in the city who have recently elected him
president of the local Lesbian and Gay Political Caucus. The "gay
rights movement in this country may be just a little over 20 years old,"
David notes, "but it has already made major progress in altering many
of the unfavorable myths and stereotypes non-gays have about lesbians and gays and their worth and value as contributing members of
society. I know there are plenty of gay men and women out there who
still won't consider seeking any kind of help from a non-gay person. I
want to be there for them as long as I can."*

Of particular interest to our discussion, of course, is the ability of non-gay and non-lesbian social workers to effectively and
compassionately handle the concerns of lesbian and gay clients,
patients, or special interest groups. Particularly with the dramatic
increase in cases of Acquired Immune Deficiency Syndrome (AIDS)
and its association with high-risk behaviors among gay males,
many more social workers have been presented with these specific
issues. And, as these opportunities have emerged, social workers
have had to simultaneously deal with their own feelings of homo-

Paying the Cost for Keeping Silent

Juan R. Palomo

I am not feeling too terribly proud of myself today. Let me explain. Recently, I wrote about Linda Morales, the Democratic activist who is a lesbian and was a grand marshal of the Gay Pride Parade.

The next day I got a call from an admirer urging me not to write any more about "the fags" because my readers were upset. I remained silent and let him go on talking until he realized I was not pleased with his call.

Over the next several days, I got several letters, some unsigned, from religious zealots, quoting the Bible to the effect that both Morales and I will end up in hell, using words such as "queers," "perverts," and "despicable creatures."

One person gave me 40 days to repent and vowed to pray for my destruction if I don't. Again, I remained silent.

The next week, a co-worker suggested we go down to Montrose "to beat up some queers."

Because I knew he was joking and because I thought it would be less of a hassle, I remained silent. A few hours later, he repeated the same remark and again, I remained silent.

Silent Much Too Long

But Sunday morning, as I read about Nancy Rodriguez, the Georgia woman who had come here to pick up the body of her 27-year-old son, Paul Broussard, I decided that I have remained silent way too long.

If you haven't heard about Paul Broussard, don't feel embarrassed. This newspaper, which has been conducting a "Search for Justice" crusade for several weeks, relegated the story to the local news section, as did the other paper.

Broussard and two friends were attacked around 3 A.M. Thursday, as they walked from a gay bar in Montrose. He and one of his friends were beaten with nail-covered two-by-fours by 10 or so young men. Broussard died several hours later.

It's being labeled a gay bashing incident, another in a series of hate-filled attacks on gay people. But it was the killing of a human being, cold and cowardly. It was an act of pure hatred committed by the 10 young

phobia—the fear or hatred of homosexuality—which are common feelings, even among lesbians and gays.

It is interesting, at least historically, that as recently as 1975, the American Psychiatric Association defined homosexual behavior as a mental disorder. However, research on sexual behavior and personal adjustment for many years demonstrated that lesbians and gays had no more symptoms of mental illness than their non-gay counterparts. Therefore, in a landmark decision in 1976, the American Psychiatric Association decided to remove homosexuality from its list of mental disorders. This pro-men, but also by their parents, their schools, their churches and their communities.

Gay activists say that if it hadn't been for their efforts to alert reporters, Broussard's death might have gone unnoticed because the police were acting as if it were just another murder.

It might as well have been, for most of official and religious Houston reacted to this latest act of brutal oppression with a thundering, deafening silence.

Had it been some white kids attacking a member of a minority group for the sole reason that he or she was a member of that group—or vice versa—this city would have been up in arms and the story would have stayed on the front page for weeks.

Every elected official and would-be elected official would be out roaming the streets in search of a TV camera, instead of reluctantly talking about it when cornered in some hallway.

But in the eyes of many, Broussard was a queer. He was a fag. He was a despicable creature, and he probably deserved to die for the fact that God made him prefer men.

The End of Silence

The right-to-lifers apparently feel he had no right to life because they too are silent.

That he was a loving son and an earnest employee, and that he loved to read books, meant nothing to this group of maniacs who attacked him, and it apparently means nothing to most of us.

His mother told The Post's Matt Schwartz that she couldn't understand how such things can happen.

Well, I can.

I can understand because I know that such things are a result of the silence of people like me. Paul Broussard died because we are cowards. We prefer to sit in our cubby holes and spend all our efforts keeping our sinking boat steady.

The gay rights activists are right: Silence does equal death.

When we fail to speak up, we are sanctioning the hatred or ignorance of people like my co-worker and my correspondents. And it is such hatred and ignorance that tells stupid kids it's OK to go around beating up the Paul Broussards of the world.

I didn't know Paul Broussard, but I am not going to let Houston forget him, or how he died—or why.

SOURCE: Houston Post, *9 July 1991.*

vides a powerful illustration of how something as critical to individual identity as sexual orientation can be defined as problematic or nonproblematic according to the judgments of other groups in society.

This has been true in the case of mental health treatment diagnosis for lesbians and gays, and will undoubtedly be the case for other groups in the future—including aging Americans, the physically and mentally handicapped, and most ethnic minorities. Changes in the demographics of our country may suggest one way some of these modifications are most likely to occur.

The New Demographics of Diversity in the United States

For decades the United States has been a nation of diverse peoples, cultures, and ethnic heritages, but the 1990 census showed more profound changes in these characteristics than at any other time in the twentieth century. In 1990, nearly one in every four Americans claimed African, Asian, Hispanic, or Native American ancestry (representing more than 63 million people). In the area of population statistics, where changes sometimes seem glacially slow, the speed at which the country's ethnic composition changed in the 1980s was breathtaking (Felicity Barringer, 1991). There is no area of future social work practice that will not be affected by these dramatic population shifts. At a minimum, agencies that served few ethnic group members will soon serve many more; those that served many may well be overwhelmed by a growing demand for services.

Of these rapidly growing ethnic groups, none is increasing faster in the United States than Hispanics—a group whose numbers now exceed 25 million, or 10 percent of the total national population. An emerging group of young Hispanic leaders is using social work community development strategies to mobilize local ethnic group members to gain a greater share of power over their own affairs.

"Hispanics are going to galvanize around a set of issues more than race," says Daniel Solis, head of Chicago's United Neighborhood Organization (UNO). "And because we're made up of different nationalities and different opinions, we're forced to do it the hard way—at the grass roots level with local institutions" (Eloise Salholz, 1990, p. 19).

Chicago is not the only city that has set itself the task of creating a workable living environment for many, diverse ethnic groups. A 1991 article in *The New Yorker* magazine suggested that

> some Americans around the country are beginning to
> articulate a belief that a livable multi-racial city or a
> multi-racial society is something we will achieve when we
> start to treat racism itself as a dangerous public-health
> problem—one that stunts human development in America
> and jeopardizes our economic security, because it

contaminates our judgement. Some Baltimoreans . . . who have been thinking about the issue are trying to prepare a strategy that splices people together in ways that simultaneously begin to blur the distinctions between "us" and "them" and between "here" and "there." It's an idea that, if it can be accomplished, might ultimately help to restrain one longtime American tendency that adds to racial tension—running away from people you don't like or are scared of. (Tony Hiss, 1991, p. 44)

Racial and ethnic tensions are not the only ones fueled by the tendency to avoid situations where individuals are different from one another. As people in our nation age, for example, problems of where these older citizens are to live have become more frequent and pressing. For example, at the turn of the century, a newborn male could expect to live to be 46 years of age, a female to 49 (David Maldonado, 1987, p. 97). Contemporary social workers are increasingly working with an everwidening range of elderly and very elderly people, including a surprising number who are 90 to 100 years of age—or even older!

In 1900, 4 percent (3.08 million people) of the total U.S. population was 65 years of age or older; by 1980, the 65 and older group had grown to over 25 million people, or 11.3 percent of the total population (David Maldonado, 1987, pp. 95–96). This not only suggests that people are living longer than ever before, but that the need for long-term care facilities, such as nursing homes, is increasing as well. The concept of long-term care now goes beyond a traditional concern with basic nursing home facilities. Demographic projections suggest that by the year 2050 the 65 and older group will represent 21.7 percent of the total population, or more than 67 million people (David Maldonado, 1987, p. 96).

The issues now at hand relate to developing and maintaining a continuum of care system that will address the whole spectrum of needs among older persons. One of the major questions is determining what types of services a diverse older population will need in the next few decades, especially as the baby boomers born in the 1940s move inexorably into the ranks of the aged. Young social workers moving from classrooms into agency practice will perhaps find a greater difference between the ages of their clients and themselves than any previous group of practitioners.

The client base for social work practitioners represents a diversity of ages, racial and ethnic backgrounds, abilities and disabilities, family structures, and sexual orientations.

Diversity and Political Correctness

Recently, you may have heard about *political correctness,* a term that probably conjures up visions of the "thought police." The term dates back to the early part of this century, but only came back into the public eye in the 1980s; it is defined as "marked by or adhering to a typically progressive orthodoxy on issues involving especially race, gender, sexual affinity or ecology" *(Random House Webster's College Dictionary).* Political correctness, according to Dinesh D'Souza (1991), has come to apply "to the assorted ideologies of the late 1960's and early 1970's: black consciousness and black power, feminism, homosexual rights, and, to a lesser degree, pacifism, environmentalism, and so on" (p. xiv). We have addressed diversity as a point of difference, and we have advocated an appreciative stance toward diversity. To some, this would represent political correctness. D'Souza asks:

> Is freedom of speech a central academic value, or only one of several competing values, so that many occasions will arise when it must be balanced against, or subordinated to, or sacrificed on the altar of other political and social values, such as appreciation for diversity? (p. xix)

We do not support the view that the ends justify the means. We do not advocate violations of First Amendment rights to free speech. As social workers, we believe in the inherent dignity and worth of all persons. We appreciate diversity in all its multifaceted dimensions. We would like to see a world in which all persons are treated with dignity and respect. We would rather hear Hispanic instead of spic, African American instead of nigger, Jewish instead of kike, gay instead of faggot, woman instead of girl, and so on. Some would say that this is sacrificing freedom of speech to the requirements of political correctness. We think it is an expression of respect. We also believe that our values and attitudes are reflected in our language. Those who allege that they are being forced to use politically correct language may be reacting to pressures toward social change. People with a vested interest in the status quo typically do not embrace change. We recognize that there is comfort in the known and in the familiar, and there is anxiety and resistance in the unknowns that change represents.

In the present era of declining resources and economic hard

times, many people in this society are frightened; though not all people fear the same things, and not all people are afraid constantly. Although fear is not the reality for all people, enough are frightened to make life conflictual and painful. White men are afraid that they will be displaced from positions of power and authority, that they will lose their accustomed roles, statuses and, potentially, their incomes, to women or racial-ethnic minorities, because these groups are perceived to be receiving preferential treatment over white men. Women— as they have been for centuries—are afraid of violence at the hands of strangers and, increasingly, are afraid of violence from those they know. Middle- and working-class women employed outside the home fear that they will not be "good enough" as mothers, and women who are homemakers fear that they will be looked down on for being "just housewives." Hispanic and African-American men fear the pervasiveness of drug addiction and violence from within their own communities, and the women fear for the safety and well-being of their children because violence is likely to erupt in school or on the streets. Heterosexuals of all racial-ethnic groups fear gay men as transmitters of HIV disease, and both gay men and lesbian women are feared for their perceived "differentness" and as a threat to traditional family models. And now, increasing numbers of Americans—of whatever ethnic group, age, or sexual orientation—are afraid that the Japanese are poised to take over the U.S. economy.

Intolerance of difference appears to be increasing, particularly in some of our nation's college campuses. This intolerance is seen in many forms. There is increased visibility among various extremist groups such as the "Skinheads," an all-white, youth-oriented neo-Nazi group that advocates white supremacy, often by use of physical violence. Political and social policy issues such as women's reproductive rights have sparked violent encounters between anti-abortion and pro-choice groups. U.S. citizens have begun to engage in "Japan bashing," not only with verbal attacks, but by literally demolishing products imported from Japan. Anti-semitism is on the rise, as evidenced by attacks on Jewish synagogues in different cities. Gay-bashing, random violent attacks on gay and lesbian persons, are on the increase. The term "hate crimes" has become part of our language.

The legacy of fear and intolerance is defensiveness and anger. If we speak out about women's issues, we are likely to be confronted angrily with, "What about *men's* issues?" If we speak in favor of diversity and multiculturalism, we are confronted by allegations of political correctness and reverse discrimination. If we speak out on behalf of gay and lesbian issues, we are either met with silence, or with "Why do they have to flaunt it?" Let us be clear: There is nothing politically correct about representing the concerns of one group at the expense of another. Nor is there anything truly feminist about a women's agenda that excludes the concerns of men. The dilemma, it seems, lies in the experience of some people who hear advocacy on behalf of one group as an attack on another group. To advocate for women is not to denigrate men. To support women's rights is not to take away men's rights.

The feminist perspective that we have integrated in this text includes a valuing and appreciation of diversity. To speak for diversity is choice enhancing, not choice reducing. Connection—through mutual, reciprocal, empathic relationships—is not only the means, but also the ends (or the confirmation) of a healthy society. This feminist perspective represents the antithesis—the opposite—of the tension and divisiveness that currently exists between and among different groups in this society. It is a perspective that emphasizes inclusion rather than exclusion. It is a world view that sees all living things as interrelated, interconnected, and interdependent. It is difficult to understand how such a view can be labeled pejoratively as political correctness. It is also unfortunate that the hostility surrounding political correctness has obscured the valid issues that truly deserve thoughtful discussion and consideration.

Having said all this, you will recall earlier in this chapter that we discussed the admonition to "start where the client is" as a necessary element in establishing good working relationships. We would be remiss if we did not acknowledge that some persons—clients, supervisors, students, faculty—will not necessarily embrace the feminist perspective that we have been using throughout this text. There is no way to know how many social work practitioners openly describe themselves as feminist social workers, or how many clients or potential clients describe themselves as feminist in their views. It is important, as in all social work practice, that we be sensitive to where other people are in their thinking, and in their developmental process of becoming. We advocate for a particular vision shaped by a feminist lens, but we cannot be effective social workers if we are intolerant of views that differ from our own.

How Does Diversity Affect What You Will Do in Practice?

It is impossible to predict whether you will encounter a great deal of diversity as a practicing social worker or whether all of your clients will be very much the same as one another—and very much like you. Remember: You must not leave yourself out of this diversity equation. It just might be that all your clients, or patients, or groups are just about the same age, from the same social class, the same ethnic background, with the same sexual orientation, and the same mental abilities. None of them may have AIDS or a physical handicap. And if they are much like you, maybe you think you won't have to worry about diversity at all. Let's consider this from another perspective.

Case

CAROL

Carol is a clinical supervisor at a large family service agency. In the past couple of days, she has received complaints from two former agency clients, both of whom worked with Jane, one of Carol's supervisees. Carol has asked Jane to come in for a conference to discuss these concerns. Carol begins by noting that some of Jane's clients quit coming to the agency after only two or three sessions.

"I just don't understand it," bemoans Jane. "When I review intake forms of potential client assignments I always try to get myself assigned to people who are a lot like me in age, ethnic background, social class, and general life-style. I just thought that having all these things in common would increase rapport and make it easier for me to help them." Carol decides to share part of a letter received by one of Jane's former clients. The client wrote: "The last straw was when my grandfather suddenly died. When I told Jane about it, she launched into how sad I must feel and how awful it must be and told me she knew *exactly* how I must feel because her grandfather died last year and she was just devastated. The fact is, I hated my grandfather. He sexually molested me from the time I was 5 years old until I was 13. As far as I'm concerned, good riddance. I'm glad he's dead. But I never got a chance to tell Jane that. There's no way she would understand. After listening to her go on and on, I even started feeling guilty for not feeling sad."

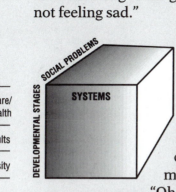

Public Welfare/
Mental Health

Adults

Incest/Diversity

Carol went on to share what Jane's other client had said: "Jane was always saying that I was just like her and so she knew exactly what I must be feeling. Most of the time I wasn't feeling anything like what she thought I was." This client related an incident during which the client had been expressing anger about her mother's constant criticism, and Jane said, "Oh but come on now . . . you're not *really* angry are you? Down deep you know your mom just wants what's best for you, don't you? I'll bet you really feel loved and cared for when she criticizes, just like I do when my mother makes suggestions about how I might do something differently in my life."

Carol was concerned. She recognized quickly that Jane had a distorted idea of what professional helping meant in a therapeutic role. Based on her responses, Jane seemed to think that telling clients she "knew just how they felt" was helpful when, in fact, her clients had not felt heard at all. Carol knew she would need to work with Jane to help her understand the importance of truly entering the reality of another person's experience, rather than diminishing it as she had been doing (quite unintentionally, no doubt).

Carol also recognized that Jane did not yet understand that there is no such thing as a human being who is "just like" any other. Jane apparently believed that by choosing clients who seemed very much like her, she would immediately and automatically know them and understand their experience. Carol had worked successfully with these kinds of issues with other supervisees. In fact, she could even recall herself struggling with feelings similar to Jane's early in her career. Carol was confident that she would help Jane grow to understand that no matter how similar another person and their experience may look to us on the surface, what goes on inside that person will be uniquely their experience. Diversity, whether or not obvious on the surface, would always exist in the uniqueness of each and every client.

New immigration laws and policies have dramatically changed the face of immigration in the last twenty years, as this naturalization ceremony in Washington, D.C., in October 1991 reflects.

Over the course of your life and your career, the people you work with may or may not be like you in many ways. Social work services are provided disproportionately to individuals with lower incomes, and most social workers are solid members of the middle class, so you may have economic differences to consider. Perhaps, as in Barbara's situation, your clients will be from a different ethnic or age group; or, like Carlos's, from both a different ethnic group and a different gender; or, like Luz's, your clients will be a different age, either younger or older. Or, perhaps like Jane, you'll need to learn that clients "just like you" really aren't clones, but unique individuals with their own stories to tell. In all of these cases, not only must you consider the problem, issue, opportunity, or concern for which your client has consulted you, but you must also consider the differences that may exist between you.

There remain several cautions about the process of addressing the issue of diversity. We must take care not to focus on differences at the expense of ignoring common human themes and similarities. In essence, we can never assume that our clients feel and experience their worlds the same way we do, no matter how similar to us any client appears to be. At the same time, we can never assume that our clients feel and experience their worlds in some totally alien and incomprehensible manner, no matter how different from us any client appears to be. Diversity is a point of difference, not a cause for fear or a justification for intolerance.

Take a few minutes and picture a world without diversity. All the lands look the same, perhaps totally arid like the desert, or completely mountainous. However you picture the country around you, it is all the same. The people in your imagined world are all the same, too—no one is average in any respect because there are no differences to average out. How do you feel picturing sameness in your entire world and sameness among all the people who inhabit it? Even when we acknowledge that intolerance of difference can result in painful conflict, we would still prefer to live in a diverse world, especially a world where diversity is appreciated.

Summary

This chapter has touched briefly on some of the characteristics of populations you will be working with as a professional social worker; it particularly highlights specific areas of difference or diversity. It is impossible to cover all of the varied ways that individuals can be different from one another yet retain their essential humanness; however, all of the demographic indicators in the United States suggest that the degree of diversity in our nation continues to increase each year. It will be a rare social worker whose career is not impacted by these important changes.

References

Alter, Jonathan. "Degrees of Discomfort: Is Homophobia Equivalent to Racism?" *Newsweek*, 12 March 1990, 27.

Barringer, Felicity. "Census Shows Profound Change in Racial Makeup of the Nation: Shift Toward Minorities Is Sharpest of the Twentieth Century." *New York Times*, Vol. III, No. 48,536 (Monday, 11 March 1991): 1.

Bloom, Martin. *Introduction to the Drama of Social Work*. Itasca, IL: F. E. Peacock, 1990.

DiNitto, Diana, and C. Aaron McNeece. *Social Work: Issues and Opportunities in a Challenging Profession*. Englewood Cliffs, NJ: Prentice-Hall, 1990.

D'Souza, Dinesh. *Illiberal Education: The Politics of Race and Sex on Campus*. New York: Vintage Books, 1991.

Green, James W. *Cultural Awareness in the Human Services*. Englewood Cliffs, NJ: Prentice-Hall, 1982.

Hiss, Tony. "Annals of Place (Baltimore)." *The New Yorker*, 29 April 1991, 40–74.

McAdoo, Harriet P. "Blacks." In *The Encyclopedia of Social Work*, 194–205. Edited by Anne Minahan. Silver Spring, MD: NASW, 1987.

Maldonado, David, Jr. "Aged." In *The Encyclopedia of Social Work*, pp. 95–106. Edited by Anne Minahan. Silver Spring, MD: NASW, 1987.

Miller, Jean Baker. *Toward A New Psychology of Women*, 2nd ed. Boston: Beacon Press, 1986.

Morales, Amando T., and Bradford W. Sheafor. *Social Work: A Profession of Many Faces*, 6th ed. Boston: Allyn & Bacon, 1992.

Salholz, Eloise. "The Push for Power: After a Decade of Disappointment, Hispanics Try to Translate Their Numbers into Political Clout." *Newsweek*, 9 April 1990, 18–20.

Solomon, Barbara B. "Human Development: Sociocultural Perspective." In *The Encyclopedia of Social Work*, 856–866. Edited by Anne Minahan. Silver Spring, MD: NASW, 1987.

Time, "The Road To Equality," Special Issue on Women, Vol. 136, Issue 19 (Fall 1990): 12–14.

Trattner, Walter I. *From Poor Law to Welfare State,* 4th ed. New York: Free Press, 1989.

Weaver, Jerry L. *National Health Policy and the Underserved: Ethnic Minorities, Women, and the Elderly.* St. Louis: C. V. Mosby, 1976.

Zastrow, Charles. *Introduction to Social Work and Social Welfare,* 5th ed. Pacific Grove, CA: Brooks/Cole, 1993.

CHAPTER 6

Values and Ethics

Introduction

In Chapter 1, we offered three broad definitions of social work. In this chapter we present a more elaborate statement of purpose for the profession. This statement provides us with a framework in which we will discuss social work values and ethics. In his 1957 article, Ernest Greenwood noted that one of the essential attributes of a profession is having its own code of ethics. As you'll see shortly, there is an overarching code of ethics developed by the National Association of Social Workers (NASW), as well as some other social work codes of ethics reflecting some different emphases. And, to help you develop a greater understanding of professional values and ethics in relation to social work practice, we will once again meet some of our intro class students as they find themselves confronted with value and ethical dilemmas.

Professional Purpose

As you have already seen, social workers have a long history and tradition relative to promoting the social welfare of all persons. This has also included an ethical responsibility to create social change, particularly for oppressed and marginalized groups. Ironically, however, agreement on a singular statement of purpose for the profession, while long sought after, has been elusive. The social work profession is unique by virtue of its person-in-environment perspective, but there are differing views about how much the emphasis should be given to the *person*, to the *environment*, or to the *interactions* between the two. Should the profession's mission be geared toward enhancing social functioning of individual persons? Toward effecting social change in the many environments in which individuals live? Or should our interventions be directed toward those intersections at which individuals and environments meet and interact?

According to the participants at the second meeting on conceptual frameworks held in Chicago in 1979, "The purpose of social work is to promote or restore a mutually beneficial interaction between individuals and society in order to improve the quality of life for everyone" (Anne Minahan, 1981, p. 6).[1] The working statement on the purpose of social work indicates that

social workers hold the following beliefs:

- The environment (social, physical, organizational) should provide the opportunity and resources for the maximum realization of the potential and aspirations of all individuals, and should provide for their common human needs and for the alleviation of distress and suffering.
- Individuals should contribute as effectively as they can to their own well-being and to the social welfare of others in their immediate environment as well as to the collective society.
- Transactions between individuals and others in their environment should enhance the dignity, individuality, and self-determination of everyone. People should be treated humanely and with justice.
- Clients of social workers may be an individual, a family, a group, a community or an organization. (Anne Minahan, 1981, p. 6)

This working statement provides a framework for our discussion of values and ethics.

Values

One of the key words in the working statement is *should*, a word that connotes a certain sense of belief about a perceived "ideal." Values reflect selected beliefs about how life *should* be. Generally speaking, values are shared ideas about what is good, right, and desirable. The authors of the Declaration of Independence, for example, held that certain "truths" were self-evident, most prominently, "that all men

[sic] are created equal, that they are endowed . . . with certain un-alienable rights, that among these are Life, Liberty, and the pursuit of Happiness."[2] These truths are, in effect, value statements that have been carried over through the years as foundations of a democratic society.

Values remain somewhat general and abstract until translated into social norms. Norms are viewed as rules, or guidelines for behavior. For example, that "all men are created equal" remained a lofty abstraction for African Americans until full equality was granted them through various civil rights legislation in the 1960s, nearly 200 years after the Declaration of Independence was signed. Women have yet to achieve full equality through law because the Equal Rights Amendment has never been passed by the necessary two-thirds majority of Congress. In essence, values are elusive and perhaps even meaningless until translated into action.

Few politicians would fail to agree with the value statement that "no child should go hungry in this country." If that same politician fails to support the Aid to Families with Dependent Children (AFDC) and food stamp programs, or to introduce other, innovative solutions to these problems, we can clearly see a contradiction between words and actions. State after state in recent history has talked about the importance (value) of taking care of its human resources, particularly children. Yet we have seen, in these same states, the refusal to find additional revenues necessary to fit actions to words. Budgets, whether federal, state, or local are one way to take a set of values and put those values into action. We might, for example, look at our federal budget and conclude that we value constructing highways and making weapons more than we value the quality of life.

For values to have real meaning in our lives, they must be translated into definitive action. Helen Harris Perlman (1976) has said, "A value has small worth except as it is moved, or is moveable, from believing into doing, from verbal affirmation into action" (p. 381). For example, to the degree that a society values an educated populace, there will be public schools and mandatory attendance laws; to the degree that a society values older persons, there will be supportive mechanisms to provide for their physical and mental health, as well as their financial needs. Just as any person's individual values exist within a context, so do the values of a profession. The values held by a particular profession exist within the context of a given society.

Women Have Never Been Full Partners in American Liberty

Still Awaiting Independence Day

By Beverly McPhail

The Fourth of July celebrations are just around the corner. And although the controversy surrounding the Martin Luther King holiday still rages in many states, the Fourth of July festivities seem rather simple and uncomplicated in comparison. Americans from all walks of life will unite to celebrate 215 years of freedom marked by the signing of the Declaration of Independence. For most Americans the biggest controversy on the Fourth will concern which fireworks display to attend or whether to barbecue hot dogs or brisket.

Yet for a certain segment of the population, the Fourth of July celebrations bring to mind a more troubling question: How many years of freedom can American women actually celebrate?

Although some people would quickly state that women are celebrating the same 215 years of freedom that all Americans share, this simply isn't the case. When our forefathers wrote "All men are created equal," they specifically meant men

while purposefully excluding women from the freedoms bestowed by the new republic. Women in early America could not vote, own property or sue in court. The exclusion of women was not merely an oversight. In March of 1776 Abigail Adams sent a letter to her husband who was attending the Continental Congress in Philadelphia. She wrote: "And by the way, in the new code of laws, which I suppose it will be necessary to make, I desire you would remember the ladies, and be more generous and favorable to them than your ancestors." Five months later the Declaration of Independence was adopted without a mention of rights or freedoms for women.

So, how many years of freedom can women celebrate on this Fourth of July? If not from 1776, perhaps women can date their independence from 1848, when Elizabeth Cady Stanton presented the Declaration of Rights and Sentiments at the nation's first women's rights convention. The Declaration

stated that "All men and women are created equal." However, this document was ridiculed and never codified so the declaration never translated into tangible freedoms for women.

Perhaps women can celebrate 71 years of freedom rather than 215 years, since in 1920 women gained the right to vote with the ratification of the 19th Amendment to the Constitution. An amendment granting women the right to vote was introduced into Congress session after session for more than 40 years before being adopted in 1920. Instead of bemoaning the extended length of time women worked to win the right to vote, perhaps women should just celebrate this day as the start of women's full participation in American democracy.

Unfortunately, though, winning the right to vote did not enable women to reap many of the benefits of a living in a free society. Women were still treated as second-class citizens and were frequent victims of economic, social and sexual discrimination.

Perhaps women can celebrate 28 years of freedom this Fourth of July, dating emancipation from the second wave of the women's movement, which is generally conceded to have begun in 1963 with the publication of *The Feminine Mystique* by Betty Friedan. On the other hand, although this book raised the nation's consciousness about sexism, new awareness didn't always translate into new attitudes or new laws.

The passage of the Equal Rights Amendment could have been a point from which to date women's full participation in a free and just society. However, the amendment was never ratified. Although first introduced in 1923 and passed by Congress in 1972, it was never ratified by the necessary three-fourths of the states. Despite an extension in 1979, the Amendment finally failed in 1982. Fear of unisex bathrooms and other ridiculous assertions kept a statement of women's equality out of the Constitution.

Perhaps this quest to pinpoint when women joined in the promises of liberty, freedom, and opportunity given to men in 1776 is a futile exercise. Perhaps the specific date

isn't important. This Fourth of July, women could forget the past slights and exclusions and just celebrate the rights and freedoms that are ours today.

But are women really free in America today? Do we have those precious personal liberties that are the hallmark of a democracy? Although women fought for their country in the Persian Gulf, female soldiers are still restricted from receiving many medals, promotions and increased pay given to men who serve in combat.

Women's personal freedoms are also restricted here at home, as women live in constant fear of being victims of violence by men. It is estimated that a rape is committed every six minutes in the United States. Three to four million women in the United States are beaten in their homes each year by their husbands, ex-husbands, or boyfriends. Domestic violence is the single largest cause of injury to women in the United States.

Women's lack of freedom and status in the United States is often more subtle than outright violence. The term "glass ceiling" was created to describe the corporate ladder structure that prevents women from rising to top executive positions. A report from the

National Institutes of Health this year revealed that only 13 percent of the annual budget on research is devoted to women's health concerns despite an increase in the number of deaths of women due to breast cancer and heart disease.

The Hate Crimes Statistics Act recently signed by President Bush directs the U.S. Department of Justice to collect statistics on crimes motivated by the victim's race, religion, ethnicity or sexual orientation, but purposely ignores gender-based crimes. The term "feminization of poverty" was coined to describe the increasing number of women who fall below the poverty line in the United States. Women who work full time still earn only 66 cents to the man's dollar.

Not only have women been denied freedoms in the past, but freedoms previously granted are being stripped away. Women's reproductive choices are being increasingly limited across the nation.

These grim realities are just a few of the indicators that women have yet to become free and equal participants in American democracy. Although women have made considerable gains since 1776, there is still a long way to go before women can be said to be full recipients of the liberty and freedom so tantalizingly promised in the Declaration of Independence. The American flag, which represents freedom for some, remains only an illusion of freedom for women, who are still frequent survivors of violence, sexism, harassment and discrimination.

The search for when women in America became full partners in the nation's democratic principles is futile when looking for the answer in the past, for that landmark has yet to occur. Women cannot rest complacently this Fourth of July, for the freedoms inherent in a democratic society are not yet ours. Women must continue to work on all fronts to achieve the rights and liberties that should be ours and will be ours one day.

McPhail is a social worker and free-lance writer living in Houston. SOURCE: Houston Post, *30 June 1991.*

Dean Hepworth and Jo Ann Larsen (1990) have observed that "professions espouse and champion selected societal values, and society in turn gives sanction and recognition to professions through supportive legislation, funding, delegation of responsibility for certain societal functions, and mechanisms for assuring that those functions are adequately discharged" (p. 9). Even though social work values have not changed appreciably over the years, the degree of tangible support, most notably supportive legislation and funding, has gone through a series of ebbs and flows over time. This has been especially apparent in the recent history of social welfare we presented in Chapter 3. These ebbs and flows have coincided with shifting societal values, which are then reflected in the positions taken by persons with decision-making authority (e.g., state legislators, members of Congress, and local members of city councils or county commissions).

Social Work Values

By this time, it may not surprise you to learn that naming social work values depends, to some extent, on who you ask or what books you read. Some authors of social work texts have differentiated between primary and instrumental values (Allen Pincus and Anne Minahan, 1973), fundamental tenets and secondary values (Scott Briar and Henry Miller, 1963), and cardinal and operational values (Dean Hepworth and Jo Ann Larsen, 1990). The NASW (1981) lists 10 overall values:

1. commitment to the primary importance of the individual in society;

2. respect for the confidentiality of relationships with clients;

3. commitment to social change to meet socially recognized needs;

4. willingness to keep personal feelings and needs separate from professional relationships;

5. willingness to transmit knowledge and skills to others;

6. respect and appreciation for individual and group differences;

7. commitment to develop clients' ability to help themselves;

8. willingness to persist in efforts on behalf of clients despite frustration;

9. commitment to social justice and the economic, physical, and mental well-being of all members of society;

10. commitment to a high standard of personal and professional conduct.

The list developed by NASW seems to describe an "ideal" social worker, rather than to provide a clear delineation of social work values. It does, however, underscore the point that identifying social work values is not as easy as we might expect. In fact, it is a somewhat arbitrary process. Acknowledging that, we would highlight the four "cardinal values" offered by Hepworth and Larsen (1990) as a point of departure for our discussion.

1. People should have access to the resources they need to meet life's challenges and difficulties as well as access to opportunities to realize their potentialities throughout their lives.
2. Every person is unique and has inherent worth; therefore, interactions with people as they pursue and utilize resources should enhance their dignity and individuality.
3. People have a right to freedom insofar as they do not infringe on the rights of others; therefore, transactions with people in the course of seeking and utilizing resources should enhance their independence and self-determination.
4. Realization of the above values should be the mutual responsibility of individual citizens and of society. Society should foster conditions and provide

opportunities for citizens to participate in the
democratic process. Citizens should fulfill their
responsibilities to society by actively participating in
the democratic process. (Dean Hepworth and Jo Ann
Larson, 1990, p. 9)

If some of these statements seem familiar to you, that is no
coincidence. Each has origins that are well-ingrained in U.S. society. Naomi Brill (1990) suggests that the dominant values of Western society can be traced to four different sources: First, the Judeo-
Christian doctrine, which suggests the inherent worth of all persons
and the notion of responsibility for others; second, the democratic
ideals identified in the Declaration of Independence; third, the puritan ethic, which suggests that "good" or moral persons work hard,
are independent and self-sufficient, and are successful because of
their own efforts; and fourth, social Darwinism, a belief in the evo-
lutionary process that suggests that the strong survive, and the weak
perish. In any discussion of values, societal and professional, there
will be echoes of these underlying values, and there will likely be
disagreement as to how these values should be translated into action.

An extremely important "value set" that shapes social work
policy and practice is the basic ideology of the social work profession. An ideology is "a system of ideas that is the product of one's
values, experiences, political persuasion, level of moral development, and aspirations for humanity" (Robert Barker, 1991, p. 109).
Competing ideologies or ideological conflicts are common. As discussed in previous chapters, the distinction made historically between the worthy and the unworthy poor reflects an ideological
conflict. Or, if we think of competing ideologies on social welfare as
a continuum, we could label one end as the *residual view* and the
other end as the *institutional view*. The residual view holds that
social welfare services should be created only "after all else has
failed." In clear contrast, the institutional view holds that social
welfare services are a natural part of society and therefore an essential right.

Although social welfare services and policies in the United
States exist within a dominant democratic and capitalistic system,
social work's predominant ideology is a liberal one. This liberal
ideology views the existence of social problems as "normal" in a

developed nation and views social welfare as a legitimate function of government. There are, of course, varying degrees of liberalism, just as there are varying degrees of conservatism. A strictly conservative ideology would, however, likely run counter to the value stances of the social work profession. Likewise (although some might disagree) an ideology that identifies capitalism as the root of all problems, and therefore sees the solutions in socialism or communism, would likely be viewed as outside the mainstream ideology of U.S. social welfare.

From among the values identified thus far, we have selected three for closer examination: (1) the inherent worth and dignity of all persons; (2) client self-determination; and (3) confidentiality. Keep in mind that any list of social work values has been developed somewhat arbitrarily. We realize, for example, that some people might question our inclusion of confidentiality as a value of equal significance. Inherent worth and dignity and self-determination are fundamental social work values. Confidentiality might just as well be considered a practice principle, rather than as a value. We have included confidentiality, however, because it is so frequently misunderstood as providing more protection to social workers than is often the case. Inherent worth and dignity is included in our discussion because it is the singular value that literally everyone includes in a list of social work values. Likewise, client self-determination is given considerable attention in the social work literature. It may also be the most complex value to apply in practice. Questions and illustrations are provided to highlight these selected values.

Inherent Worth and Dignity of All Persons

This value suggests that *all* persons, by definition, have inherent worth and dignity as human beings on this planet. Regardless of gender, race, ethnicity, culture or national origin, sexual orientation, age, religion, physical or mental handicap, all persons are worthwhile inherently, and all persons are entitled to dignity in their unique personhood. Initially this value can be difficult to understand. The key to understanding this value is the ability to separate, at least intellectually, a person's behavior from that person's inherent essence of humanity.

You might, for example, be wondering how social workers see inherent worth and dignity in a client who has sexually abused a child, or in a probationer who has killed someone. As social workers, we actually see two dimensions of that individual. Yes, we see behavior that we may find abhorrent or repugnant. But we also see a person, a unique individual with their own life history, their own experiences in the world, and their own feelings and thoughts. No two people are exactly alike, no matter how similar their upbringing may have been, no matter how many commonalities we may see on the surface. To help people, we must embrace their inherent worth and dignity as individuals, despite the fact that we may not like or approve of their behavior.

We demonstrate regard for all persons by trying to understand them. This is not always easy. And this does not mean that we give up or forget our own beliefs and values. Social workers are, after all, individual human beings with their own life histories, experiences, thoughts, feelings, beliefs, and attitudes. When our clients appear to have different histories from ours, or when their beliefs and values differ from ours, we are challenged to put ours aside in order to understand theirs. This is the essence of empathic connection, which we view as "entering" the experience of another person in order to truly understand them.

If we cannot truly understand another person's experience, it is unlikely that we can value them as human beings. And if we cannot value our clients as human beings, it is even less likely that we can help them. The value of inherent worth and dignity is the foundation of any kind of interpersonal helping. It is our education and training that teach us to separate the value of human beings from their behavior. Without our belief in the inherent worth of all persons, there would be many who would never be helped. As a result, there are many who would continue to harm and many more who would continue to be harmed. This ability to separate the worth of individuals from our reactions to their behavior is among the most difficult lessons for us to learn, but it is also among the most important.

After their first class lecture on values, some of the students went over to the Union for coffee. They were strangely quiet as they walked across campus, a stark contrast to their usual animated verbal bantering. Once gathered around their usual table, cups in hand, LaDonna spoke up. "I really don't know if I can go 'round respecting bigots and racists! I've lived too long and seen too much hate in my time. I just don't know how to respect that kind of thing." Jahad, not always regular at these afterclass meetings, was even more emphatic than LaDonna. "No way! I figure what I'll do is stay as far away from 'em as I can. . . . I'm gonna be the best social worker I can and work with my own people, in my own community."

Jennifer found herself feeling uneasy and was hesitant to speak up for fear of offending her classmates. Finally, she said, "Well, wait a minute. What I got about this inherent dignity and worth stuff was we have to respect human beings as part of our universe, but nobody has to respect racism or bigotry. It's like somehow figuring a way to separate the person from the behavior, isn't it?" Tricia chimed in, "Yeh, maybe that's it, but when I think about my biological father being on drugs, and all the pain that he caused people, I don't know if I can separate the person from that kind of destructive behavior. It just doesn't sound that simple to me."

The discussion went on for several minutes and David, usually an active participant, had been quiet the whole time. "You know, I kind of have to agree with LaDonna and Jahad. When you live your life as the object of so many people's hatred, for no reason except your skin isn't white, or in my case, because of who I choose to love, then I think it's asking a whole lot of us to value the inherent dignity and worth of all people. Maybe if everyone was that way I could handle it alot better, but for some of us, it's a real one-sided deal, you know?"

The group fell silent, not quite knowing how to respond. Each of them did recognize that this value was really going to be a challenge.

Self-Determination

Clients' self-determination is defined as their prerogative to make their own decisions and choices. This not only includes choices or decisions about the course of intervention, but about all aspects of their life. The social work literature is replete with thought-provoking, philosophical treatises about the nature of self-determination.[3] Helen Harris Perlman (1965), an esteemed social work educator, has identified the essential nature of self-determination: "I *am* because I *will* is the essence of self-determination: 'I am because I will to choose, to decide, to be responsible for, a cause of, the consequences that follow on my actions'" (p. 410). This statement acknowledges that we may decide and we may choose, but we must also be prepared to accept responsibility for the consequences of our decisions and choices. As an abstract value, self-determination is easy to support; translating it into practice is often very difficult. This difficulty emanates from the contradictions inherent in self-determination.

First we must consider the fact that each of us lives in a social context, interacting constantly with other persons. As a result, any decision we make about our lives will affect the lives of those around us. Second, we must acknowledge that social workers operate in a divided reality. On the one hand, we are to serve our clients, to advocate for them, to help them improve the quality of their lives. On the other hand, we represent our agencies and our agencies reflect—to varying degrees—the norms of the community in which we live. In some situations, what may seem best for our client may be at odds with community norms or agency standards. According to Sharon Freedberg (1989), a tension results in which "social workers thus strive for a balance between responsibility to the community and responsibility to the self-determination of the individual client system" (p. 33).

As social workers our responsibility is to maximize the client's opportunities for self-determination (Sharon Freedberg, 1989). This means we take into account all that we know about our clients and, in light of what we know about them, we attempt to empower them to make their own choices and decisions. Thus, our role in client self-determination involves providing information, identifying possible consequences, and exploring alternatives with our clients. The self-determining client will then have been empowered to make an *informed* choice. Without a full exploration of options, it is unlikely that we can say a client has really exercised self-determination.

As a social work value, client self-determination can challenge us personally, much as we have already described in the value of inherent worth and dignity. What do we do when a client makes a decision that *we* think is a rather poor choice? Let's look at a situation that illustrates this dilemma.

Case

KATHY

*B*efore going back to school for her MSW, Kathy had volunteered in a shelter for battered women. She had become increasingly interested in the problem of violence against women after reading a news story about a woman who killed her live-in boyfriend. The woman had been convicted of murder and sentenced to prison, even though testimony from the trial indicated that she had been battered throughout her relationship with this man. Kathy had found herself wondering why anyone would stay in an abusive, violent relationship. She also felt guilty for thinking that way, so she decided to see what she could learn by volunteering to work with the women in the local shelter.

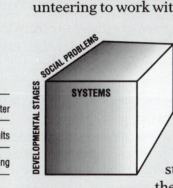

Women's Shelter

Adults

Crime and Battering

Kathy quickly became one of the best volunteers in the shelter. She was warm and supportive, and a natural listener. Over time, as she heard more and more from the women about the horrendous abuse they suffered, and as she saw the same bruised faces reappear over time, she found herself increasingly frustrated by their ambivalence about leaving their abusers. She wanted to scream, "Get out of there!" and have each of them do exactly that. She didn't want to hear how the abusers were always "sorry" afterward, she didn't want to hear how many times they promised "never to do it again." And, perhaps most of all, she didn't want to hear these women talk about how they "really do love him" as they planned to go back.

In one of her very first MSW courses, Kathy was introduced to the social work value of client self-determination. She recognized it immediately. Lost in thoughts of the battered women she had seen, she realized that she somehow had known—intuitively—the value of respecting the client's right to decide. She felt somewhat better remembering that she had never given in to the temptation of screaming "Get out of there!" She also felt worse, recognizing that she didn't—at the time—know how to empower clients to exercise their right of self-determination. Now she was getting the picture.

The "picture" that Kathy had begun to see more clearly is the value of client self-determination. Imagine yourself as a battered woman. You have been injured physically and you have left your own home in fear to come to this shelter. Concerned and well-intended Kathy succumbs to her frustration and says "Get out of there!" How might you feel? What effect might Kathy's advice have on you? Although we understand Kathy's feelings of frustration and concern, it is not very likely that you would feel understood, let alone empowered to make a sound decision. You might feel like leaving the shelter to get away from this person who obviously does not understand what you are going through. Kathy's well intended advice may have resulted in exactly the opposite outcome of what she wants for you.

Given the complex dynamics of abusive relationships, we know that most battered women are likely to return home any number of times before they feel empowered to leave. Adding shame to the problems of a battered woman is neither helpful, nor empowering, and it may cause her to be less likely to seek help if and when the abuse occurs again. When she needs more help in the future, she may be less likely to ask for it.

It is difficult for social workers to stand by and watch clients make choices that may be life threatening. This is certainly the case with battering, which tends to escalate in severity over time. Nonetheless, our job is to understand our client's experience, to provide her with useful information about her options—including the consequences of these options—and to help her become sufficiently empowered to make her own best choice at this moment in time. We may not always agree with our clients' choices, but we must respect their right to make them. We can only do the best we can at any moment in time. If we have done our best, then we can only trust that our clients are doing their very best as well.

This example has explored a kind of classic conflict with client self-determination. Whenever we hear ourselves telling a client "What you really should do is . . . ," or "I don't think that's a good idea at all," we're in the process of potentially violating client self-determination. These statements reflect a lack of respect for the right of clients to be self-determining. They are also disempowering and they undermine the client's opportunity for growth. This, however, is not the only way in which client self-determination can be misused.

Case

JASON

J ason remembered the time his parents made him see a therapist when he was in the ninth grade. Born into a family that stressed structure, orderliness, and achievement, Jason just didn't seem to fit in with his laid-back attitude. When his midterm report card came home with barely passing grades and very unexceptional marks in citizenship, his parents took him to a therapist.

That first meeting came back to him clearly now. Jason remembered his parents telling Don, the therapist, about his grades, his disorganization, and his "who cares?" attitude—all in great detail—while he sat silently. "We just don't know how to get through to him how important all this is for his future," they lamented. After Don asked them to step out for a few minutes, Jason found himself looking at Don and wondering "Now what?" They both remained silent for what Jason thought was forever.

Finally Don asked, "So what's going on here?" In his typical fashion (and not unlike many adolescents), Jason shrugged his shoulders, looked at the floor, and said "I dunno." Don sat quietly for a minute, then asked, "What do you think the problem is?" Jason didn't know what to say because he didn't exactly know why he was there. He felt Don's eyes boring holes into him and that made him uncomfortable. "It sounds to me like your parents are really concerned about you." "I guess so," Jason said. "Well, how can I help?" Don asked. "Beats me," Jason mumbled to himself.

Jason remembered sitting through that session wondering, Why am I here? What's wrong with me that my parents made me come? What am I supposed to be doing?

In his attempt to be respectful of Jason, and in trying to allow complete client self-determination, Don failed to see Jason's need for information and structure. Don's style was low-key and reflective, but when faced with a client like Jason, he did not know how to connect with him. Don's approach with clients, maintaining a passive, reflective communication style, is intended to help them "work through" their issues or problems without being led. This approach may be quite effective with clients who are insight-oriented, verbal, and articulate. However, for those who do not relate well to "talking therapy," too much respect for or emphasis on self-determination may be counterproductive.

In working with adolescents, it is important to recognize that they are not likely to "open up" immediately to a stranger, particularly when the stranger is a social worker or therapist. In fact, in almost any unclear or unstructured situation, all but the most assertive individuals are likely to be reserved and unsure of themselves. Don would have done better to have explained some basic things to Jason right away. You might think of this as the journalism model of "who, what, when, where, why, and how," except it is the social worker who is providing the answers before asking questions of the client.

For example, Don might have said, "Jason, I imagine you're wondering why you're here and what it is we're supposed to do together, so let me tell you a few things about who I am first." He might have then explained who he was in that setting (a social worker/therapist who tries to help families work out problems and conflicts). He might also have explained that he works with lots of families, that he knows it can be confusing and scary to see a therapist, and that seeing a therapist does not mean you are "crazy" or "bad." Don would also have done well to explain that he was not "taking sides," because it is likely that an adolescent like Jason might expect an adult to take his parents' side. Jason would also need to know that Don saw him as a participant, rather than as an object in the resolution of the family conflict. Don would need to assure Jason that his perceptions and opinions mattered and that he would have choices in how the family conflict could be addressed.

If Don had taken a few minutes to provide this kind of information, he would have provided something else that is equally important. He would have provided structure to an otherwise unknown situation, and by doing so, he would likely have decreased Jason's anxiety at finding himself in that office. These few examples suggest that structure is very important in the beginning of a relationship, particularly with an adolescent who is unlikely to be trusting or forthcoming with any information. This also demonstrates how the value of client self-determination can be integrated into our work with clients who are not knowledgeable or sophisticated about therapy. In our scenario, Don was trying to be respectful of

Jason, trying to allow for client self-determination. But our clients cannot really be self-determining unless they understand who we are and what our work with them is about. Only when they are completely informed can they fully participate in the work to be done, including making their own self-determined choices.

As social workers, we see many people who, for a wide range of reasons, are involved in situations or behaviors that place them at risk. The risk of permanent injury—psychological as well as physical—or death, increases over time for battered women. The adolescent experimenting with drugs is at risk for addiction, school failure, and trouble with the law. Our role, relative to self-determination, is not to tell our clients what to do or what not to do, but to explore all the options and to identify the likely consequences of their choices. This is not always easy, particularly when clients make choices that, in our view, are unhealthy—whether physically, psychologically, or both.

Confidentiality

Protection of information provided by or received about clients is the essence of confidentiality. "Confidentiality means safeguarding from disclosure personal information that the client reveals in the context of the professional relationship" (Jill Kagle, 1991, p. 165). It means any information shared within the helping relationship is to be kept confidential by the social worker except for specific, compelling, professional circumstances; these specific circumstances or limits must be discussed with the client in the earliest stage of the professional relationship. Recognizing that the quality of the professional helping relationship is critical, and that honest communication is the foundation for this kind of relationship, clients must be helped to feel secure that their lives will *not* be the subject of idle talk or coffee room gossip. Confidentiality emanates from the belief in clients' right to privacy, and is supported through the NASW Code of Ethics.

There are specific situations in which confidentiality is limited. These generally include situations where, in the social worker's judgment, the client is at risk for self-inflicted harm or harm to others. The suicidal person is an example of someone demonstrating potential harm to self. An example of potential harm to others is the client who threatens to kill a partner if that person leaves. In these situations, the practitioner may need to advise the client that confidentiality cannot be maintained. This places the practitioner in a position of assessing the degree of perceived risk, which is a difficult but not necessarily uncommon task.

There are also specific settings in which confidentiality is limited or where it does not apply. These settings include inpatient hospitals, medical or psychiatric, and various residential treatment programs where a team of professionals is providing services. In such instances, it is permissible for social workers, physicians—including psychiatrists—nurses, psychologists, and others participating as a treatment team to discuss the patient/client's progress, concerns, and plans. This is part of a coordinated treatment approach.

The limits of confidentiality are also apparent in cases of child abuse or neglect. Not only do social workers have an ethical obligation to report actual or suspected incidents of child abuse or neglect, but all states have laws requiring any person having knowledge of child abuse to notify the local authorities at Children's Protective Services. Finally, the limits of confidentiality are different in the case of persons who, by virtue of age (e.g., minors) or mental handicap (e.g., persons certified as mentally ill or incompetent), do not have the same rights and protections as others.

A common misunderstanding of confidentiality is its confusion with the protection afforded by *privileged communication.* Privileged communication is granted through state statute and protects persons, such as physicians and lawyers, from having to divulge any information shared by the patient or client. For a communication to be considered privileged, it must be made with the intention and assurance that it will not be disclosed to anyone. Social workers enjoy this protection of privileged communication in about half of the states that have licensure.

This protection rests on a legal basis and therefore prevents a physician or attorney from having to testify or provide information about a patient/client in a court of law; however, such a protection is not afforded to all social workers. In fact, in most states social workers can be subpoenaed to testify in a variety of situations—for example, divorce or child custody—affecting their clients, and this can occur against the wishes of the client and the practitioner. The records that are kept as part of the client's file in an employing agency can also be subpoenaed, and we are required by law to produce them. The honest sharing of information is crucial in social work, thus the lack of privileged communication may negatively effect our ability to help. Nonetheless, our clients have a right to know the limits of confidentiality. It is clearly our responsibility to inform them of this early in the working relationship.

Personal and Professional Values

So far, we have treated the subject of values as if we assume that our personal values are quite congruent with those advocated by the social work profession. Realistically, we recognize that this is not always the case. There are, for example, "splinter" professional organizations, such as the North American Association of Christians in Social Work (NACSW), and the National Association of Black Social Workers (NABSW), which have their own statement of values emphasizing a certain ideological set of beliefs on which their practice is based.

Membership in the NACSW is open to "persons who have accepted Jesus Christ as Savior and Lord," who support the objectives of the association and agree with its Statement of Faith and Practice. This statement includes tenets emphasizing Christian beliefs, tenets emphasizing human relationship and responsibilities, and tenets emphasizing vocation. The NABSW was formed in 1968 in an effort to deal with problems of concern to the black community, to promote programs servicing blacks, and to assist black social workers. The association has its own code of ethics, holds annual conventions, and publishes its own journal, *Black Caucus* (Robert Barker, 1991). Some social workers feel that splinter groups weaken the status and unity of the profession's largest association, the NASW. Others feel these groups serve a valuable function by providing a forum for social workers with special interests or values that differ from those of the NASW.

Knowing Ourselves

We believe strongly that all practicing social workers, as well as those of you who may be considering entering the field, must take a long and careful look at their own beliefs, attitudes, and values. This is neither a simple, nor a quick process. To look at our own beliefs, attitudes, and values requires first that we identify what they are. This often sounds far easier than it really is.

A beginning step might be to consider a very fundamental question: What is my philosophy of life? This, of course, assumes that each person has a philosophy. What we are referring to is a sense of what gives meaning to your life. The French philosopher Descartes stated, "I think, therefore, I am," but this is barely a beginning to the process of self-knowledge and self-awareness.

Naomi Brill (1990) has addressed the importance of self-awareness for those who want to "work with people." She suggests that each of us ask ourselves some basic questions:

- How do I think and feel about myself?
- How do I deal with my own fundamental needs?
- What is my value system, and how does it define my behavior and my relationships with other people?
- How do I relate to the society in which I live and work?
- What is my life-style?
- What is my basic philosophy?
- What do I present—and represent—to those with whom I work? (p. 19)

These are important questions for us. In the fourth century B.C., Socrates said that "the unexamined life is not worth living." No matter what our career or professional choices are, there is fundamental truth in this view for all humans on the planet. To go through our lives without ever knowing ourselves is a great and fundamental loss. We each have the gifts of intelligence and curiosity; we have the ability to think and to feel. What a loss it would be to go through the world unconscious of ourselves, not knowing who we are and what we truly believe. Second, our failure to examine our own beliefs, attitudes, and values can lead to major, unanticipated confrontations with the reality of social work and the demands that we accept when joining this profession. As stated succinctly by Brill:

> People entering human service should be aware of their personal value systems; they also need to be able to assess the consistency of their values with those upon which human services are based. The harboring of internal inconsistencies does not lead to personal or job satisfaction or to mental health. (p. 268)

As we examine our personal values in relation to those of the profession, it would be wise to ask ourselves whether our political ideology is congruent with overarching social work values. Finally, it is important to assess our personal values in relation to specific agency policies and norms because this arena may present some unanticipated conflicts.

In summary, values help define what is good and desirable in a society. In social work, professional values influence and guide us in practice. Whereas it is relatively easy to espouse the appropriate values in the abstract, the realities of individual and social problems often present us with difficult professional decisions. We have acknowledged that some social workers—as individuals—may hold personal beliefs and values that differ from those advocated by the National Association of Social Workers as a whole. As a result, we have argued that knowing ourselves, which is the essence of self-awareness, is critically important in order to serve our clients professionally.

Manhattan borough president Ruth Messinger speaks at a Henry Street Settlement–sponsored forum, "Women Speak Out About AIDS," in November 1991.

Social Work Ethics

In the general sense, ethics is the philosophy of morality, a set of principles related to what is believed to be right and wrong. In an applied profession such as social work, ethics are seen as values in relation to action or performance. A code of ethics is a series of statements that takes abstract values and principles, and connects them to actual behavior. Professional codes of ethics are designed to provide clear guidelines for ethical practice. Regardless of which profession you examine (e.g., medicine, law, social work), each has a code of ethics that delineates what practitioners may and may not do to be considered within the bounds of ethical conduct.

Charles Levy (1976) stated that social work ethics serve three essential professional purposes: "It is a guide to professional conduct, it is a set of principles that social workers can apply in the performance of the social work function, and it is a set of criteria by which social work practice can be evaluated" (p. 108).

NASW Codes of Ethics: 1960 and 1980

Our earlier discussion centered around general values and values that are identified inherently with the profession of social work. We indicated that abstract values must be translated into action before they are truly meaningful in practice. It is through the National Association of Social Workers (NASW) Code of Ethics that this translation can best be examined. The NASW was formed in 1955, but it took a full five years to develop the first code of ethics. The first code was adopted by the NASW Delegate Assembly on 13 October 1960 and was amended on 11 April 1967. This original social work code of ethics reflected not only an emerging professional identity, but also a set of philosophical beliefs about the nature of what social work should be. The original code reflected a strong sense of idealism, as these excerpts illustrate:

> Social work is based on humanitarian, democratic ideals. Professional social workers are dedicated to service for the welfare of mankind [sic]; to the disciplined use of a recognized body of knowledge about human beings and their interactions; and to the marshalling of community resources to promote the well-being of all without discrimination. Social work practice is a public trust that

requires of its practitioners integrity, compassion, belief in the dignity and worth of human beings, respect for individual differences, a commitment to service, and a dedication to truth. It requires mastery of a body of knowledge and skill gained through a professional education and experience. It requires also recognition of the limitations of present knowledge and skill and of the services we are now equipped to give. The end sought is the performance of a service with integrity and competence. (NASW, 1977, pp. 1066–1067)

The original text continues with a set of statements that NASW members are committed to uphold and abide by:

As a member of the National Association of Social Workers I commit myself to conduct my professional relationships in accord with the code and subscribe to the following statements:

- I regard as my primary obligation the welfare of the individual or group served, which includes action for improving social conditions.
- I will not discriminate because of race, color, religion, age, sex, or national ancestry, and in my job capacity will work to prevent and eliminate social discrimination in rendering services, work assignments, and in employment practices.
- I give precedence to my professional responsibility over my personal interests.
- I hold myself responsible for the quality and extent of the service I perform.
- I respect the privacy of the people I serve.
- I use in a responsible manner information gained in professional relationships.
- I treat with respect the findings, views, and actions of colleagues and use appropriate channels to express judgment on these matters.
- I practice social work within the recognized knowledge and competence of the profession.
- I recognize my professional responsibility to add my ideas and findings to the body of social work knowledge and practice.

- I accept responsibility to help protect the community against unethical practice by any individuals or organizations engaged in social welfare activities.
- I stand ready to give appropriate professional service in public emergencies.
- I distinguish clearly, in public, between my statements and actions as an individual and as a representative of an organization.
- I support the principal that professional practice requires professional education.
- I accept responsibility for working toward the creation and maintenance of conditions within agencies which enable social workers to conduct themselves in keeping with this code.
- I contribute my knowledge, skills, and support to programs of human welfare. (NASW, 1977, p. 1067)

Reflecting on these statements now, it is as if they represent a bygone age of innocence in which inspiration was commendable, idealism was accepted, and trust abounded. It is true that the profession had yet to recognize and respond to discrimination based on sexual orientation, marital status, political belief, or mental or physical handicap. Nonetheless, there seemed to be a sense that social workers, once enlightened, would respond empathically. As this first code was being formulated, our nation had yet to see the beginnings of a secret war in Southeast Asia. We had not yet experienced the assassinations of a president, a pacifist civil rights leader, and a former attorney general. The second wave of feminism had not yet appeared, and only the beginnings of a black civil rights movement were visible in the South.

The intervening years between the formulation of the first and the current social work codes of ethics were not kind to our values and beliefs about social justice. Social activism increased substantially, but so did civil disorder. A general sense of disillusionment and distrust came to characterize many persons who came of age in the decades of the 1960s and 1970s, and the formulation of the revised social work code of ethics seems to reflect this shift.

The current code, adopted in 1979 by the NASW Delegate Assembly, effective 1 July 1980, reflects a different time and a different world, both professionally and personally. The world reflected in the current code is shaped by the social and political realities between 1960 and 1980, an historical period characterized by social movements, political scandals, and a morally and politically divisive undeclared war, all of which served to highlight ethical issues nationally.

In our view, the current code seems far removed from the first. It has evolved far beyond a set of guidelines to resemble a codified set of rules. The establishment of explicit procedures further reflects the shift from idealism to "legalism," as the NASW established its own committee on inquiry to hear complaints alleging ethical violations. In addition, the revised code contains fewer articulations of principles relating to promoting the general welfare of society. Compared to the first code, there are fewer prescriptions for social workers to engage in political advocacy in the current code. In all probability, this reflects the political climate of the 1970s. Whether or not stated explicitly, advocacy still remains an integral part of social work practice.

The following excerpts are from the preamble of the 1980 NASW Code of Ethics. They illustrate the stark contrast between the ethical concerns of the profession now as compared with 30 years ago.

> This code is intended to serve as a guide to the everyday conduct of members of the social work profession and as a basis for the adjudication of issues in ethics when the conduct of social workers is alleged to deviate from the standards expressed or implied in this code. It represents standards of ethical behavior for social workers in professional relationships with those served, with colleagues, with employers, with other individuals and professions, and with the community and society as a whole. It also embodies standards of ethical behavior governing individual conduct to the extent that such conduct is associated with an individual's status and identity as a social worker. (NASW, 1991, p. 221)

We recognize that society has generally become increasingly litigious over the past two decades, yet the legalistic tone of the document is still startling. This legalistic tone probably reflects our national inclination to resolve differences through the courts, rather than through interpersonal discussion, negotiation, mediation, and accommodation. It is, nonetheless, a regrettable situation.

Summary of Major Principles of the Present NASW Code of Ethics

    I. The Social Worker's Conduct and Comportment as a Social Worker

        A. Propriety. The social worker should maintain high standards of personal conduct in the capacity or identity as social worker.

        B. Competence and Professional Development. The social worker should strive to become and remain proficient in professional practice and the performance of professional functions.

        C. Service. The social worker should regard as primary the service obligation of the social work profession.

        D. Integrity. The social worker should act in accordance with the highest standards of professional integrity.

        E. Scholarship and Research. The social worker engaged in study and research should be guided by the conventions of scholarly inquiry.

    II. The Social Worker's Ethical Responsibility to Clients

        F. Primacy of Clients' Interests. The social worker's primary responsibility is to clients.

        G. Rights and Prerogatives of Clients. The social worker should make every effort to foster maximum self-determination on the part of clients.

        H. Confidentiality and Privacy. The social worker should respect the privacy of clients and hold in confidence all information obtained in the course of professional service.

        I. Fees. When setting fees, the social worker should ensure that they are fair, reasonable, considerate, and

Major shifts in emphasis are not difficult to identify. The first code advises us to accept "responsibility to help protect the community against unethical practice by any individuals or organizations engaged in social welfare activities." In contrast, the preamble to the current code states that "social workers are required to cooperate in its [the code] implementation and abide by any disciplinary rulings based on it. They should also take adequate measures to *discourage, prevent, expose,* and *correct* the unethical conduct of

commensurate with the service performed and with
due regard for the clients' ability to pay.

III. The Social Worker's Ethical Responsibility to Colleagues

J. Respect, Fairness, and Courtesy. The social worker
should treat colleagues with respect, courtesy, fairness, and good faith.

K. Dealing with Colleagues' Clients. The social worker
has the responsibility to relate to the clients of colleagues with full professional consideration.

IV. The Social Worker's Ethical Responsibility to Employers
and Employing Organizations

L. Commitments to Employing Organizations. The social worker should adhere to commitments made to
the employing organizations.

V. The Social Worker's Ethical Responsibility to the Social
Work Profession

M. Maintaining the Integrity of the Profession. The social worker should uphold and advance the values,
ethics, knowledge, and mission of the profession.

N. Community Service. The social worker should assist
the profession in making social services available to
the general public.

O. Development of Knowledge. The social worker
should take responsibility for identifying, developing, and fully utilizing knowledge for professional
practice.

VI. The Social Worker's Ethical Responsibility to Society

P. Promoting the General Welfare. The social worker
should promote the general welfare of society.
(NASW, 1991)

NOTE: See Appendix for the entire text.

colleagues" (emphasis added). It strikes us as a sad commentary
that scandals such as Watergate and Iran-Contra have left a legacy
wherein ethical codes must require professionals to consider exposing their colleagues on the basis of unethical conduct. Further, although some might find it absurd that professional social workers
would have to be told that sexual activity with clients is unethical,
even this must now be stated explicitly (see Appendix, II, F, 5).

The revised code has grown from the original series of 15

statements to a lengthy, complex document that is subdivided several times to include no fewer than 69 specific statements. Historians and other social scientists may, one day, be able to evaluate the social and political changes that so powerfully altered the ethical climate of the country between 1960 and 1980. Whatever they find, we can at least see that social workers were attempting to confront the ethical issues that have come to characterize this nation in the last decades of the twentieth century. In our view that is a positive move on the part of our profession.

Values and Ethics: Some Illustrations

Few social workers are prepared fully for the kinds of value and ethical confrontations that are likely to occur in practice. Similarly, it would be impossible to provide an adequate set of examples to illustrate each of these, as new developments serve to create new dilemmas faster than they can be addressed. Nonetheless, several illustrations are provided of what may be considered classic practice dilemmas that have their origins in the realm of values and ethics.

There is not a single person reading this text who has not already faced some ethical decisions in life. Someone offers to give you the answers on a homework assignment. Your instructor accidentally leaves the answer key to the final exam out on the desk. A student, who last semester took the same course you are in now, offers to let you use her term paper. These illustrate possible ethical dilemmas faced by students. They represent situations where we must decide between what is ethically right and wrong. In social work, ethical decisions are often far more complex and multidimensional. They may not, as in the examples given, be totally black or white, right or wrong. Instead, they may look gray, and we may find ourselves able to argue on both sides of the issue.

Mandatory AIDS Testing

Consider a very current ethical issue faced by health care practitioners. Should mandatory testing for the HIV (AIDS) virus be required for practicing doctors, nurses, and dentists? Make a list that would argue in favor of mandatory testing. Now make a list that would argue against. After looking at your two lists, are you prepared to take a clear position in favor of or against mandatory testing? The morally right or ethical decision in this case is still subject to debate.

How you came to decide is just as important as your decision. Assuming you feel ready to take a position, how did you decide what it would be? What factors influenced you most? Do the social work values of self-determination and confidentiality play a part in this illustration? Did you consider the health care providers right to privacy? Did you decide that the patient's right to know was of greatest significance? Most importantly, can you see how other people might argue just as forcefully for another position?

Program Funding

Case

ETTA

*E*tta was no stranger to the struggles for financial support. As a social worker in a neonatal intensive care unit years ago, she knew how difficult it was to maintain funding for certain kinds of programs. Her work had involved counseling with mothers whose infants were low birthweight babies or, more often, babies born addicted to crack cocaine as a result of their mother's addiction. Etta had heard the public outrage at those mothers time and time again, particularly when it came time to renew the annual budget. "Everybody feels sorry for the babies, sure, but what about those mothers?" Etta asked. "Who's going to help them? Who's going to teach them job skills and give them hope so they won't be out doin' crack?"

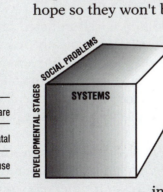

Health Care

Prenatal

Substance Abuse

Etta knew that continued funding for intensive neoanatal care wasn't in jeopardy because everyone saw the children as innocent victims. The problem was getting people to recognize that the mothers were in need of help. Public sentiment ran high against "crack mothers" and "social degenerates" who the media described as more interested in drugs than in the health of their own children. Etta understood the lure of drugs, particularly in low income communities and she know that prevention programs were a critical need in dealing with the problem.

In preparing her presentation to the funding source—the group that would either approve or reject her funding proposal for a community-based drug prevention program—Etta realized that she was facing a real dilemma. Some funding source members had been quoted by the media as stating they would only support her proposal if the program design included mandatory counseling about birth control and abortion for all acknowledged drug using clients. Etta had problems with this. Clients might well stay away from the program altogether, or be unwilling to provide accurate information about possible drug use. Beyond this, Etta felt it was inappropriate for the funders to dictate program policy, particularly when that policy could result in value conflicts, ethical questions, and violations of client self-determination.

Etta wasn't sure how to deal with this. On the one hand, she didn't think she could accept this policy in good conscience. On the other hand, there weren't many options for funding this kind of program. If you were Etta, what would you do?

Suicide

One of the most serious and troubling value and ethics conflicts relative to client self-determination is the case of suicide. Is the deliberate act of killing oneself to be permitted under the value of client self-determination? Or do social workers have a responsibility to intervene and try to stop this? If society, as a whole, suggests that killing—whether this killing is self-inflicted or the killing of another person—is morally wrong and socially unacceptable, then where is the social worker's responsibility? Are we responsible to the individual client? To society at large? To the client's family or friends? Does it make a difference why the client wishes to die? Would we evaluate self-determination differently depending on the circumstances?

Some social workers would say, without hesitation, that suicide is a reflection of the clients' temporary mental instability, in which case we have a responsibility to intervene to protect clients from themselves. Other practitioners take the position that there is such a thing as "rational suicide," a situation involving certain specific circumstances such as terminal illness. If a person is suffering from inoperable cancer or from a fully developed case of AIDS, and there is no hope for recovery, is it possible for that individual to choose, quite rationally, not to live any longer? The quality of life could be a major variable in such situations. If you believe in the inherent worth and dignity of all persons, do you support a terminally ill client's "right" to die with dignity, if "with dignity" means at a time, and in a place, and by means of their own? If you say yes, how far might you go to support this value? Although no one has the right, legally, to assist a person in actively committing suicide, how far would you go to support their efforts? What is the ethical direction to take?

Bioethics

Bioethics is a specialized area of ethics focusing on the moral, ethical, and legal dilemmas that have been created by massive technological developments in the field of medicine. With the advances in medical technology in recent years, bioethical issues have evolved as never before. The professional literature on bioethics has grown substantially, especially as more and more social workers have entered the health and medical areas of social work practice.[4] Bioethical issues cut across the values and ethics of social work, raising questions that were little more than science fiction fantasy a generation ago.

Current medical technology has confounded the essential definitions of life and death by making it possible to maintain a person on life support systems, even though the person is clinically "brain dead." Which is to be honored, brain death or heart death? Organ transplants allow many thousands of persons to live longer and healthier lives. Yet who decides which individual should receive a particular organ when there are many who need it? These issues will require the most careful consideration among our finest thinkers because our responses will ultimately effect all aspects of social welfare over time.

Political Activism

This may be like the glass half-empty or the glass half-full perception. Those who react negatively when they hear the word *politics* likely see the half-empty glass, even when we speak of politically oriented social work. Those committed to social change in the legislative arena, however, likely envision political social work as the glass half-full, and embrace the opportunity to significantly affect social policies. We believe it is important to separate the opportunities from the negative connotations of the words *politics* or *political.*

The fact is, any arena of social work practice, be it agency administration, clinical services, research, or community organization, is susceptible to unethical practices and value conflicts. It is not the setting or the method that determines vulnerability to ethical violations or value conflicts. It is, as always, people who behave unethically or who succumb to projecting their values inappropriately on others. As we have noted before, social workers are fallible human beings. Nonetheless, we take a strong position that social workers have a special responsibility to act ethically and to uphold the values of the profession.

If ethical violations occur, if value conflicts arise, we are not free to look the other way. We have an obligation to speak out and to address the situation. This is true in all arenas of social work practice, including political social work. It is our position that political activism, directed toward the achievement of social work goals, grounded in the values and ethics of the profession, is congruent with the profession's standards. It is our hope that the negative connotations of politics can be offset, and that political social work will be seen as an opportunity to effect institutionalized change.

Summary

Social work is a value-laden profession. Can practitioners really operate as if they are free of biases? Not at all. Those who enter the profession are often already making a value statement by their choice of work; not all persons are attracted to working with oppressed or disadvantaged groups, nor do all persons have a commitment to working with the tragic human problems that social workers—even those in private settings—see everyday.

Those who engage in macro practice are attempting to influence policy development; they are trying to achieve a world characterized by equality and social justice. This reflects a commitment to specific values. Those engaged in micro practice are trying to help clients enhance their social functioning, whether that is through the provision of concrete services such as financial aid, or whether it is through the resolution of deeply rooted interpersonal problems. This, too, is a reflection of values. Values influence our practice and ethics direct how we practice. Still, social workers are human beings with their own issues, their own attitudes and beliefs. We have advocated that each of us acknowledge our personal values, understand how they fit within the values and ethics of our chosen profession, and remain mindful of our responsibility to our clients.

Notes

1. This particular meeting was a follow-up to efforts initiated in 1974 by the NASW Publications Committee and the editorial board of *Social Work* to further explore the purpose and objectives of the profession. The January 1981 edition of *Social Work* was the second special issue on conceptual frameworks, the first having been published in September 1977.

   You may want to review the following classic works that reflect the profession's struggle to clarify its status, purpose, and objectives. Abraham Flexner, "Is Social Work a Profession?", in *Proceedings of the National Conference on Charities and Corrections, 1915*, pp. 575–590 (Chicago: University of Chicago Press, 1916); Porter R. Lee, "Social Work: Cause and Function," in *Proceedings of the National Conference of Social Work, 1929* (Chicago: University of Chicago Press, 1930); *Social Casework: Generic and Specific, A Report of the Milford Conference* (1929; reprint, Washington, D.C.: National Association of Social Workers, 1974); Ernest V. Hollis and Alice L. Taylor, *Social Work Education in the United States* (New York: Columbia University Press, 1951); Subcommittee on the Working Definition of Social Work Practice for the Commission on Social Work Practice, National Association of Social Workers, "Working Definition of Social Work Practice," as printed in Harriett M. Bartlett, "Toward Clarification and Improvement of Social Work Practice," *Social Work*, Vol. 3, No. 2 (April 1958); William E. Gordon, "A Critique of the Working Definition," *Social Work*, Vol. 7, No. 4 (Oct. 1962): 3–13. Additionally, see Donald Brieland, "Historical Overview," *Social Work*, Vol. 22, No. 5 (Sept. 1977): 341–346, for a brief overview of these works.

2. Not only were women invisible in the Declaration of Independence, but African Americans were counted as three-fifths of a white person in determining taxation and representation in the U.S. Constitution. In the same section, "Indians not taxed" were excluded explicitly (1788,

Article 1, Section 3). The so-called "three-fifths" standard was eliminated in 1868 through passage of the Fourteenth Amendment (Section 2) to the Constitution. It was not until 1870 that the right to vote was granted to citizens irrespective of "race, color, or previous condition of servitude" (Fifteenth Amendment, Section 1). It was not until the Nineteenth Amendment was passed in 1920 that women had the right to vote. Section 1 read: "The right of citizens of the United States to vote shall not be denied or abridged by the United States of by any State on account of sex." Section 2 stated: "Congress shall have power to enforce this article by appropriate legislation."

The brief chronology would not be complete without noting that the first equal rights (for women) amendment to the Constitution was introduced in 1923, but was not passed by Congress until 1972. At that time it was turned over to the states for ratification. The ERA never was ratified by the necessary three-fourths of the states, and it died away for good in 1982.

3. See, for example: Saul Bernstein, "Self-Determination: King or Citizen in the Realm of Values?", *Social Work*, Vol. 5, No. 1 (Jan. 1960): 3–8; Frederic G. Reamer, "The Concept of Paternalism in Social Work," *Social Service Review*, Vol. 57, No. 2 (June 1983): 254–271; F. E. McDermott, *Self-Determination in Social Work* (London: Routledge & Kegan Paul, 1975); Alan Keith-Lucas, "A Critique of the Principle of Client Self-Determination," *Social Work*, Vol. 8, No. 3 (July 1963): 66–71; David Soyer, "The Right to Fail," *Social Work*, Vol. 8, No. 3 (July 1963): 72–78; Julie S. Abramson, "Participation of Elderly Patients in Discharge Planning: Is Self-Determination a Reality?" *Social Work*, Vol. 33, No. 5 (Sept.-Oct. 1988): 443–448; Sharon Freedberg, "Self-Determination: Historical Perspectives and Effects on Current Practice," *Social Work*, Vol. 34, No. 1 (Jan. 1989): 33–38.

4. See, for example, Frederic G. Reamer, "The Emergence of Bioethics in Social Work," *Health and Social Work*, Vol. 10, No. 4 (Fall 1985): 271–281; J. W. Ross, "Ethical Conflicts in Medical Social Work: Pediatric Cancer as a Prototype," *Health and Social Work*, Vol. 7, No. 2 (May 1982): 95–102; M. D. Hiller, ed., *Medical Ethics and the Law* (Cambridge, MA: Ballinger Publishing, 1981); Marcia Abramson and Rita Beck Black, "Extending the Boundaries of Life: Implications for Practice," *Health and Social Work*, Vol. 10, No. 3 (Summer 1985): 165–173; Karen A. Holmes, "Euthanasia: A Social Work Perspective," *Health and Social Work*, Vol. 5, No. 4 (Nov. 1980): 5–12; Sheldon R. Gelman, "Life vs. Death: The Value of Ethical Uncertainty," *Health and Social Work*, Vol. 11, No. 2 (Spring 1986): 118–125; Robert M. Veatch, *Death, Dying and the Biological Revolution* (New Haven, CT: Yale University Press, 1976).

References

Barker, Robert L. *The Social Work Dictionary,* 2nd ed. Silver Spring, MD: NASW, 1991.

Briar, Scott, and Henry Miller. *Problems and Issues in Social Casework.* New York: Columbia University Press, 1971.

Brill, Naomi I. *Working with People: The Helping Process,* 4th ed. New York: Longman, 1990.

"Code of Ethics." In *The Encyclopedia of Social Work,* pp. 1066–1067. Edited by John B. Turner. Washington, DC: NASW, 1977.

Freedberg, Sharon. "Self-Determination: Historical Perspectives and Effects on Current Practice." *Social Work,* Vol. 34, No. 1 (Jan. 1989): 33–38.

Greenwood, Ernest. "Attributes of a Profession." *Social Work,* Vol. 2, No. 3 (July 1957): 45–55.

Hepworth, Dean, and Jo Ann Larsen. *Direct Social Work Practice: Theory and Skills,* 3rd ed. Belmont, CA: Wadsworth, 1990.

Kagle, Jill Doner. *Social Work Records.* Belmont, CA: Wadsworth, 1991.

Levy, Charles. *Social Work Ethics.* New York: Human Sciences Press, 1976.

Minahan, Anne. "Purpose and Objectives of Social Work Revisited. *Social Work,* Vol. 26, No. 1 (Jan. 1981): 5–6.

"NASW Code of Ethics." In *Social Work Speaks: NASW Policy Statements, 2nd ed.,* pp. 221–225. Silver Spring, MD: NASW, 1991.

———. *Standards for the Classification of Social Work Practice.* Silver Spring, MD: NASW, 1981.

Perlman, Helen Harris. "Believing and Doing: Values in Social Work Education." *Social Casework,* Vol. 57, No. 6 (June 1976): 381–390.

———. "Self-Determination: Reality or Illusion?" *Social Service Review,* Vol. 39, No. 4 (Dec. 1965): 410–421.

Pincus, Allan, and Anne Minahan. *Social Work Practice: Model and Method.* Itasca, IL: F. E. Peacock, 1973.

CHAPTER 7

Knowledge Base

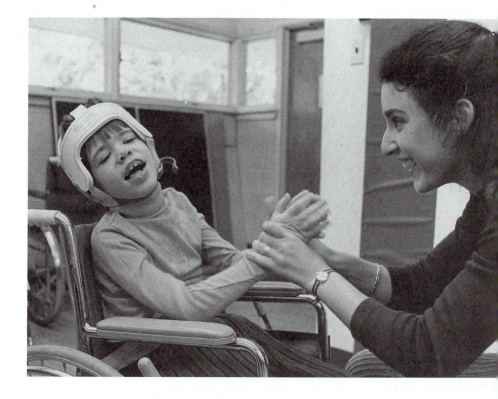

Introduction

The profession of social work could be described as having an identity problem. By this we mean that it is sometimes difficult to identify exactly what it is that social workers *do*. Some of this problem is related, at least in part, to the fact that social workers perform so many different tasks, and are found in a wide variety of different practice settings, many of which were described in Chapter 4. Another aspect of the issue relates to the fact that some of the important building blocks of the profession's knowledge base have been "borrowed" from other disciplines. The term *knowledge base* refers to the information—concepts, theories, and research—that a profession uses to guide its activities.

For example, in medical schools, students study anatomy, physiology, and other specific subjects that all relate clearly to the *practice* of medicine. Computer science students study principles of computer programming (i.e., computer languages) and the ways in which computers can be used to process, or *work with*, information. Social work students, however, are often surprised to find how much diverse knowledge and information from many disciplines they are expected to learn in order to *do social work*. There is theoretical knowledge about functional or normal behavior, about dysfunctional or abnormal behavior, and about specific interventive or therapeutic skills. But a great deal of content is devoted to the study of social institutions and their multifaceted functions; to social welfare policies and social welfare delivery systems; to research methodologies; and to the values and ethics that underpin social work *practice*.

Clearly, no single academic discipline or knowledge base can provide all this information. As a result, the knowledge base for social work practice, whether at the entry level of the BSW or at the advanced level of the MSW, is borrowed from several different disciplines to fully prepare students for the demands of professional practice.

This chapter describes the primary knowledge bases on which social work education has historically relied: sociology, psychology, economics, political science, anthropology, and more recently, human biology. Each of these disciplines has contributed to our professional preparation and development and has helped to inform our practice in the complex world of real human beings and organizations. Another section of the chapter is devoted to a discussion of related knowledge areas. These include literature, history, philosophy, theology, and women's studies. These have yet to be considered a formal part of the social work knowledge base, but we believe that each has something important to offer us as social workers. A brief discussion of social work's developing knowledge base is also included in the chapter.

Borrowed Knowledge

Early in its evolution as a profession, social work was seen as applied sociology, translating the theoretical knowledge of an essentially academic discipline into work with oppressed, needy individuals, groups, and organizations. During this early period of development, which will be detailed more completely in Chapter 11, the profession discovered that the knowledge base in many theoretical fields was useful as a basis for developing approaches and techniques to helping people and understanding their problems in social functioning. Although social work now generates much of its own knowledge base, the field remains shaped by this historical store of information and is open to incorporating contemporary knowledge of other disciplines—sociology, psychology, economics, political science, anthropology, and human biology.

Sociology

Simply stated, sociology is the discipline directed toward the study and interpretation of the relationships between people and their environments, particularly at the societal or macrolevel of analysis.

Society itself is viewed as a functional group, albeit a very large one, in which all members, in different ways, seek to maintain and perpetuate themselves and their interests. The astute reader will already have a sense of the considerable complexity involved in such large-scale analysis. In addition to general sociology, many colleges and universities offer courses or majors in urban sociology, clinical or applied sociology, criminal justice, and anthropology.

Sociological theory has contributed a great deal to social work education and practice. For example, concepts such as power, social control, inequality, and stratification, social movements, class, and culture have their origins in sociological theory, and they have contributed significantly to social work practice.

To illustrate, sociological theory suggests that power, which was discussed in Chapter 5 in terms of minority status, is the ability to dominate, coerce, or control the behavior of others; that is, it is essentially the ability to interfere with the freedom of others. At first this might seem to be an abstract concept, yet social workers deal with issues of power everyday when they see abused children, battered women, and victims of incestuous or sexual assault. Each of these is clearly the result of an *abuse of power,* whether that power is manifested by the authority vested in a role such as parent–child, or by the vestiges of English Common Law translated into the legal marriage contract,[1] or by greater physical size or strength.

It is not only the social worker working with the abused child or the battered woman who needs to understand the concept of power. Those who practice in the area of policy development or in the political area of legislative change must also grasp what power means, where it originates, how it is manifested, and thus, how it can be regulated.

Case

RYAN

Ryan gazed out the window of his campaign office and noticed that half-a-dozen women from the near Northside neighborhood were beginning to arrive, even though it was still half an hour before his campaign steering committee was scheduled to meet. He waved them to the circle of gray metal chairs as he sat down in one.

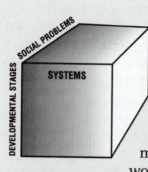

Political Activism

All Ages

Gender Issues/Diversity

Anabella, the most verbal of the six, spoke up immediately. "Ryan, we want to know how you're going to run against this woman who filed as a candidate yesterday? Your position on the issues is much more in line with what the women of this district want. But I'm worried that alot of the voters, especially women, might support her just because she's a woman."

Ryan paused a moment to gather his thoughts. "I'm not sure just yet what approach we'll use," he said, shifting his language from the first person "I" to the more inclusive "we." Participating in a workshop on oppression last year, Ryan had become sensitized to the significance of language, and he had learned that the inclusive term "we" was an important method of empowerment. "One thing is clear, the era of male-only political races is a thing of the past. We need to appreciate this opportunity to debate the issues with a competent candidate of either gender. There's no doubt about it, the balance of political power in this country is definitely shifting."

After the meeting had ended, Ryan sat quietly at his desk. Alone with his thoughts, he wondered how it would be running against a woman opponent. He knew Anabella was right that there might be some women who would support a woman candidate solely on the basis of gender. He also knew he was committed to learning about and understanding the issues that seemed of greatest concern to his potential constituents, both women and men. His steering committee, with a racial-ethnic mix and with a majority of women, had been chosen carefully. Ryan understood that he—as a white, middle-class, Protestant male—could not fully understand everyone's experiences, but he was willing to learn. Feeling somewhat overwhelmed, he thought, "I guess I should start with some basics. I need to explore the demographics of this district." Ryan was very sure that gender, age, and level of education were all important factors in whether people voted.

For practicing social workers, as well as hopeful politicians, an understanding and analysis of power is absolutely necessary in order to identify ways in which larger scale social changes can be initiated. At the most basic level, defining a particular phenomenon as a problem or as normal behavior is rooted in the concept of power. In this case, we are referring to the power to define.

You will recall the example discussed in Chapter 5 describing the American Psychiatric Association's (APA) power to define homosexual behavior as a mental disorder. Prior to 1976, the group decided that such behavior was not normal; in other words, it was a disorder. But in 1976, a majority voted to define homosexuality as normal and not a mental disorder. As another example, violence against women, particularly rape and battering, was not defined as a significant social problem until the 1970s when feminist sociologists began to study this phenomenon. Violence against women was subsequently redefined, not as the idiosyncratic behavior of a few "sick" men, but as a reflection of society's attitudes that devalue women, and as an extension of male power abuse and domination over women. [2]

"Power," according to Ellen Boneparth and Emily Stoper, "has been a thorny problem for the women's movement" (1988, p. 18). As an oppressed group in society, women have suffered from powerlessness; yet getting more power is a simplistic solution that would serve only to perpetuate the existing oppressive hierarchical system. The feminist perspective advocates equal power and equal participation, not a reverse of one gender's power over the other. A feminist analysis of power distinguishes between power *over* and power *for*, the latter speaking to a vision of using power for the greater good, including equality and justice among all persons. This suggests that power, in and of itself, is not inherently negative. It is the abuse of power that causes damage—politically, economically, and psychologically—to those who are less powerful.

In social work, the term *empowerment* has now been incorporated into our language as a professional goal. We speak of empowering communities, organizations, and individuals, which reflects our commitment to help all persons achieve their optimal level of social functioning—that is, to be able to exercise personal power over their own lives. Empowerment acknowledges the strength of clients, recognizes that they may have had nothing to do with having "caused" their problems, yet assumes that they are expected to take responsibility for and participate in the solution.

In addition to macrolevel theoretical concepts, sociological theory also provides substantive knowledge about particular social problems. Social workers need this substantive knowledge in order to understand the problems that we see in practice—whether our practice is with Children's Protective Services, hospital emergency rooms, public schools, employee assistance programs, chemical dependency units, or in program development, policy making, or legislative change. We must understand the larger picture of how society and its institutions are structured, how these structures manifest and maintain inequality, and how change can be effected in order to help all persons achieve their optimal level of social functioning, which is, after all, the ultimate goal of social work.

Psychology

If we placed the knowledge bases of social work on a continuum of large-scale to small-scale analysis, sociology would clearly be toward the large-scale side, whereas psychology, with its focus on individuals and their internal world, would be placed toward the other side. Sociology examines the interplay between people and their external environments, and we might say that psychology studies the interplay between people and their internal environments; that is, how people behave based on internal needs or drives, motivations, conflicts, and cognitive and emotional processes.

Traditionally, psychologists have placed considerable importance on the development of scientifically based methodologies. Depending on your point of view, a rather scientific approach can leave you more or less comfortable with the resulting theoretical bases and subsequent therapeutic efforts. This is similar to the long-standing debate in social work about whether clinical or therapeutic practice is science or art. With respect to psychology, all psychologists are concerned with human and/or animal behavior; however, there are different schools of psychological thought that significantly influence one's choice of theory and technique. Not all psychologists share the same theoretical frame of reference (neither do all social workers for that matter).

For example, behavioral psychologists operating from an objective perspective consider their unit of study to be human *behavior*, that which can be observed, defined operationally, quantified (i.e., measured or counted), and changed. Behaviorists tend to be less concerned with intrapsychic (internal) dynamics, believing es-

study of eight-four boys whose development Kohlberg followed for over twenty years. (p. 18)

Gilligan's (1982) work represents a new era in developmental theory.

The disparity between women's experience and the representation of human development, noted throughout the psychological literature, has generally been seen to signify a problem in women's development. Instead, the failure of women to fit existing models of human growth may point to a problem in the representation, in the conception of human condition, an omission of certain truths about life. (pp. 1–2)

According to Gilligan's central assumption, "the way people talk about their lives is of significance, [because] the language they use and the connections they make reveal the world that they see and in which they act" (p. 2). She explains that "the failure to see the different reality of women's lives and to hear the differences in their voices stems in part from the assumption that there is a single mode of social experience and interpretation" (p. 173).

Other theorists, such as Jean Baker Miller, Judith Jordan, Alexandra Kaplan, Janet Surrey, and Irene Stiver at the Stone Center at Wellesley College, have continued this knowledge-building process. Referring to their work as "self-in-relation" theories, the Stone Center group (Jordan et al., 1991) has taken issue with models of "human" development that fail to include women's experiences and result in women being seen as deficient when compared to a male-defined yardstick of normal or healthy development. Unlike most developmental theories that focus on the need to separate (i.e., from mother in infancy and childhood, from family in adolescence), the Stone Center group suggests that women's development occurs in relation to others throughout the life cycle. And, like Gilligan, they have sought to understand women's experience by talking with and listening to women, an approach that, unfortunately, has not been used consistently by others.

It is not only in our psychological or developmental theories that women have been ignored. All parts of our culture—history, literature, art, journalism—have been accustomed to using the supposedly generic "mankind," which we were told "of course" included women, even though women's contributions are far less frequently acknowledged. In a presentation at the Menninger Foundation,[3] social worker Lois Braverman addressed this point. She stated that what is defined or described as truly significant is found at "the hub," and that a feminist perspective asks us to reexamine what we see as the center (or the hub), and what we see as peripheral (or away from the center, on the edge). According to Braverman, whatever is defined as outside the hub is what gets "prefixed." Women must be "exceptional" women to be included at the hub. Men, most especially white men, whether or not exceptional, are simply assumed to be at the center of whatever is defined as important. Braverman notes that the centrality of the white male hub has also placed all but the most notable persons of color and their many contributions at the periphery.

Let's follow Braverman's suggestion for a few minutes. As you think about most of your textbooks, or as you read the newspaper, what is being said about men? What is—or is not—being said about women? As you look at the psychological literature, do you see as many women scholars and theorists as men? As you examine your history textbooks, do you find that women's contributions to our culture, or to scientific achievement, are as well represented as those of men? What about art and literature? As you consider these questions, also notice how often you see the following: "John Smith, white scientist and inventor of the hydrophlam, ..." Does that

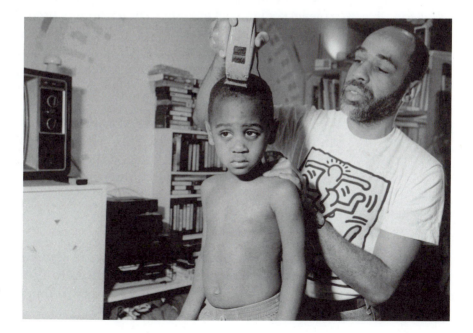

An alternative family—a gay father and his son— represents a form of diversity in our world.

strike you as odd? If so, it's probably because we rarely see a white man "prefixed." In all probability, if our sentence had read "John Smith, scientist and inventor . . ."—like you would normally see it written—you would have *assumed* John Smith was white. White people need no prefix; unless we're told to the contrary, we assume the person is white. Men need no prefix; unless the name tells us otherwise, we assume the person is male. Heterosexuals need no prefix; unless we think to ask, we assume that everyone is straight.

If women and men speak in different voices, it is likely that there may be other voices as well. People of color may speak in voices different from white people; gay men may speak differently from straight women and men, and from lesbian women as well. Obviously, the number of combinations of voices could become overwhelming, but there is a simple way to handle this: Listen to the voices of others who are different from you. They will tell you their experience. Through that dialogue you will come to know and—we hope—appreciate the rich diversity of all humankind.

Macro–Micro Tensions in Social Work

The differently focused perspectives offered by sociology on one hand, and psychology on the other, have not only contributed to the theoretical knowledge base of social work, but their inclusion has also contributed to an historical tension between micro- and macrolevel social workers. *Micro practitioners* tend to rely more on the internal world perspective of psychology because their work is focused on the problems of individuals, couples, families, and small groups. *Macro practitioners* tend to rely more on the larger environmental perspective of sociology because their work is focused on larger system change.

Theoretical frameworks provide the "lenses" through which individuals view their world. Thus, a sociological lens sharpens the focus on the environment outside the individual whereas the psychological lens focuses on the internal world of the individual.

Case

CARLOS

Carlos had become acutely aware of increased reports of domestic violence in his community. He also knew that unemployment had risen during the same period and he wondered if the two issues were related. He scheduled an open meeting at the community center where he worked to discuss training and job searches.

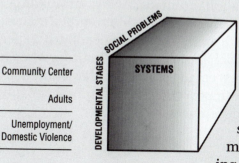

Community Center

Adults

Unemployment/ Domestic Violence

The room was packed on the night of the meeting. After a brief opening from Carlos, people discussed, with much emotion, their anger at a plant closing, and their frustration with the lack of information about jobs or the need for new skills. Together they continued to make suggestions about what the variety of community agencies might do to provide training, information, or job search skills. A small group eagerly agreed to work with Carlos to pursue these ideas.

Case

NANCY

Nancy had become acutely aware of increased reports of domestic violence in her community. She also knew that unemployment had risen during the same period and she wondered if the two issues were related. She thought she would ask a few of the couples who were in therapy if stress from unemployment or the fear of unemployment was effecting their marriages. Couple after couple described escalating tensions that were often acted out in violent outbursts of anger.

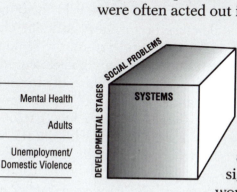

Mental Health

Adults

Unemployment/ Domestic Violence

Nancy realized that her clients needed to be able to share their feelings about loss of self-worth or fear of economic crises and to learn how to deal with these stressors in nonviolent ways. She scheduled a series of group sessions to focus on effective stress and anger management. So many people signed up, she realized more sessions would need to be scheduled.

There is a debate (not a new debate, however) between these "camps." This debate centers on whether the more effective way to enhance people's social functioning is by helping individuals to change (micro), or by changing the social environment and institutions in which individuals live (macro). It is an ongoing conflict that, unfortunately, has tended to pit one group against another. In reality, there are many different ways we can effect positive change. This kind of conflict, although intellectually stimulating and thought-provoking, has too often polarized both practitioners and social work educators; much energy has been needlessly expended in battles over which approach is most correct. In times when funding for social programs is especially scarce, neither approach may receive adequate financial support because unsympathetic funding sources can exploit these differences.

Economics

This discipline is closely related to sociology in that its focus is on large systems. The study of economics involves examining the ways in which goods and resources are produced, distributed, and consumed in a society in order to promote and maintain the material welfare. The relevance of economics to social work may not be immediately apparent if you view the whole of social work practice as in the therapeutic role, yet an understanding of basic economic structural issues is important in all social work practice.

For example, individual clients may come to us in an agency setting with financial problems that are the result of large-scale corporate layoffs. If we fail to understand the context in which such realities occur, we may be able to appreciate the very meaning of this experience for the middle-class or formerly affluent client. Equally important is the need for us to understand the structural aspects of our economic system that essentially guarantee unemployment or underemployment for certain members of our society. This is an arena in which policy analysts must examine the multifaceted and sometimes conflicting interests of a society that, on one hand, speaks to equal opportunity for all citizens while, at the same time, promulgates policies that structure inequality into the fabric of the economic system.

As we have seen in the previous chapters, social work has a strong historical tradition and commitment to helping poor and oppressed persons. This does not mean that all social workers must have an additional degree in economics. But it does suggest that knowledge from this discipline provides a sound foundation for understanding and appreciating the economic contexts in which our clients live, and how this ultimately affects certain groups in positive and negative ways.

"Don't tell me about economics," thought Tricia. "I feel poor enough. I'm a part-time student, I can only work part-time, and I'm a single mother of a handicapped child. It would help if I could get insurance for my little girl, but I can't because of something called 'pre-existing conditions' and because I don't work full-time. I have a lot of sympathy and understanding for people who are just barely scraping by, because that's me, most of the time. Sometimes I think about what it would be like to live in a country with national health insurance. At least then my daughter's medical needs could be met and I could finish school in less than seven years and get a real full-time job."

There are many fascinating social work value and ethics issues interwoven throughout the structure and policies of an economic system. For a moment, think of yourself as a single parent. You want to work to support yourself and your child without public assistance. Assume that you have the skills necessary to obtain a job that will pay you $1,200 a month, well above the federally defined poverty level, and assume that your child is physically healthy. However, your child is only three, too young for regular public school, and your community offers only private child-care services that range in cost from $2 to $5 an hour. Calculating your actual work hours at 40 per week, plus commuting time, child care will cost you $84 to $210 per week, or $336 to $840 per month. Would it pay you to hold down your full-time job and try to be self-supporting? It does not require a great deal of mathematical skill to note that child-care costs alone—that is, excluding the absolute basic costs of rent, utilities, and groceries—would leave you wondering whether you can afford to go to work!

This example illustrates how the economic structure, the availability (or nonavailability) of support services, and social policy can interact to produce disincentives for employment. This is the result of an economic system that is market oriented and traditionally focused. The U.S. economic system is built on the notion that a free and unregulated marketplace will best meet the needs of the population. Of course this capitalist theory assumes that consumers of goods and services have equal information, equal access, and equal ability to purchase goods and services. Furthermore, our economic system continues to operate on the definition of the traditional family, historically viewed as a unit comprised of two heterosexual spouses—the male as primary wage-earner, female as primary child caretaker—and their offspring. This definition remains despite recent demographic data indicating that fewer than half of Americans now live in this traditional nuclear family unit.

Unfortunately, wishful thinking and turning away from reality creates large gaps in needed services. The millions of people who do not fit the traditional family model cannot benefit from policies that do not reflect the reality of their lives. Policies that truly valued the diverse kinds of family units that now exist might include a national policy enabling single parents to attend school or job training programs, hold down jobs *and* provide for safe, affordable child care, or a national policy allowing gay men and lesbian women to include their life partners as spouses on their health insurance— policies that acknowledge the diversity of family forms as they actually exist. They would also facilitate client self-determination and would reward rather than penalize people who want to work.

Social workers frequently see clients in various Catch-22 situations, not only in public assistance programs, but increasingly among the "newly" unemployed or underemployed, who are the displaced workers who have lost their jobs to technology or to the ebb and flow of the country's economy. Auto workers from Detroit with 15 and 20 years on the job found themselves forced to leave the area in search of employment in the late 1970s and early 1980s. The problem? U.S. car manufacturers did not recognize the increasing dissatisfaction of U.S. car buyers, who began purchasing more reliable Japanese imports in great numbers.

The problem widened as unemployed workers from the Midwest and Northeast moved toward the Southwest in hopes of finding jobs, just when the economy of the oil-producing states bottomed out along with the price of oil. The result? Great numbers of unemployed from out of state added to the increasing numbers of unemployed in another hard hit region, and social workers added new terms to their language: the displaced middle class, the formerly affluent, the new poor. For the first time in their lives, many of these people had to ask for help, even for basic necessities like food and shelter; for many, this was the end of the great American dream. Underlying faults in the structure of the U.S. economic system can be identified as the cause of the disillusionment and pain on the faces of clients being served by social workers.

If you recall the discussion in Chapter 3 of major social policies—such as the 1935 Social Security Act and the 1964 Equal Opportunity Act—you can reflect on the competing economic theories that were part of their implementation. Or, consider the conflicting opinions that you hear or read about nationalized health care or governmentally supported child care. These two policies are clearly derived from an economic theory that does not presume equality in opportunity or purchasing power. Socialism, in economic terms, represents greater government regulation in pricing and delivery of certain essential goods and services.

Political Science

Political science is closely aligned with sociology and economics. Its primary unit of focus is the structure and functions of government. "The government" is comprised of those persons, both elected and appointed, who formulate laws, policies, and procedures for the operation of a specific entity (i.e., the federal government handles affairs that pertain to the nation; state governments deal with individual states; likewise for counties, parishes or cities, and so on). An understanding of the structure and functions of governments is critical for all social workers, especially those practicing at the community or macro change levels. To effect change in a system, we must first understand the structure and functions of that system in order to determine the best strategy to use. This is equally true for agency managers and administrators as it is for neighborhood or community organizers, and for legislative lobbyists.

Sometimes when systems change is discussed in relation to government or political entities, the question is raised as to whether change in a system is best effected from the inside or outside. Much of this discussion also addresses whether incremental (i.e., slow, step-by-step) change is possible, likely, or preferable, or whether it is necessary to eliminate existing systems or structures, and essentially start over with a new model, more along the lines of a revolution.

Such discussions have been heard less often among social workers in the last 20 years, perhaps reflecting the more introspective mood of the country in general. This relative quiet may also be related to a shift within the profession, a sense of general concern among social workers regarding the public's often misinformed perception of social work (a topic that we will discuss extensively in Chapter 13). Image issues have prompted many practitioners to consider moving toward private practice settings in an attempt to

Senator Barbara Mikulski (D-MD) received her MSW from the University of Maryland School of Social Work in 1965 and was elected to the U.S. Senate in 1986, after several terms in the House of Representatives. Mikulski is the first woman to have won a statewide election in Maryland.

shed, at least in part, the stereotype of social workers as "bleeding hearts" or "rabble rousers." If increasing numbers of practitioners continue this movement, fewer are left to tackle the structural or systemic problems created by ill-informed policymakers and politicians.

Nonetheless, social workers who support the position of change from within a system often seek managerial or administrative positions in social service agencies. In so doing, they can exercise a degree of authority and influence through policy development, and they can help shape the nature and direction of service delivery efforts. Increasing numbers of social workers, such as

Maryland Congressperson Barbara Mikulski, have moved further into the realm of elected political office as a way of effecting larger scale social change.

An NASW publication lists 113 social workers in elected state, county, municipal, and local offices in 1991. This document is the first of its kind, and acknowledges that political social work is indeed an important arena of social work practice. On the other hand, there are great numbers of practitioners who continue to work from outside the target system, believing that if they are part of the system, their ability to effect change will be compromised. Whether or not working from the inside, change-focused practitioners must have a sound knowledge of how political systems operate.

Anthropology

Anthropology is also related to sociology. It is traditionally viewed as the study of primitive cultures and the peoples within them. Much like sociology and psychology, however, there are several different specialty areas within the discipline; for example, social and cultural anthropology have made and continue to make substantial knowledge contributions to social work. These areas once focused almost exclusively on primitive cultures, but now include the study of contemporary cultures as well. Clearly, any discipline that offers theory and knowledge aimed at understanding the nature of humankind will be of value to social workers.

An appreciation of the vast diversity of life-styles within and among different groups is an important part of what we discussed in Chapter 5. This appreciative stance evolves largely from the social work values and ethics discussed in Chapter 6. The study of different cultures, whether primitive or contemporary, distant or within our own land, offers us the opportunity to gain an appreciation for the richness of human diversity, to examine our own attitudes and beliefs about what is right, normal, or appropriate. This kind of expanded thinking helps make each of us a more sensitive and self-aware practitioner.

Human Biology

Human biology has recently been defined as a requirement in accredited undergraduate social work education programs and as a prerequisite for admission to accredited MSW programs. Its inclusion as a required area of study suggests that social workers must know and understand basic biological or physiological functioning, particularly as this relates to human growth and development through the life cycle. Knowledge about human biology is more substantive than theoretical. It provides a solid foundation for later study of content related to psychological development.

Substantive content included in human biology may include information about major illnesses (e.g., cancer, heart disease, stroke, HIV/AIDS, mental disorders) and their treatment. It may also include information on frequently prescribed psychoactive drugs, the conditions for which they are prescribed, and common side effects. As social workers, we also need to know the signs or symptoms of health conditions common to particular age groups. For example, older persons may report a number of health problems and they may be taking several prescription and over-the-counter medications. These individuals may accidentally overdose or experience adverse effects due to the interaction of medications unless someone—typically the social worker—monitors the situation.

Understanding human biology does not qualify us to diagnose medical problems. It does give us the foundation to know when a referral to a physician or psychiatrist is in order. It also helps us differentiate physical or biological problems from psychological problems.

Case

FRANCES

*F*rances loves working with older people. Though she didn't get her MSW until she was in her fifties, she knew the direction she wanted to take with her career. Her outgoing personality mixed with an everpresent dry sense of humor made her a favorite with the staff and patients at the nursing home where she was a consultant. Armed with her enthusiasm and knowledge, Frances was also in demand as a guest lecturer in social work, gerontology, nursing, and public health classes.

With just a touch of intimidation she would begin: "Do you know that the average older American takes three times as many drugs as the average American? Do you know that between 75 and 81 percent of people over the age of 65 take at least one prescription drug, and that Medicare recipients not living in institutions receive an average of 17.9 prescriptions every year?"

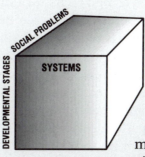

Health Care

Older Adults

Problems of Aging

She would pause to let those numbers sink in. The discussion that followed often centered around potential consequences of drug misuse, the economics of health care, and the pervasiveness of ageism. "If a teenager acts kind of crazy, we say that's 'just adolescence,' but when an old person acts strange, we want to medicate them! What does that say about our attitudes toward older folks?"

Frances was not simply educating in her presentations; she was raising consciousness and advocating on behalf of a group of persons that is growing larger every day. Current demographic projections show there are more of us aging (i.e., many of the baby boom generation are now over 40) and more of us are living longer than ever before. Frances knows that she'll have plenty to do as long as she wants to do it.[4]

Social work education programs have struggled not only to find a place for human biology content in their crowded curricula, but also to identify the most relevant content in a very broad and changing area. An understanding of human sexuality helps us work better with clients who lack basic information about sexual functioning, contraception, or sexually transmitted diseases. Understanding some fundamentals of nutrition can be helpful in assessing client functioning, as can knowledge about the effects of stress on the human body. And, in an era marked by the emergence of HIV/AIDS—the greatest public health threat in this century—everyone, and certainly every social worker, should know the essential facts of HIV transmission, the physical manifestations of the virus, and the various treatment options.[5]

Issues Related to "Borrowing" Knowledge

The knowledge contributions of the disciplines discussed thus far represent a traditional view of what social workers are believed to need. In fact, social work education has relied extensively on knowledge from these areas. This liberal borrowing has been both a blessing and a curse. Some have criticized us for failing to depend on a unique knowledge base, whereas others see little point in "re-inventing the wheel" when there is so much relevant knowledge available from other disciplines. A few critics have argued that we have taken too liberally from some areas (e.g., psychology) to the detriment of others (e.g., sociology, economics, political science), and that this has resulted in an overemphasis on a micro or clinical focus at the expense of larger scale social change. This is a theme of the micro–macro strains within the social work profession noted earlier. These strains actually do reflect a significant, real, and ongoing struggle within the profession.

Our profession is unique in its global goal of enhancing social functioning, which, by definition, includes achieving social justice. Our profession is unique in viewing people within their social environment. The fact is, a broad base of knowledge, borrowed or developed from within, is absolutely necessary to prepare us for effective and ethical practice. There is ample opportunity for all who wish to contribute to achieving these goals. Even though we may use different methods, even though our client groups may be of different sizes, and even though we may see the "cause" of individual and social problems differently, each of us who shares a vision of a healthy and just society has a place in this profession.

Related Knowledge

The aforementioned disciplines are those most frequently recommended to undergraduate students considering a degree or career in social work. It is not, we recognize, a short list. Still, there are several other knowledge areas that we believe can contribute to the process of becoming the "ideal" social worker. For example, we believe that well-read practitioners are especially skilled and highly sensitive. Aside from life experience and the wisdom of age, what better educational ground is there than novels that deal with the essential struggles of the human spirit? Classic and contemporary literature, poems, and dramas are rich in their treatment of the human condition. Biographies and autobiographies offer insight into the lives of real people who have confronted life's challenges. A study of the public and private lives of such persons offers a rich opportunity to examine and ponder the complexities of human behavior.

History, too, flawed and incomplete as it may be, teaches us a great deal about ourselves as a nation, including how we have grown and changed. Family units of a century ago bear little resemblance to those we see now. Urbanization, industrialization, and then technological advances have forever altered and, in some cases, eliminated the traditional functions of the American family. To fully understand and appreciate who we are now, and how we got this way, we must have a sense of our collective and individual roots. Furthermore, the historical accounts of other cultures or nations with whom we share this planet offer us insight into different ways of being and behaving, ways that we might find puzzling, disturbing, or perhaps only interesting, but that nevertheless help broaden our vision beyond the limited scope of our own experience.

Beyond literature and history are the areas of philosophy and theology, which provide us with greater, often unanswerable, but perennially challenging questions as to the essential meaning of life. Too often it seems that social workers, like other professionals, are caught up in their work, sometimes feeling overwhelmed, becoming detached from their clients and, ultimately, detached from themselves. The practice issues that confront social workers are the essential issues of the human condition: basic human needs for food and shelter, as well as needs for love, health, connection, and relationship. No one is exempt from having these basic human needs and it is in the best interest of all concerned—ourselves and our clients—if we are clear on what we believe and what we value in life.

Finally, it will come as no surprise that we see women's studies as excellent background for social work practice. Most social work practitioners are women. Most clients are women. Women's studies provides useful knowledge to help us understand why this might be the case.

Although it is not possible to describe the content of all women's studies courses or programs because they range from an approach of "selected women's issues" to an analysis of evolving feminist philosophies, there is a growing body of readily available literature. Regardless of whether one chooses to enroll in formal courses or to use the self-selection approach at a local bookstore, literature by women about women's experience will help inform our practice efforts. [6] And, even in a knowledge area that is still evolving, there are a number of "classic" works to stimulate new ways of thinking about old issues. [7] In addition to theoretically oriented works, you can also select problem specific readings, such as violence against women (e.g., sexual assault, battering, pornography, incest, sexual abuse), addictions (e.g., alcohol or other drugs), and eating disorders (e.g., anorexia, bulimia), or identity specific material, such as women of color, lesbian women, or older women. [8]

A Strictly Social Work Body of Knowledge

Despite social work's historical and contemporary use of knowledge developed in other fields, our profession has been engaged in its own knowledge development as well. This knowledge has been developed by both social work practitioners and educators, and it is used by professionals in many disciplines. Persons working in the alcohol treatment programs are likely familiar with (MSW) Claudia Bepko's work with Jo Ann Krestan (1985, 1990) on treating alcoholic families and codependency. Social worker Claudia Black (1982) has produced groundbreaking work on Adult Children of Alcoholics (AcoAs). Many other contemporary social work educators and practitioners have made substantial contributions as well.

However, our process of knowledge development is not just a recent trend. The first publication that attempted to describe a social casework approach to helping was Mary Richmond's *Social Diagnosis,* published in 1917. Since then, social work publications such as books and journals have proliferated, providing a wide variety of forums for analysis, discussion, and dissemination of ideas. Some journals focus on practice with specific populations—for example, the very young, the very old, hospitalized individuals, and so on—but others are quite generic, featuring a wide variety of articles in each issue, covering a range of populations, practice methods, or theoretical approaches. [9] For the most part, these articles are written by social workers and describe some aspect of their experiences in practice; however, a growing number of these articles are beginning to be modeled after the scientific studies of other disciplines, with more use of experimental, hypotheses-testing methods found in the so-called hard sciences.

In addition to the large numbers of books and discipline specific journals, the profession also has its own two-volume *Encyclopedia of Social Work* published by the National Association of Social Workers (NASW). Currently in its 18th edition, this encyclopedia is updated regularly to reflect the changes in social work as they evolve in our society. *The Social Work Dictionary* (Robert L. Barker, 1991) is yet another helpful reference published by the NASW.

Social Work Education

Knowledge integration has been and continues to be a major task for social workers. What may interest you as an Introduction to Social Work student is how these knowledge bases have been incorporated into social work education. If you are enrolled in an accredited BSW program, your advisor has undoubtedly told you that there are many required courses for the social work major. These courses fall into the following curricular categories: social welfare policy and services, human behavior and the social environment, social work practice, research, and field instruction. Let's examine each of these content areas briefly.

Social welfare policy and services (often called SWPS and pronounced "swaps") courses explore how social welfare policy is formulated, examine the various effects that policy has in relation to social service delivery systems, and provide skills in policy analysis. Knowledge is drawn from literature on the historical and philosophical tradition of the social work profession, including values and ethics, as well as from current policy issues.

Human behavior and the social environment (usually shortened to HBSE, or "hub-see") courses deal with the question of why people behave as they do. HBSE courses are theoretical in nature and help us to understand individual, group, and organizational behavior from the microlevel (individual and family) to the macrolevel (societal). Knowledge is drawn from psychological, biological, sociological, political, and economic theories.

In contrast, *social work practice* courses focus on skill development, ranging from essential interpersonal skills to specific practice principles of selected models of intervention. In a given course, content may be limited to practice with individuals, groups, or families and in a separate course, the focus would be on the skill base of community or administrative practice. Knowledge is again drawn from the social and behavioral sciences, as well as from the profession's value base and code of ethics.

Research courses provide the knowledge and skill needed in order to read, understand, and interpret published research studies. Such courses also make us aware that there are many different ways to "know what we know." Research methods help us learn how to conduct research and how our findings can be used to improve our practice, to analyze policies, and to evaluate our programs.

Field instruction courses, sometimes called practica, focus on the application of knowledge and skill in social work practice. These courses give students the opportunity to actually work in a social welfare setting and, under the supervision of a qualified social worker, to provide services. Because they take place in real-life social work settings, field courses are an excellent way for students to examine their interest in pursuing a career in social work.

Taken as a package, the social work curriculum is comprehensive and multifaceted. In addition to required courses in the areas we have identified, students can enroll in a variety of elective courses that address their particular interests. And, as we have noted previously, there are many choices of content area that would provide an excellent foundation for the person interested in social work.

Summary

The vast knowledge base of social work continues to expand. This chapter has provided an overview of the knowledge contributions from those disciplines—sociology, psychology, economics, political science, anthropology, and human biology—that have most clearly influenced social work. We have also discussed related areas that we believe hold promise for expanding our current perspectives.

The profession's tendency to borrow knowledge from other disciplines has at various times been criticized, and at other times been celebrated. Our diversity as practitioners has required us to use knowledge from whatever fields would best help us achieve the profession's ultimate goal of social justice. As we move toward the end of the twentieth century, our profession has developed to the point where we can identify our knowledge base and see it reflected in social work education programs across the country.

Notes

1. From early English Common Law, we inherited the "Rule of Thumb" that stated a man could beat his wife and children with a switch (i.e., a slender whip or tree limb) no larger around than his thumb. Also included was the definition of wives and children as chattel, or the property of the husband. This is a revealing example of how power, used

sentially that human behavior is the result of individual learning, and that which has been learned can, therefore, be unlearned.

In contrast, the most well-known and, no doubt, the most influential school of thought in psychology is the psychoanalytic, developed by Sigmund Freud in the late nineteenth and early twentieth centuries. The most prominent schools of thought evolving and branching out from early psychoanalytic theory are ego psychology, object relations theory, and self psychology. The intricacies of these theoretical models are beyond the scope of this book, but we can say that the specific unit of attention among psychoanalysts operating within a subjective/empathic framework is the individual's dynamic internal life, particularly unconscious motivation and conflict, and experience of self.

In a different frame of reference, theories about human development through the life cycle have come primarily from "developmental psychologists" such as Erik Erikson. Erikson (1950) introduced a psychosocial developmental model that includes eight stages of life span development. According to this model, each stage is characterized by a crisis point that must be mastered before moving on to the next stage. Another theorist, Jean Piaget, is well known for his theory of cognitive development. Piaget (1952) suggested that all people learn how to think in essentially the same ways, and go through the same four cognitive stages of development in the same order. Other theorists, such as Lawrence Kohlberg, have addressed moral development. Kohlberg (1969, 1981) proposed a path of moral development that includes six stages within three levels.

As stage theories, each of the developmental models noted has been criticized as too linear (i.e., they tend to suggest that "normal" development be viewed as a straight line progression from the first stage through the last). Other criticisms have been more pointed. Carol Gilligan (1982), a former student of Kohlberg's, identifies a clear gender bias prevalent among current developmental theories:

> While in Piaget's account (1932) of the moral judgment of the child, girls are an aside, a curiosity to whom he devotes four brief entries in an index that omits "boys" altogether because "the child" is assumed to be male, in the research from which Kohlberg derives his theory, females simply do not exist. Kohlberg's (1958, 1981) six stages that describe the development of moral judgment from childhood to adulthood are based empirically on a

abusively, has been codified into law and, as a result, has served to reinforce inequality.

2. See, for example, Diana E. H. Russell, *The Politics of Rape* (New York: Stein & Day, 1975); Susan Brownmiller, *Against Our Will: Men, Women and Rape* (New York: Simon & Schuster, 1975); Lenore E. Walker, *The Battered Women* (New York: Harper & Row, 1979); and *The Battered Women Syndrome* (New York: Springer, 1984); and Joyce E. Williams and Karen A. Holmes, *The Second Assault: Rape and Public Attitudes* (Westport, CT: Greenwood Press, 1981).

3. "Women in Context" Conference, Menninger Clinic, Topeka, Kansas, December 1983. Braverman's lecture was videotaped and produced as "A Feminist Perspective: Implications for Therapists."

4. Statistical data used by Frances are from Mary Ann Matteson, and Eleanor S. McConnell, *Gerontological Nursing: Concepts and Practice* (Philadelphia: W. B. Saunders, 1988), as cited by Harriette C. Johnson et al., "Strengthening the 'Bio' in the Biopsychosocial Paradigm," *Journal of Social Work Education*, Vol. 26, No. 2 (Spring/Summer 1990): 109–123.

5. An excellent resource for creative ways in which to integrate content on AIDS is Adele Weiner, "Incorporating AIDS Content Across the BSW Curriculum," *Journal of Social Work Education*, Vol. 26, No. 2 (Spring/Summer 1990): 162–176.

6. Any woman born and raised into a culture that has historically devalued women (such as ours) will have internalized, to varying degrees, the beliefs and values of that culture. Simply because a book is written "by a woman" about "women's experience," we cannot assume that the author has dealt with her own internalized devaluation of herself. This society (unfortunately, we are not unique in this) has been characterized by misogynist (i.e., meaning literally, "woman-hating") attitudes. Unless we have dealt with our own issues, everything we see and do will be influenced by these pervasive attitudes.

7. Recommendations include: Betty Friedan, *The Feminine Mystique* (New York: Dell Publishing, 1963); Kate Millett, *Sexual Politics* (Garden City, NY: Doubleday & Co., 1970); Nancy Chodorow, *The Reproduction of Mothering: Psychoanalysis and the Sociology of Gender* (Berkeley: University of California Press, 1978); Carol Gilligan, *In a Different Voice: Psychological Theory and Women's Development* (Cambridge: Harvard University Press, 1982); Jean Baker Miller, *Toward a New Psychology of Women* (Boston: Beacon Press, 1986); and Mary Field Belenky, Blythe McVicker Clinchy, Nancy Rule Goldberger, and Jill Mattuck Tarule, *Women's Ways of Knowing: The Development of Self, Voice, and Mind* (New York: Basic Books, 1986); Catharine A. MacKinnon, *Feminism Unmodified: Discourses on Life and Law* (Cambridge: Harvard University Press, 1987); Susan Faludi, *Backlash: The Undeclared War Against American Women* (New York: Crown, 1991).

8. Some topic-specific suggested readings not mentioned elsewhere:

Violence

Bass, Ellen, and Laura Davis. *The Courage to Heal: A Guide for Women Survivors of Child Sexual Abuse.* New York: Harper & Row, 1989.

Herman, Judith. *Father-Daughter Incest.* Cambridge: Harvard University Press, 1981.

Russell, Diana E. H. *Sexual Exploitation: Rape, Child Sexual Abuse, Sexual Harassment.* Newbury Park, CA: Sage, 1984.

Schechter, Sue. *Women and Male Violence: The Visions and Struggles of the Battered Women's Movement.* Boston: South End Press, 1982.

Yllo, D., and Michelle Bograd. *Feminist Perspectives on Wife Abuse.* Beverly Hills, CA: Sage, 1988.

Addictions

Chernin, Kim. *The Obsession: Reflections on the Tyranny of Slenderness.* New York: Harper & Row, 1981.

———. *The Hungry Self: Women, Eating and Identity.* New York: Random House, 1985.

Kasl, Charlotte Davis. *Women, Sex, and Addiction: A Search for Love and Power.* New York: Harper & Row, 1990.

Orbach, Susie. *Hunger Strike: The Anorectic's Struggle as a Metaphor for Our Age.* New York: W. W. Norton, 1986.

Women of Color

Comas-Diaz, L. *Cross-Cultural Mental Health Treatment.* New York: John Wiley, 1988.

Giddings, P. *When and Where I Enter: The Impact of Black Women on Race and Sex in America.* New York: Bantam Books, 1985.

Naylor, Gloria. *The Women of Brewster Place.* New York: Penguin, 1980.

Pinderhughes, E. *Understanding Race, Ethnicity, and Power.* New York: Free Press, 1989.

Stack, Carol. *All Our Kin: Strategies for Survival in a Black Community.* New York: Harper & Row, 1974.

Lesbian Women

Barrett, Martha Barron. *Invisible Lives: The Truth About Millions of Women Loving Women.* New York: Harper & Row, 1990.

Boston Lesbian Psychologies Collective, eds. *Lesbian Psychologies: Explorations and Challenges.* Chicago: University of Illinois Press, 1987.

Cruikshank, Margaret. *Lesbian Studies: Present and Future.* New York: Feminist Press, 1982.

Pharr, Suzanne. *Homophobia: A Weapon of Sexism.* Inverness, CA: Chardon Press, 1988.

Older Women/Ageism

Macdonald, Barbara, with Cynthia Rich. *Look Me in the Eye: Old Women, Aging and Ageism.* San Francisco: Spinsters, Inc., 1983.

9. NASW publishes four journals: *Social Work* (free to all NASW members);

Health and Social Work (focusing on health and mental health practice); *Social Work in Education* (for school social workers, educators, and administrators); and *Social Work Research and Abstracts* (includes research articles as well as abstracts of all articles published in major social work journals). The Council on Social Work Education publishes the *Journal of Social Work Education* (free to members of CSWE) and Haworth Press publishes a variety of specialty journals: *Social Work in Health Care, Administration in Social Work, Computers in Human Services, Journal of Gay and Lesbian Social Services, Journal of Gerontological Social Work, Journal of Multicultural Social Work, Social Work with Groups,* and others. Sage Publications has *Affilia: Journal of Women and Social Work, Hispanic Journal of Behavioral Sciences, Journal of Aging and Health, Journal of Black Studies, Journal of Interpersonal Violence,* and others. There are actually hundreds of professional journals. We just wanted to give you a head start on a few.

References

Barker, Robert L. *The Social Work Dictionary,* 2nd ed. Silver Springs, MD: NASW, 1991.

Bepko, Claudia, with Jo Ann Krestan. *The Responsibility Trap: A Blueprint for Treating the Alcoholic Family.* New York: Free Press, 1985.

———. *Too Good for Her Own Good: Breaking Free from the Burden of Female Responsibility.* New York: Harper & Row, 1990.

Black, Claudia. *It Will Never Happen to Me.* Denver: MAC, 1982.

Boneparth, Ellen, and Emily Stoper. *Women, Power and Policy: Toward the Year 2000,* 2nd ed. New York: Pergamon Press, 1988.

Erickson, Erik H. *Childhood and Society.* New York: W. W. Norton, 1950.

Gilligan, Carol. *In a Different Voice: Psychological Theory and Women's Development.* Cambridge: Harvard University Press, 1982.

Jordan, Judith, Alexandra G. Kaplan, Jean Baker Miller, Irene Stiver, and Janet Surrey. *Women's Growth in Connection: Writings from the Stone Center.* New York: Guilford Publications, 1991.

Kohlberg, Lawrence. "The Development of Modes of Thinking and Choices in Years 10 to 16." Ph.D. Diss., University of Chicago, 1958.

———. *Stages in the Development of Moral Thought and Action.* New York: Holt, Rinehart & Winston, 1969.

———. *The Philosophy of Moral Development.* New York: Harper & Row, 1981.

National Association of Social Workers (NASW). *Social Workers Serving in Elective Offices, 1991.* Silver Spring, MD: NASW, 1991.

Piaget, Jean. *The Origins of Intelligence in Children.* New York: International Universities Press, 1952.

———. *The Moral Judgment of the Child* (1932). New York: Free Press, 1965.

Richmond, Mary E. *Social Diagnosis.* New York: Free Press, 1917.

Social Work Practice: Methods

How is the actual practice of social work organized? Do social workers really have a distinct perspective, that is, a unique way of seeing the world? What are the actual skills needed to *do* social work practice? Unit III contains three chapters that answer these questions. Chapter 8 provides an overview of significant organizing concepts and terms used in describing social work practice. Chapter 9 identifies and describes the basic generalist skills that are the foundation for all our practice efforts. Chapter 10 provides an overview of advanced practice skills in social work.

Conceptual Framework

Introduction

To this point, you have learned about the origins of social welfare and you have seen how basic human needs are addressed through a variety of practice opportunities. You have also become familiar with the profession's appreciation of diversity, and learned about the knowledge base of social work as well as the values and ethics that are central to the profession. In this chapter, we will provide a framework for understanding how social work practice is organized around certain concepts and perspectives. In particular, you will be introduced to the person-in-environment perspective, a systems theory framework, and an overview of the levels and methods of intervention that organize social work practice.

Person-in-Environment Perspective

Everyone is born into a family of some kind, and that family is located geographically in a particular neighborhood or community that is a part of a larger city, state, region, and so on. Each of these variations interacts to affect the individual and vice versa. Does it matter whether you were raised by a single mother or by an adoptive family? What effect does it have on your life potential if you are born into an impoverished rural family rather than into a wealthy family living in Manhattan? Do you think your life would be different if you had been born in Saudi Arabia? in Soweto? You can begin to appreciate the interactive influences and the connections between individuals and their environments by imagining your own answers to these questions.

One of the unique things about social workers is the way in which they are taught to view the world. You will recall from Chapter 7 that sociologists study groups and societies to understand how and why they operate as they do, and that psychologists and psychiatrists focus on the pathology or illness of an individual or small group in order to understand and cure them. Both these disciplines play an important role in understanding human behavior, yet they often fail to integrate their views into a total picture. It is social workers who are taught to look simultaneously at both the person and the environment. Social workers see people as they interact with, and are affected by, their environment. We acknowledge explicitly that no one lives in a social vacuum. This is referred to as the *person-in-environment perspective*. This is a truly dynamic, living picture that takes into account not only who a person is as an individual human being, but also what external influences are likely to be playing a part in that person's overall life.

Some of you may be thinking this perspective seems obvious, yet even social workers have had to struggle to grasp its importance. This struggle is reflected in our earlier history, as evidenced by the split between the Charity Organization Societies and the Settlement Movement; the former viewed the roots of human misery in the weak moral character of some individuals, whereas the latter saw the roots of people's problems as located in a society that allowed basic human needs to go unmet. Throughout the 1920s, the profession struggled with the conflicts presented by this dichotomy, and it grew and matured as a result. However, it was not until the 1960s that a conceptual framework for eliminating this dichotomous thinking began to get the attention of social workers. This framework is known as *systems theory*.

Systems Theory

If we take the person-in-environment perspective a step further, we can introduce systems theory as a conceptual framework for social work practice. The concept of systems originated in the fields of biology and medicine, but it has been applied widely in many other disciplines, including social work. A systems approach is important because it tells us that (1) people and their environments are in constant interaction with one another; (2) searching for cause–effect explanations *only* in people or *only* in their environments is seeing just a part of the big picture; and (3) our attention must be directed toward the dynamic totality of what we see. As noted by Naomi Brill (1990), "The crucial role played by social forces, both through the environment and through the impact of other persons on individual functioning, cannot be ignored. In order to be effective, we need to be able to deal with the totality of the person—the sum of both the inborn internal self and the socially determined facets of the individual" (p. 104).

Even though it is called a theory, systems is not so much a formal theory as it is a *framework* or an *approach* for seeing and understanding. This framework helps us to take in large amounts of information about the world and make sense of it. A systems approach also enables us to examine the interaction and the connections between people and their social environments instead of looking only at one or the other, as if people and their environments were separate, autonomous entities. There are, however, two primary criticisms of this model. First, although a systems approach helps us to examine, understand, and make sense of a situation, it does not tell us what to do about it. Second, some social workers find the language of systems to be unduly complex and mechanistic. Despite these criticisms, however, the systems approach seems well established as a conceptual framework in social work.

Webster's unabridged dictionary includes 13 definitions of the word *system*. The first states that a system is "a set or arrangement of things so related or connected as to form a unity or organic whole." This definition suggests that the parts of a system may be live or inanimate, and that the parts must be related or connected in some meaningful way that creates a whole. As used in social work, a system is often described as a set of interrelated and interdependent parts that have common or shared properties. Figure 8.1 illustrates how systems can be represented graphically. First, the total individual is a whole system, made up of physical, spiritual, intellectual, psychological, and social components. The individual is also made of biological subsystems such as the circulatory system, the digestive system, and the reproductive system. Finally the individual is also a part of larger systems such as a family, a neighborhood, and a community. Perhaps a brief overview of selected systems terminology will clarify this further.

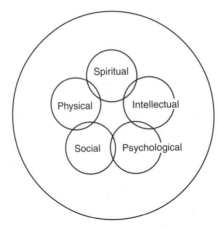

The Total Individual, a System

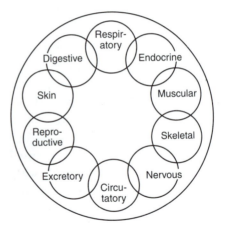

Human Beings, Biological Systems

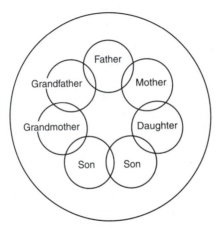

A Family System

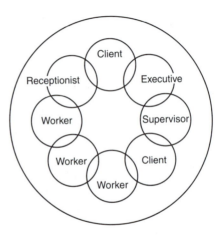

An Agency System

FIGURE 8.1 Systems,
Their Parts, and Their
Boundaries (Source:
Naomi Brill, *Working
with People: The
Helping Process,* 4th
ed. Copyright © 1990
by Longman Publishing
Group.)

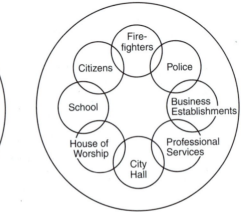

A Neighborhood System

A Community System

Systems Theory Terminology

Focal or Target System.   This simply refers to the system or unit on which we are focused at the moment. The focal system of a teacher may be the student or the class; for the probation officer it may be the probationer; for the social worker in children's protective services it may be the child(ren), the parents, or the whole family. You will notice that the focal system can be of any size; that is, we may focus on only an individual or we might focus on the family as a total unit comprised of all individual members. In social work practice, our client is often our focal system, but a client can be an individual, a group, family, community, or even a larger system.

Subsystems.   A subsystem is a part of component of a larger system. Stated another way, a subsystem can be viewed as a system within a system. Biological subsystems of humans include the respiratory, circulatory, or nervous systems, all the way down in size to atoms and molecules. Families are systems comprised of subsystems, such as one or more parents or parent figures, one or more children, and, often, one or more related persons (such as grandparents, aunts, uncles, cousins, etc.). To determine the subsystem of a community, think of all the parts that make up that larger system. For example, a given community would include the people who live there, educational systems that provide schools, the law enforcement or criminal justice system that provides protection or corrections services, the health and welfare systems designed to meet human needs, and so on. Each of these community subsystems can be broken down into smaller subsystems when that is necessary to fully understand the total picture.

Suprasystem.   Just as a subsystem is a smaller part of a whole, a suprasystem is a larger, more encompassing whole. That is, a suprasystem involves a large-scale unit of analysis, such as a nation or an entire culture. A nation, then, because it is such a large entity, would have multiple layers of subsystems: states, counties, cities, communities, neighborhoods, households, and so forth.

Boundaries.   A boundary is a limit setter, a point that keeps any part of a system (or subsystem) enclosed or contained. The simplest kind is a geographical boundary. The points at which states in the United States are separated and distinguished from one another are state boundaries and, on a smaller level, there are county lines and city limits. It is important to recognize that a boundary, in systems terms, is not necessarily the same as a *barrier*. A barrier suggests blockage, whereas a boundary is simply a line of demarcation; barriers tend to prevent movement from one place to another and boundaries mark off the end of one place and the beginning of another. In our example of a geographical boundary, we can drive across city limits or state lines without being blocked off by barriers.

Homeostasis. This term refers to the need for all systems to maintain a steady state of functioning. Related to this is *equilibrium,* a term that suggests balance within the system and balance with other systems. No system is absolutely static; a static system cannot develop and, as a result, it will die. A steady state of flux or movement is necessary for any system to survive. This is why a system with an overly rigid or a closed boundary cannot remain healthy or survive. Without some energy flow, without some movement, a system will reach *entropy,* or the state of chaos or disorganization. Overly rigid boundaries that severely limit the energy flow into and out of a system create or exacerbate entropy.

Equifinality. This is among the more immediately relevant systems terms for social workers. It means that there are many different ways to achieve the same goal, even when we begin at different places. For example, a social worker in the corrections field would likely say that the goal of our correctional system is to rehabilitate offenders. The concept of equifinality suggests that rehabilitation could be achieved by incarcerating the offender, by placing the offender on probation, by providing job training and placement of the offender, by requiring drug treatment, or perhaps, by some combination of these measures. Depending on the nature of the crime and one's philosophical beliefs about human nature and rehabilitation, there are many potential paths toward the same ultimate goal.

Systems Theory Assumptions

Finally, there are several assumptions about systems that have influenced social workers' thinking:

1. Functioning or change in one part of a system affects all other parts of that system.

2. In order to survive, a system must have goals and attain those goals.

3. Systems must have input—some form of energy—from the external environment.

4. A system must have throughput, or a way of processing input.

5. Systems must produce output, which then becomes input for other systems; this reinforces the cyclical or interactive nature of systems.

6. Related to input, throughput, and output is the notion that there must be feedback from the environment.

7. Systems are self-regulating in that they can adjust and readjust following a disturbance or disruption of steady-state functioning.

Relevance of Systems Theory to Social Work.   With this background in mind, consider some examples of how a systems framework operates. You are a school social worker. Your primary role is to work with children identified by teachers as "acting out" or "disruptive." What would your first thoughts be about the nature of a given child's problem? If you immediately thought the child might suffer from Attention Deficit Hyperactivity Disorder (ADHD), you might be correct. However, before making that judgment, it would be critically important to use a systems framework to examine the larger picture of the child's current situation. You would, for example, want to know something about the family itself: How many parent figures are in the child's life? How is the relationship between parents and among others in the family? What is the family's financial status? Have there been any major changes in the family, such as loss of a job, relationship change or ending, death, birth of a child, or illness? To move to a diagnosis of the individual child is to move prematurely and in a shortsighted manner that fails to take into account all the home factors that could influence or account for the disruptive behavior at school.

Moreover, we cannot overlook possible physiological factors related to the child: For example, is there a pattern in the timing of the disruptive behavior? If you found that the disruptive behavior *invariably* occurred in the afternoon, perhaps there is a connection with too much sugar in the school lunch. Furthermore, the classroom environment itself, including the teacher and the other students, needs to be examined as possible interactive influences on the child's behavior. In fact, as we have noted previously, how a problem is defined and who does the defining can influence the entire situation. Disruptive behavior to one teacher may be viewed as "energetic creativity" by another.

This illustrates how seeing the child as a system, complete with his own unique physiological make-up, *and* seeing him simultaneously as part of other systems—such as a family or a member of a specific classroom—can influence our assessment of the problem. It might even be a good idea to look at the community in which the school is located, because community attitudes often influence our definitions of appropriate or inappropriate behavior. There may be, for example, greater latitude in what is defined as appropriate in a public school compared with a private military boarding school. The whole picture of children in their environment(s) and the complexities of the individual need to be addressed.

Using a systems framework may seem to result in overwhelming amounts of information, yet it becomes second nature in practice and actually helps us to create order out of apparent chaos. A social worker's process of seeing the totality of a situation is not unlike that of a detective trying to solve a mystery. Armed with a mental checklist, the goal of the detective is to narrow the number of possible suspects in order to identify the culprit; or, in the case of social work, to narrow down the possible causes in order to identify the target of our intervention.

Levels of Intervention

Having provided an overview of the systems approach, we will now turn to a discussion of how social work practice is structured or organized. We often speak of structuring practice according to the level of intervention: *micro, meso,* or *macro.* These terms have nothing to do with the magnitude of change. Instead they relate to the size of the *client system* (remember that this also referred to as the focal or target system). Identifying oneself as a micro, meso, or macro practitioner is a self-description that indicates the size or type of client system with which one works. It is also suggestive of the kinds of skills that are needed to work at each of the different levels of intervention.

Micro is from the Greek *mikros,* meaning small. Social workers who practice at the microlevel are working with focal systems that are individuals, small groups, or families. Sometimes microlevel intervention is called *clinical social work,* not because the work is done in a clinic setting per se, but because the focus of the work is with an individual, a group, or a family. Meso is from the Greek *mesos,* meaning middle. A social worker who operates primarily at the mesolevel works to effect change with larger systems, such as neighborhoods or communities. Finally, macro is from the Greek *makros,* which means long as in extent, or large. A macrolevel practitioner is someone whose focus is on effecting change in large social systems, for example, by influencing the passage of legislation that will ultimately impact thousands or even millions of people.

There has been a tendency to dichotomize or split micro and macro practice. We see this as unfortunate, if not inappropriate. Social work practice is not, and should not be, a choice between working with small client groups with limited goals versus changing society into a grand and perfect world. When levels of intervention are polarized into micro versus macro, it suggests an artificial choice where one level seems better than another. This is an overly simplistic and ultimately divisive way to conceptualize social work practice, and it is contrary to the mission of the profession.

Think back to the working definition in Chapter 6: "The purpose of social work is to *promote* or *restore* a mutually beneficial interaction between individuals and society in order *to improve the quality of life for everyone"* (Minahan, 1981, p. 6, emphases added). We would suggest that the words "to promote or restore" reflect support for both micro- and macrolevels of intervention. It also seems very clear that intervention at all levels is absolutely necessary in order "to improve the quality of life for everyone."

Although all social workers need to develop knowledge and skills for practice across all three levels of intervention, the reality is that most do tend to select and work primarily at one. In light of the fact that there are more unmet human needs than any single profession can possibly handle, social workers can essentially pick and choose the level of intervention they prefer and develop their strongest skills in that area.

Recognizing that many students are attracted to social work because they have a general notion of wanting to help people, it may be useful to discuss how helping is viewed at the three different levels of intervention. For example, if you have ever heard or said to yourself, "What we need to do is change the system!", you may well be hearing a budding macro practitioner. The social worker focusing on the macrolevel of intervention sees the world in terms of large systems, and looks for ways to influence policies and practices that are unjust, discriminatory, or otherwise detrimental to the well-being of large numbers of persons. The macro practitioner often takes the role of social activist by trying to draw attention to large-scale social problems, such as poverty, illiteracy, homelessness, substance abuse, crime, and so forth.

At the macrolevel, the roots of these problems are often viewed as failures in existing social policy or as problems that have in some way become institutionalized by our society. The macro practitioner intervenes with social institutions such as government agencies, schools, or the media in an attempt to influence them to become more responsive to human needs. In comparison, microlevel practitioners may well see the roots of these large-scale social problems in much the same way as their macro colleagues, but their approach is more likely to involve direct work with the people who are poor, illiterate, homeless, addicted, or victimized. In a nutshell, macro practitioners work to change policies and micro practitioners work to change people.

Is there a right way to approach these problems? To respond affirmatively is to revert back to the split between the Charity Organization Societies and the Settlement Movement proponents. Instead, it seems preferable to acknowledge that both approaches are viable and necessary. Rather than create unnecessary splits, we would suggest a more appreciative stance that supports efforts at all appropriate levels of intervention.

Methods of Intervention

We now move to specific types of intervention. In social work, these are called *methods*. Traditionally, social work methods have included social casework, social group work, and community organizing and planning. In the early years of the profession's development, each of these methods was clearly placed into a corresponding level of intervention: casework was done at the micro level of intervention, group work was at the meso level, and community organization was considered at the macro level of intervention. More recently, however, we are likely to see casework and group work considered micro level of intervention, community organization as meso level, and practice aimed at changes at the state, national, or even international levels would be viewed as macro level intervention.

Social Casework

Social casework is a method unique to social work; that is, no other profession lays claim to doing social casework. In its original usage, the term was meant to reflect a dual focus on the individual case, but with an eye toward the person-in-environment; hence, the inclusion of the word "social." Casework involves direct contact with the individual and may have any number of specific goals. In general, casework is intended to help individuals resolve interpersonal or situational problems in living. Those who identify themselves as caseworkers are often employed in public settings such as human resources departments (or, what some people continue to refer to as the welfare department). With increasing frequency, however, fewer social workers speak of doing casework, and prefer to say they do clinical social work or individual therapy.

Casework is the inclusive, general term applied to the social work method that involves direct, individual helping. There is, however, no one universally accepted model of social casework. The origins of social casework are found in Charity Organization Societies' concept of the "friendly visitor." In the late 1800s, concerned by the increasing numbers of poor and destitute in urban areas, affluent women volunteered to serve as friendly visitors.

> Working with one, two, or even three families . . . the visitor assumed a responsibility that was intended to be long term, even permanent. Friendly visitors were to encourage improvements in housekeeping and hygiene and advise on problems of home management. Especially they were to assist family members to obtain work, drawing on their own contacts to arrange employment or apprenticeships for boys and place girls in domestic service. As a result, or so the theory ran, poor families would learn that the well-to-do were not enemies, and the

wealthy would come to appreciate the fortitude of the poor as they observed how they coped with life's hardships. (Verl Lewis, 1977, p. 99)

From this foundation, the method of social casework evolved and was articulated by Mary Richmond (1917, 1922). Richmond defined social casework as "those processes which develop personality through adjustments consciously effected, individual by individual, between men and their social environment" (Dorothy Becker, 1977, p. 1224). In the years since, several different models of casework have been developed by social workers. Those most clearly viewed as models of social casework (as opposed to models of individual therapy, for example) are the psychosocial, functionalist, problem-solving, and task-centered models.

Psychosocial casework evolved in the 1930s and was often referred to as the "diagnostic school" due to the emphasis placed on diagnosis. Even while stressing the importance of diagnosis, however, proponents of the psychosocial model have always viewed assessment as including the dualistic person-in-situation perspective. That is, although the caseworker gives careful attention to diagnosing the individual's problem and to helping the client develop insight, the treatment process also includes situational or environmental interventions on behalf of the client. Hence, the linkage of "psycho" referring the individual's internal personality dynamics, and "social," referring to the individual's external environment. With early influences from Freudian psychoanalytic theory and work by Mary Richmond, Gordon Hamilton (1937, 1940) originally developed the foundation for this model and Florence Hollis ([1965, 1972] 1981) provided later refinements.

During the same time, the *functionalist* model evolved through the work of faculty at the University of Pennsylvania School of Social Work. Concern over some of the Freudian influences (for example, a rather deterministic or mechanistic view of humankind) that were integrated into the psychosocial model, the functionalists identified the purpose of all social work "as being the release of human power in individuals, groups and communities for personal fulfillment and social good and the release of social power for the creation of the kind of society, social policy, and social institutions that make self-realization most possible for all men" (Ruth Smalley and Tybel Bloom, 1977, p. 1282). The functionalist model

Mary E. Richmond
(1861–1928).
Pioneering practitioner,
educator, and
theoretician of the
Charity Organization
Society.

emphasizes the potential for growth, the role of the agency as providing focus and direction to the helping effort, and highlights process as the interactional medium for casework. With early influences by Otto Rank, Jessie Taft (1937) and Virginia Robinson (1936, 1950) were pioneers in the development of this model, followed by Ruth Smalley (1967) in the 1950s.

The name Helen Harris Perlman is nearly synonymous with the *problem-solving* model of casework. This model emerged in the early 1950s and diverged from the diagnostic school of psychosocial casework. Perlman suggested that all human living is a problem-solving process and that "cure" is, therefore, not a viable goal. The "chief aim of the problem solving model is to help individuals or families cope with whatever they are *currently* finding insurmountable and to do so in ways that will make maximum use of their conscious efforts, choices, and competences" (Helen Harris Perlman, 1977, p. 1292). Emphasis is placed on the "four P's": "A *person* beset with a *problem* seeks some solution from a *place* (a social agency or some other social institution) and is proffered help by a social worker whose professional *process* simultaneously engages his problem-solving powers and/or supplements his problem-solving resources" (Helen Harris Perlman, 1977, p. 1292).

In the mid-1960s, largely due to the overloads being experienced by many social welfare agencies, William Reid began to test a new casework model to determine whether clients would benefit equally from brief, highly focused service as opposed to more prevalent models of longer term intervention. Developed in collaboration with Laura Epstein, Reid called this the *task-centered* model: "The model was based on the proposition that effectiveness of interpersonal treatment is relatively short-lived—that is, that the most benefit clients will derive from such treatment will be derived within a relatively few sessions and relatively brief period of time" (William Reid, 1986, p. 270). In practice, the social worker "helps the client identify specific problems that arise from unrealized wants and are defined in terms of specific conditions to be changed" (Francis Turner, 1986, p. 271). Intervention is focused on helping the client identify the specific problem(s), agreeing explicitly on how to work—task by task—to correct the problem, and following through with those tasks between sessions.

These four models of casework represent various shifts in the social work profession over time. Even more drastic shifts have occurred in recent years. These shifts have brought other models, primarily therapy models, of practice into the repertoire of social workers. Some, such as the range of behavioral therapies, have become a mainstay in some social work practice settings. Others, such as transactional analysis or reality therapy, have lost much of their popularity; only some of their basic concepts or techniques continue to be used.

Social Group Work

There are several different terms used to describe the work that social workers perform with groups. *Social group work, social work with groups,* and *group therapy* are among the most common terms. For many, the first two are used interchangeably, whereas group therapy remains a distinct type of practice within a group setting. Group therapy is a practice method also used by psychologists, psychiatrists, and psychiatric nurses. In general, social group work is based on the belief that groups are an effective and efficient medium in which to achieve individual and group objectives. They are also viewed as more cost effective in that greater numbers of people can be helped at one time; in casework or other individual intervention only one person is seen at a time.

According to James Whittaker and Elizabeth Tracy (1989), there are four distinguishing features of social group work: (1) "the group as a whole and the development of individuals as group members; (2) the development of mutual aid/support among and within the group; (3) the power of group process over the life of the group; (4) the development of an autonomous group" (p. 242). Without stating it explicitly, these features suggest how important the group can be in helping people by providing a supportive atmosphere that focuses on relationship within a group. This may, in part, account for the enormous popularity of self-help groups in the past decade.

Self-help groups are, by definition, groups that do not involve a professional leader or facilitator. They are often behaviorally focused, such as groups organized for the purpose of helping members lose weight or quit smoking. Or they may be 12-step "recovery" groups that have been patterned after Alcoholics Anonymous (e.g., Al-Anon for families of alcoholics; Adult Children of Alcoholics, ACoA; Incest Survivors Anonymous, ISA; or Codependents Anonymous, CODA; etc.). Recovery groups bring together people who are struggling with the negative effects of a shared problem or experience to reduce their sense of isolation and to enhance their personal recovery. Social workers often recommend that clients participate in such groups as an adjunct to professional intervention.

Case

NANCY

Nancy's experience with groups was extensive. As a BSW social worker she organized and facilitated educationally focused groups for prospective adoptive parents. These groups were designed to help them explore their motivation for adopting and to prepare them for the demands of the adoption process. In her six years with Catholic Social Services, Nancy facilitated several couples groups in which the focus was on enhancing communication patterns, and she also designed an educational series on parenting skills for groups of pregnant teens.

In her more recent move into private practice, Nancy again found herself drawn toward working with clients in groups. Although she had initially expected to limit her practice to couples and families, she had a number of individual women clients, all of whom had early histories of incest or sexual abuse. From the extensive reading she had done, plus what she had learned from her own recovery experience, Nancy was well aware that isolation and shame were two common characteristics of abuse survivors. Recognizing that groups were the ideal medium for reducing isolation and addressing shame issues through sharing experiences, Nancy decided to organize a survivors group. Three of her own individual clients were far enough along in their recovery process to benefit from a group approach; once she let her colleagues know that she was organizing a survivor's group, she had more referrals than she could handle.

Despite her vast knowledge and experience, as the time came for the first session of the group, Nancy felt some anxiety. This was, after all, her first therapy group in her own practice. Unlike her previous agency-based work, now she had no supervisor next door, nor any colleague nearby. She was becoming acutely aware of what her colleagues meant when they spoke of their isolation in practice on their own. Fortunately, at least in this case, the first group session went well and Nancy's anxiety level decreased in the first few minutes.

SOCIAL PROBLEMS

SYSTEMS

DEVELOPMENTAL STAGES

Private Practice/
Group Work

Adult Women

Sexual Abuse

In the first session, Nancy went over the ground rules, most of which were already known as Nancy had previously met with each prospective group member. Each member was given time to introduce herself to the group. As a therapy group, membership was closed. This meant that members were expected to remain with the group for an agreed-on number of sessions, and no new members would be added during that time. In this case, the group contract involved an agreement by all eight members to attend group once a week for 12 weeks with each session lasting an hour and a half. As survivors, the members shared common experiences or sets of experiences involving incest or sexual abuse, and the group's focus was on recovery from the effects of these experiences.

As the group became increasingly cohesive after the first few sessions, Nancy could see that this was going to be a powerful therapeutic experience for all involved. The recovery process, as she well knew, could often be long and emotionally painful, and survivors in recovery need massive support. For this reason, Nancy also encouraged the group members to attend carefully selected self-help recovery groups like Incest Survivors Anonymous (ISA) while they participated in her group. As helpful as the therapy group might be, Nancy hoped that members would take advantage of all available support to sustain their recovery process.

After a particularly draining but productive session one evening, Nancy sat in her office and marveled at the inner strength and resilience of the women. She also thought back several years to her own recovery work and wondered how it might have been different had there been self-help groups available then. After a moment or two, Nancy let out a sigh—part satisfaction and part fatigue—then packed up her things and headed toward her car, reminding herself that "we're all just doing the best we can."

In social work, the origins of social group work can be traced to the settlement house movement of the late nineteenth century. Many settlement house workers chose the group medium to teach basic life skills to the great numbers of new immigrants to U.S. cities. They also organized recreational groups for children, something that both the YMCA and YWCA had been doing since shortly after the Civil War. The settlement workers also used groups as a way of bringing people together to address common problems within a neighborhood or community. According to Ruth Middleman and Gale Goldberg (1987), the "concerns of early group work focused on the Americanization of immigrants, the acculturation of rural arrivals to the urban scene, social reform, the problems of social isolation as a function of industrialization, character-building, leisure-time interests and skills, and recreation" (p. 715).

The popularity of social group work as a practice method crystallized in 1937 with the formation of the American Association for the Study of Group Work, one of the seven associations that eventually merged to form the NASW in 1955. During the 1950s and 1960s, group work's focus was expanded to more of a problem orientation and several specific models were developed. The *social goals model* drew on the work of early theorists like Grace Coyle (1948) and maintained a focus on influencing groups toward democratic values, social conscience, and social action for the "common good." Socialization was emphasized, as was individual growth, development, and learning. The focus was similar to that of the group work of earlier settlement house programs. The *remedial model*, formulated by Robert Vinter in the late 1950s, laid the foundation for what we now call group therapy. As developed by Vinter (1967), the remedial model included psychoanalytic concepts and concepts drawn from ego psychology to help individuals achieve their treatment goals within the group setting. Others might refer to this model as rehabilitative in that its goals are to effect change among individuals within the group. A third model, developed by William Schwartz (1971), is the *reciprocal* or *interactionist* model. It relies heavily on systems theory concepts and emphasizes the interdependence between individuals and the various systems with which they interact. The goal is helping group members with similar problems or circumstances to get what they need from the systems resources that are available.

Charles Zastrow (1989) has identified other varieties of groups in social work: "social conversation, recreation-skill building, educational, problem-solving and decision-making, self-help, socialization, therapeutic, and sensitivity and encounter" (p. 7). The major point to emphasize about group work, whatever the model, is the essential belief that the group is an excellent medium for growth, development, and change. Merely by participating in a group, it is possible for people to learn about appropriate and inap-

Group therapy, like all forms of social work practice, includes clients of all life stages.

propriate behavior, to enhance communication skills, and to develop greater awareness of relationships between and among individuals. In addition, as you will see in the next section, when sufficient numbers of individuals join together with a common cause or problem, collective or group action is an effective means for accomplishing specific goals.

BSW practitioners are involved in a variety of group activities. If you work in a hospital setting, you might develop support groups for persons with cancer, or in a school setting, you might have groups designed to help prevent kids from dropping out. Some groups in school or community settings are educationally focused, as in the case of teen mothers who need help in learning about prenatal care, and teen parents who need information about child development. Social workers who are involved with child welfare agencies often spend time in developing educational groups for parents in an effort to prevent child abuse. Persons working in mental health and mental retardation facilities may have groups designed to teach basic life skills to the retarded or chronically mentally ill. Finally, an overview of groups in social work would not be complete without noting that essentially all agency-based practice will involve staff meetings and perhaps committees, which are both types of groups.

Community Organizing

Like social casework, no other profession trains individuals to do community organizing. While volunteers, political activists, or even community nurse practitioners or urban planners may undertake some of these roles, no other profession has the same history and continuing commitment to this method. Community organizing, as a method of social work practice, includes at least three specific strategies: (1) locality development, (2) social planning, and (3) social action. By whatever specific label, community organization is intervention performed at the community level and is directed toward influencing institutions and solving community welfare problems.

Community organization, as a social work practice method, developed simultaneously with social casework through both the Charity Organization Societies and the settlement house movement. It was first systematically studied as a practice methodology in the 1939 Lane Report, although it was not until 1947 that its theoretical underpinnings were analyzed (Wilber Newstetter, 1948; Kenneth Pray, 1948). That the COS and Settlement House Movement spawned the community organization method, side by side with social casework and group work, is not as surprising as it might seem initially.

As we have noted several times, from its earliest history, social work has had two, sometimes competing, goals: care of troubled individuals and the elimination of social conditions that bring about individual hardship. Currently this would be described as the competing goals of treatment and social reform. However, even Mary Richmond, who devoted her skills to the development and improvement of the casework method, declared:

> I have spent twenty-five years of my life in an attempt to get social casework accepted as a valid process in social work. Now I shall spend the rest of my life in trying to demonstrate to social caseworkers that there is more to

social work than social casework. (Frank Bruno, 1948, p. 186)

It is also important to note that all forms of community organizing (by whatever name) require analytic as well as interpersonal skills and they include a problem-solving process not unlike casework and group work.

This problem-solving process includes: (1) defining or uncovering the problem; (2) building the structural and communication links for action on the problem; (3) laying out the alternative options; (4) adopting a strategy or policy; (5) developing a plan and implementing it; and (6) receiving feedback, monitoring progress, and redefining the problem (Joan Ecklein and Armand Lauffer, 1971; Fred Cox et. al., 1987; Jack Rothman and John E. Tropman, 1987).

Case

ETTA

*E*tta felt at home in her old neighborhood church. She had always experienced a sense of belonging and inner strength as she listened to the choir and the impassioned words of the pastor. Now it was her turn to speak to the assembled group, to ask them to come together and organize around a problem that was hurting the entire neighborhood. "Crack cocaine is killing our babies," she said softly. "Our children are being taken from us. Nearly every day we see people runnin', we hear guns goin' off, we hear the cryin' and we know. We know that someone's been hurt, maybe killed because of crack cocaine. And we've got to do something to stop it. The police can't do it. The politicians can't do it. We've got to do it for ourselves, and for our children."

Heads nodded as the church members listened. Etta knew that everyone in the audience had already been touched in some way by the growing problem of crack cocaine. Etta said that the only way to save the neighborhood was to organize like other communities and neighborhoods had done. Abandoned homes had become "crack houses," meeting places where the sale and use of crack cocaine

Community Organization

Adults/Adolescents

Substance Abuse

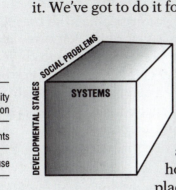

was an everyday occurrence. Crack users were getting younger and younger and the dealers seemed to be on every corner, day and night. As drug use increased, so did the number of burglaries and assaults. Dealers fought among themselves over territorial rights and longtime residents of the neighborhood began to live in fear.

Etta described how other communities had organized to rid their neighborhoods of crack dealers and crack houses. She laid out a plan for people to come together and clean up the abandoned houses. She talked about confronting the city council about the fact that buildings long scheduled for demolition had been ignored and left to be taken over by dealers. She talked of the strength in numbers and asked the assembled group for their active support. "Our church," she said, "is strong because our people are strong. We can work together to fight this problem. Reverend Williams is willing to help us organize and he is willing to come with me when I talk to the city council next month. We need to show them—the dealers and the politicians—that we aren't gonna sit by and let our children die."

After the service, Etta stayed to meet with anyone who was willing and able to get involved. By the time she left, three task groups had been organized, each with an identified group leader. One group, headed by one of the oldest neighborhood residents, would talk with people who missed Etta's presentation and enlist their help; another group, headed by the pastor's nephew, would set up a meeting with the precinct captain of the police department to inform him of the neighborhood's action and identify the need for additional law enforcement support; the third group was headed by a husband-wife team who volunteered to develop a cleanup strategy involving young people from the neighborhood.

As each of the groups engaged in their own organizing and planning, Etta and Pastor Williams discussed their strategy for getting on next month's city council agenda. They both realized that the problems facing the neighborhood were not simply going to disappear, but they were encouraged by the high level of energy that could already be felt in the room.

The general community organization method includes several different approaches or models. First consider the *locality* or *community development* approach. This model assumes that community change can best occur through widespread participation in goal setting and action. Themes of self-help, development of indigenous leadership, democratic procedures, and voluntary cooperation are essential components in this model. Its major purpose is to change human attitudes and behaviors through education to stimulate self-development and awareness. There have been elements of this model throughout social work history, but the height of this type of community organization occurred during the 1960s and was supported by many of the goals of the Economic Opportunity Act. Specific examples include tenants' rights associations, neighborhood improvement associations, and the creation of multiservice centers.

The *social planning* model utilizes a more technical process of problem solving with regard to social problems. It emphasizes rational and deliberately planned change, and whereas community participation may be an element, expert planners are viewed as the leaders of this change effort. The goals of this model are to improve social conditions by changing the policies of formal organizations so that the amount, the quality, the accessibility, and/or the range of services and facilities provided is expanded. Community Planning Councils, as part of or separate from United Way, are an example of an entire agency whose function is to assess community need and coordinate activities to meet those needs. Large public and not-for-profit agencies employ social workers in planning roles. This type of community organizing increased in demand and stature during the 1970s with the requirements of Title XX for needs assessment and program evaluation.

Social action, the third model of community organization, attempts to make fundamental changes in major institutions or community practices. Its ultimate aim is the redistribution of power, resources, or decision making within the community. The goals are reform of major legal and functional systems of a society. Political activism and lobbying are central components of this model. Saul Alinsky's Back of the Yards Movement, originated in the 1930s, and the National Welfare Rights Organization, originated in the 1960s, are excellent examples of this model. Currently, social action efforts at national coalition building are underway by the Child Welfare League of America and the Children's Defense Fund in an effort to influence federal legislation. These efforts include widespread lobbying for new or substantially different legis-

Discrimination and oppression have been confronted through social activism. Here, Coretta Scott King and Cesar Chavez, head of the National Farm Workers union, lead a 1960s boycott of lettuce to protest the pay and working conditions for farm laborers.

lation or appropriations related to the health and welfare of our nation's children.

Each of these three models—locality or community development, social planning, and social action—has a slightly different focus and each includes somewhat different strategies to achieve its goals. However, they all share a common ultimate goal: social reform as a way to improve the quality of life for all persons. Locality or community development requires some planning techniques; social planners will need to utilize social action methods if institutional barriers are met; social action workers may need to start with a locality-based group to determine effective strategies. In addition, a given project may begin using one model and, over time, move to another model.

As emphasized earlier, by whatever label, these models are aimed at larger systems than individuals and families and have reform as a goal. The emphasis, acceptance, and popularity of each model has shifted over time, but in some fashion each has continued solidly within the profession of social work as a necessary and important method of intervention.

Summary

Social workers view the world from an interactive approach called the person-in-environment perspective. People live in various environments, they are affected by their environments, and they, in turn, affect their environments. Systems theory, used as an approach to making sense of the world, helps us to maintain a focus on the person-in-environment. Although some people have expressed discomfort with the mechanistic language of systems, it has provided social workers with a viable conceptual framework for handling large amounts of information in meaningful and effective ways.

The actual practice of social work has been organized around levels of intervention—micro, meso, and macro—as well as corresponding methods of intervention—casework, group work, and community organizing. We have defined and described the three levels of intervention in social work, and we have presented brief overviews of selected models of casework, group work, and community organizing. The long-standing strain between the competing goals of individual treatment and social reform was acknowledged, although we would hope that social workers will not feel compelled to choose one over the other.

References

Becker, Dorothy G. "Mary E. Richmond." In *Encyclopedia of Social Work*, 17th ed., 1224–1225. Edited by John B. Turner. Washington, D.C.: NASW, 1977.

Brill, Naomi I. *Working With People: The Helping Process*, 4th ed. New York: Longman, 1990.

Bruno, Frank J. *Trends in Social Work*. New York: Columbia University Press, 1948.

Cox, Fred M., John L. Erlich, Jack Rothman, and John E. Tropman, eds. *Strategies of Community Organization*, 4th ed. Itasca, IL: F. E. Peacock, 1987.

Coyle, Grace. *Group Work with American Youth*. New York: Harper and Brothers, 1948.

Ecklein, Joan, and Armand Lauffer. *Community Organizers and Social Planners: A Volume of Case and Illustrative Materials*. New York: John Wiley, 1971.

Hamilton, Gordon. "Basic Concepts in Social Casework." *The Family*, Vol. 18, No. 5 (July 1937): 147–156.

————. *Theory and Practice of Social Casework*. New York: Columbia University Press, 1940; rev. ed., 1951.

Hollis, Florence. *Casework: A Psychosocial Therapy*. New York: Random House, 1965; 2nd ed., 1972; 3rd ed., 1981.

Lane, Robert P. J. "The Field of Community Organization." In *Proceedings of the National Conference of Social Work 1939*, 495–511. New York: Columbia University Press, 1940.

Lewis, Verl S. "Charity Organization Society." In *Encyclopedia of Social Work*, 17th ed., edited by John B. Turner, 96–100. Washington, D.C.: NASW, 1977.

Middleman, Ruth R., and Gale Goldberg. "Social Work Practice with Groups." In *Encyclopedia of Social Work*, 18th ed., 714–729. Edited by Anne Minahan. Silver Spring, MD: NASW, 1987.

Minahan, Anne. "Purpose and Objectives of Social Work Revisisted. *Social Work*, Vol. 26, No. 1 (Jan. 1981): 5–6.

Newstetter, Wilber I. "The Social Intergroup Work Process." In *Proceeding of the National Conference of Social Work 1947*, 205–217. New York: Columbia University Press, 1948.

Perlman, Helen Harris. "Social Casework: The Problem-Solving Approach." In *Encyclopedia of Social Work*, 17th ed., 1290–1299. Edited by John B. Turner. Washington, D.C.: NASW, 1977.

Pray, Kenneth L. M. "When is Community Organization Social Work Practice?" In *Proceeding of the National Conference of Social Work, 1947*, 194–204. New York: Columbia University Press, 1948.

Reid, William. "Task-Centered Social Work." In *Social Work Treatment: Interlocking Theoretical Approaches*, 267–295. Edited by Francis J. Turner. New York: Free Press, 1986.

Richmond, Mary E. *Social Diagnosis*. New York: Russell Sage Foundation, 1917.

————. *What Is Social Case Work?* New York: Russell Sage Foundation, 1922.

Robinson, Virginia P. *The Dynamics of Supervision Under Functional Controls*. Philadelphia: University of Pennsylvania Press, 1950.

————. *Supervision in Social Case Work.* Chapel Hill: University of North Carolina Press, 1936.

Rothman, Jack, and John E. Tropman. "Models of Community Organization and Macro Practice Perspectives: Their Mixing and Phasing." In *Strategies of Community Organization,* 4th ed., 3–26. Edited by Fred Cox, John Erlich, Jack Rothman, and John E. Tropman. Itasca, IL: F. E. Peacock, 1987.

Schwartz, William, and Zalba, Serapio (eds.). *The Practice of Group Work.* New York: Columbia University Press, 1971.

Smalley, Ruth E. *Theory for Social Work Practice.* New York: Columbia University Press, 1967.

Smalley, Ruth E., and Tybel Bloom. "Social Casework: The Functional Approach." In *Encyclopedia of Social Work,* 17th ed., 1280–1290. Edited by John B. Turner. Washington, D.C.: NASW, 1977.

Taft, Jessie. "The Relation of Function to Process in Social Case Work." *Journal of Social Work Process,* I, 1937.

Turner, Francis J., ed. *Social Work Treatment: Interlocking Theoretical Approaches.* New York: Free Press, 1986.

Vinter, Robert (ed.). *Readings in Group Work Practice.* Ann Arbor: Campus Publishers, 1967.

Whittaker, James K., and Elizabeth M. Tracy. *Social Treatment: An Introduction to Interpersonal Helping in Social Work Practice,* 2nd ed. New York: Aldine De Gruyer, 1989.

Zastrow, Charles. *Social Work with Groups,* 2nd ed. Chicago: Nelson-Hall, 1989.

CHAPTER 9

Generalist Skills

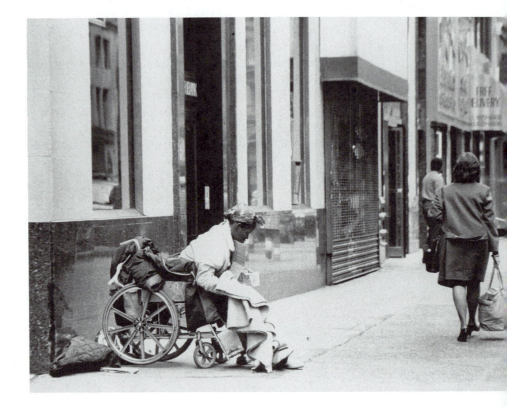

Introduction

As you have no doubt noticed by now, defining exactly what a social worker does is a challenge, in part because social workers are found in so many different settings, doing so many different kinds of tasks. Early in this text, you were introduced to a number of students considering a commitment to social work. You've also met several former students and you have seen their various career choices develop over a 10-year period. As described, no two of them were doing exactly the same practice in the same kind of setting. Given that reality, what are the essential, fundamental skills of social work practice? In an attempt to answer this, we will discuss the structure of social work education and how BSW and MSW practice differ. Then, in some detail, we will identify and describe the professional helping relationship and the generic skills that serve as the foundation for all social work practice.

Social Work Education

All academic or professional education programs are characterized by hierarchical structures, and social work is no different. That is, within traditional four-year colleges or universities, the first degree granted is the bachelor of arts (BA) or of science (BS), with a specific major field of study. For most people, this is where formal education ends and "life education" takes over. For those interested in social work as a major field of study, however, there were no accredited[1] bachelor's programs until 1974. Although there were social work *courses* prior to 1974, and there were undergraduate social work *programs* prior to that time, the Council on Social Work

Education (CSWE) did not agree to accredit BSW programs until that time. There are a number of historical reasons for this.

Prior to 1974, the Master of Social Work (MSW) had been the only formal or official degree in preparation for social work practice. While there was early disagreement as to whether this should be a one- or a two-year graduate degree, by the mid-1950s, when the CSWE was organized, the two-year MSW was a fact of social work education. It has remained so, with the understanding that the MSW is the terminal, or final, practice degree. This means that the MSW degree prepares you to do advanced social work practice while the BSW prepares you for entry-level social work practice. Among social work educators, it is becoming increasingly difficult to find teaching positions without a doctoral degree, but for applied practice, the MSW remains the terminal (or final) degree.[2]

What specifically differentiates the BSW from the MSW social worker besides two more years of school? Bachelor's level education for social work certainly includes all the content of any undergraduate program: courses from the liberal arts, social and behavioral sciences, human or biological sciences, foreign languages, and all the knowledge that produces an informed, well-rounded citizen. As you will recall from Chapter 7, social work majors are required by CSWE accreditation standards to take courses in specific content areas. These include human behavior and the social environment (HBSE), social welfare policy (SWPS), social work methods, research, and field practicum (a supervised, agency-based experience similar to an internship). Courses in these areas constitute the *foundation* knowledge and skills for social work practice and, in fact, one or two semesters of MSW study include similar content. This is why the CSWE requires MSW programs to consider advanced standing status (i.e., waiver of certain foundation courses) to students holding the BSW degree earned in an accredited undergraduate program.

The MSW program, in the very early stages of study, is similar in content to the BSW, but the program moves quickly into more advanced (as opposed to foundation) material, and provides a greater range of specialization opportunities. Whereas the particular areas of specialization among MSW programs vary, each will produce an MSW graduate with advanced practice skills, even if the program describes itself as producing "advanced generalists."

In summary, BSWs, having mastered the necessary and sufficient foundation skills, are prepared for entry-level practice. MSWs are prepared for advanced practice, having engaged in more in-depth and concentrated study. Their concentrated study often includes a specific field of practice specialization such as mental health, health care, or gerontology, or a method specialization such as individual practice or administration.

BSW and MSW: Implications for Practice

What this means in terms of actual employment is that BSWs may work in correctional settings such as juvenile or adult probation; in public assistance programs such as Aid to Families with Dependent Children (AFDC) or food stamp offices; in state or county child welfare or children's protective services; in public or private hospices, nursing homes, and hospitals; in residential settings for children or adolescents; in rehabilitation programs with visually impaired, hearing impaired, or physically challenged persons; in substance abuse treatment programs; in emergency shelters for battered women and children; in neighborhood health and family planning clinics; in refugee relocation centers; in delinquency prevention organizations; and in an increasing number of public schools. This list, although lengthy, is still not exhaustive; it is intended only to illustrate the breadth of settings in which BSWs begin to practice.

It is not uncommon to find BSWs working along side MSW practitioners. However, the specific roles and functions of the two will differ. In probation, for example, the MSW is more likely to be a supervisor or administrator, whereas the BSW will be involved directly with clients helping them learn to productively redirect their lives in society. This often involves helping probationers get into substance abuse treatment programs, complete their education, and find jobs. The same is often true of social workers in Children's Protective Services where BSWs may be involved most heavily in the intake and investigative stages, and MSWs may be supervisors or administrators, or in some cases, they are involved in more specialized, intensive family intervention programs.

All social work practitioners share a common frame of reference with respect to social work values and ethics, an understanding of the professional helping relationship, and a set of essential skills and techniques that underlie all practice efforts. Having already discussed values and ethics in Chapter 6, we will now turn our attention to the professional helping relationship.

Professional Helping Relationships in Social Work

The term *professional helping relationship* is used to identify a particular kind of relationship that is different from the relationships we have in our personal lives. These differences are important because they guide us in our work, reminding us that social work practice is based on more than good intentions. Though we are not criticizing good intentions, it is our knowledge base and skill, our professional values and ethics that move us into professional practice. Let us first start with a discussion of helping relationships in social work.

Characteristics of Helping Relationships

Relationships of any kind involve connection between or among people. In social work, relationship involves dynamic interaction and is the medium through which our intervention occurs. Not surprisingly, most of what has been written about professional helping relationships is directed toward our one-on-one, family or small group helping or therapeutic relationships. We need to recognize, however, that the element of relationship is just as crucial to the meso or macro practitioner. Working to change social policy or to organize large numbers of people to achieve a community goal still begins with and is founded on our ability to establish and maintain relationships. Felix Biestek (1954) used an analogy to summarize the importance of relationship between clients and workers: "it is the *soul* of casework, while the processes of study, diagnosis, and treatment may be considered the body" (p. 57). Biestek focuses on the casework relationship, but we would argue that relationship is the soul of *any* effective social work intervention.

Much has been written about the elements or characteristics of helping relationships. Alan Keith-Lucas (1972), for example, has said that helping relationships are mutual, though they are not consistently pleasant or friendly; they involve feeling as well as knowledge and they exist for a particular purpose—to help a person or groups of people to make choices that will improve their lives. Real choice, to Keith-Lucas, is a major element of helping relationships and he notes that helping relationships, because they are purposeful, are bounded by time and space.

Biestek (1954) identified seven elements of the casework relationship: (1) purposeful expression of feelings; (2) controlled emotional involvement; (3) acceptance; (4) individualization; (5) nonjudgmental attitude; (6) client self-determination; and (7) confidentiality (p. 60). Similarly, Naomi Brill (1990) identified characteristics of the helping relationship as accepting; dynamic; emotional; purposeful, time-limited, and unequal; honest, realistic, responsible, and safe; and authoritative (p. 89). As you can see there is overlap among these lists. This suggests that there is a high degree of consensus about the elements or characteristics of helping relationships.

Although there is considerable agreement about how we describe helping relationships, actually establishing and maintaining them is largely a question of skill. This is an area that we will discuss in some detail immediately after we identify the phases of the helping relationship.

Phases of Professional Helping Relationships

What we do in social work is characterized by phases of intervention and tasks or skills of intervention. This means that through each phase of our work we need specific skills in order to accomplish our tasks. If we were to envision everything in life as series of phases, we could reduce it all simply to beginnings, middles, and endings. Books and plays begin with a preface or a prologue and end with a conclusion or an epilogue. Our lives are characterized by our having been born (beginning), by living (middle), and by dying (ending). In the process, we experience the same phases over and over in numerous ways during the course of our lives.

Table 9.1 PHASES AND TASKS OF HELPING RELATIONSHIPS

Tasks	Phases		
	Beginning: *Relating*	Middle: *Resolving*	End: *Terminating*
RELATIONSHIP BUILDING:	Communication via listening, via observing	Enhance relationship and communication	Review process and progress
	Establish trust, rapport, and empathic connection		Acknowledge feelings about ending
ASSESSMENT PROCESS:	Gather information, identify presenting problem, identify and analyze dynamics	Refine assessment (continually)	
DETERMINATION OF GOALS:	Set goals, contract	Identify and work through obstacles	Assess and evaluate change(s)
ASSESSMENT SUMMARY:	Includes analysis of situation and stated plan of action	Implement plan	Plan for follow-up (as needed)

Similarly, the social work helping relationship has identifiable phases, each accompanied by a particular set of tasks. These are shown in Table 9.1.

Beginning Phase   In the very beginning, our tasks are to establish effective communication and build rapport in order to engage with the client in the change effort. At the same time, we begin to move toward some understanding of and agreement about the nature of the problem at hand. Why has this person appeared in our practice setting at this particular moment in time? The answer to this question is viewed as the *presenting problem,* or the essential or apparent reason for seeking help at this moment. As the presenting problem is considered, the social worker's task is to begin the process of assessment. The term *assessment* means to size up, to make sense of the client's presenting problem. As you can see from the table, assessment is never a static, moment-in-time pronouncement. We make initial assessments, and we continue to assess movement, obstacles to change, and perhaps totally new dimensions of the problem as new information emerges. However, when the initial assessment has been made and there is some degree of mutual understanding of the nature of the problem, then a plan for intervening or changing the situation is developed mutually. This marks the last part of the beginning phase.

Middle Phase   The middle phase of implementation is often referred to as the "working phase," although that seems to undermine the importance of all the efforts that contribute to relationship building, problem definition, and assessment in the beginning. These are obviously elements that require work, skill, and effort as well. For example, if the client terminates as a result of communication problems, the so-called working phase will not take place. Ironically, with so much said about the beginning phase, it may involve less time than the middle phase of helping. Often, depending on the specific boundaries of one's practice, the beginning is as brief as one meeting, as might be the case for a consultant who is designing an in-service training program for agency staff.

The length of the middle phase may also have to do with the infinite complexity of the human condition wherein change, even when viewed as healthy, desirable, and perhaps even mandatory, is resisted. For many, a known problem is at least predictable and is less terrifying than that which remains unknown or beyond our current ability to envision. Again, depending on the nature of your practice, the middle phase of implementation may take a relatively short-time (e.g., a telephone hotline crisis intervention setting may actually include all phases in a single phone call), or it may take years (e.g., the lobbyist who advocates for years to accomplish passage of a national health policy).

Ending Phase: Termination   The last phase is termination, the point at which the work at hand has been accomplished, and it is time to end the helping relationship. Just as there is a human tendency to resist change in general, many of us resist terminations because they require us to say goodbye to meaningful relationships and work. Each of us is confronted with many terminations or endings in our lives: graduations, moves, job changes, children leaving home, friends and loved ones moving away or dying, relationships that do not work out, and, ultimately, even our own death. In a healthy process of termination, we review where we started, where we have been, and now, where we are going. We leave no dangling strings, no important words unsaid, no unfinished business. This applies to the community planner who has developed and received approval and funding for a major low income housing project, as much as to the hospice social worker who accompanies a person with AIDS through the process of dying.

Helping relationships are the primary medium through which intervention and change occur. As such, they hold an esteemed position of importance in our work. Still, there are other factors that determine the success of our efforts, not the least of which is our skill base. The following section takes us from an understanding of the helping relationship into a discussion of the essential foundation skills we need to engage in social work practice.

Generalist Practice Skills

In Chapter 7, we provided an overview of the numerous disciplines from which social work has borrowed to create a social work knowledge base, primarily a theoretical knowledge base. Theoretical knowledge is of great intrinsic value and helps us understand and appreciate the human condition. But to prepare ourselves to do social work, we need to translate theory into practice, moving from the *what* of knowing, to the *how* of applying what we know. This is called *prescriptive knowledge,* or knowledge that prescribes or tells us what to do.

The remainder of this chapter is focused on prescriptive knowledge in the form of generalist skills, the essentials and fundamentals that every social worker needs, regardless of practice setting, client group, level, or method of intervention. These are organized under the headings of communication and relationship skills, analytic thinking and assessment skills, and interventive skills.

Communication

Each of us has experienced a serious "failure" to communicate. For a moment, try to remember a specific time when you could not get another person to understand you, no matter how hard you tried. Replay that experience in your mind. Pay close attention to how you feel. In these moments we may feel impatient, frustrated, angry—or perhaps confused, sad, even hopeless or despairing.

In all human endeavors, but especially in social work practice, communication is an absolutely essential skill. Without effective communication (and that is really the focus here), we cannot engage in, or even establish, a relationship with others. Keeping in mind that the essential function of communication is *understanding one another*, there are many complexities in this process. To communicate with and to fully understand one another requires us to recognize several things.

First we need to realize that we are never *not* communicating, and that communication is a *process* that is never static. Whether or not we are speaking, we are still communicating with nonverbal messages through body language and facial expressions. In fact, most times, our nonverbal messages are more accurate or true reflections of what we think or feel than the words we speak. Second, the *content* of both verbal and nonverbal communication reflects not only what we think, but also something about who we are, what we value or believe in, and what attitudes or biases we hold. Third, whether expressed openly or not, *feelings* are always present, and unless brought into our dialogue and identified, confusion and misunderstanding can result. Finally, because the helping relationship between social worker and client is, by definition, *unequal*, there is a greater potential for miscommunication or misunderstanding.

This inherent inequality of the helping relationship must be recognized as a source of potential communication barriers or breakdowns. Consider, for example, how we describe our roles: We are the "helpers," the service providers, the people assumed to have the necessary knowledge and skill to help. Our clients are in need of help, the people assumed to have unmet needs for concrete services (e.g., financial assistance, health care, information, and referral) or for other services such as counseling or therapeutic intervention. It is important to the relationship that we be aware and mindful of how the client feels about these unequal positions.

In our Western culture, for example, persons in need of help are often seen as weak or inadequate, and, as a result, the role of asking for and receiving help creates discomfort for many.[3] Our society places a great deal of emphasis on the Puritan or Protestant work ethic, a philosophical position that suggests if we work hard enough, we will succeed; conversely, if we do not succeed, if we need to ask for help, then we feel we must not have worked hard enough, or we have failed in some fundamental way. (Perhaps you can recall a clear reflection of this position in the Elizabethan Poor Laws discussed in Chapter 2, where distinctions were made between the worthy and the unworthy poor.)

These basic concepts begin to sensitize us to how truly complicated effective communication is, but there are other factors that affect communication, including gender, ethnicity, culture, and socioeconomic status differences between or among the participants. For instance, men have been socialized more strongly than women to believe that asking for help is a reflection of personal failure. Much to the detriment of their mental health, men in this society have been taught that they must be strong, and that to show their feelings is to be weak. This makes it difficult for them to seek help at all or, if they do, to be comfortable in even identifying, much less expressing, what they feel. Furthermore, there are racial, ethnic, religious, or cultural differences where there are clear prohibitions against or stigma attached to seeking help, particularly outside of one's own community.

Case

BARBARA

*B*arbara could feel tension in the air as soon as she greeted Carol at the door. Carol was approaching the end of her mandatory six-month new employee probationary period with the company in which Barbara worked in the Employee Assistance Program (EAP). Barbara recalled that Carol had introduced herself with great poise and self-assurance when they had first met just months earlier, and she was struck with how different Carol now seemed. Both the poise and the self-assurance seemed to have disappeared; in their place were tension, anxiety, and apprehension. "Well," Barbara thought to herself, "I guess those feelings are understandable. After all, this isn't a social visit, and Carol knows that being referred to me by her supervisor can mean trouble, especially just before her probationary period ends."

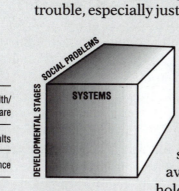

Barbara started by reintroducing herself, and explained to Carol why she had been referred to the EAP. As she described the supervisor's concerns about Carol's absenteeism and frequent late arrivals to the office, Barbara was conscious of modulating her voice into a soothing and reassuring tone. She was also aware of maintaining a delicate balance— holding eye contact while not appearing to stare at a client who, obviously, already felt self-conscious and anxious.

After offering Carol a cup of coffee, which was declined, Barbara began. "Carol, your supervisor, Ms. Powers, wanted me to see you because she's concerned about you. As I understand it, your initial job performance was really outstanding and you rarely missed a day of work. But in the past couple of months, the quality of your work has changed quite a bit, you've called in sick several times and it looks like you've had a lot of trouble getting to the office before 9:15 or 9:30. I hope you know that our basic concern is seeing you succeed. I see you as someone with a lot of potential and . . ." Before Barbara could finish her sentence, Carol had dissolved into tears.

As the tears diminished, so did much of Carol's anxiety and apprehension. Composing herself carefully, and drying her eyes with a tissue, Carol finally said: "My work *is* really important to me. It's the *only* thing in my life that I seem to be good at. I don't want to lose my job; I don't know what I'd do if that happened." Barbara sat quietly yet attentively, noting the urgency in Carol's voice, as well as the seemingly incongruous statement that work was "the only thing" that Carol felt she was "good at." Barbara thought to herself, "Here's this very competent, articulate woman feeling like work is the only thing she's good at—I wonder what that's about." Pausing to be sure that Carol had finished speaking, Barbara said: "I heard you say that work is the only thing in your life that you seem to be good at. Can you tell me a little more about what that means to you?"

The session seemed to move quickly as Carol described feelings of shame, worthlessness, and despair in relation to her marriage. As Barbara understood it, Carol had gotten married at about the same time that she had taken this job. Since meeting Frank as an eleventh grader, she hadn't dated anyone else. And, while she had always known him to be possessive and jealous, she had told herself that was because Frank really loved her. Listening attentively, what Barbara heard Carol describe was a man who abused alcohol, flew into rages, and accused his wife of having affairs despite all denials to the contrary. Barbara knew that spouse abuse, whether physical or verbal, often results in diminished self-esteem, feelings of shame, and a sense of worthlessness. Carol's recent patterns of missing work, tardiness, and impaired work performance were likely clues to an abusive relationship with Frank.

Although Barbara suspected that she had uncovered the root of the work-related problems, she now needed to consider how Carol's needs could best be met. To what extent could Carol's situation be resolved in the limited number of sessions that Barbara could provide within the EAP guidelines? Would it be better to provide outside referrals? Recognizing that Barbara had apparently been successful in establishing a beginning working relationship with Carol, what do you see as the pros and cons to these options?

Relationship Building

Effective communication is absolutely necessary in the process of relationship building. The creation of a viable helping relationship, whether therapeutically focused or focused on the provision of concrete services, also involves establishing rapport and engaging with the client.

In order to establish rapport and engage with the client, the social worker needs to develop finely tuned *listening skills*. This may sound simplistic, but it is another skill that is far more difficult to master than it might seem. Perhaps the best way to capture the essence of listening skills is found in Theodore Reik's *Listening with the Third Ear* (1948), in which he speaks of the need to "hear" that which is *not* being said by using the "third ear." Examining this further, we need to focus attentively (not intrusively, however) on the client's words, timing, and tone of voice, as well as nonverbal cues. And, although this may sound as if it is directed only toward one-on-one social work practice, keep in mind that staff meetings, committee work, and administration, as well as legislative lobbying, all require the same ability to communicate—that is, to understand and to be understood by others.

It is through this focused attention on the client that we begin to establish *rapport*. Taken from the French, rapport refers to a close or sympathetic relationship. When we use the term in practice, it generally means "hitting it off" or "clicking." It is our ability to establish rapport that creates the context for the development of an empathic relationship. And, as noted previously, *relationship* is the medium through which our intervention occurs. Ultimately, relationship is the ideal growth medium for human beings. According to women theorists at the Stone Center (Judith Jordan et al., 1991), there are five positive outcomes of good relationships: an increase in zest and vitality, increased empowerment to act, an enlarged picture of ourselves and of others, increased self-worth (i.e., confidence, competence, integrity), and an increased desire for more rather than less connection.

It is worth noting that these positive outcomes are as relevant to our personal relationships as they are to describing productive social work helping relationships. Our goal in practice, of course, is not simply productive relationships, but helping relationships characterized by empathic connection. Empathy reflects an authentic mutual experience of connection created when we can truly and subjectively grasp the client's feelings and perceptions, and can convey this to clients so they experience our "being with" them.

Judith Jordan, Janet Surrey, and Alexandra Kaplan (1983) describe empathy as a complex cognitive and affective process—

that is, a "feeling/thought," which is a term originated by Jean Baker Miller. According to Jordan, empathy involves: (1) the motivation to understand another person's inner state, (2) the capacity to perceive cues to another's state, (3) the capacity to surrender emotionally to another's inner state, (4) feeling joined or connected with another as a result, and (5) communicating understanding of the other's inner state. Conversely, when we try to force others into seeing the world as we do, when we try to fit the client's reality into our own definitions, the result is an empathic failure. Unless this empathic failure is mended, the client will likely leave. The tragedy for many clients, particularly those with limited resources, is being left without choices as to other persons or agencies that can meet their needs.

Finally, a unique quality of social work relationship building is the integration of the values and ethics described in Chapter 6. Treating our clients as persons with inherent dignity and worth, and respecting their right to make choices (self-determination) will further the establishment of solid working relationships. With all this considered, when we are communicating effectively, when we really understand and appreciate the client's reality, when we demonstrate respect for the client, we are engaged in a helping professional relationship.

Analytic Thinking and Assessment

The careful observer of human behavior will have already noticed, perhaps with amazement, the many different ways in which different people perceive and describe the same reality. Just as there are many ways of perceiving and describing various phenomena in the world, there are different ways of cognitively processing that which one perceives. That is, our thinking styles may range from basic, such as, B follows A; to complex, such as, how is it that B follows A? As educators, we have wondered whether the person with the more complex thinking style is the one who will produce the better client assessments. To the extent that this is true, it is probably because a good assessment requires careful listening, interpretation, plus comfort with our own intuitive ("gut") feelings.

You will recall that assessment in social work practice is a process that involves information gathering *plus* an analysis of that information. This enables us to reach a clear understanding of the presenting problems and the accompanying dynamics. The primary purpose of assessment is to understand enough to then develop a plan of intervention. Although there may be a tendency to think of assessment as a purely clinical term, this is misleading. Administrators, managers, supervisors, community organizers, and program developers all do assessments. Granted, they may be assessing groups such as boards of directors, staff groups, city councils, neighborhoods, or potential funding sources rather than individual clients. They may sometimes also use different language, such as information gathering, data collection, or fact finding, but the process used and the skills needed are essentially identical to that of the clinical practitioner. In all these cases we are attempting to get enough relevant information to understand the nature of the problem and the dynamics (i.e., what are the related issues that are coming into play here?), so we can begin developing a way to resolve the problem.

Initial assessments, although often impressionistic, are sometimes just as accurate as those that we ponder for hours. In fact, one of the most frequent pitfalls of the inexperienced practitioner is confusing the collection of incredible amounts of information with assessment. The absence of an initial assessment—even after several sessions of information gathering—is sometimes explained by saying "I really don't have all the information yet." Perhaps it is like the cultural message to us as consumers that "more" is automatically "better." The fact is, we never really feel we know all we need to know. Our challenge is to gather the most relevant information available and do the best we can in that moment. It is understood that this is difficult, that it feels risky and threatening. Yet that is the nature of our practice. If we continue to gather information and continue to wait for our comfort level to increase, we might never move ahead. Many facts do not make an assessment. It is the analysis, the interpretation and the meaning of the information, that ultimately constitute the assessment. This is why the skills of analytic thinking are so important.

In common usage, the terms *analytic* and *intuitive* are often viewed as nearly opposites. Analytic, for example, suggests a process in which component parts are separated in order to examine each piece one by one, whereas intuitive suggests a process where there is an almost immediate seeing or sense of knowing the whole. These terms suggest two very different processes, but we believe that learning to think analytically can help compensate for under-developed intuitive abilities.

Suanna Wilson's Analytical Thinking Model. Suanna Wilson (1980) has formulated an Analytical Thinking Model (ATM) for teaching social work students how to develop sound assessments. As you can see, the process of assessment is broken down into a series of steps. Although you may initially find it difficult to move so tediously, step-by-step, it is a model that will help improve essential assessment skills in practice. Additionally, the Analytical Thinking Model has been modified for use in both clinical and in larger systems assessments.

The Analytical Thinking Model

A professional helping person must learn how to think analytically before effective diagnostic statements can be produced. Analytical thinking refers to the ability to take a situation apart so that its dynamics can be studied meaningfully and the appropriate "solution" selected. Achieving this ability does not mean that the practitioner will also be able to diagnose. Even after the worker has learned to analyze a situation, he may not be able to select the appropriate diagnostic label to apply to what he is recording or observing. His ability to do this will depend upon his knowledge of the dynamics of human behavior. However, the analytical thinking process will lay the groundwork for application of this knowledge.

The following method is suggested for analyzing case situations. The professional or student should put himself through this process in preparation for writing the diagnostic summary and treatment plan that will be placed in the formal case record. As the worker goes through the process, his "answers" should be put in writing on a worksheet and then summarized to make up the formal diagnostic summary and treatment plan. This process could easily take several hours, obviously impractical for daily social work practice. The goal is that the worker learn the thinking process and eventually be able to do it automatically, in his head, as he works with clients and prepares written diagnostic statements. Once learned, the Analytical Thinking Model (ATM) approach should take no more time than that currently being used to arrive at diagnostic assessment and service plans.

1. Review mentally everything that is known about the case up to the point that you are preparing to do a diagnostic summary.

2. List, in outline form, ten to fifteen key facts known about the case. Do not give impressions or analyses. Try to select only the major facts that are known about the client and/or his situation. This requires sorting out what is relevant from what is not. If some significant information about the case is unknown, this could be a key fact that should be listed.

3. Review the list of facts you have written down. *THINK: What feelings might the client be experiencing, knowing what I know about him?* Focus on the client *only*—do not describe feelings of family members or others, though the client's attitudes toward these people might be included here. List individually each feeling you think the client might have, and *for each feeling:*

   (a) State who or what the feeling might be directed at. This will not be appropriate for all feelings (such as guilt or depression), but would apply to feelings such as anger, resentment, and love.

   (b) State why you think he might have the feeling.

   (c) State how the feeling might be manifested behaviorally. In other words, how might the client express his feeling? What kinds of behavior or actions would tell you that the feeling is present? It might be helpful to review mentally the common ways that most people might deal with, express, or not express, the feeling, and then consider how your particular client might express the feeling.

You will get your ideas about the kinds of feelings your client may be experiencing and the ways in which he might express them from several sources:

   (a) Your own personal life experience. A review of how you have handled certain feelings may help you iden-

tify feelings and potential behaviors on the part of your client.

(b) Your professional work experience. This has put you in touch with many people, experiencing and expressing many diverse feelings. If you have several months' experience, you are probably able to identify patterns that tend to produce certain kinds of feelings or cause people to express them in certain ways.

(c) Your knowledge of the client's specific situation. This could include what others have told you about him, past case records, statements he has made, or nonverbal communication you have observed.

(d) Your knowledge of human behavior in general. Classes taken, preparation for a professional degree, attendance at workshops or training sessions given by an agency, and readings could inform you how most people in the client's situation would probably feel or behave. Bear in mind that you are thinking theoretically at this point. You are not wholly certain your client has the feelings you have identified, but are simply listing all possible feelings he *might* have. As you get to know him better, some of your ideas will either be substantiated or eliminated.

It is important in this step to list *all* possible feelings you think your client might have. This means you may need to read some literature about the environmental, physiological, emotional, or cultural factors that are known to be affecting your client in order to determine what kinds of feelings and reactions a person in your client's situation might be expected to have.

4. Consider who are the "significant others" in the client's life. Select one or two persons with whom he relates most closely and go through step 3 with them. In view of the key facts known about the client and his situation, the possible feelings he might be experiencing as a result, and the associated behaviors, what are the major feelings that these significant others might be having? Look at and describe the actual or possible interactional patterns between the client and these other persons. Bear in mind that the professional helping person can also be a significant other with feelings.

5. *Develop a treatment plan.*

   (a) *List all possible case outcomes or treatment goals, regardless of whether they appear realistic or unrealistic.* (For example, "get Mr. S. to go to a nursing home"; "remove six-year-old Sarah from the home"; "help Mrs. J. prepare for her death due to her illness." These should be broad, basic objectives or outcomes. Do not list subgoals or steps for achieving the outcomes listed.

   (b) *Label each plan or outcome suggested in (a) as either realistic or unrealistic.* Also determine which outcomes or goals are unrealistic to plan for consciously, but may happen anyway due to circumstances beyond the client's or the worker's control. For example, Mrs. S. has been an alcoholic for fifty years and is now seventy. It is not realistic to expect her to stop drinking at this point. But, as her health deteriorates, she may be forced into an inpatient medical facility where she is unable to obtain alcohol, thus bringing about an involuntary withdrawal from alcohol.

   (c) *For each realistic goal: (1) state the goal; (2) break it down into subgoals that must be achieved before the overall goal can be accomplished; and (3) state exactly what specific treatment techniques will be used to accomplish the goal or subgoals.* For example, a realistic goal might be for Mrs. C. to gain better control over her children and use more effective parenting techniques. However, a subgoal might be to help her alleviate her depression and feel better about herself as a step toward helping her relate more effectively to her children. If a treatment technique such as "empathy" is listed, state exactly *how* you would communicate empathy to this particular client in this particular situation. What would you say or do? Or, exactly how would you get your client to "ventilate unexpressed feelings of anger" if you have put that down as one of your goals or treatment plan objectives?

   (d) *Rank the treatment goals in order of priority.* Which ones will you work on first? Watch for some goals that, if accomplished, would automatically bring about accomplishment or progress toward achieving other goals.

    (e) For each treatment goal, give an estimate of the length of time you feel it will take to accomplish the goal.

    6. *Finally, write a diagnostic statement that summarizes your main thoughts in steps 2 through 4. Also make a heading of "treatment plan" and summarize what you came up with in step 5.* Only the written material you produce in this final step should be placed in the official case record. The worksheets from steps 1 through 5 should not become part of the permanent case file. They should be kept in a secure location in a separate folder until no longer needed by the worker, at which time they should be destroyed.

Application of the Analytical Thinking Model to a Supervisory-Administrative (Large-Systems) Problem

Supervisory and administrative staff in the helping professions are often faced with difficult decisions. Human elements can make such decisions most difficult for the individual who is especially attuned to human needs and is professionally trained to "be a helping person." When such decisions are rendered, the employee, the supervisor himself, upper-level administrators, consumers, and others may be affected. What is needed is an objective, *structured* method of attacking the problem.

    Analytical thinking refers to the ability to take a problem situation apart so that its dynamics can be studied objectively and meaningfully and the appropriate "solution" selected. Until the analytical thinking method is learned, the supervisor-administrator should write each step out on paper. This forces thinking to be definite, organized, and to the point. The basic steps are as follows:

    1. *Review mentally everything that is known about the situation or problem.*

    2. *List ten to fifteen key facts known about the situation or* *problem.* Use outline form. Do not give impressions or analyses. Sort out the relevant from the irrelevant factors in the situation.

3. *What feelings might the key person in the situation be experiencing? List each feeling individually, and for each one:*

    (a) State who or what the feeling might be directed at. If you have listed "anger" as a feeling that your supervisee might have, state who or what he might be angry at, and so on.

    (b) State why you think the feeling might be present.

    (c) State how the feeling might be manifested behaviorally. How might the supervisee express his feelings? What kinds of behaviors or actions would tell you that the feeling is present? What are some of the ways that supervisees deal with and express feelings of anger, for example, toward a supervisor?

4. *What feelings might the person who will have to make the decision or take the necessary action have in this situation?* (In a supervisory problem this would be the supervisor; in an administrative situation it could be the administrator or perhaps the department or agency collectively.)

5. *What feelings might significant others be experiencing in this situation?* Select *only* significant others whose feelings are *relevant* to the problem at hand. A number of significant persons may have feelings (e.g., the family of the employee in a supervisory problem), but these feelings might not necessarily affect the handling of the problem. Consider: *should* family feelings about a supervisee's dismissal determine what action the supervisor should take? Typical significant others whose feelings might be relevant could include co-workers, the administration, clients, other agencies, the community, the taxpayers (in a government agency), or funding and accrediting bodies.

6. *List all possible solutions or actions that might be taken to resolve the problem.* List all possible alternatives, even those that may seem undesirable or impossible. Do not permit the reality constraints of the system to limit your creative thinking in this step.

7. *For each possible action listed in step 6, list all possible repercussions, both positive and negative, that might occur if the action were to be taken.* Be sure to consider the reactions of persons identified in steps 3, 4, and 5 as you work on this step. At the

completion of this step, label each possible action as realistic or unrealistic, desirable or undesirable.

8. Select the option, solution, or possible action that comes closest to resolving the problem and has the fewest potentially negative factors that would make it impossible or undesirable to accomplish or implement.

SOURCE: *Reprinted with permission of The Free Press, a Division of Macmillan, Inc. from RECORDING: Guidelines for Social Workers by Suanna J. Wilson. Copyright © 1976, 1980 by Suanna J. Wilson.*

Like other generic skills, assessments are done at all levels of practice (i.e., micro, meso, and macro), and across a range of specific practice settings. Even though the ATM was formulated primarily in teaching clinical assessment, the same analytic thinking skills are needed by practitioners doing social work with communities, agency boards, committees, or legislatures. Although the size of the group may vary, how we go about making sense of the dynamics we see involves the same intuitive and analytic processes.

Goal Setting and Contracting. Based on the initial assessment, both practitioner and client have come to some agreement about the problem at hand, and have mutually identified the best possible outcome of intervention. This "best possible outcome" then is the goal of intervention. This essentially asks the question: How will things look, feel, or be different for this client (regardless of whether the client is an individual, a community, or a nation) when the presenting problem has been resolved? This is the goal toward which the actual intervention is directed.

The assessment summary ends with an outline of the intervention plan, and this often includes a *contract,* sometimes called a service contract (Beulah Compton and Burt Galaway, 1989, p. 471). The contract is a set of statements that reflect our mutual understanding of the goals and how each participant will be involved in achieving them. Depending on the setting in which you practice, a contract may or may not be written, it may or may not even be discussed explicitly.[4]

For instance, in the case of the AFDC social worker, your role in meeting client needs involves determining whether applicants meet the stated criteria for service. In this case, explicit contracting is not necessary because the request for help is clear (financial assistance), the desired goal is obvious (receipt of financial help), and your role and functions are inherent in the agency's stated purpose. A different example would be the social worker in a juvenile probation setting. In this case, a discussion of the "ground rules" (e.g., when you will meet, where, how frequently, for how long, what will happen in sessions) not only clarifies the working contract, but also has therapeutic value in setting clear boundaries and expectations. As you saw in the case of Jason and Don in Chapter 6, setting boundaries and discussing expectations are particularly important in working with adolescents.

Given that helping relationships in social work are purposeful (i.e., they exist for a particular reason), mutuality in defining intervention goals and agreeing on how they are to be reached is an integral part of the helping relationship. This helps remind us that helping relationships are best viewed as partnerships in which both persons or groups work together to reach their goals. This is reflected further throughout the following illustrations of selected BSW practice roles and functions.

Selected Practice Roles of BSWs

In Chapter 4 we identified some of the many practice opportunities for BSWs beginning their careers. As noted, there are numerous opportunities to work in a variety of roles using different interventive strategies. The following section includes representative, though not inclusive, social work roles and functions in selected practice situations. Social work is challenging partly because there are always opportunities for creative approaches. As a result, modifications of and additions to these roles can certainly be made as long as good judgment is exercised in thinking through your plan.

We have selected three roles for brief discussion: *information and referral, case management,* and *advocacy.* These particular roles have been selected because they are used essentially in all practice settings.

Information and Referral

Social workers are expected to know a great deal about a great many things (as you now know from reading this far). Critical knowledge areas for social workers include the structure and function of various systems (e.g., economic, political, social, service delivery), the interaction between individuals and their environments (i.e., educational systems, health and correctional systems, family and community systems), and the values and ethics of the profession. All social workers must, at the very least, be familiar with these knowledge areas. Whether clients are sent to our agencies involuntarily, such as probation, or whether they are seeking help on their own, they often have needs that can be met—at least in part—by the provision of information, and frequently by referral to other services.

The social worker in Children's Protective Services (CPS) may be initially investigating allegations of abuse or neglect, but will frequently be involved in providing information at some point. In cases of abuse or neglect, necessary information could be fundamental, such as parenting education aimed at helping clients to learn nonabusive, health promoting methods of child rearing. Many persons reported to CPS have their own personal histories of abuse or neglect. Although this does not excuse abusive or neglectful treatment of their children, it does suggest that lack of information may lie, at least partially, at the root of the problem. If your own experience of "normal" parenting was characterized by abuse or neglect, how would you be expected to know any different? It seems more than a little ironic to us that nearly every job, occupation, or profession requires at least minimal education or training, with the exception of child rearing and parenting!

Most CPS workers typically have heavy caseloads that prohibit indepth direct intervention. Thus, a frequent role for them is referral. Having assessed the individual client and their situation, the worker explores available community resources that can be called on to help resolve the problem. The well-informed CPS worker knows that Parents Anonymous (PA) is a no fee, self-help, support group for parents with a history of having abused or neglected their children. Referring the client to this kind of support service is certainly an appropriate role in this case. As you can see, the information and referral role requires an accurate assessment of client needs, knowledge of community resources, and the skills to access these resources.

Case Management

Many times clients present us with multiple problems that call for a variety of different services to meet their needs. To most people, the vast networks of social, health, and legal services are large, impersonal, and confusing. Many people have no idea where or how to locate particular services they might need and, as a result, human needs often go unmet. The tragedy is that many services exist, but cannot be located or accessed by those who need them. Social workers employed as case managers are involved in linking clients with the services and resources they need.

Like information and referral, case management requires us to have extensive knowledge of community resources and services. However, the role and responsibility of the case manager extends beyond providing information. Case managers are often involved in the initial assessment where the client's needs are identified. Then, it is the case manager who is ultimately responsible for seeing that the client is (1) connected to the appropriate service provider(s) and that (2) appropriate services are actually being received. Case managers are the persons who prevent endless bureaucratic runarounds and keep an eye on the progress of clients as they receive services from a variety of providers.

Case management is a critical role that requires coordination and monitoring skills. Coordination is important to ensure that each of the clients' needs is being met without duplication of services. Likewise, monitoring is important as an ongoing process that holds each service provider accountable for doing what they are expected to do. Case managers are typically involved in coordinating and monitoring service delivery, rather than providing direct services themselves. Initially they may work directly with clients to determine what services are needed, but their primary roles and functions are to (1) identify the appropriate service providers, (2) link clients with those providers, (3) continue to coordinate services as needs change, and (4) continually monitor progress.

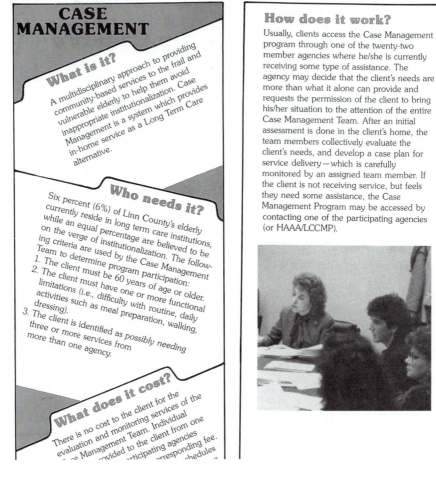

CASE MANAGEMENT

What is it?

A multidisciplinary approach to providing community-based services to the frail and vulnerable elderly to help them avoid inappropriate institutionalization. Case Management is a system which provides in-home service as a Long Term Care alternative.

Who needs it?

Six percent (6%) of Linn County's elderly currently reside in long term care institutions, while an equal percentage are believed to be on the verge of institutionalization. The following criteria are used by the Case Management Team to determine program participation:
1. The client must be 60 years of age or older.
2. The client must have one or more functional limitations (i.e., difficulty with routine, daily activities such as meal preparation, walking, dressing).
3. The client is identified as possibly needing three or more services from more than one agency.

What does it cost?

There is no cost to the client for the evaluation and monitoring services of the Case Management Team. Individual ... provided to the client from one ... ticipating agencies ... corresponding fee. ... hedules ...

How does it work?

Usually, clients access the Case Management program through one of the twenty-two member agencies where he/she is currently receiving some type of assistance. The agency may decide that the client's needs are more than what it alone can provide and requests the permission of the client to bring his/her situation to the attention of the entire Case Management Team. After an initial assessment is done in the client's home, the team members collectively evaluate the client's needs, and develop a case plan for service delivery—which is carefully monitored by an assigned team member. If the client is not receiving service, but feels they need some assistance, the Case Management Program may be accessed by contacting one of the participating agencies (or HAAA/LCCMP).

Integrated, holistic case management is an important and valued role for social workers in our increasingly complex service delivery system.

Case management has been an important and needed function in social work for some time, but it has taken on even greater significance because the maze of human services delivery systems has become increasingly complex. In addition, client needs have become more multidimensional and complicated. Persons with HIV disease, for example, have numerous problems that cannot be met by a single provider or an individual agency.

Clients with HIV disease need medical services and medications, as well as therapeutic or supportive counseling. Over time, if the HIV disease progresses into AIDS, clients may suffer from specific illnesses such as Kaposi's sarcoma, or pneumocystic pneumonia. As a result, they may be periodically hospitalized for treatment, they may be unable to work, or they may lose their jobs due to prejudice or fear on the part of employers. As their financial resources are diminished through unemployment and there is an accompanying loss of insurance benefits, their medical and hospitalization needs increase. The loss of income also often results in clients being unable to make mortgage or rent payments for housing.

Case managers are frequently employed by agencies that specialize in working with HIV-positive and AIDS clients. Case managers assess client needs, then connect clients with the appropriate service deliverers or resources such as physicians, Supplemental Security Income (SSI) offices, the housing authority, hospice care, and, in cases where discrimination has occurred, legal aid or civil rights attorneys. Other important services for persons with HIV disease are nutritional and wellness programs, transportation services for those unable to drive, and intervention on behalf of clients with insurance companies. The multidimensional needs of persons with HIV provide us with an example of the critical importance of case management as a contemporary social work role.

Advocacy

Just as information and referral is related to case management, advocacy is related to both roles discussed previously. In fact, some case managers include advocacy as part of their responsibility to clients. In social work, much has been written about the role of advocacy at both the micro- and the macrolevels of intervention. An advocate "is one that pleads the cause of another" as in the case of an attorney. Another definition of advocate is "one who argues for, defends, maintains, or recommends a cause or proposal" (Karen A. Holmes, 1981, p. 33). This suggests a distinction between two kinds or levels of advocacy in social work practice. One is called *case advocacy*, which is described as action taken on behalf of a specific client. The other is *class advocacy*, which is action taken to effect change in policies, practices, or laws affecting all persons in a specific class or group (Karen A. Holmes, 1981, p. 33).

While the case manager is assessing, linking, coordinating, and monitoring services to clients, the advocate is going a step further. The advocate is committed to ensuring that service delivery systems are responsive to clients' needs, and that clients receive all the benefits and services to which they are rightfully entitled. On an

A demonstration by Act-Up in New York City. The "Silence=Death" emblem suggests the consequences of *not* actively protesting perceived injustices—in this case, the lack of government attention to AIDS.

individual level, case managers can and do engage in advocacy on behalf of specific clients who are not being served appropriately.

Take, for example, a client who needs home health care and financial assistance. The case manager has linked the client with a home health care provider and has helped the client apply for disability benefits. However, the home health aide informs the case manager that the client's home has no running water because the utility bills have not been paid for several months. Obviously this is an obstacle to the delivery of home health care services. The case manager may move into the role of advocate to convince the water department that they will be paid when disability checks arrive, and that this client *must* have water in the home. This would be an example of case advocacy where the case manager "pleads the cause" of the client and argues on the client's behalf for the delivery of a particular service. As you can see, the role of case advocate may also function as part of case management.

Class advocacy, on the other hand, is more often related to performing as a lobbyist or an activist, working on behalf of entire groups of persons who are trying to deal with underdeveloped or unresponsive systems. In the 1970s, sexual assault was identified as a major social problem affecting women. Many groups across the country organized to advocate for more sensitive treatment of victims from the medical, law enforcement, and legal-judicial systems. In the 1980s, similar advocacy efforts were made on behalf of battered women, and in the 1990s, increasing attention has been given to advocacy efforts on behalf of children, persons with HIV disease, and crime victims, among others.

To engage in either case or class advocacy, social workers must know and understand service delivery systems, as well as interpersonal and organizational dynamics. They must have a thorough understanding of the policies, regulations, and appeals processes of the agencies and systems with which they come in contact. Skills in organizing and data gathering are as critical as interpersonal and public relations skills. Further, to engage successfully in advocacy efforts, social workers must have a degree of comfort in taking a definite stand on an issue or a cause. This requires a certain amount of assertiveness because confrontation may result from or be a part of our advocacy efforts.

The advocacy role in social work is as important now as it was in the 1960s. Service delivery systems have become more, not less, complicated; attitudes that block clients access to services have become more, not less entrenched. In view of the profession's values and code of ethics, it is easy to see how advocacy cuts across all social work practice, regardless of our setting, client group, or level of intervention.

Summary

Since 1974, accredited social work education programs have prepared bachelor's level (BSW) social work practitioners. This degree is viewed as an entry-level practice degree, and BSWs may find themselves working along side or under the supervision of MSWs. However, both share a common educational foundation of skills. These include knowledge of the characteristics of professional helping relationships, the phases of helping relationships, and the skill base needed to establish helping relationships. Communication, relationship building, analytic thinking, and assessment are skills that provide the basis for generalist social work practice. Finally, the generalist social work roles of information and referral, case management, and advocacy were introduced.

Notes

1. Accreditation can be described as a "stamp of approval" from a group or organization sanctioned to bestow such approval. The Council on Social Work Education (CSWE), through its Commission on Accreditation, is the body that is responsible for accrediting social work programs at the BSW and MSW levels. Ironically, doctoral programs in social work are not within the purview of CSWE. Accreditation is a quality control measure, ensuring that the policies of the accrediting body are being adhered to by the degree-granting program. This strengthens the degree because potential employers know that a graduate from an accredited BSW or MSW program has mastered specific knowledge and skills. Accreditation also makes these degrees rather "portable" in that a BSW from a small, relatively unknown school is seen as having the same essential preparation as a BSW from a large, well-known institution.

2. The doctorate in social work, whether the PhD (Doctor of Philosophy) or DSW (Doctor of Social Work), is more an academic than an applied degree. Typically most people who pursue a doctorate in social work want to teach at the university level, conduct advanced research, or engage in policy analysis. In this respect social work is different from disciplines like clinical psychology, where a doctorate is required for practice.

3. For an excellent discussion of the dynamics involved, see Alan Keith-Lucas, *Giving and Taking Help* (Chapel Hill: University of North Carolina Press, 1972). Of particular interest are the chapters "The Nature of Help," "Taking Help," and "The Helping Relationship."

4. For an extensive discussion of contracting, see Anthony Maluccio and Wilma Marlow, "The Case for the Contract," *Social Work*, Vol. 19, No. 1, (Jan. 1974): 28–36.

References

Biestek, Felix P. "An Analysis of the Casework Relationship." *Social Casework*, Vol. 35, No. 2 (Feb. 1954): 57–61.

Brill, Naomi I. *Working with People: The Helping Process*, 4th ed. New York: Longman, 1990.

Compton, Beulah, and Burt Galaway. *Social Work Processes*. Belmont, CA: Wadsworth, 1989.

Holmes, Karen A. "Services for Victims of Rape: A Dualistic Practice Model," *Social Casework*, Vol. 62, No. 1 (Jan. 1981): 30–39.

Jordan, Judith, Janet Surrey, and Alexandra Kaplan. "Women and Empathy," Stone Center Work in Progress 82–02. Wellesley, MA: Stone Center for Developmental Services and Studies, 1983.

Keith-Lucas, Alan. *Giving and Taking Help*. Chapel Hill: University of North Carolina Press, 1972.

Reik, Theodore. *Listening with the Third Ear*. New York: Grove Press, 1948.

Wilson, Suanna. *Recording: Guidelines for Social Workers*. New York: Free Press, 1980.

CHAPTER 10

Advanced Methods

Introduction

This chapter builds on the generalist skills discussed in Chapter 9, and provides an overview of advanced methods. Although this text has been written primarily for undergraduates who may be working toward a BSW to prepare for entry-level practice, we thought you would find it informative to have a discussion of the advanced methods that evolve from the MSW level. We have developed the chapter along the lines of micro and macro methods, although this distinction is made only for the sake of clarity and is not meant to suggest that we support separating or polarizing micro and macro intervention.

Each section follows the same format beginning with an overview, evolution, and a discussion of advanced methods for micro and macro practice. Attention is also given to preparing for micro and macro practice, selected practice roles, as well as the influence of gender. To provide a framework for this content, we will first focus on a discussion of generalist versus advanced practice.

Generalist versus Advanced Practice

The BSW degree, by definition, is the necessary preparation for entry-level social work positions. The generalist skills of BSW practice are solid grounding for work with a variety of client problems and a variety of client groups, yet they are bounded by their generalist nature. That is, generalist education is intended to prepare social workers for the provision of direct services that rely primarily on task-centered or problem-solving models of practice. Examples would include providing *concrete* services such as financial assistance in departments of human resources, information and referral services, resource identification for posthospitalization placement, and intake work that identifies a client's presenting problem(s).

In comparison, the MSW degree is defined as the necessary degree for advanced, or specialized practice. Specializations, as you will recall from Chapter 4, may be defined by methods (i.e., casework, group work, planning, administration), by fields of practice (i.e., health, mental health, gerontology, corrections), or by problem focus (i.e., substance abuse, poverty). As a result, there are educational differences in the depth of substantive knowledge, as well as in the range of theoretical knowledge regarding human behavior and specific interventive models.

As you have probably gathered by now, unlike some other professions, such as teaching or nursing, social work education in the United States began at the graduate level. Consequently, the skills described in the last chapter were, and still are, part of the foundation for graduate social work education. The events that led to the development and accreditation of undergraduate social work programs occurred in the 1960s. As you will recall from Chapter 3, as public sector social services expanded, and as federally funded community action programs proliferated, the demand for social service workers far exceeded the numbers of trained personnel available. Furthermore, a substantial number of the positions in the expanding job market did not really require the complexity of knowledge and skill characteristic of the MSW. Thus the impetus for professional social work education at the undergraduate level with the goal of preparing students for entry-level practice. The Council on Social Work Education (CSWE) responded and as of 1974 BSW programs could be accredited.

Whereas some would say the council's response was painfully slow, others might suggest that the decision was premature and ill conceived. Critics tended to say that there was inadequate attention given to conceptualizing the distinctions between BSW and MSW education. It is interesting to note that the entire structure of social work education was changed not primarily in response to emerging theoretical influences, but in response to the receipt of federal funds that led to vast expansion of the human service job market. Because the structure of social work education was changed in this way, there continues to be some confusion as to the specific differences between the skills and methods of entry-level BSWs and advanced-level MSWs.

Further complicating the picture of social work practice is the variety and breadth of practice opportunities—as illustrated in Chapter 4—and the richness of roles and functions that we hope are apparent from all that you have now read. Advanced social work practice, historically and in the present, is comprised of methods related to both direct and indirect service to clients. Despite arguments to the contrary, there is no definitive argument that social work began solely as a direct service or clinical profession. Social work practice, even at the turn of the twentieth century, incorporated both clinical and nonclinical elements.

If you recall, even within the elements of the laws that proceeded from the Elizabethan Poor Law, practice included direct intervention with the individual or family (micro), as well as intervention with larger systems such as legislative work, or practice with organizations such as the churches (macro). The Charity Organization Societies (COS) in England and in the United States continued to utilize both methods simultaneously. COS workers were engaged in "case finding" and investigating the conditions of the poor (micro) as well as the coordination of efforts (macro).

Although you may read and hear that one of these methods, micro or macro, was formalized and preceded the other, we would argue that both methods have been present in social work practice since it was first recognized as such. We would also argue that both will continue to be necessary to achieve the overall goals of the profession in the future. It is logical that helping individuals in need cannot be accomplished without attending to the functions of documenting need and service delivery; accounting for the expenditure of public or private funds in service delivery; managing the facilities and staff to provide support to the direct service workers; and advocating for client needs to policymakers.

This seeming tension between proponents of micro intervention and proponents of macro intervention is, we believe, an unfortunate, if not inappropriate and unnecessary kind of dichotomy. Social work practice is not, or should not be, a choice between working with small client groups with limited goals versus changing society into a grand and perfect world. The apparent polarized conception of micro *versus* macro practice seems to suggest an artificial choice of one level of intervention as better than another. Not only is this overly simplistic and ultimately rather divisive, but it is contrary to the mission of the profession. Referring back to the working definition at the beginning of Chapter 4, "the purpose of social work is to *promote* or *restore* a mutually beneficial interaction between individuals and society in order to *improve the quality of life for everyone*" (Minahan, 1981, p. 6, emphases added). By emphasizing the words "to promote or restore" we see support for both micro- and macrolevels of intervention. Further, it is very clear that intervention at both levels is absolutely necessary in order to "improve the quality of life for everyone."

Realistically, it is often difficult to delineate exactly where micro and macro methods begin and end. In the last chapter, for example, we discussed how advocacy includes case advocacy, a micro intervention, as well as class advocacy at the macrolevel. Similarly, we have noted that it is also sometimes difficult to distinguish where generalist (BSW) practice ends and where advanced or specialized (MSW) practice begins. An example might help you begin to think about these differences.

BSWs have the essential and appropriate skills to provide information and referral services. This means (1) they are sufficiently skilled in interviewing techniques to identify a client's problem; (2) they are knowledgeable about community resources or they know how to go about finding those resources; (3) they are able, through relationship skills, to support and encourage the client to follow through on the client's own behalf; and (4) they can provide follow-up to assure that the client has connected with the appropriate service. However, if a client needs ongoing therapy, then the client would be referred to an MSW for that level of specialized clinical (micro) skill. Or, if the BSW worker cannot find an appropriate service, the information about this service gap would likely be turned over to a social work planner or lobbyist (macro practitioner) who would have the specialized skills to address this service gap.

Micro Practice: An Overview

Micro practice is a generic term that suggests several things: (1) that our target group will be an individual, a couple, a group, or a family; (2) that service will be directed to benefit the target group specifically; and (3) that the goal of intervention will be to enhance the quality of life and overall social functioning of the client in the environment. Therefore, micro and macro methods share the same essential goal, but they differ in terms of their target group, in the degree to which they focus on direct versus indirect service delivery and client contact, and in how they achieve their goals. This much is clear, but there is confusion about micro social work methods. This confusion is the result of using an array of different terms to describe the same activities. For example, some social workers say they do casework and others say they are direct practitioners; some say they are clinical social workers and others describe themselves as psychotherapists.

The Evolution of Micro Practice

As you now know, attending to social welfare concerns and providing humane services to people in need is not new. However, in the history of social work practice, the publication of *Social Diagnosis* by Mary Richmond in 1917 is considered to mark the beginning of social casework as a specific method. Richmond's book essentially laid the groundwork for the training of "friendly visitors," and put forth the notion that there was a *method* to these efforts.

According to Carol H. Meyer (1987), "At least two major themes from Richmond's work have persisted: the need to individualize people (thus, the term 'casework'), and the need to understand, or diagnose, their situations" (p. 410). Interestingly, in her choice of terminology—that is, diagnosis—Richmond set in motion a metaphor with the medical profession, a comparison that continues to be the subject of considerable debate among social workers. Specifically, the medical model as it is called, tends to address physiological dysfunction in a sequence of diagnosis, treatment, and cure. This suggests, implicitly, that persons are either sick or healthy. Furthermore, the medical model has tended to maintain a rather myopic focus on the patient, giving little attention, until recent years, to all the myriad variables in the environment that affect physical health.

Another critical factor during this time was the work of Sigmund Freud, particularly his theory of personality and identification of defense mechanisms. Whereas Richmond's work described a method of working with people, Freudian theory was seen as contributing to an understanding of human behavior. Freudian psychoanalytic theory garnered a great deal of positive support from social workers eager to understand the "whys" of human problems. Although there is a rich history in the evolution of micro practice theories and methods, it is sufficient to say here that the influence of Freudian and neo-Freudian theories remained entrenched in social work until the 1960s.

In the meantime, other methods such as social group work and social work with families were evolving within the profession. Group work is generally viewed as having evolved in the 1930s, though it came into its own as a specific social work method after World War II. Social work with families, although not new to the profession, became an identified practice area in the mid-1950s, as the child guidance movement gained widespread acceptance. By the 1960s, family treatment had become something of a specialized area within the mental health field, and programs specifically designed for those interested in family therapy were developed.

However, as the social activism of this period evolved, social work's attention was turned to the War on Poverty, civil rights, and large-scale social change. As a result, casework in particular—but other micro methods as well—were criticized heavily by many for their lack of attention to larger social concerns. The provision of direct services to individuals, even financial assistance, was viewed as "Band-Aid therapy" that failed to attend to the root causes of poverty while making only the most basic level of survival possible.

Advanced Micro Practice Methods

Traditionally, micro methods have included social casework and social group work. Current terminology for advanced micro practice in the 1990s would likely be clinical social work, individual, group, or family therapy. Although work with individuals dates back to the origins of casework in the early 1900s, the profession has seen major philosophical shifts toward therapy as an appropriate role and function of advanced practice in recent years. Moreover, increasing numbers of persons now view the MSW degree as a viable professional education for private practice, a major shift from the profession's early focus on social reform, and a shift that has created heated debate within the profession.

Within this debate, critics of social workers in private practice lament what they label as self-serving efforts to separate from the profession's historical commitment to the disadvantaged. They believe that private, for-profit social work practice is antithetical to the values of the profession, and that this produces a discriminatory service delivery system based on ability to pay. It is true that private practice social workers typically see clients who are middle income or above, but the other side of the debate asks why social workers should provide their services for free, or at reduced rates. If their services are equal to those of psychologists or family therapists, why should social workers be singled out to charge less?

Yet another argument comes out of a feminist analysis. That is, social work, like the nursing and teaching professions, has traditionally been devalued, at least in part because women have been the primary service deliverers. Specifically, "women's work" (i.e., educating the young, caring for the sick, helping people in need) has traditionally been viewed as less important than the work of men. Nancy Chodorow (1978) has conceptualized this as "being versus doing," with men seen as the "doers" and women as concerned with "being." A feminist analysis suggests that women, the traditional caregivers of society, are entitled to appropriate compensation for the services they provide, and this certainly extends to professional social workers in private practice.

Roles of Micro Practitioners

In advanced practice, whether in a public agency or in a private setting, the primary role is often that of social work therapist. This may involve work with individuals, couples, groups, or families, or all the above. The goal of therapy may range from recovery from substance abuse, to improving family relationships, to recovery from a childhood trauma such as incest. Some agencies, like some individual practitioners, have a particular focus based on the client group (e.g., child guidance clinic, adolescent treatment facility, chronically mentally ill, etc.), or on the presenting problem (e.g., addictions, medical crises, childhood trauma, etc.).

Supervision is another role in advanced micro practice. It is not uncommon for agency practitioners skilled in individual, group, and family work to find themselves being promoted to a supervisory level, too often without specific educational preparation. The supervisory role often includes educational components aimed at improving the quality of services being provided by those under one's supervision. As such, some consider supervision to be an indirect method of practice because direct client contact occurs less frequently.

It is likely that education for advanced micro practice in the 1990s will continue to reflect the influence of the debate surrounding social workers in private practice. MSW curricula that include specific models of individual, group, and family therapy, as well as fields of practice specializations, such as health and gerontology, are likely to solidify further as necessary preparation for advanced practice. This does not, however, obviate the need for education related to professional values and ethics, the history of social welfare, social welfare policy, or research—all of which are required components of MSW programs. Nor should curricula fail to include content and skills on the methods and arenas of macrolevel practice.

Regardless of public or private setting, and regardless of preferred methods, social workers will continue to share the same historical traditions, the same unique person-in-environment perspective, and the same goal of improving the quality of life for all persons. To argue further about whether one method is preferable to another, to argue further about the appropriate settings for social workers, is to risk becoming divisive among ourselves in an era when the needs have never been greater, and, frankly, when our clients need all the help we can offer.

Life Experience and Gender in Micro Practice

In our view, the process of life experience enhances an individual's capacity for advanced clinical practice beyond what is gained from professional education. We believe that it is too simplistic to suggest that more education is automatically better. Furthermore, life experience is more than the sum total of our age in years. Both young and old may bring rich life experience to clinical work. We believe this should be highlighted as an important foundation for social work practice, particularly at the advanced microlevel.

The experience of women illustrates this point. Women tend to learn and know a great deal from their experiences (even though they may not recognize the value of their own experiences), regardless of their chosen roles in life. If we examine the life experience of a woman who has married and had children, we would see someone who has spent many hours developing and using a variety of communication skills, setting limits and boundaries, teaching, listening, comforting, and healing. This woman has developed interpersonal skills with adults, with infants, with growing children through various developmental stages. She has experience in financial planning and budgeting, and most certainly in organizing. She may well have exceptionally strong management skills in running an entire operation (i.e., the household).

This woman has already developed many skills that, with additional theoretical grounding, make her an excellent candidate for advanced social work practice. From her own life, she knows experientially about a range of human feeling that encompasses joy to sadness, exhilaration to despair, and fulfillment to loss. Without having experienced this range of feeling, we can only try to guess or imagine what the experience might be; we cannot, in fact, empathize fully with a feeling that we have never experienced. Does this suggest that advanced micro practitioners need to have encountered every experience that a client might bring to us? Obviously not. It is necessary to be able to identify a similar feeling in our own experience and transfer it to the experience of the client. For example, if we are working with a person suffering from a terminal illness, we do not need to share the illness to understand and empathize; but if we have felt threat, loss, and fear when a friend or family member was dying, from our own experience we know something about how this feels. We can relate more sensitively to clients when we are able to draw on our own life experience.

Issues of Empathy and Gender in Micro Practice

Empathy, as noted in Chapter 9, is a cornerstone to effective social work, yet its importance is particularly critical in advanced micro practice. The success of therapeutic intervention with individuals, couples, groups, or families is dependent on establishing empathic connections. It is, therefore, of considerable interest that research findings suggest that females tend to score higher than males on measures of empathy. For example, Martin Hoffman (1977) conducted a review of the literature on empathy and noted: "What is most striking about the empathy findings is the fact that in every case, regardless of the age of the subjects or the measures used, the females obtained higher scores than did the males" (p. 715). While he acknowledges that the variations in scores were not always striking, he adds: "Nevertheless, females did obtain higher scores in 16 out of 16 independent samples. The probability of this occurring by chance is only 1 out of 64,000" (p. 715). Further, in a study on the impact of social work education on empathy, Thomas Keefe (1975) states, "One last serendipitous finding was a slightly higher level of empathy for female students than for male students" (pp. 73–74). These gender-based differences related to empathy can be explained only partially by the differential socialization of females and males in this society, because some of Hoffman's findings were based on infant research and, presumably, the effects of socialization would not yet have been discernible.

The implications of these findings on empathy are rather intriguing when applied to micro and macro practice. In particular, we recognize that advanced micro and macro methods are divided not only by what the practitioner does, but often by who the practitioner is; that is, most direct service delivery social workers are women and most macro practitioners are men. In light of the research on empathy, perhaps this is not surprising. Perhaps this suggests a "good fit," in that women seem to bring unique strengths to the interpersonal relationship arena. However, it seems rather ironic that a profession that began through the efforts of women as "friendly visitors" and social reformers has become a profession that can often be characterized as "male dominated." Despite the fact that most social workers are women, and despite the fact that most recipients of social work services are female, men still hold most of the positions viewed as inherently more important or more powerful. Once again (or still), women's work remains primarily in the realm of direct service, supported by Nancy Chodorow's conception of women's "being"—caring for, nurturing, and helping others—whereas men's realm remains in the world of "doing"—as agency administrators, managers, or executive directors.

In this discussion, care must be taken to note that "being," as used here, is also doing, albeit a different kind of "doing" than is typically valued in this society. This notion of being, as part of advanced clinical practice, is extraordinarily difficult, yet extremely important. It requires that the social work therapist "be with" the client subjectively in the client's experience. This is quite different qualitatively than "doing" something with or to the client. It requires "being close" rather than distant, connected rather than separate. Each of these terms reflects different approaches (or, if you will, ways of being) and each is suggestive of the different kinds of skills needed by persons involved in advanced micro and advanced macro practice.

Macro Practice: An Overview

As noted in earlier chapters, advanced macro professional techniques and methodologies have, from the early days of Charity Organization Societies and settlement homes, been part of the practice of social work and among the roles and functions of social work practitioners. Despite those early beginnings, however, in varying forms macro practice has often had to vie for attention in graduate schools' curricula; for equal professional stature in classification and licensure activities; and for legitimation as a real social work method. Also, not surprisingly, given the variation of practice contexts as well as changing social, political, and economic conditions, macro practice has had changing theoretical bases and different foci for practitioner's roles.

Although we have included macro practice in this chapter on advanced methods, suggestive of MSW preparation, this distinction is neither completely accurate nor valid. As discussed in the micro section, the distinction between generalist and advanced is neither uniformly agreed on nor consistent. As a result, some methodologies commonly described as macro practice are clearly also part of the generalist model discussed in Chapter 9, whereas others fall more clearly and consistently in a graduate program as advanced practice skills and roles.

So, what is macro practice? Under that general rubric has been included advocacy roles such as community organizer and lobbyist; social planning roles such as program planner and program evaluator; and management roles such as program director, consultant, and executive. What do all of these roles have in common? What they share are two important elements that relate them to social work professionally and combine them under this generic macro label.

First, the relationship between these methods and social work practice exists because of the arenas in which they take place: public social services and not-for-profit social services. Second, their connectedness to each other comes because in all cases they can be viewed as "indirect services" in that they may not as directly relate to and interact with social service clients. However, they are legitimate social work functions because they clearly have the same goals as micro practice: client advocacy, social justice, the improvement of social functioning, and the enhancement of the quality of life.

The Evolution of Macro Practice

As was illustrated in Chapters 2 and 3, the history of macro methods is as old as the profession. The roots of both social planning and community organizing can be traced back to the Charity Organization Societies that assessed needs, gathered resources, and coordinated the delivery of social services.

So, whereas the roots of casework can be traced to turn-of-the-century case finding techniques, so, too, can the beginnings of macro practice. Despite this early beginning, these macro functions were not viewed as central and legitimate roles, but as peripheral to the primary functions, and/or as "citizen" roles.

Consequently, through the early decades of the century, as social work emerged from the "friendly visitors" to university-based graduate professional education, social activism was present in labor union movements, in efforts to initiate child labor laws, in attempts to improve the conditions of the institutionalized mentally ill, and in juvenile delinquency prevention programs. However, it was not until World War II that community organization was recognized within social work education as a formal method of social work.

Built around a conflict strategy, Saul Alinsky's community

An April 1992 pro-choice march in Washington, D.C. drew an estimated 500,000 demonstrators.

organization model was developed in the early 1930s, but did not catch on until the 1960s. In the 1950s and 1960s, social activist roles became more important as society increasingly became aware of poverty and racism and took action to reduce or eliminate both. Community organization, as a fully developed and legitimated method in graduate schools of social work, saw its peak in the curricula of the 1960s, and, not surprisingly, the community organizers saw peak levels of employment during that same period. The civil rights movement and the "maximum feasible citizen participation" mandates of the Economic Opportunity Act of 1964 pushed the recognition of community organization as a separate field of specialization by CSWE in 1967.

The era of increased accountability for social services came with the country's realization that the War on Poverty had not eradicated poverty, civil rights legislation had not eradicated discrimination, and huge federal dollars had been poured into public social services. This forced the profession and graduate social work education to examine the relevance of community organization models in a society that was demanding increased fiscal accountability and sophisticated methods of program evaluation, including cost benefit analyses. Seemingly overnight, macro curricula changed from community organizing, with class advocacy as its primary principle, to a planning and management focus with human relations principles. In fact, by the 1980s the term *community organization* had been almost obliterated from our social work vocabulary, and was replaced by terms such as *community development* and *social planning* (Ralph Kramer and Harry Specht, 1983).

What the 1980s brought was a retrenchment of public dollars, despite the previously noted increased demands and consequent implementation of significantly improved accountability mechanisms in social services. It is impossible to describe in simple terms where this led macro practice and macro curriculum, but the 1980s spawned two more disparate variations. The first was an increased emphasis on political activist skills. This change evolved from the realization that social workers must be in the forefront of stopping the drastic federal and state social service budget reductions, which only led to increased social problems. The second was an increased focus on more sophisticated management techniques emphasizing management information systems, human relations management, and fiscal management.

Advanced Macro Practice Methods

In addition to some of these technical and methodological concerns, there has been divergence and disagreement among administrators, social planners, and community organizers, especially with respect to their attitudes and values. The administrative group criticizes the community organizers for being too radical and unrealistic, whereas the administrators are accused of being antagonistic to change and the planners are charged with selling out to community economic power brokers. It is possible that some of this friction has inhibited the constructive thinking and conceptualization about important linkages among what otherwise appears to be conceptually distinct and sometimes competitive practice arenas.

Clearly the dilemmas arise in large part from the historical development of these macro methods. What was appropriate for the 1960s and a progressive context of social change was not appropriate in the 1980s. Likewise, the 1980s was a decade characterized by fiscal conservatism and by attacks on the welfare state, and the macro methods needed then may or may not be appropriate for the 1990s and beyond. Moreover, macro content is as affected by regional and local differences as is micro content. Organizing within the context of New York City and Chicago (from which many community organization texts and, therefore, methodologies are derived) is not the same as organizing in Houston or in Miami. As a result, the 1990s macro student must recognize that the techniques of the 1960s evolved within a rather specific and essentially liberal context. This suggests that sensitivity to the current context and climate is critical.

To be appropriate for the 1990s and beyond, community organization methods have been modified, though not all modifications are simply conservative revisions. Indeed, the fundamental purpose of community organizing—no matter what macro context or agency/organization situation in which practitioners find themselves—is a commitment to broader values and progressive objectives. This commitment still includes our efforts to create a more humane, equitable, and democratic society, which is the same commitment that guides all social work practice.

The dilemmas encountered with some of our social planning and policy analysis models have been the transference of ideologies and techniques from other fields without including the lens of social work values and ethics. For example, when the 1970s demanded increased fiscal and performance accountability, the scurry to utilize cost effectiveness and cost benefit analyses in not-for-profit social services did not take into account the critical and very difficult questions of how anyone places a market value on a life saved, or on an education completed. It was equally problematic that the transference of traditional managerial principles was done without the same thoughtfulness in applicability and relatedness. Worker performance measures became equivalent to output production and time efficiency studies required logging activities by categories. Consequently, the age-old battle heightened: Would employees' time be spent most meaningfully in direct services to clients? in record keeping? in collateral contacts? in advocacy?

Case

LUZ

*T*o Luz, there was no such thing as "luck." She was a person who had planned each step of her life with care and attention to detail. Now, as she sat in the executive director's office of the Multi-County Mental Health Center for Northeast Region II, *her* office, she began to review the personal journal that she had kept during her first year in this administrative position. "What pleases me most," read the journal from her first month, "is how committed this staff is to meeting the needs of these rural counties. The resources are not abundant, but if I could put a price on dedication, this agency would be rich."

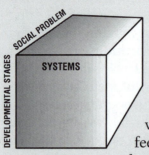

Mental Health/Administration

Adults

Gender/Ethnic Issues

Reading on, Luz saw her own anxious words leap off the page. "March 27, 1992. Tonight I make my first presentation to the Board of Directors. I still worry I will not be seen as a 'real' executive. Part of me knows that this is the group that approved hiring me, so why am I worried, but another part of me feels like this is a test. I don't really know these people, mostly business and corporate types, mostly men who are older than I am. Are they really ready for a woman as the executive director of this agency? Am I really ready? I like being the first—first woman, first Hispanic—in this position, but I feel a burden, as if I am carrying the weight of *all* women and *all* Hispanics with me. I need to remember that a little anxiety is normal for me when I'm doing a major presentation, that I'll be fine after the first few minutes. After all, I've planned and worked a long time to get where I am, and *I can do the job.*"

Luz could now smile as she remembered that first meeting. The board was impressed not only with her work on the revised agency mission statement and the development of new program goals, but they responded well to her presentation style, which was both warm and engaging with no sacrifice of quality or substance. She flipped through her journal and stopped on an entry from May, 1992. "I wish they had taught me more about time management and stress reduction when I was in school. I feel like I'm juggling 10 projects at once and facing too many deadlines! Why did I think that being an administrator meant I'd have all the help in the world and all I'd have to do was 'administer'? All this week I've kept my appointments to a minimum so I can work on preparing the annual budget, but at the end of the day the budget hasn't moved very far and I'm not sure where my time has gone. I haven't been able to cross anything off my To Do list for days! Guess it's time to remind myself that I can, and should, set better limits. I don't need to respond to everyone's crisis like it's my own. In fact, maybe that's not even really helpful. Maybe when I get involved with staff issues I'm giving clinical supervisors the message that I don't think they can work it out themselves. Sounds like something I'd better think about—where's the line between being supportive and disempowering people?"

All in all, Luz thought to herself, "This has been quite a year. I've developed a solid working relationship with the board. They have supported me on nearly every request I took to them. (Except for a new building—oh well, maybe after the annual campaign next year!) Our expanded outreach programs have located more and more people in need (I guess that's a mixed blessing), particularly in the hard-to-reach, underserved rural areas. We've hired three new BSWs and each one has become a major team player in our direct services mental health program. And next month, the evaluation of our new outreach program gets underway."

Now, speaking out loud to no one except herself, Luz said, "I think moving into administration was a good choice." Then, turning to her computer, Luz pulled up the file "To Do Lists" and started setting her next priorities.

Within the context of administration, what has long faced the profession of social work is the job competition, particularly at the higher levels of management, with MBA's and MPA's. Unfortunately, even in the 1990s, the general public and even the social work profession have often seen the routes to high level executive positions in social service agencies either through non-social work education (as noted earlier), or in the historical and traditional method of organizational ascendancy: Good caseworkers are moved up to become supervisors. Particularly since the 1970s and throughout the 1980s, more graduate programs have focused on management techniques, specifically in the not-for-profit arena, and have attempted to train executives within an MSW program. There are assumptions, quite obviously, that the preferred training is the combination of social work values and generalist practice skills accompanied by appropriate managerial skills.

The last combination of role sets to be discussed in advanced macro practice is in the political arena. Although this is a set of roles as historically congruent and related to social work practice as any other, it also, surprisingly, has been the role set causing the greatest amount of internal professional controversy. The necessity for political action by a profession that acknowledges its roots in advocacy has conflicted with the concerns that political skills and political values may be antithetical to those of the larger profession.

Like community organization, political social work roles have most frequently been viewed as citizen roles. The methodologies have been questioned, and, in the 1990s, political social work has not yet been legitimated as a method of practice (Karen Haynes and James Mickelson, 1991). In fact, the NASW has just begun to include data about social workers in elected or appointed political positions as career categories.

However, despite these shifts in the primary focus of macro practice and the apparent divisions within, national data indicate that approximately 15 percent of all MSW students choose macro practice as their methodological specialization. This percentage has remained consistent over the past 10 to 15 years. Furthermore, however a particular graduate program may choose to identify its macro specialization (administration and planning; planning and management; political social work; community organizing), there are common elements to the preparation for this advanced practice specialization.

Roles of Macro Practitioners

So where do we find these macro practitioners in the 1990s? In any community, macro practitioners may fill the roles of program directors, executive directors, and consultants; they may be found in positions with community development corporations, hunger and homeless coalitions, or working with professional associations or labor unions. Equally likely would be macro practitioners in program planning, program evaluation, and policy analysis positions, particularly in larger public as well as not-for-profit agencies. Finally, it would be hoped that we would find some macro practitioners in the political arena as campaign coordinators, as candidates, or serving in elected offices; or in appointed positions such as state mental health commissioners, as legislative aides, and in key advisory or staff positions.

This description makes it obvious that these roles are no more or less diverse than the roles of micro practitioners; these roles are equally essential for exercising the profession's commitment to social justice and to the enhancement of the quality of life.

Knowledge and Gender in Macro Practice

As in the case with micro practice, knowledge gained through life experience is a valued foundation for our work at the macrolevel. The self-assurance of the manager or the assertiveness of the lobbyist are bolstered through experience, and help us build on our formal knowledge. There are also issues related to gender that we feel are important to note in our discussion of macro practice.

Knowledge for Macro Practice

It is probably evident, given the role sets among macro practitioners just described, that the necessary knowledge base is diverse and broad. As indicated in Chapter 7, knowledge bases for all social work practice have been drawn from a multitude of disciplines, predominantly in the social and behavioral sciences. This is equally true for macro as well as micro theoretical bases.

At the macrolevel, the history of social movements and social change, and theoretical concepts such as power and conflict, are underpinnings of the community organizing and social activists' role sets. In addition, theories from management and political science help direct the focus of many of the social planning and policy analysis role sets. Administrative specializations within graduate curriculums draw heavily from industrial psychology, organizational development, and personnel management. Political social work roles, in addition, draw from political science as well as law.

Suffice it to say that many of the theoretical bases for macro practice build on the generalist base and systems theory framework. Macro practice, indeed, builds on: (1) the person-in-environment perspective, with emphasis on environmental intervention; (2) the interpersonal communication and relationship skills for use in management, committee work, and constituency building; and (3) the analysis of policy to effect social change.

Gender Issues in Macro Practice

There is an apparent gender-related dilemma in macro practice. Although women comprise over 75 percent of the professional social work labor force, men are disproportionately represented in the macro arenas of practice. There are several possible explanations for this situation: (1) Women tend to choose practice roles that emphasize relational connections; (2) women are more interested in part-time employment; and (3) to achieve greater professional status, men have actively been sought out to fill these roles.

It is equally likely that, as the profession began its dramatic push toward professionalism and scientific practice, men became preferred in managerial positions, and male professors (and there were many more male than female professors) were more likely to advise male students toward macro practice concentrations and macro practice careers.

Whatever the history and the reason, women have recently begun moving into managerial and administrative positions in social service settings. There are currently more women faculty in social work programs (although significantly fewer are tenured compared to men), and approximately 65 percent of all doctoral students enrolled in social work are women (CSWE, 1991). As more women become leaders in practice and in education, it will be interesting to compare data on the specializations that women and men choose. If women do not choose to specialize in macro practice because they see it as incompatible with their values or with their management style, then the profession will be challenged to highlight the similarities between micro and macro practice and to clarify that, although the means (micro or macro strategies) may differ, the ends are ultimately the same. Further, we would hope that social work managers and administrators will continue to link their own skills in interpersonal relationships with a desire to nurture or support their employees in the management arena. This we believe will influence management and administration practice toward the creation of more humanistic macro practice models.

Conclusion

Neither micro nor macro methods, nor the role sets within them, are inherently better or more necessary to the professional practice of social work. In the real world of practice after completing an MSW, many social workers find themselves needing some combination of these methods to be successful. For example, the agency-based therapist still needs the knowledge base and the skills to understand how organizations are structured to deliver services and achieve certain goals. The therapist needs to have an understanding of policies (city, county, state, federal) that influence agency regulations and affect client choices. Likewise, the macro practitioner needs the knowledge of how group process works in order to deal with agency task forces or community groups.

As we read in Chapter 1, Luz began her career in clinical social work, but planned carefully during her MSW program, enrolling in administrative courses to pave the way to an agency executive position. Nancy knew she needed not only practice skills, but knowledge about budgets, public relations, and marketing to establish and maintain a successful private practice. Ryan expertly combined his undergraduate activism with advocacy skills to become successful in the political arena after completing his MSW degree.

The aforementioned generalist skills as well as the generic problem-solving approach are common to both advanced micro and macro methods of practice. Defining the problem, considering alternatives, analyzing predictable outcomes, developing interventive techniques, and monitoring the follow-through are the common steps of any social work method. Both micro and macro practice build on generalist knowledge and skills and each method is enhanced by the other. The quality of advanced macro practice is enhanced by incorporating essential micro skills and, likewise, micro practice is enhanced by careful consideration of the macro "bigger picture."

Summary

Advanced micro and macro practice methods have been reviewed to demonstrate both commonalities and differences. The two primary levels of social work education were discussed as preparation for entry-level practice (BSW) or for advanced practice (MSW). Both micro and macro practitioners share the same global, professional goal of achieving a more just society by improving the quality of life for all persons. These groups essentially differ only in the means or methods by which they work to achieve this goal. The range of human needs that challenge professional social workers calls for knowledge, expertise, and commitment from practitioners at both the micro- and macrolevels of intervention.

References

Alinsky, Saul D. *Reveille for Radicals.* New York: Vintage Books, 1969.
———. *Rules for Radicals: A Pragmatic Primer for Realistic Radicals.* New York: Vintage Books, 1971.
Chodorow, Nancy. *The Reproduction of Mothering: Psychoanalysis and the Sociology of Gender.* Berkeley, CA: University of California Press, 1978.
Council on Social Work Education (CSWE). *Statistics on Social Work Education in the United States: 1990.* Alexandria, VA: Council on Social Work Education, 1991.
Haynes, Karen S., and James S. Mickelson. *Affecting Change: Social Workers in the Political Arena,* 2nd ed. New York: Longman, 1991.
Hoffman, Martin L. "Sex Differences in Empathy and Related Behaviors," *Psychological Bulletin,* Vol. 84, No. 4 (1977): 712–722.
Keefe, Thomas. "Empathy and Social Work Education: A Study." *Journal of Education for Social Work,* Vol. 11, No. 3 (Fall 1975): 69–75.

Kramer, Ralph, and Harry Specht, eds. *Readings in Community Organization Practice,* 3rd ed. Englewood Cliffs, NJ: Prentice-Hall, 1983.

Meyer, Carol H. "Direct Practice in Social Work: Overview." In *Encyclopedia of Social Work,* 18th ed., 409–422. Edited by Anne Minahan. Silver Spring, MD: NASW, 1987.

Minahan, Anne. "Purpose and Objectives of Social Work Revisited." *Social Work,* Vol. 26, No. 1 (Jan. 1981): 5–6.

Richmond, Mary E. *Social Diagnosis.* New York: Russell Sage Foundation, 1917.

UNIT FOUR

The Changing Profession of Social Work

When and how does an occupation become a profession? What occurs in the development to support this as a goal? What are current professional issues as we face the year 2000? What is social work's professional identification? Chapter 11 provides a historical perspective to the evolution of social work as a profession. Chapter 12 illustrates current and future issues within the profession and Chapter 13 describes action steps for the profession to improve its identity. Chapter 14 predicts future challenges and growth.

The Profession of Social Work

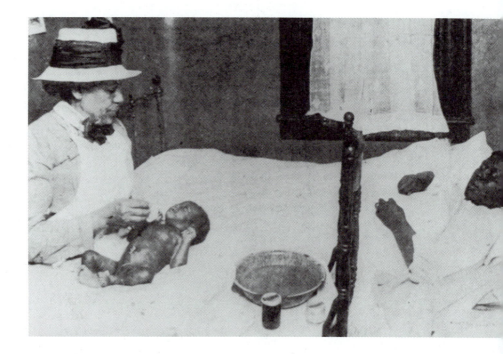

Introduction

*The professor watches David, LaDonna, Kimberley, and Lisa in ani-
mated conversation at the back of the classroom. Their camaraderie
has been satisfying, as has their interest in continuing studies in social
work. She knows that these four have all registered for the next social
work course.*

*With only a quarter of the semester to finish, the professor looks
forward to seeing some of them again in a future class. She begins:*

*"I know that we have spent some time, maybe more time than
some of you had hoped, on the history of social welfare abroad and in
the United States. Whereas the history of the profession is inextricably
linked to these events, looking at that history separately will allow us
to take away another perspective. Social workers sometimes forget
that our professional history is really only 100 years old and significant professionalization has occurred during the last 40 years. Social
work is a comparatively young profession."*

Professional Beginnings: 1890–1930

If you reflect back to what you learned in Chapter 2, you will recall
that this time period represented a time of national expansion
through immigration, increased westward movement, industrialization, and several economic recessions. Rugged individualism
paralleled increasing recognition of social and individual problems.

It was a period in which women's roles were changing due to
urbanization, industrialization, and World War I. It was also a period during which social work education and professional social
work began to take shape.

Many of the initiatives that led to the establishment of these

The first YMCA, founded in 1844 in the City of London.

new social welfare organizations and the emergence of the new profession of social work came from a relatively select group of individuals. Both men and women were involved in these efforts, but women's contributions are especially noteworthy because they came at a time when few women had career options, and those available careers did not include expectations of female leadership or high visibility.

In describing the emergence of social work, it is important to acknowledge the work of men such as Clifford Beers, Richard C. Cabot, Edward T. Devine, Harry Hopkins, and Ernest Greenwood.

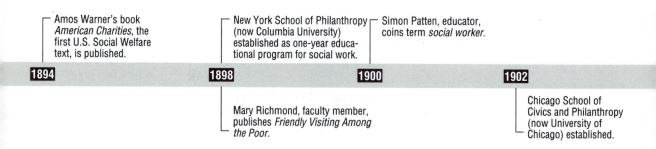

Amos Warner's book *American Charities*, the first U.S. Social Welfare text, is published.

New York School of Philanthropy (now Columbia University) established as one-year educational program for social work.

Simon Patten, educator, coins term *social worker*.

1894

1898

1900

1902

Mary Richmond, faculty member, publishes *Friendly Visiting Among the Poor.*

Chicago School of Civics and Philanthropy (now University of Chicago) established.

But we will also look at the many women who served in positions of leadership and authority: in charities and hospital social work—Ida Cannon, Mary Jarrett, Mary Richmond; in settlements—Jane Addams, Mary McDowell, Lillian Wald; in education—Edith Abbott, Sophonisba Breckenridge, Grace Coyle, Mary Parker Follett; in public administration—Grace Abbott, Julia Lathrop, Frances Perkins, Jeannette Rankin, Barbara Mikulski; and in social action and reform—nearly all of these women, plus the indomitable Florence Kelley, played significant roles (Clark Chambers, 1986, p. 7).

Social Work Practice Developments

In the United States, the profession of social work grew directly and simultaneously out of the work of both the Charity Organization Societies and the settlements at the turn of the twentieth century. As described in Chapters 2 and 10, these movements began the formalization of services, and have been referred to as initiating casework, groupwork, and community organization. Services that had previously been fragmented and delivered in an unplanned fashion, predominantly by female friendly visitors, became formalized organizations with paid employees—mostly women—delivering more standardized services.

At the same time that social work education was becoming more formalized, a number of significant developments were occurring in practice settings. Medical social work was introduced in 1905 at Boston's Massachusetts General Hospital by Dr. Richard C. Cabot, who hired Ida M. Cannon to work in the hospital's outpatient department. The first psychiatric social worker, Mary Jarrett, was also hired at Massachusetts General. The country's newly established juvenile court system employed social workers as family caseworkers and child welfare specialists. In public school settings, social workers worked as visiting teachers dealing with those "for

Social Work Department established at Massachusetts General Hospital.

Abraham Flexner, in speech to National Conference on Social Welfare, declares that social work is not a profession.

American Association of Hospital Social Workers formed (later the American Association of Medical Social Workers).

1905   **1915**   **1917**   **1918**

Mary Richmond publishes *Social Diagnosis* as an answer to Flexner.

National Social Workers Exchange (later American Association of Social Workers) founded.

Smith College establishes first program for psychiatric social workers.

whom neither the attendance officer, school nurse, nor classroom teacher was equipped" (Roy Lubove, 1965, p. 39). In 1918 the American Association of Hospital Social Workers was organized, followed by the National Association of School Social Workers in 1919. Social work was first practiced in "host" settings such as hospitals, jails, and schools, so social workers formed associations around those common settings. By 1921 the National Social Workers Exchange became the American Association of Social Workers, the first national professional social work association.

Social workers found themselves providing services in institutions such as hospitals, courts, and schools where a variety of other professionals worked, and where their own professional status began to take on particular significance. Most were eager to disassociate themselves from the unpaid, untrained volunteers in Charity Organization Societies and settlements. Many felt that the existence of formal, university-based training for social work, along with paid employment in the field, were evidence that social work had achieved the status of a profession. To confirm this perception, the National Conference on Charities and Corrections invited Abraham Flexner, the leading authority of the day on medical education, to speak at their 1915 meeting. Those who hoped Flexner would legitimize social work's status as a profession were disappointed by his address, "Is Social Work a Profession?"

Flexner had a fixed notion of what constituted a profession. He stated that professions "involve essentially intellectual operations with large individual responsibility, derive their raw material from science and learning, this material they work up to a practical and definite end, possess an educationally communicable technique, tend to self organization, and are becoming increasingly altruistic in motivation" (Abraham Flexner, 1916, p. 580). Flexner's judgment that social work did not meet these criteria had signifi-

Association of Training Schools for Professional Social Work (later the American Association of Schools of Social Work, now the Council on Social Work Education).

American Association of Social Workers formed.

James Tufts publishes report on social work education, *Education and Training for Social Work*, which recommends individual as well as societal change.

1919　　　　　　　**1921**　　　　　　　**1923**

Social Workers in schools organize the National Association of Visiting Teachers.

Eduard Lindeman publishes *The Community*, which includes first delineation of community organization.

cant impact. Social workers diligently struggled to satisfy the criteria with the hope of helping social work achieve recognition as a full-fledged profession.

Each twentieth-century accomplishment in the field of social work—from the establishment of the National Association of Social Workers to an emphasis on the integration of scientific research and practice—has been celebrated as another step in the battle for recognition. It was not until several decades later, in the 1950s and 1960s, that questions were raised about the accuracy of the criteria or the appropriateness of allowing a medical educator to be the judge of social work. After closer scrutiny, it became evident that these standards were established to protect and enhance the status of medicine against the claims of other occupational groups (David Austin, 1983, p. 373).

On balance, it was not so much the inability of social work to satisfy Flexner's criteria—if indeed they were appropriate criteria in the first place—that prevented social work from achieving a professional identity. There were a variety of other obstacles as well, not the least of which was the perception of social work as predominately a "woman's occupation." In this respect, social work was not alone. This was a problem shared by nursing, library science, and primary and secondary education; each of these professions sought professional status and the recognition and acceptance that comes with it.

Social casework embraced Freudian concepts in the 1920s, partly in an attempt to satisfy Flexner's criteria for a unifying body of knowledge. It was soon evident, however, that the fields of social work practice had become so varied that the term *casework* had become virtually meaningless, except in specific agency contexts. Even the American Association of Social Workers could not bring about agreement on the essential features of casework practice.

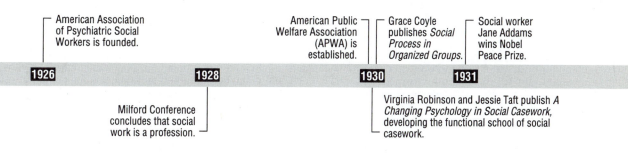

American Association of Psychiatric Social Workers is founded.

American Public Welfare Association (APWA) is established.

Grace Coyle publishes *Social Process in Organized Groups.*

Social worker Jane Addams wins Nobel Peace Prize.

1926   **1928**   **1930**   **1931**

Milford Conference concludes that social work is a profession.

Virginia Robinson and Jessie Taft publish *A Changing Psychology in Social Casework,* developing the functional school of social casework.

From 1923 to 1929, professional leaders met annually at the Milford Conference to redefine the generic basis of casework. The final 1928 conference report defined the distinguishing characteristic of social casework as the capacity of individuals to structure their social activities within a given environment. This definition was a departure from Mary Richmond's original emphasis on the reciprocal relationship between individuals and their social environments (Donald Brieland, 1987, p. 744).

Social Work Education

The emerging profession of social work strengthened its identity by initiating formal training as a requirement for employment. At the 1897 National Conference on Charities and Corrections, Mary Richmond, then director of the Baltimore Charity Organization Society, outlined the concept of organized training for charity workers. The following year, Edward T. Devine, executive director of the New York COS, initiated a six-week summer training program for social workers called the New York School of Applied Philanthropy, with Richmond as one of the instructors. By 1910, the program had expanded to a two-year program of preparation for practice in a field that was increasingly being called "social work."

By 1912, the basic thrust of social work education was established. The practice and educational communities debated whether social work education should focus on social analysis and reform, or on the dissemination of practice wisdom for case work with individuals and families; an agreement was developed favoring the latter.

This position had been strongly advocated by Richmond, who came to the New York COS in 1905 to be on the editorial staff of

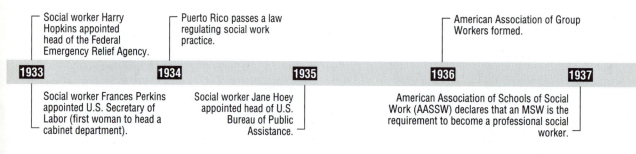

Social worker Harry Hopkins appointed head of the Federal Emergency Relief Agency.

Puerto Rico passes a law regulating social work practice.

American Association of Group Workers formed.

1933 **1934** **1935** **1936** **1937**

Social worker Frances Perkins appointed U.S. Secretary of Labor (first woman to head a cabinet department).

Social worker Jane Hoey appointed head of U.S. Bureau of Public Assistance.

American Association of Schools of Social Work (AASSW) declares that an MSW is the requirement to become a professional social worker.

Charities and the Commons, the first professional social work journal. Using the journal as a platform, she argued for an emphasis on the practical preparation of social workers, and used case records as teaching materials to draw on the professional experience of practitioners. This position also argued for a strong emphasis on field work experience for students and a close working relationship with existing social welfare agencies. Richmond also discouraged the affiliation of social work training with established universities, which she felt would place too much emphasis on traditional intellectual training and too little emphasis on practice competence developed through applied field work.

In the end, Richmond's point of view with respect to case work emphasis, communication of the collective wisdom of practitioners, and inclusion of significant field experience prevailed, even though training for the new profession rapidly became linked with colleges and universities. By 1919, the 17 schools of social work in the United States formed the Association of Training Schools for Professional Social Work (the precursor to the current Council on Social Work Education). By 1923, 13 of these schools were affiliated with or located in universities. In 1927 the Association of Training Schools became the American Association of Schools of Social Work (AASSW).

Among the most striking features of the educational model developed during these years are its resilience and its longevity. As David Austin (1983) has noted:

> Edward Devine's speech on the curriculum of the
> professional school of social work at the 1915 national
> conference (of Charities and Corrections) reflected the
> developments at the New York School. That speech, taken

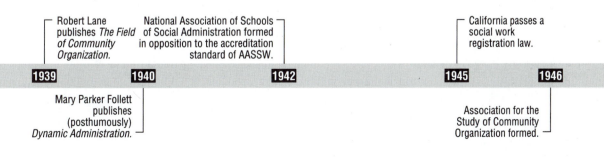

Robert Lane publishes *The Field of Community Organization.*

National Association of Schools of Social Administration formed in opposition to the accreditation standard of AASSW.

California passes a social work registration law.

1939   1940   1942   1945   1946

Mary Parker Follett publishes (posthumously) *Dynamic Administration.*

Association for the Study of Community Organization formed.

together with statements that followed by faculty members from schools of social work in Boston and St. Louis, could readily serve as an outline for a School of Social Work accreditation review today. Social work education was for persons (primarily women) who were college graduates. It involved a combination of field work and academic classes. The program preferably would take two years, with the first year being general and the second year providing for specialization. Devine suggested that the first priority among curriculum subjects was a "course which deals with individuals and families and their complicated disabilities." "Of such a course directed field work in organized charity, probation, medical social service, etc. is an essential part." After the study of family rehabilitation, the next important element was "the history and nature of social movements." Specialized studies in such subjects as health and hygiene, social legislation, and penology might be included, as well as courses in social statistics and administrative problems. (p. 360)

"Geez," says Jennifer, *"it doesn't look like much has changed in education. That's the kind of curriculum my sister had in her BSW program."*

Tricia responds, *"Well, it seems that we've learned all semester that social work is a balance of knowing and doing and has developed from lots of different theories. I guess that's as true today as it was in the 1920s."*

"But it seemed like there were more social reformers then," sighed Kimberley.

"Take heart," the professor cautions, *"there have been changes and there still are social reformers in our profession."*

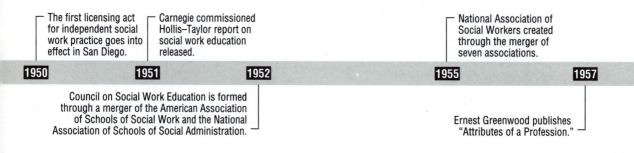

The first licensing act for independent social work practice goes into effect in San Diego.

Carnegie commissioned Hollis–Taylor report on social work education released.

National Association of Social Workers created through the merger of seven associations.

1950   **1951**   **1952**   **1955**   **1957**

Council on Social Work Education is formed through a merger of the American Association of Schools of Social Work and the National Association of Schools of Social Administration.

Ernest Greenwood publishes "Attributes of a Profession."

Women in the Profession

During this time period, the first "social workers" were often part of the first generation of graduates from the new women's colleges in New England and the Middle Atlantic states. Most came from middle-class and upper-middle-class backgrounds and were seeking careers rather than the traditional path to marriage, family, and homemaking. Although a handful of talented and assertive women in that generation became doctors, lawyers, and even preachers, these professions were relatively closed to them. Even fewer women were able to establish careers in business, engineering, science, or government service.

In contrast, women constituted the vast majority of persons engaged in service professions such as nursing, teaching, and library work, although the administrative structures in these fields were dominated by men. Consequently, social work was one of the few developing professions where women had an opportunity to pursue a career and to achieve a leadership position.

In the years between 1890 and 1930, social work created a trend all its own among developing professions in that women, as well as men, became administrators of social agencies, directors of field work, chairs of academic and agency departments, deans of schools of social work, and heads of government bureaus. Equally with men, women initiated research projects; authored books and articles; and advocated for public policies bearing on social welfare in housing, conditions of labor, schooling, public health, mother's assistance, juvenile justice, and children's codes.

As has already been noted, from social work's beginnings, far more women than men have been involved either as volunteers or as paid employees. It is interesting to note that for a number of years, roughly between 1915 and 1930, women were equally represented

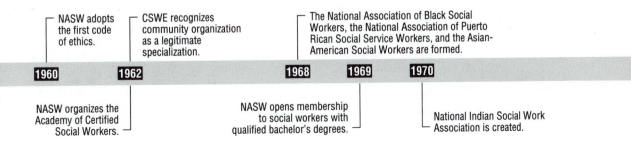

NASW adopts the first code of ethics.

CSWE recognizes community organization as a legitimate specialization.

The National Association of Black Social Workers, the National Association of Puerto Rican Social Service Workers, and the Asian-American Social Workers are formed.

1960   1962   1968   1969   1970

NASW organizes the Academy of Certified Social Workers.

NASW opens membership to social workers with qualified bachelor's degrees.

National Indian Social Work Association is created.

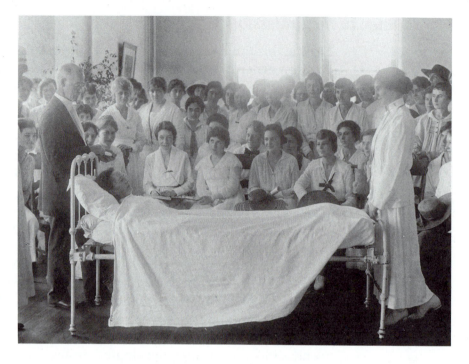

Dr. John A. Houston conducting a Smith School for Social Work class in psychiatry at Northampton State Hospital, 1918.

in leadership roles. Both men and women in this period began to consider social work as a career, and to depend on the salary they received as a social worker to support themselves and their dependents.

Many of the social workers of this period, both women and men, were remarkable individuals. In particular, considering the historical context, the decisions made by many women were rather extraordinary. Not only did these women move outside the cultural expectations in accepting full-time, paid employment in

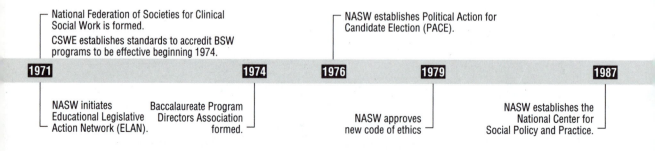

National Federation of Societies for Clinical Social Work is formed.
CSWE establishes standards to accredit BSW programs to be effective beginning 1974.

NASW establishes Political Action for Candidate Election (PACE).

1971   **1974**   **1976**   **1979**   **1987**

NASW initiates Educational Legislative Action Network (ELAN).

Baccalaureate Program Directors Association formed.

NASW approves new code of ethics

NASW establishes the National Center for Social Policy and Practice.

the community, but they also adopted personal life-styles that were at odds with the prevailing norms for females of the era, norms that revered marriage and child bearing as women's primary responsibilities.

> Congregate living in many settlement houses provided a kind of surrogate extended family, knit by mutual affection and grounded in shared values and shared experiences, for many women who had settled into neighborhood work as a career and as a way of life. In such environments, very special friendships were often formed that served to sustain and comfort each partner and to strengthen her in personal and social encounters. . . . We do not know how extensive such arrangements were—extensive enough in that generation to inspire their designation as "Boston marriages"—and there are many examples from among prominent social work leaders. "Lesbian" was not yet a term used to describe such relationships, yet it seems logical to speculate that some companionships undoubtedly involved sexual intimacy and that many of them reflected those emotional ties that define women-loving women. The kind of sharing and reciprocal caring that mark such relationships between two human beings was likely to be of crucial significance in the course of personal and professional lives. (Clark Chambers, 1986, p. 19)

Despite these women's personal lives, they remained committed to professional activities that supported and reinforced a traditional family ethic—an ethic based on the dominant ideology of "proper" family and work roles as defined by a patriarchal society and the social, political, and economic needs of capitalism (Mimi Abramovitz, 1988). Many social workers understandably shared the cultural assumptions that surrounded them and justified careers in human service for women because such work exemplified the values of nurturance and care. But unlike all other professions and semiprofessions in that generation, social work provided authentic opportunities for women to achieve positions of responsibility and power (Clark Chambers, 1986, p. 21).

Social Work Expansion: The 1930s and 1940s

As the nation sank into the Great Depression, which was set off by the stock market crash in 1929, social work and social workers rose to the challenge of confronting society's ills. And when numerous public social programs emerged from New Deal legislation, there were far too few professional social workers to fill all of these newly created positions.

The field of social work began to undergo a number of dramatic changes during this period, due in large part to the nation's depressed economic conditions and to a variety of internal professional struggles. Confronted with large-scale social problems such as unemployment and poverty, the profession had to face the reality that casework could not adequately address these problems. In these times, unemployment and the consequent poverty could not be seen as the result of weak moral character or individual failure. Social workers could—and did—help individuals and families through these difficult times, but the newly created public social programs required different sets of practice skills.

Social Work Practice Developments

Not surprisingly, many social workers of the era were less concerned with the features of casework than with the emerging methods of social group work. Whereas most caseworkers and casework agencies had roots in the charity organization movement, social group work evolved out of the settlements. Grace Coyle was a leading figure in the group work movement. The term *group work* was first used in 1927 at Western Reserve University. By 1937, 13 institutions, 10 of them schools of social work, were offering instruction in group work practice.

The National Conference on Social Work added a group work section in 1935, and the National Association for the Study of Group Work was organized a year later. The method gained further strength in the 1940s as it proved an effective vehicle for providing psychotherapeutic services to large numbers of war-shocked survivors in Veteran's Administration facilities.

The depression era also saw the further development of community work. During World War I, Community Chests (precursor to United Way) had developed as a mechanism for coordinated fund raising in communities. The Depression, the continuing growth of large urban areas, and the labor movement focused attention on problems such as poverty, unemployment, and discrimination—problems that required community action rather than casework services alone. The identification of community organization as a method of social work practice was somewhat slower to evolve and somewhat less well-defined than those of casework and group work. But by 1946, the Association for the Study of Community Organization, another outgrowth of a section of the national conference, was formed. Sophonisba Breckenridge, Mary Parker Follett, and Edith Abbott were early social workers who advocated for broadening the profession's base to include concerns with social policy and administration. Breckenridge developed the first social welfare administration course in 1921 at the University of Chicago School of Civics and Philanthropy. Follett published the first book on administration several years later, but her work did not enjoy general acceptance until after her death.

Social Work Education

By 1932 a minimum curriculum in the social work programs included at least one academic year of course work and field instruction. Accreditation of these programs was initiated. In 1935, the American Association of Schools of Social Work (AASSW) established the rule that only training programs affiliated with universities and colleges could be accredited. Soon after, the AASSW decided that accredited programs must require two years of postbaccalaureate study.

However, many public institutions of higher education had attempted to meet the demand in the fast growing public sector through a different format: a four-year undergraduate program, followed by a one-year master's program. Because these programs did not meet the AASSW requirements for accreditation, these schools formed the National Association of Schools of Social Administration (NASSA) in 1942. Predictably, these conflicting standards caused confusion. So in 1946 these two groups came together through a grant by the Carnegie Corporation to study social work education.

Women in the Profession

Women retained positions of prominence and leadership in social work until approximately 1930. At that time, men began to emerge into leadership positions in disproportionate numbers. As in law, medicine, and higher education, men became directors of agencies and graduate schools, and moved into directing public policy and welfare administration. A number of factors contributed to the dissolution of the unique partnership between women and men that had existed for some four decades. One factor was the gradual fading of the residence principle in settlement houses. This weakened the morale of settlement workers, particularly the women, and diluted the sense of shared mission and purpose that came from living together under the same roof. Another factor was depression employment rules, which explicitly favored men on the grounds that they were the chief wage earners for families, and should therefore have higher priority than women for jobs.

Still another factor may have been a double standard in the growing acceptance of dual roles for women, at home and in the workplace. Although dual roles became more acceptable, there was still an expectation that women who worked would give priority to family needs over career needs when the two conflicted. In an earlier time, women had to choose between marriages and careers; many prominent social work leaders chose to direct their energies to the profession and achieved high visibility, autonomy, and leadership positions in the process. From 1930 on, many women attempted to combine both roles. They left supervisory, administrative, and leadership posts to the men in social work who could pursue them full-time. Women, on the other hand, worked part-time, or temporarily left the field to bear and rear children.

Finally, social work was continuing to try to meet the requirements of a profession during this period, and the models from other professions suggested that male executives would garner more respect. In fact, the number of male students studying macro practices was disproportionate to the total male enrollment in social work programs. And these macro areas better prepared them for these leadership positions. According to some social scientists near midcentury, the efforts of social work to achieve professional status were doomed because of the overrepresentation of women in its ranks (Amitai Etzioni, 1969).

Of course, there were some women who continued to hold on to tradition: Margaret Berry, Helen Hall, and Helen Harris in the settlement movement; Eveline Burns, Jane Hoey, Katherine Oettinger, and Frances Perkins in social policy and administration; Gisela Konopka, Helen Harris Perlman, Charlotte Towle, Elizabeth Wisner, and Gertrude Wilson in education. But the imbalance in influence, power, deference, and rewards between male and female social workers eventually became unmistakable.

Jason, with that look of confusion says, "But isn't social work still considered a woman's profession? I don't understand how you could be saying that men are more in control."

David responds, "When I was looking for services for my partner, Gary, I got a directory of social services in this community. It surprised me that more than 75 percent of our agencies have male executive directors."

"But that's because men can make hard decisions, deal with budgets . . . ," Jason replies, but the class stops him with a collective groan.

Social Work Comes of Age: The 1950s through the 1970s

Although the 1950s witnessed a temporary backlash against public welfare, for the most part, these decades spawned major expansion of public social services. The Economic Opportunity Act of 1964, the Title XX amendments to the Social Security Act of 1974, as well as the creation of formal structures at federal and state levels to deliver social services represent major developments in social welfare policy. These are detailed in Chapter 3, so this will serve as a reminder that this period encompassed the largest expansion of the

U.S. Welfare State, the enhanced diversification of the professional labor force, and the initiation of undergraduate accredited programs in social work.

Social Work Practice Developments

The 1950s were a period when social work made significant strides in professional development. The following seven separate social work organizations that represented specialized areas of practice, interests, or expertise combined forces in 1955 to form the National Association of Social Workers (NASW): the American Association of Medical Social Workers, the National Association of School Social Workers, the American Association of Social Workers, the American Association of Psychiatric Social Workers, the American Association of Group Workers, the Association for the Study of Community Organization, and the Social Work Research Group.

All members of the previous organizations automatically became members of the NASW. Thereafter, all new members were required to hold a graduate degree from an accredited school of social work. Between 1955 and 1965, membership in NASW increased dramatically. The organization immediately began to publish *Social Work,* which was careful to note that one of Flexner's six criteria was satisfied by the development of the NASW as a single, unified professional organization. One of the most significant articles to appear in the new journal was Ernest Greenwood's "Attributes of a Profession" (1957). Like Flexner, Greenwood proposed five critical attributes of a profession. However, unlike Flexner, Greenwood had no difficulty in determining that social work already exhibited most of these attributes and was therefore clearly a profession. One of Greenwood's professional attributes was the presence of a regulative code of ethics; and, although social work did not have such a code in 1957, this was soon remedied when the first NASW Code of Ethics was adopted in 1960.

Other significant developments in the 1960s included substantial growth in the demand for social workers, particularly for workers with specialized training in administration. The division of labor between men and women in social work became even more clearly demarcated in this period as proportionally more men opted for educational programs preparing them for administration, and proportionally more women chose to prepare for direct practice careers. This effect was exacerbated as efforts to recruit more males into social work were stepped up, in no small part as an attempt to elevate the profession's credibility and standing in the public mind, as well as to stimulate higher salaries.

With a greater demand for social workers, more and more universities developed graduate programs awarding the MSW degree. By 1976, there were 82 accredited schools in 37 states, Washington D.C., and Puerto Rico. Despite the increased numbers of accredited graduate schools, and the marginally enhanced professional status for social work, not enough males or females were entering into graduate programs. As a result, in 1969, the NASW made an unprecedented move and broadened its definition of professional practice to include those who had completed an approved bachelor's level course of study in social work at an approved undergraduate institution.

Also recognizing the need for more organized political efforts, the NASW established the Educational Legislative Action Network (ELAN) in 1974 and the Political Action for Candidate Election (PACE) in 1976. These actions set the model for states to follow and legitimized previously unstructured and unprioritized activities.

Social Work Education

To understand the full implication of the NASW's redefinition, we need to discuss the Ernest Hollis and Alice Taylor report. This 1951 Carnegie commissioned study recommended unifying educational standards and led to the official merger of the AASSW and the NASSA into the Council on Social Work Education (CSWE) in 1952. This report, authored by Ernest Hollis and Alice Taylor, recommended a two-year graduate-level training program as the minimum requirement for professional practice. The overall effect of the Hollis–Taylor report, combined with the establishment of the CSWE, was to eliminate bachelor-level social workers from the ranks of social work professionals for nearly 20 years (Ernest Hollis and Alice Taylor, 1951).

Lisa's hand goes up. "Do you mean that no one could be a social worker without an MSW?" she asks incredulously.

"That seems very elitist," LaDonna comments.

"And overqualified for some work," Tricia adds.

"You're all correct, but let's wait to see if there is any explanation," the Professor concludes.

At this time, accreditation of schools of social work was carried out under the authority of the CSWE. However, with the NASW decision to admit bachelor-level members in 1969, the CSWE moved rapidly to create and adopt standards to accredit BSW programs by 1974. The CSWE board of directors further approved action that "advanced standing" of up to one year could be granted to BSW students who entered accredited MSW programs from CSWE approved programs. By 1980, more than 167 BSW programs had become accredited in 47 states, Washington D.C., and Puerto Rico.

These developments had several effects. The social work profession was now accessible to many individuals who could not afford graduate education, to those living where there was no available program, and to those who were turned off by the elitist reputation of graduate school. The acceptance of bachelor-level training as the minimum requirement for professional practice resulted in significantly broadening social work's sphere of influence in social welfare and in the human services. BSW programs tended to attract students who were ethnically, racially, socially, and economically more diverse than those in MSW programs. As a result, their inclusion gave social work a "new face" that was more likely to be male, more likely to be African-American, Hispanic, Asian, or Native American, and perhaps more likely to have been touched by poverty or near poverty.

Doctoral education in social work also increased during this period. Until 1965, there were approximately 17 doctoral programs in the United States. These programs offered either a PhD or a DSW degree with the different degrees reflecting more about the institution in which they were housed than a substantive difference in the program of study. By the end of the 1970s, there were almost 40 doctoral programs.

However, the doctoral degree is not a professional practice degree. Rather it prepares the student for teaching, research, or policy analysis. Thus the CSWE does not accredit doctoral programs, and the MSW remains the terminal professional degree.

There is little doubt that growth in doctoral education during this period was caused by the increased demand for social work educators in the BSW programs as well as increased demands for researchers and policy analysts in the public sector.

Women in the Profession

Although the vast majority of students entering MSW and BSW programs were still female during this time period, women continued to lose ground in leadership positions. One survey of over 800 agencies showed that the percentage of female executives had decreased from 60 percent in 1957 to 16 percent in 1976 (John Szakacs, 1977). It is generally acknowledged that male social workers move into administrative and supervisory positions earlier in their careers and at a much faster rate than women (Mary Valentich and James Gripton, 1978, p. 108).

Both cause and result of this situation is the relative absence of women in significant administrative positions to act as role models and mentors for junior women and to encourage women to enter the macro tract in their graduate programs (Karen Haynes, 1989, pp. 44–45). On the other hand, one positive trend was the increased number of women faculty in social work programs, particularly in the newly emerging BSW programs.

Women in Leadership

Council on Social Work Education (1952)

Helen Wright, president, 1952–1954
Jane Hoey, president, 1956–1958
Grace Coyle, president, 1958–1960
Ruth Smalley, president, 1960–1963
Katherine Kendall, executive director, 1963–1966
Lillian Ripple, acting executive director, 1971–1972
Dorothy Bird Daly, president, 1978–1981
Diane Bernard, interim executive director, 1985–1986
Eunice Shatz, executive director, 1986–1988

Rochelle Gershenow, acting executive director, July
1988–August 1988
Julia Norlin, president, 1989–1992

National Association of Social Workers (1955)

Helen Cassidy, president, 1966–1967
Maryann Mahaffey, president, 1975–1977
Nancy Humphreys, president, 1979–1981
Maryann Quaranta, president, 1981–1983
Dorothy Harris, president, 1983–1985
Annette Maxey, president, 1985–1986
Suzanne Dworak-Peck, president, 1987–1989
Barbara White, president, 1991–1993

*National Association of Deans and Directors of
Social Work Programs* (1980)

Ione Vargas, president, 1981–1983
June Hopps, president, 1987–1989

Association of Baccalaureate Program Directors
(1974)

Trueheart Titzl, president, 1974–1975
Mary Ellen Elwell, president, 1978–1981
Ann McEllean, president, 1981–1983
Judy Norlin, president, 1985–1987
Kay Hoffman, president, 1989–1991

To highlight this point, three of the four presidents of the Association of Baccalaureate Program Directors (BPD) from its founding in 1974 through 1991 were female. By contrast, the NASW had had no female executive directors since its inception in 1955 through 1980, and only 3 of the 15 nationally elected presidents of the NASW were female during this same time frame. The CSWE had 6 executive directors from its beginning in 1952 until 1980, and only 2 were female. The CSWE fared better in the representation of women as elected presidents; during this same period, 5 of 10

CSWE presidents were female. The graduate programs had a very loosely affiliated group with no formalized structure and leadership.

Social Work, the New Federalism, and Beyond: 1980 to Present

As the 1970s drew to a close, it was evident that whereas public support of services had expanded, these public social services had not replaced the traditional not-for-profit services. Furthermore, the enormous federal deficit had become an issue in the presidential platform of the 1980 election. Candidate Reagan's agenda, as noted in Chapter 3 relied on privatization models.

This solution blamed escalating public social service costs on the social work profession. Politicians suggested welfare reform rather than programs targeting illiteracy, high school dropouts, teen pregnancies, and unemployment (Karen Haynes and James Mickelson, 1992, p. 170).

Once elected, President Reagan chose to reduce the deficit by slashing domestic social services. Despite language about "safety nets" for the "worthy poor," the passage of the Gramm–Rudman Balanced Budget and Emergency Deficit Control Act of 1985 was followed by cuts in program funding and levels of benefits.

Proponents argued that there would be no cuts in essential programs for the truly needy because state and local governments and philanthropic associations would replace the lost federal dollars. Further, they argued, "waste" and "fraud" would be reduced. Although these targeted reductions were not directed to the not-for-profit sector, the trickle down effect nonetheless reduced the numbers of people eligible for public services; reduced the numbers and diversity of public social services; and, consequently, increased the demands on the not-for-profit sector. The planned agenda was to return to the private philanthropic model, but the ability of the private sector to replace these cuts in federal expenditures was greatly diminished by the economic recession and the emergence of new social problems. As a result, ironically, the 1980s witnessed an attack on public social services simultaneous with the emergence of large-scale social problems such as AIDS, homelessness, and hunger.

The 1992 election raised domestic issues to priority positions within the campaigns, specifically the economy and health care. This election also represented the first since the NASW's inception where the professional association made an early endorsement in the presidential race for the winning candidate. Social work Political Action Committee (PAC) support and social workers in many state campaign efforts for Bill Clinton at least promise that our professional voice may be heard in a national arena.

Social Work Practice Developments

One extremely detrimental effect on social work practice during the 1970s and 1980s was declassification of social service positions. This will be covered in more detail in Chapter 12; briefly, according to successful arguments, professionally educated social workers were not interested in public social services; on-the-job training was sufficient; and professionally educated employees were overqualified. Thus, by reducing educational qualifications, salaries could be reduced. Consequently, budget reductions and declassification activities spoiled a pivotal moment; the opportunity was lost for enough professional social workers in high enough places in the public sector to make a difference.

As noted in Chapter 3, the profession once again confronted the dilemma of either being agents of social control or agents of social change, and chose the former role. The question of whether this model allowed social work to survive and allowed clients to be served or whether we gave in to political pressure, and which path would have benefited clients most, may never be answered (Karen Haynes and James Mickelson, 1992, p. 177).

On the other hand, the 1980s, more than any decade in our professional history, signaled the achievement of increased public sanction of our professional status through the passage of state statutes regarding the legal regulation of social work practice. By 1992, all states had passed such legislation.

The 1980s began a resurgence of advocacy, which has continued into the 1990s. More articles and books were published about advocacy and political skills, including Steve Burghardt's *The Other Side of Organizing;* Robert Fisher's *Let the People Decide: Neighborhood Organizing in America;* Karen Haynes and James Mickelson's *Affecting Change: Social Workers in the Political Arena;*

and Maryann Mahaffey and John Hanks's *Practical Politics: Social Work and Political Responsibility.*

Coalitions formed on local, state, and national levels to combat the attacks of this new federalism. Generations United merged previously competing interests of children and the aged. The national Children's Defense Fund and Child Welfare League assumed stronger leads in the public policy debate. This may be the one positive outcome of the Reagan era.

Social Work Education

As an illustration of this return to advocacy, in 1982 the Council on Social Work Education included in its curriculum policy statement the assertion that students should be prepared "to exert leadership and influence as legislative and social advocates, lobbyists, and expert advisors to policy makers and administrators" in ways that "will further the achievement of social work goals and purposes." Furthermore, increased interest in social work education is well documented through the enrollment and admissions application data collected by CSWE.

Moreover, the managerial and bureaucratic language of the 1970s began to be replaced in the curriculum and writings with the language of advocacy. In a 1989 survey, 42 of 100 MSW graduate schools had courses on community organization, advocacy, and/or planned change (Kenneth Cornman, 1989). In fact, one MSW program has established a specialization in political social work.

During this same time frame, the formal acceptance of part-time social work education occurred, an acknowledgment of the increased demand for professionally educated social workers with the economic realities of the severe shortage of student stipends and agency educational leaves. The growth of social work educational programs at all three educational levels continued, although a few BSW programs collapsed under the weight of higher education budget reductions. In 1992, there were approximately 103 accredited MSW programs, 375 accredited BSW programs, and 49 doctoral programs in the United States. A total of 32,325 students were enrolled in BSW programs, 29,368 were enrolled in MSW programs, and 2,100 were enrolled in doctoral programs (CSWE, 1991).

Women in the Profession

Although the statistics on the number of female students in BSW and MSW programs did not significantly change during this time period, the number of females entering and completing doctoral programs in social work increased. In 1990, 67.8 percent of doctoral students were female, whereas two decades previously this percentage would have been reversed (CSWE, 1991). This trend will provide a strong counterargument to the traditional explanation that few women hold doctorates and thus few women rise to the rank of full professors in social work higher education, or become administrators or agency executives.

In fact, in BSW programs, the number of female faculty at two of the three academic ranks was higher than for male faculty: Thirty-three percent of the full professors, 50 percent of the associate professors, and 63 percent of the assistant professors were female. Also during this time frame, three of six BPD presidents were female.

However, within the graduate programs, the number of female faculty at all academic ranks was substantially lower than for male faculty: Thirty-three percent of full professors, 42 percent of associate professors, and 60 percent of the assistant professors were female in graduate and joint programs (CSWE, 1990). Leadership in the National Association of Deans and Directors (NADD) also reflected these statistics. The NADD became more structured during the early 1980s and since that time has had six presidents, but only two females. However, it is also true that the numbers of female deans in graduate programs increased threefold from 1980 to present.

During this time frame the NASW did not include many women in leadership positions. Although in the early 1990s over 70 percent of the NASW membership was female, to date, the NASW has had—in its 25-year history—only one female executive director (who served only one year). However, four of the six presidents who have served since 1981 have been women.

Of the five CSWE executive directors during this time frame, three were women (however, two of the three were Acting); of the six presidents, two were women. We would be remiss if we did not mention that social worker Barbara Mikulski (D-MD), who served from 1976 to 1986 in the U.S. House of Representatives, became the first social worker elected to the U.S. Senate in 1987. Women's roles in social work were changing once again.

"Why are we making such a big deal about the number of women in leadership positions in social work? I guess I thought the current concerns were to attract more men into the field," Jahad interjects.

"Yeah," agrees Jason. "I'm constantly getting kidded about being in this class with all these women."

"Well, let me tell you, if I hadn't heard Etta talking about her career and her education, I might not be here today. It was important for me to see a successful black woman. Then, I believed I might be able to do it too," LaDonna entered forcefully.

"The profession wants and needs talented and committed people, both female and male. We don't want to discourage men from thinking about social work because it's 'woman's work,' nor do we want women to believe that administration and politics are 'men's work.' We'll be talking more about some of these issues in the remaining weeks of class."

Summary

In the 100 years of the development of social work in the United States, the movement from the "charity" model to formalized and professional services is well established. The more serious professionalization, however, started in the mid-1950s.

Clearly, in its early development, our profession has withstood attempts to dismantle its services, reduce its importance, and smear its reputation. Social work's ability to withstand this pressure and to use it to examine its educational structure and underpinnings, its professional membership, and its primary commitment seems to predict that it will continue to move forward not only to gain increased stature but to significantly contribute to the programs and the conscience of this country.

As we observed in Chapters 2 and 3, the history of the profession, its services, the educational system, and its workers are both reflective of and reactive to larger social and demographic issues.

References

Abramovitz, Mimi. *Regulating the Lives of Women: Social Welfare Policy from Colonial Times to the Present.* Boston, MA: South End Press, 1988.

Austin, David. "The Flexner Myth and the History of Social Work." *Social Service Review*, Vol. 57 (Sept. 1983): 357–376.

Brieland, Donald. "History and Evolution of Social Work Practice." In *Encyclopedia of Social Work*, 18th ed., 739–754. Edited by Anne Minahan. Silver Spring, MD: NASW, 1987.

Burghardt, Steve. *The Other Side of Organizing: Resolving the Personal Dilemmas and the Political Demands of Daily Practice.* Cambridge, MA: Schenkman Publishing, 1982.

Chambers, Clark. "Women in the Creation of the Profession of Social Work." *Social Service Review*, Vol. 60 (March 1986): 7.

Cornman, Kenneth. *Community Organization Reference Manual for Social Work Graduate Schools.* New Jersey: Rutgers University, 1989.

Council on Social Work Education (CSWE). *Statistics on Social Work Education in the United States: 1990.* Alexandria, VA: CSWE, 1991.

Etzioni, Amitai, ed. *The Semi-Professions and Their Organizations: Teachers, Nurses, Social Workers.* New York: Free Press, 1969.

Fisher, Robert. *Let the People Decide: Neighborhood Organizing in America.* Boston: Twayne, 1984.

Flexner, Abraham. "Is Social Work a Profession?" In *Proceedings of the National Conference of Charities and Corrections 1915*, 576–590. Chicago: Hildmann, 1916.

Greenwood, Ernest. "Attributes of a Profession." *Social Work*, Vol. 2, No. 3 (July 1957): 45–55.

Haynes, Karen S. *Women Managers in Human Services.* New York: Springer Publishing, 1989.

Haynes, Karen S., and James S. Mickelson. *Affecting Change: Social Workers in the Political Arena.* New York: Longman, 1991.

———. "Social Work and the Reagan Era: Challenges to the Profession." *Sociology and Social Welfare on "The Reagan Legacy,"* Vol. 19, No. 1 (1992): 169–183.

Hollis, Ernest, and Alice Taylor. *Social Work Education in the United States.* New York: Columbia University Press, 1951.

Lubove, Roy. *The Professional Altruist, The Emergence of Social Work as a Career, 1880–1930.* Cambridge: Harvard University Press, 1965.

Mahaffey, Maryann, and John Hanks, eds. *Practical Politics: Social Work and Political Responsibility.* Silver Spring, MD: NASW, 1982.

Szakacs, John. "Survey Indicates Social Work Women Losing Ground in Leadership." *NASW News*, Vol. 22, No. 4 (1977).

Valentich, Mary, and James Gripton. "Sexism and Sex Differences in Career Management of Social Workers." *Social Science Journal,* Vol. 15, No. 2 (1978): 101–111.

CHAPTER 12

Current Issues

Introduction

" 'Social Worker Lets Child Die at Hands of Parents,' " the professor reads from one of the local newspapers. "Our U.S. Representative to Congress has once again declared that cuts in domestic social service programs can be replaced by volunteer efforts and private contributions. Our state legislature has been embattled around the issue of increasing salaries for state social service employees and some believe that we should reduce the state qualifications for these jobs.

"Whereas I do not necessarily see these news stories as positive, they are, indeed, representative of the kinds of issues facing the profession today. You know that I have planned for this all semester. I'm very pleased that our new NASW state president, Chris Nash, agreed to do this teleconference with us this morning on some of these issues. I trust that you all remember the process and the protocol. Let's see if Ms. Nash is in the state office headquarters."

The equipment on, Ms. Nash begins, "Good morning. I'm delighted to have this opportunity to talk with you about our profession and its challenges. Please feel comfortable to interrupt whenever you have questions.

"Current professional issues can be addressed in many ways. One way is to identify specific concerns that directly affect practicing social workers. Another way is to describe a set of issues that include the context of social work practice. A third category is to group issues that have been of professional concern nationally; and another is to describe concerns of both the profession and the public.

"Included in practitioner concerns are paperwork and technology, worker motivation, and new client problems. Within the organizational issues are those issues related to job descriptions, performance evaluation, and some workplace problems. Professional issues center around quality control and within this topic I will identify strategies such as service delivery effectiveness, personnel classifica-

tion, and legal regulation of practice. Last to be discussed is funding issues within which I have included the issues related to obtaining and maintaining funding, the difficulties of mixed funding, and accountability. Although each category could include quite a lengthy list, I've chosen a limited number for discussion today.

"The strategies by which any profession chooses to address client problems are also inextricably woven with the legal, fiscal, organizational, and managerial issues, with which the profession must deal. I believe that these are not only some of the current issues, but also likely future issues. By discussing these we can predict more fully the nature and context of social work practice for the twenty-first century."

"But I Want to Work with People": *Practitioner Concerns*

Realistically, the concerns of practitioners cannot be separated from the other issues identified earlier because each set of issues influences the other interactively. We know, for example, that practitioners are very concerned about limited funding. Not only does funding affect the quality of services and service delivery efforts overall, but it influences practitioner's very employment possibilities and financial well-being. Similarly, legal regulation of social work practice, although an issue of professional concern for over two decades, can enhance or limit status and employment opportunities for social workers.

However, we wanted to begin this chapter where most social workers are concerned first—with individual practitioner issues. That is, what do social workers struggle with in their practice? What do they worry about? On a daily basis, what are their frustrations and needs? What are the demands and rewards of practice?

Paperwork

We have never met anyone who went into social work so they could "do paperwork." Nonetheless, paperwork, especially in an era of increasing accountability, is a time-consuming reality of social work practice. New social workers often lament the time spent in record keeping and various forms of recording, time that they would prefer to spend working directly with clients. Each agency is likely to have its own policies for record keeping, some requiring only essential client information, some requiring ongoing, detailed progress notes. Keep in mind that whatever the requirements, our clients would be ill-served if no records existed when workers change or when service is interrupted unexpectedly for reasons beyond our control.

This paperwork expanded as a result of several factors: the growth in the public sector and the need for accountability; the initiation of information systems for both client and management; and at varying times, the concern about misuse of services on one end of the pendulum to the concern with reducing fragmentation of service delivery on the other. Also, the professionalization of the field prompted the initiation of more thorough "process recordings." Students and new professionals, in particular, would have a record of service delivered, as well as the interactive processes that were part of that intervention. Knowledge development brings with it the need for increased demographic information and social histories so that patterns can be traced. In addition, recording information about clients served, progress made, or barriers identified serves as an important data base for researchers, policymakers, and program evaluators. It represents the basic material for funding and provides examples for the media.

Accountability may require the need to periodically determine and monitor client eligibility, which translates into repeatedly asking for the same information and employing techniques to verify that information. The result, as well as the complaint, is that social workers spend more time reporting on their interactions with clients than in direct service to those clients.

There is no formula for the percentage of time spent with clients versus paperwork, but it would appear that a balance should be maintained. When professionals spend more time in documentation and clerical functions than in service delivery, that time is nonproductive, wasteful, and as noted earlier, may be another explanation for employee dissatisfaction and consequent "burnout." However, in order to provide quality and individualized service a paper trail is necessary.

"But if you have to spend all your time filling out forms, how can you really be helping people? And, it sounds like paperwork is likely to increase," Tricia inquires.

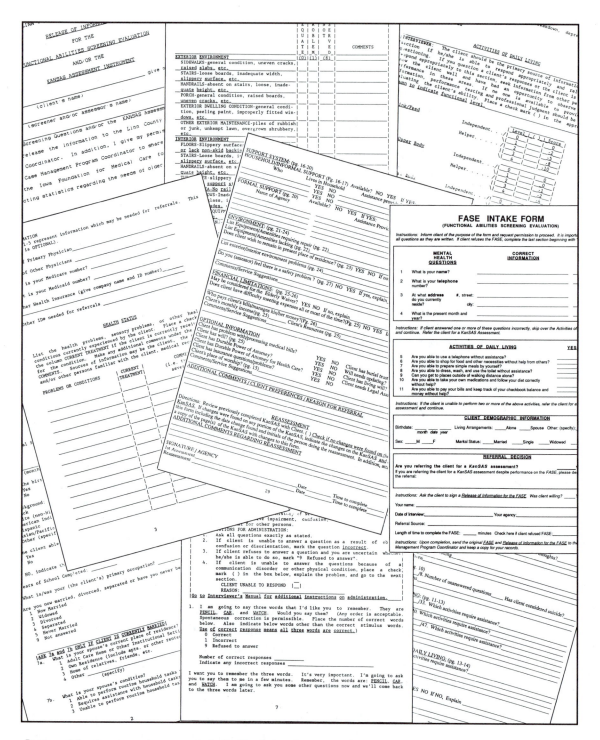

Paperwork has become a clear presence in the life of virtually every social work practitioner.

"Well, let me answer that question a couple of ways," President Nash replies. "You expect your University to keep a paper trail of your progress, don't you? You expect your doctor or dentist to have records of when you've been ill; what you're allergic to; and emergency contact numbers. I know that I expect that in order to get good service. Paperwork demands might increase, but technology, which I'm just about to discuss, ought to help keep the time spent on it in balance."

Technology

Many social workers had great hopes that using computers would simplify record keeping and overall data management, but the initial transition or start-up time for those unfamiliar with computer technology has, in fact, become a stress-inducing process. Over time this will likely change. New practitioners will come to their jobs with computer skills in hand, but, for now, the benefits of computer technology have yet to be fully realized in most agencies.

Social work agencies have been moving, perhaps with some reluctance, into the age of computer technology. The first uses of this technology in social service agencies have been in the management arena with the computerization of personnel and financial records. This has been helpful in managing personnel data, in compiling information needed to demonstrate financial accountability, and in reducing some administrative costs. The computerization of agencies has not so directly benefited the front-line service delivery personnel. In fact, from the practitioner's perspective, there are several concerns about computerization.

Some practitioners have raised concerns about the confidentiality of client records, as well as with the lack of professional judgment when computer programs for assessment or diagnosis are used. Concerns about who might have access (or who might be able to gain unauthorized access) to computerized client files are legitimate given the reality of playful or malicious "hackers," who find it a challenge to enter confidential file systems.

The ability to centralize client information across large geographic regions and/or beyond an organization's boundaries is far easier with computerization. Although this may achieve the goal of coordination of services, it may also be used to prevent clients from being served by multiple agencies.

Further, the use of "canned" assessment or diagnostic software may be viewed as potentially threatening to the practitioner–

client relationship. Some have raised questions as to whether any computer program can individualize clients and their particular problems as well as a competent, caring social worker. Others wonder, "If reasonably valid assessments can be generated from data entered into a computer, then what'll happen to me?" Although this concern may seem farfetched to some, it raises some intriguing questions as to the nature of social work practice. If few enter the profession of social work in order to "do paperwork," fewer yet want to work with computers rather than people.

David interjects, "I left my job, which included a lot of high tech stuff in order to really get involved, really make a difference. Do I have to go back to interacting with a computer?"

"Well, to some extent, yes," President Nash replies carefully. "You, perhaps more than others in this class, probably also realize how efficient a machine can be in retrieving information; in analyzing some of this information; and, provided the information entered is accurate, that the computer has better memory."

"But", Lisa jumps in, "if computers can diagnose client problems, will there be any jobs for us?"

With a grin, President Nash replies, "I'm sure that you all know something about the sophisticated diagnostic technology now available in the medical field, yet the demand for nurses and doctors has not decreased. Why universities, such as your own, have sophisticated computer labs with self-instruction for a variety of courses, yet the need for faculty to interpret and interact is perhaps more important than ever."

The Impact of New Client Problems

At this point in the history of humankind, is there anything really new? As we think about this, and about the nature of human suffering, we have to say "no, but yes." The kinds of social problems seen by the new MSW of the 1960s—racism and poverty, for example—were not new then, and they still exist today. For the new BSW or MSW in the 1990s, the range of contemporary social problems has changed somewhat, but most of all, the range has increased. Racism and poverty are still with us, perhaps less visibly in some cases, but undoubtedly more insidiously ingrained.

What is new on the list of social problems and concerns of social workers? We would suggest the following, all of which have been identified explicitly within the past 25 years: HIV disease, "discovered" in the early 1980s; sexism, "named" in the second wave of feminism in the 1970s; violence against women—battering, sexual assault/rape, incest—also "named" in the second wave of feminism, plus sexual harassment, most explicitly identified by Anita Hill following the nomination of Clarence Thomas to the U.S. Supreme Court in 1991; homelessness, "visible" as of the early 1980s; disappearing health insurance, seen not only among the homeless, but the newly unemployed of the recession in the early 1990s; alcoholism, "crack" cocaine addiction, and the vast array of addictive and dysfunctional family systems, each "named" in the growing recovery movements of the late 1980s.

Each of these "new" client problems raises challenges to social work practitioners, not the least of which is trying to keep up with an everexpanding knowledge base. With new client problems comes the need to know more—about the nature of the problem itself, about the needs of clients with this problem, about the appropriate skills necessary for effective intervention, and about the community resources available. It seems that as soon as we begin to feel confident about what we now know, there are new issues facing us. This speaks to the importance of continuing education for all practitioners. The reality of our work demands continual updating of substantive knowledge, theoretical frameworks, and skills. Our professional education and training, whether at the BSW or the MSW level, is best viewed as a beginning, not as an end. Our professional degrees might better be viewed as "licenses to learn," not only because it is impossible to know all we need to know, but also because what we know becomes out of date all too quickly.

"My mother, who's a social worker, says that probably the most valuable part of her social worker training was the skills part and knowing where to go to find answers to new questions," Jennifer offers supportively.

"Absolutely correct," President Nash agrees, "your social work degree will be invaluable irrespective of changing client or social problems because it will teach you very important knowledge and skills that are transferable to other clients, other problems, and other places."

"Even like working with starving kids in Somalia?" Lisa jumps in.

"Yes."

Burnout

Burnout refers to a form of depression and apathy resulting from on-the-job stress and frustration. It leaves workers unmotivated, uncreative, and often unresponsive, characteristics that are both individually and organizationally counterproductive.

To understand why social workers can become burned out, take a look first at *motivation.* Although there are more than 100 definitions of motivation, probably the simplest has to do with a willingness to work. Most motivational theories separate intrinsic from extrinsic motivation. Intrinsic motivation stems from our willingness to work to satisfy our own needs for growth and challenge, whereas extrinsic motivation results from rewards provided by others. Simply stated, intrinsic motivation comes from internal sources and extrinsic motivation comes from external sources.

There are several different, and somewhat competing, theories of motivation. Some theories of worker's satisfaction suggest that extrinsic factors such as salary, job security, and status can serve as "dissatisfiers," and intrinsic factors such as job content, what we do in our work and how well we feel we do it, may serve as motivators.

So, why do social workers experience burnout or become unmotivated? Historically, it has been assumed that people who enter the profession of social work are intrinsically motivated by altruism, the desire to do good things without expecting specific rewards. However, as we have just described, motivation is likely not that simple, and altruism may need to be balanced by a decent salary and public esteem.

We will explore—and discard—some of these salary and image problems in the next chapter. Why have enrollments in social work programs increased nationally in the late 1980s and early 1990s? Because there are many intrinsic rewards that we hope you have recognized by now. Management literature identifies a variety of strategies to address motivational issues, including task and job enlargement, participatory management styles, bonuses, standardized promotional criteria and intervals, continuous feedback and incentive systems, and "top performers of the month."

Realistically, we cannot generalize the motivations for an entire social work labor force, nor can we identify a single strategy that will work. However, it is useful to keep in mind that both intrinsic and extrinsic motivators, in some balance, are essential for the well-being of all employees. And because an organization is only as effective and productive as its employees, this balance of motivators is crucial to the success of an organization.

"I don't know how I could not get stressed out and down working with people with such terrible problems day after day and probably not getting paid too well," Jason says with discouragement.

Before President Nash can respond, Jahad responds, "I'll tell you, it's hard to describe the feeling, but it's pretty powerful, when a young kid, who looks certain to become a school dropout and a gang member, turns around and gets a scholarship to college and you had something to do with it. Besides, the salaries aren't that bad and I'd rather be working at something meaningful for a little less money, than making more money and not feeling good inside."

The class and President Nash are quiet a moment. "Yes," President Nash says quietly, "that's why I'm so proud to be a social worker."

"You Can't Do It Alone":
Organizational Issues

Despite increasing interest among social work practitioners in private practice, most social work practice occurs within an organization or agency structure. *Organizations,* by definition, have structure, lines of authority, and differential roles among their members. Organizations are comprised of individuals, each of whom may have a slightly different vision of how the work of the organization is to be conducted. Social workers, particularly those just entering their first agency employment, are often concerned with some very basic questions. Why are there so many rules? What exactly am I expected to do? How will I know if I'm doing a good job? What if I have problems on the job?

Organizational Policies

Agencies often orient new employees (and students as well) by using their policy manual and discussing the rules. This is probably not the most engaging way to excite people about the organization's mission and purpose, but knowing the rules is a necessary part of organizational life. If you are asking why, think about what happens when two or more people live together without rules. You soon realize that disruptions and disagreements may result. For example, can everyone just come and go as they please or will that disturb others' privacy? Who is paying what bills? Are all residents responsible for their own food, for throwing out their own garbage, for cleaning up after themselves, or do these chores get assigned, rotated, or paid for?

Sometimes social workers feel that organizational policies (rules) are barriers rather than facilitators to helping clients. In a few instances this might be correct, but most of these policies serve important functions. One set of policies usually relates to general rules for all personnel: working hours, flex time, vacation, and sick leave. A second set of policies relates to the financial operation of the organization: salary, salary increments, pay periods, and reimbursable expenditures. Perhaps with the exceptions of flex time and salary increments, these policies are usually the least controversial and the best understood.

A third set of policies relates to client service: eligibility requirements, types of service available, payment of services, and length of service. A fourth set of policies, and often externally demanded by funding sources, include data collection regarding clients, services provided, service gaps, and worker timesheets.

Job Descriptions

"What exactly am I expected to do?" is a question of very personal and critical significance. You might be surprised (and dismayed) to know that not all social service agencies have clear and specific job descriptions. To address this problem, increasing numbers of social service agencies have begun to develop what is called task-based job descriptions. Why? Because these:

1. serve to clarify job expectations since job descriptions are often vague and incomplete;
2. facilitate worker evaluations since there are specific competencies necessary for assessing outcome;
3. relate tasks to job and not to worker to improve continuity during staff turnover;
4. provide information to assess staffing needs;
5. better link the work performed by staff and the goals of the agency;

6. are useful in identifying training needs;
7. provide a benchmark for ensuring equitability of work performed and salary levels. (Peter Pecora and Michael Austin, 1987, pp. 24–25)

It may seem obvious that individuals in any organization need to have precise and clear job descriptions. Lack of clarity and specificity in job descriptions contributes to burnout and also leads to an inability to accurately and comparably assess an employee's performance. If you are not clear about the tasks involved in your job and how these tasks relate to the larger organizational mission, it will be difficult, if not impossible, for you to know what to do and to have a sense of accomplishment and significance to the organization.

In the same way, it will be impossible for managers to track the flow of work, to make new assignments, to devise plans for restructuring, if these job descriptions are nonexistent. If all of these reasons were not sufficient in and of themselves, human service agencies are often measured for their success and/or excellence by the abilities of staff members to deliver specific services to designated clients with particular problems. Therefore, without job descriptions, there are no mechanisms for measuring success.

"I know that this may sound strange or too basic to you," President Nash continues, *"but I can't begin to tell you how many inquiries our state office gets for help in writing agency job descriptions. I also would have to be honest in telling you that some of the grievances filed with our state chapter by social workers are the result of poor or no job descriptions."*

Kimberley pipes in, "I'm still not sure that I understand what all the emphasis on job descriptions is about—I know what social workers are supposed to do."

"Well, I know what social workers, in general, do also," President Nash follows up with a bit of a smile, *"but the questions that come to our state office include questions like:*

Is it my job, while assessing a client's readiness for treatment, to provide information and referral to other community services?

Should it be part of my job to serve on a community-based needs assessment team just because I provide services to the targeted client group?

Is talking to the media part of my job?"

Performance Evaluation

How will I know if I'm doing a good job? Well, by now you should know that the first ingredient is a clear job description. This is an essential element for fair performance evaluations provided these precise job descriptions are written so that the professional elements of practice are highlighted and the mechanistic and technical elements of positions are minimized (Michael Fabricant, 1985, p. 391).

Contrary to some workers' fears, the more explicit these job descriptions are, the less anxious the worker is likely to feel. Without this specified precision, evaluations might inappropriately include personality attributes, compatibility with other employees, personal style and dress—qualities that are not essential to the satisfactory completion of the job. Good performance evaluations should provide legal protection for employers and employees, as well as a sound basis for growth opportunities and developmental training for employees.

As more organizations and agencies move toward task-specific job descriptions, fewer practitioners may feel concerned with the ambiguity of what they are expected to do and how their performance will be evaluated. Also, as noted earlier, it may help reduce burnout by providing higher intrinsic motivation through the successful performance of tasks and the realization of their relation to the organization's goals.

This time the professor interrupts, "Interestingly, I had a good example just two weeks ago about how lack of performance evaluation criteria affects motivation. Nancy, an alumna of this program, who some of you have met, is now in private practice. One reason she established a private practice was to have more autonomy and less accountability to all of the organizational 'red tape' that we've been talking about. She called because she was very discouraged and was finding her private practice unmotivating. As we talked, it became very clear to me that she was feeling unsuccessful mostly because she had established no guidelines for herself to measure success.

"I tried to ask her whether she had ever established for herself how many clients she would consider to be successful or if a certain type of client problem or problem mix might be considered successful. Did they all have to be fee paying clients or had she established any percentage for pro bono work?

"I pushed a bit harder. Did she consider 'success' a few sessions or many? Had she established client specific goals? Was she leaving herself any time for professional development? for mentoring others?"

Job Problems

It is not our intent, nor is it our belief, that social service agencies have any more on-the-job problems than other places of employment. In fact, because of their mission and the skills of their professional employees, they may have fewer. However, problems do occur and there are remedies.

Disagreements can occur in agencies about job descriptions, particularly if they are not specific, and about job performance and consequent salary decisions. Usually agencies have internal policies to "grieve" or bring complaints in these areas to agency administrators and to the governing body.

Sometimes employees become concerned with agency issues that are not only related to them, but have to do with the functioning of an entire unit or the entire organization. These may be routine policy changes that would be discussed at staff meetings, or they may be ethical issues that might be brought to NASW.

Unfortunately, another job-related problem has to do with sexist practices in social service agencies. As we have noted, although the majority of the social work labor force is female, males occupy leadership and managerial positions in disproportionate numbers. This has been described as "an effort to defeminize social work; that is, make it more intellectual, rationale, scientific and administrative—in short, give it more male qualities" (Janet Chafetz, 1972, p. 18; Barbara Collins, 1986). Numerous studies have found significant differences between male and female salaries in social work at all levels of employment, even when career tenure, educational level, family status, family commitment, and job mobility were controlled (Martha Williams, Liz Ho, and Lucy Fieldler, 1974, p. 465; Reginald York, H. Carl Henley, and Dorothy Gamble, 1985, pp. 9–12).

These barriers may exist in the formal organizational structure, or in the attitude and behaviors of others; they may represent barriers not only to entry into managerial positions, but also to upward mobility. Specific barriers may be related to the absence of clear job descriptions, the unequal allocation of task assignments, the absence of a cohesive peer group, supervision that is too direct or controlling, or collegial attitudes that do not take women managers seriously. These factors may impede female social workers' career paths and/or create such job dissatisfaction that burnout or turnover result (Karen Haynes, 1983). Other problems, such as the lack of career planning, the absence of mentors and role models, or the absence of formal and legitimated networking opportunities continue to be barriers that may keep more women from seeking or achieving administrative positions (Diane Kravetz and Carol Austin, 1984, pp. 32–35; Karen Haynes, 1989, pp. 5–7).

"That seems awfully negative about male administrators and male colleagues," LaDonna notes. *"In my experience, I have worked for some female bosses who weren't too supportive of women."*

"Excellent point," President Nash comments. *"I probably did overemphasize to make my point that female social workers need to be aware of these barriers and learn some strategies, for themselves and for their organizations, to overcome them."*

Doing It Well: Professional Priorities

A major issue for any profession is the ability to control, monitor, and document the quality of services. *Quality control* refers to the desire to provide the best and the most consistent standard of services to one's client group. Within the broad category of quality control is a group of related variables, including the qualifications of service deliverers, protection of the profession's title and practice, specific standards of service (i.e., staff to client ratios), appropriate treatments, and measurement of outcomes.

Compared to the professions of law and medicine, quality control issues in social work are more complex. For example, as we have discussed in previous chapters, early social services of various kinds were often delivered by volunteers, by paraprofessionals, and/or by indigenous workers. Given the historical context, in fact, many common human needs that would otherwise have gone unnoticed and unmet were met through the efforts of these committed and altruistic, albeit untrained, individuals. Thus, no one would question the need for a physician to have completed medical school successfully in order to practice medicine, yet many do not seem to acknowledge the education and training necessary to practice social work.

As social work has matured as a profession, we have tried to educate society about the importance of professional education for social workers. Of course, along with the need for professional education and training comes the need for an appropriate level of financial compensation. Society questions the necessity of compensating social workers much more than it does physicians or lawyers. In the public eye, at least, it seems that social work's history of volunteerism and altruism haunts the profession. We are expected, in some measure, to place our interests secondary to the interests of our clients or to the interests of society. Some believe that advocating higher salaries may be viewed as self-serving or as contrary to our tradition of benevolence and charity. Yet as a profession, we are no less entitled to reasonable compensation for services delivered than any other profession. As we will see, however, there are other obstacles to quality control within the profession of social work, not the least of which is the criteria for success.

Service Delivery Effectiveness

With the age of accountability, questions have arisen about the success of social services. The questions are overdue and the funders, whether private individuals, not-for-profit boards, or the public, deserve responses to questions such as "Is our money helping? how many? how much?" These questions are and will remain difficult ones, both conceptually as well as empirically.

The effectiveness of service delivery can be measured in a variety of ways (see also chap. 9). Most frequently, the questions for evaluation center around the following:

1. Effort—How much resources are we putting in?

2. Effectiveness—Is it working, with whom, how, for how long?

3. Efficiency—How much is it costing to cure one client; to prevent one case of child abuse; to rehabilitate a juvenile delinquent?

4. Quality—Do the standards for service provision assure quality?

What these questions clearly bring to the front is the need for social work agencies to define their programmatic goals in operationally measurable and realistic terms. Although this sounds very straightforward, it may be the most difficult part of any program evaluation effort. Effectiveness (does it work?) is the most commonly asked question, but also one of the most difficult to measure.

"I guess I still don't get it. Why is it so hard to measure what you're doing and if it's working?" Jahad asks.

"Let's take a couple of examples. You would assume that our state Children's Protective Services agency is clear that it's primary goal is the prevention and treatment of child abuse. Does the agency mean that it wants to prevent child abuse from occurring at all? Or prevent its repeated occurrence? The former goal is extremely difficult to measure. How do we know that we have prevented child abuse? The mechanisms for evaluating success are likely either to be indirect methods—such as pre- and posttest of parental knowledge of child development and behavior, for example—or dependent on macro indices—such as numbers of reported cases of child abuse. If we find less child abuse between two points in time through these methods, we cannot know with certainty that the program was effective.

"Another mental health clinic program might have a stated goal of reducing marital stress due to interpersonal relations. The measure of success might be that the couple remains together in the relationship, or that the couple becomes separated. Diametrically opposed outcomes might both be indicators of success. These are both sets of questions related to effectiveness."

If the primary question is effort (how much), then we need to ask questions relative to resources and inputs: How many hours of professional time has it taken to deliver the services? How much clerical and administrative support is necessary to deliver the services? How much in the way of capital equipment is necessary? How much volunteer time is used? These are important data sets, but too often "How much does it take to provide the service?" is substituted for the real question, "Was the service successful?" Using effort as a primary evaluative measure might drive agencies to hire less qualified persons or to substitute volunteers for professionals.

This is a particular problem when an agency wants to answer efficiency questions, because efficiency is the ratio of effort to effectiveness. Therefore, the lower the effort, the better the ratio. Funders are likely to be impressed.

It is difficult to measure success, then, because the constructs are complex and often require very indirect measures. The inferences made must, by their very nature, be tentative, and the conclusions drawn relative to efficiency are laden with inherent value biases.

Personnel Classification

To provide quality services, an agency, or a profession, must have personnel who are appropriately trained and educated for the tasks. As we have repeatedly noted, the social services profession, because of its historical development, has lacked this kind of control. Over the last 30 years, social work positions have been *declassified* at an alarming rate across the country. Declassification refers to the lowering of the required qualifications for a given job position. In summary, the reasons for these efforts have been:

1. The mushrooming of public programs has called for expanded staffing. MSWs and BSWs have been either unavailable, uninterested in public social services, or too few in number to fill vacancies.

2. Many positions have been filled by "human service" staff with the assumption that on-the-job training is sufficient.

3. As unions become the bargaining agents for state employees, they emphasize promotion through experience and do not support professional education.

4. In some states, state personnel departments use BSW and MSW employees interchangeably; they assume then that the master's level is superfluous to providing direct service.

5. Quantitative accountability on the job (how many) has become the norm for evaluation; qualitative intervention (how well) is rarely measured or recognized.

6. Legislation and administrative rules have allowed "equivalences" to social work education to stand.

7. Fewer resources have been available, and this has led to a justification for lowering standards.

These declassification efforts have denigrated social work education, and social work functions have been redefined so that in some cases they are eliminated entirely. This sounds rather bleak, but it is important to note that the NASW and its membership continue to work against the declassification of social work roles, functions, and positions. The NASW has, for example, held two national conferences on validation of state civil social work employment, and several state NASW chapters organized efforts directed toward declassification concerns.

In 1973, NASW developed a policy statement that presented a

classification structure for preprofessional levels of social service workers. In September 1981, the NASW revised this statement utilizing a model that objectively established the levels of education, training, experience, skills, and knowledge needed for adequate performance at identified levels of competency. This process was accomplished through evaluation-based research known as *validation studies,* which examine the skills necessary to perform tasks rather than what the applicant is capable of learning to do while on the job. These standards were intended to serve as a national model for the design of personnel classification systems.

NASW Standards for Social Service Manpower

1. The tasks and functions of a job should be derived from the goals and objectives of the job.

2. Each function and task has a range and continuum of required knowledge, skills, and abilities related to its effective performance.

3. There is an interrelated system of practice skills based on the complexity of tasks in social services.

4. Competence is developmental and dynamic within each level of practice.

5. The levels of competence in social work are based on six factors:

    a. Knowledge
    b. Responsibility
    c. Skill
    d. Situational complexity
    e. Social consequences
    f. Client vulnerability
    g. Social purpose

6. The certification of a professional's qualifications may be acquired from a school of social work, a governmental body, or a professional organization.

SOURCE: NASW Standards for the Classification of Social Work Practice, Policy Statement 4, *1981.*

The professor offers an example. "Do you remember that we read about our state examining the job qualifications for entry positions in nursing homes for social workers? Do you remember that they wanted to eliminate the need for applicants to hold a BSW and wanted applicants to have just two years of college, an associate's (AA) degree? That's an excellent example of declassification. Fortunately, our state office mounted a lobbying effort to successfully defeat that attempt."

Legal Regulation

Social work has been recognized as a profession since the early part of the twentieth century, but serious and consistent efforts for legal regulation of social work practice did not begin until the 1970s. The National Association of Social Workers voted in favor of a model legal regulation bill in 1971, basing its position on the efforts to improve and monitor the quality of services to clients. Laws to regulate social work practice have been on the legislative agenda of some states in literally almost every session since that date. Today, all states legally regulate social work practice in one form or another.

Some of the most frequently cited reasons for legal regulation are:

1. Consumer Protection. Professionals perform functions too complex for most consumers to adequately evaluate; legal regulation guarantees professional competence.

2. Professional Standards and Quality Control. These provide a public, legal definition of the practice and require that certain standards be met.

3. Reduction of Declassification Activities. This policy assures that professional education is a qualification for hiring and promotion.

4. Confidentiality. The courts are more likely to uphold privileged communication if a profession is regulated and has established procedures to maintain confidentiality.

5. Third Party Payments. Legal regulation is usually required to extend insurance coverage to social workers.

As we have noted, the legal regulation statutes vary from state to state. Three categories of legal regulation may apply to any profession: registration, certification, and licensure.

Registration provides the most limited degree of regulatory power. The state simply establishes a self-identified registry of people who perform a certain service. Although there may be some specific requirements for registration, these are typically quite limited and unregistered professionals are seldom penalized by the state unless they claim to be registered.

Certification is more rigorous. The state declares that a certified person is competent to perform a certain service; competence may be defined and tested by the state, but only in relation to the use of a specific title. Persons who are not certified cannot use the same title as certified persons, but they are not prohibited from providing the same or similar services.

Licensure is the most rigorous form of legal regulation. It gives the state the authority to (1) define who can perform a certain activity; (2) specify the requirements for knowledge and skills, including how these are to be obtained and demonstrated; and (3) enforce the definition of standards and behavior expected in a profession. Licensure protects both the title and the job activity. As a result, licensure combines registration and certification with control over a profession (David Hardcastle, 1977, pp. 14–19).

However, depending on the various sections of a licensure bill, even this form of legal regulation may be insufficient for the ultimate protection of clients. For example, depending on the inclusion and then the description of these sections, a licensure bill may be more or less effective in the protection of practice and the concomitant quality control of social services.

Licensure bills generally include sections on:

1. Privileged communication
2. Reciprocity
3. Exemption
4. Renewal
5. Levels of practice
6. Administration
7. Definition of practice

Exemption clauses may be provided for one or more of three categories of people. First, in a policy often known as "grandparenting," individuals who have been practicing for some time before the enactment of a licensure bill may be permitted to continue, even though the bill requires more education than they possess. Second, practitioners in certain other professions, such as the ministry, marriage counseling, family and child counseling, and psychiatry, are often exempted from social work licensure requirements. And finally, in perhaps the most serious form of exemption, some states allow all state agency employees to practice social work without meeting licensure requirements.

"Why is that such a problem?" Jason asks.

"Because then the people who really need to be protected by the state, like kids, don't get quality service," Tricia retorts heatedly.

"And the media then labels these employees social workers when any mistakes are made," President Nash comments somewhat heatedly as well.

Licensure acts often contain several levels of practice based on varying educational requirements and skills. Social work licensing statutes commonly provide for two or three levels of practice. These include the certified social worker (usually MSW), social worker (usually BSW), and social work associate (AA). Incorporating multilevels of practice in a licensing act recognizes the complexity of tasks and the diversity of skills necessary for their successful accomplishment.

Probably one of the most important sections of a bill is the definition of *practice*. This provision clarifies for the public the duties and functions of the profession. Social work is commonly defined as an institutional method of helping people to enhance their social functioning and to resolve their social problems. Although the definition of practice is the portion of the bill that most clearly helps to protect the practice, it is often the most difficult provision on which to achieve internal consensus and external acceptance.

Arguments that are used to object to, or to reduce the effectiveness of, social work legal regulation bills often include the fact that other mechanisms already exist to provide the same function. There are, for example, state agency regulations, supervision, professional standard review organizations, professional codes of ethics, and professional grievance processes.

"I've also heard some talk that licensure is discriminatory and exclusionary," LaDonna says matter of factly.

"Yes, those charges have been made by organizations representing minority populations in many states. To the extent that the whole rationale for licensure is to exclude persons without the prerequisite knowledge and skills from practicing and to the extent that higher

education in this country is still not equally accessible to minorities, the charge is true. The real issue for our profession is to work to assure greater equality of educational opportunities while still protecting our clients," President Nash answers.

Who Pays? Public Concerns

By the beginning of the 1980s and based on Ronald Reagan's campaign promises, the public had accepted the notion that a disproportionate and detrimental amount of federal dollars were going to social services. As we have already described in Chapter 3, the promise—made and kept—was to reduce these federal levels of public social service expenditure. Those concerned about the inadequacy of the "safety net" were assured that the private sector would move in to replace the lost federal dollars. That did not happen.

There was a problem with that argument because the gap was far larger than the level of private philanthropy in the past. A second problem was the failure to realize that, if the public had been convinced that too many tax dollars were spent in social services, these monies had been spent wastefully, and there were indeed "lazy and no good" people living off the public dole, then that public was certainly unlikely to give its own hard earned dollars to those same organizations and individuals. Add to all this the fact that the national economy was in a recession. Increases in savings, not philanthropic giving, were the pattern, and higher rates of unemployment left fewer people willing or able to give.

Finally, the argument of returning decision making, and bill paying, to the lowest level of government was supported by the notion that it would empower communities. But the communities in the greatest need also had the fewest resources to contribute. Communities with high rates of unemployment were often also communities with high crime rates, high teenage pregnancy rates, high school dropout rates, and high incidences of drug usage. The inner cities, most negatively affected by these problems, did not have the tax base to pay for the solutions.

With the emergence of the New Federalism in the 1980s, the solution of privatization became increasingly popular. The view emerged that the private sector and the marketplace were better mechanisms to insure efficient use of funds, nonmonopolistic service delivery, and accountability based on profit to insure better services. But that solution raises the same concerns today as it has historically: How can the private marketplace provide services to involuntary clients, to low income and poor clients, to clients in need of protection? In response to this paradox, some social service agencies, following the private health care model, have created a two-tiered system of delivery, which basically returns to categorizing worthy and unworthy recipients. Some administrators and providers appear to be more accountable to the profit motive than to enhancing social functioning and the quality of life.

Social services face the twenty-first century with multiple, unstable sources of funding. Dependent on political whim and shifting personal and social values, agencies confront the same old question of whether social services are rights or luxuries.

Obtaining and Maintaining Funding

We need do little more than read the daily newspaper to see accounts of limited funding availability and cutbacks to social services. As social problems and human needs increase, so does competition for available funds. Those seeking funds from various levels of government may be fighting others for those same dollars. For example, with a finite financial base, a state legislature may be examining competing proposals requesting funds for new state prisons, for highway repair, or for health care for indigent persons.

Obtaining funding through legislative groups is likely to mean being skillful in political processes such as lobbying, as well as being dependent on the rise and fall of city or state coffers and the political ideology of the times. Public funds may be allocated on a per capita basis, or on an incidence or prevalence of the problem basis, or due to the influence of a particular city or state legislator. Once obtained, maintenance of these funds requires, usually, the annual or biennial submission of new budget requests with substantial justification for each request. Obviously, each renewal is as dependent on the aforementioned factors as the legitimacy and the validity of the budget request itself.

Likewise, an initial request to the United Way for an allocation must begin with the agency meeting the United Way's admission criteria. Once met, the budget requests and all of the supportive documentation goes to a United Way allocation panel. Each United Way annually prioritizes services based on changing community needs or sentiments. Thus, obtaining an initial allocation from the United Way is as dependent on whether your agency's services happen to be congruent with the United Way's priority settings as it is to whether this is a critically important service.

The allocation process of the United Way usually includes panels of volunteers—who are not professional social workers—who review the written material, often make a site visit to the agency, and make a recommendation for the level of funding. As with legislators, these people may be influenced by personal preferences and/or individual knowledge of an agency's services. Once initial funding from the United Way has been obtained, there is an annual budget request cycle without guarantee of stable, much less increasing, funding over time.

Funding from private or corporate foundations is usually for the purpose of initial or demonstration funding in order for that service to either become self-sustaining or to find other stable and consistent sources. Foundations change their priorities, so success in obtaining foundation funding can be highly dependent on the congruence of the request with the foundation mission, and may be based on personal connections.

Fees for service, a more recent but expanding source of revenue for many social service agencies, entail alot of paperwork. Because paying clients can take themselves elsewhere if they begin to dislike the service provision, or can stop service if their source of monies declines, it is not a stable source of revenue. Although many insurance carriers over recent decades have begun to reimburse for social work services, attempts to contain health care costs have reduced mental health coverage in general. Policies that include mental health coverage include annual limits, a lifetime maximum, and a co-payment requirement of 20 to 50 percent. Finally an obvious, but important, point about the fee-for-service funding base: Most people who are insured are part of the labor force. Consequently, if these people are laid off or become unemployed, they quickly lose their insurance coverage and their ability to pay fees for service.

A critical current and future issue for the profession is the amount of time and expertise necessary to obtain and then annually request renewal of funding. It would seem much more efficient to require the accountability annually but to allocate funding for multiyear time frames, thereby reducing the annual time and energy demands relative to obtaining funds.

Lisa says, "I remember when Etta came to class. One of the things she spoke to us about was how many funding sources were involved in several of the children's health services in town. I was amazed that there were so many! I can't remember them all, but I know that it was client fees, United Way, Medicaid, SSI, and a grant."

"That's why it's so important for us to try to convince funders to keep the record keeping simple, to ask for the same information, and to collect that information only one time," President Nash interjects.

Mixed Funding Sources

In the early years of social service delivery, financial support typically came from a single source. The churches funded church-related services, the National Benevolence Societies paid for their own private services, and even when the public sector got involved, funds were entirely local, supporting local services for local citizens. These were simple models of funding with one source of money and one line of accountability.

The "community chests" and "united fund drives" of the 1920s began the change, but the most dramatic changes occurred in the 1930s when the federal government got involved in developing and funding national programs to intervene in the Great Depression. Increasing federal involvement in social service programs during the 1960s and 1970s, directed federal dollars to the states and cities, but frequently required "matching" state and/or local dollars. The more that different levels of government were involved, the more complicated the lines of accountability became. Add to this the constantly changing pockets of money from private foundations and United Ways, and we have a complicated and often confusing array of funding formulas and requirements.

Each source that provides funding dollars for social welfare programs may require that certain conditions be met. The following list illustrates some possible conditions to be met by an agency receiving funds from multiple sources in the 1990s:

1. delineation of clients to be served: by gender, age, race/ethnicity, presenting problem, geographic setting;

2. specific operating procedures: agency hours and place of service delivery;

3. types of services delivered: information and referral only;

4. *staffing:* qualifications, staff to client ratios, salary ranges;

5. *documentation of service delivery:* number of clients served, client data bases, explanations or descriptions of services delivered, including specific dates and times;

6. *evaluation methods:* definition of "successful outcomes," frequency of evaluations, identification of evaluative tools.

Sometimes, especially for small agencies, the number of conditions imposed by their funding sources are too costly or too complicated to implement. As a result, agencies may decide not to pursue particular funding opportunities, especially if the available funds are limited. When several funding sources are involved, each with its own set of service conditions and reporting requirements, we can begin to see the time and energy required to account for the funds received by the agency.

Accountability

In the last 20 years, *accountability* has become a major concern in all arenas of health, education, and welfare service delivery. Health insurance companies are requiring greater accountability of hospitals and physicians. The taxpaying public is requiring greater accountability from public school administrators and teachers. And, in social work, funding sources are requiring greater accountability from service delivery agencies. Those who pay the bills want to know if their money is being spent appropriately and for the purpose for which it was intended—the essence of the concept of accountability. Monies provided to deliver social services, whether from private or from government (city, county, state, federal) sources, ought to be accounted for in a routine manner. Although few would disagree with this position, coming to a clear agreement about what accountability means and how it can be documented in social service delivery is yet another matter.

Does accountability mean an audit trail of how funds were spent, including data on the proportion of dollars spent on salaries, administrative versus direct service costs, money spent on equipment, the costs of ongoing general maintenance, and operating expenses? The most likely answer is yes to all of these things. Does accountability also include providing data on how many clients were seen, at what time, for how long, and by whom? The answer to this is less clear and, even if we were to answer yes, there might be problems in agreeing on whether this information would be meaningful in any way. Does accountability include measurements of success in service delivery? Increasingly, funding sources are saying yes to this, yet as we have just discussed, defining success in social services may be extremely difficult.

Definition and measurement are far easier when we are simply counting the dollars spent on prenatal care, the costs to immunize children against childhood illness, the monies spent on the food stamp programs. It is in the area of qualitative measurement that accountability becomes very complex. For example, how do we measure prevention? If troubled adolescents remain in school, can we say that it is only our particular service or program that has prevented truancy, or delinquency? As yet, there is no simple definition of therapeutic success in our work. When our services are less tangible—such as counseling or therapy, rather than the tangible provision of money, food, or shelter—can we count the number of hours spent and determine whether funding has been used wisely?

"Isn't it fair that these agencies have to be accountable for the public and private monies they get? I don't think that's such a terrible thing to ask," Jason says with exasperation.

"Of course, you're right. The funders, whether taxpayers or private contributors, have a right to know where and how their money has been spent. It is our professional concern as social workers to identify the questions to ask, not the duty of other people from different backgrounds who have limited knowledge of the complexity of our services. Why should business people, accountants in particular, be determining these questions?" President Nash asks Jason—without understanding why the class is laughing.

Summary

Although this chapter has focused on issues, we have no intention of discouraging you from entering the social work profession. All professions encounter issues and the challenge to a profession is to maintain the main principles of professional practice while being flexible to changes in technology, policies, the labor force, and social needs and problems.

We hope that we have accurately described practitioner, organizational, professional, and funding issues as well as solutions or strategies to cope with these. We are aware that these may exhibit themselves somewhat differently depending on the specific field of practice, client population, or geographic area of service delivery.

It is unlikely that these issues will be resolved in the foreseeable future. Until there is widespread support for the notion of social welfare as a human right rather than a luxury, obtaining the needed monies for social service programs will remain a competitive process characterized by limited success. And until there is legal regulation of social work practice—comprehensive licensing laws—quality control will be compromised.

Each issue serves to remind us of the work that still needs to be done, yet we maintain a sense of optimism that the social work profession stands ready to continue its work. There may never be a time in our profession's history where we can say we have come so far, yet still have so much to do. Positive changes have already occurred in some areas even though more needs to be done. It is important to acknowledge that no progress can be made until issues or concerns have been clearly identified. We believe that we have named many in this chapter. One might also conclude that some of these problems, such as the difficulty to differentiate the social work labor force or the issues arising from the technological age, actually come as a result of some positive trends. Other issues, such as employee benefits and worker motivation, are neither new nor likely to change.

"Unless there are any more questions, I'd like to end this teleconference on a positive and challenging note. In my position, I talk with many groups in our state and the nation, and I remind them to celebrate, not that there is still human suffering, but that there are still individuals and organizations whose major purpose is to alleviate that suffering.

"I tell them to celebrate that social workers are people dedicated to service for the welfare of humanity; to the disciplined use of a recognized body of knowledge about human beings and their interactions; and to the marshaling of community resources to promote the well-being of all without discrimination.

"I remind them to celebrate that our profession, as it continues to mature, can trace the development of ideas and the effectiveness of strategies, such that our professional field will build on itself; newer minds will deal with older problems and we can add chapters to the evolving history of how people help people.

"And I celebrate that some of you will add new ideas and diversified skills to an already talented and dedicated cadre of social workers.

Therefore, I hope if you choose social work as your profession—a profession that will provide you with a career unparalleled by challenges and enriched by the commitment to human dignity and social justice—that you will retain your passion for and your commitment to improving the quality of life.

"And finally, if you make that choice, I hope you remain as proud as I am of being a social worker.

"Thank you. I enjoyed our conversation."

References

Chafetz, Janet. "Women in Social Work." *Social Work*, Vol. 17, No. 5 (Sept. 1972): 12–18.

Collins, Barbara. "Defining Feminist Social Work." *Social Work*, Vol. 31, No. 3 (May-June 1986): 214–219.

Fabricant, Michael. "The Industrialization of Social Work Practice." *Social Work*, Vol. 30, No. 5 (Sept.-Oct. 1985): 389–395.

Hardcastle, David. "Public Regulation of Social Work." *Social Work*, Vol. 22, No. 1 (Jan. 1977): 14–19.

Haynes, Karen S. "Sexual Differences in Social Work Administrator's Job Satisfaction." *Journal of Social Service Research*, Vol. 16, No. 3/4 (1983): 57–74.

———. *Women Managers in Human Services*. New York: Springer Publishers, 1989.

Kravetz, Diane, and Carol Austin. "Women's Issues in Social Service Administration: The Views and Experiences of Women Administrators." *Administration in Social Work*, Vol. 8, No. 4 (1984): 25–38.

NASW Standards for the Classification of Social Work Practice, Policy Statement 4. Washington, D.C.: NASW 1981.

Pecora, Peter J., and Michael J. Austin. *Managing Human Service Personnel*. California: Sage, 1987.

Williams, Martha, Liz Ho, and Lucy Fielder. "Career Patterns: More Grist for Women's Liberation." *Social Work*, Vol. 19, No. 4 (July 1974): 463–466.

York, Reginald O., H. Carl Henley, and Dorothy N. Gamble. "Barriers to the Advancement of Women in Social Work Administration." *Journal of Social Service Research*, Vol. 9, No. 1 (1985): 1–15.

CHAPTER 13

Professional Identification

Introduction

The name tags at the social work conference read:

"I am Julie, social worker and director of the Early Adolescent Program at the Children's Museum."

"I am Ryan, social worker and candidate for state representative."

"I am Luz, social worker and executive director of the mental health clinic."

"I am Nancy, social worker and family counselor."

"I am Bill, social worker and AIDS activist."

"I am Judy, social worker and Children's Protective Service worker."

"I am Carlos, social worker and a barrio organizer."

"I am Barbara, social worker and Employee Assistance Program supervisor."

"I am Etta, social worker and advocate for children's health."

"I am Molly, social worker and a nationally syndicated columnist."

"I am Sheila, social worker and city councilperson."

"I am George, social worker and a union dispute mediator."

"I am Patricia Sue, executive director of the Campfire Girls."

After "social worker," other name tags read "dance therapist"; "professor"; "organizational consultant"; "deputy director, State Department of Health"; "district manager, congressional office." To an outsider, the diversity of positions, skills, roles, and titles might be more apparent; to the assembled group, the commonality of skills and mission provide cohesion and comfort.

The day long program that has brought this group together provides ample opportunity to "catch up and network," but the central theme this year, "Enhancing our Public Image," has been a draw as well. Before we "listen in" on the conference, let's underscore that all members of this group are professional social workers, holding BSWs and/or MSWs. They are part of a large labor force that works in the not-for-profit sector of family and children's services, mental health clinics, hospitals, refugee services, adoption agencies, and information and referral services. Their numbers are expanded by those who work in the public sector: in juvenile and adult probation services, in public child and adult protective services, in public schools, in state hospitals for the mentally ill, and in social security offices. In the 1990s, social workers can be found in private residential facilities, such as psychiatric hospitals and nursing homes; in day-care centers; in private and group practice; or in the corporate world in personnel divisions, employee assistance programs, or in public and/or community relations departments. Increasingly, social workers are involved in electoral politics: running for office, managing a campaign, being employed as a legislative aid.

Not surprisingly, the majority of the attendees are female. Some of these social workers are young and recently out of an undergraduate program; some have completed an MSW degree, usually after some social service experience. Others are middle-age job changers with considerable previous life and/or job experiences. Some entered professional educational programs after years of rich volunteer experience. Some are students, encouraged to attend by their professor to continue to get more information about the pro-

Headed for the future: Social work students celebrate their graduation.

fession. They are white, black, brown, Native American, and Asian American. They are of every nationality, socioeconomic background, and from every geographic origin.

How, from this incredible diversity, can a common professional identity emerge?

Now, let's listen in.

Common Identity. *The first set of five panelists on the program have been given the task to draw from the specifics of their current jobs, the commonalities of skills, knowledge, and values from the profession; to identify how professional social work education prepared them for these specific jobs; and to describe what keeps them connected to the profession.*

Julie, director of the Early Adolescent Program at the Children's Museum, speaks first. Her current job, which she has held for two years, is managerial in description, but builds heavily on generic social work skills and knowledge. "To be able to create programs to engage children, at any age, one must know something about developmental stages; must be able to identify possible causes for behaviors, such as boredom or defiance; and must learn how to design and finance programs to achieve these goals. It's hard for me to imagine any other educational background that could have prepared me as well. I know that I was competing with alot of others from varying backgrounds, but I still believe that it was my ability to take the broader view—the person-in-environment perspective—that gave me the edge in the job interview."

Molly, a nationally syndicated columnist, jumps in next. "Well, it wasn't easy to become a syndicated columnist—I didn't go to graduate school in social work for that purpose. But, I found with my undergraduate journalism degree that it seemed a natural to take the issues I was learning about in social work to the public from a social worker's perspective. For me, the common identity has been around the mission of the profession, a mission that strives for social justice and human dignity and a mission that operates on the general principle of advocacy for clients. I get angry when I read stereotypical and incorrect media reports about us or our clients. I decided to advocate for our clients while educating the public through the media."

There's a pause and Bill, an AIDS activist, begins, softly at first, "I am still sometimes amazed that my position with the Greater AIDS Foundation is real. For me, it represents the most meaningful combination of personal life experience with professional skills and commitment. I can remember when I had to hide the fact that I was gay. I can *remember the depression and anger when several of my friends died. Fortunately, I sought counseling and the 'therapist,' a social worker, told me about social work. In that anger, I thought that theoretical and conceptual 'book' stuff was getting in the way of 'doing.' I desperately wanted to make a difference. However, I learned that I had to know something before I did something. In my current job, there is a constant need to keep informed about state and federal policies, current research findings, funding opportunities, and recent practice innovations. Probably what was and continues to be most important for me is the fact that social work combines caring and advocating."*

Patricia Sue, executive director of the Campfire Girls, smiles and says, "I couldn't think of a more perfect way to combine my continuing interest in children with my respect and concern for the environment. Although my position wasn't advertised to require social work education, I was encouraged to apply by a mentor who thought that I would be perfect for the position. Although I don't work as directly with the girls as I would like, I find my knowledge in human development essential for program planning, and the policy perspective an asset in grant writing, policy initiation, and fund raising. I also realize that content on the political process not only helped me with fund raising, but has come in handy working with my board."

"I protect our children," Judy, senior Children's Protective Service worker, adds. "Every day I have to make critical decisions that affect children's lives. My days are harried and often stressful, but I always feel that I'm right in there on the front line, working with some of the most vulnerable of our client populations. I knew that this was the kind of work I wanted to do when I entered the social work program. Not only does my job demand knowledge about family dynamics and child development, but also about community resources. Because I've had several job offers over the years, I also know that if I ever want a change, my education and professional experience will be extremely marketable."

During these presentations, heads in the audience are nodding. The moderator of the panel sums it up nicely, "I believe that these panelists have provided excellent and diverse examples of our common professional identity: The values, the knowledge, and the skills that we learn through class and field work, through on-the-job training, and through continuing education have as their common root a mission of social justice and human dignity. These panelists also underscored the strength of our professional preparation for examining the big picture and for linking private troubles to public issues. Directly or indirectly, I believe that they all validated the marketability of our social work degrees."

The Public Image

Despite the common, strong, and proud professional identity described at our social work conference, the identity of social work in the public's mind is less clear and sometimes less positive. It is not our intent to dwell on the negative or to deter any of you from a choice of social work as a career, but because we suspect that you will encounter some of these misconceptions and stereotypes, it is our intent to provide you with strategies to combat them.

Why else is this important? There are several reasons. First, the stereotypes of who social workers are and what they do can be erroneous and yet, like many stereotypes, persistent. But more than that, these persistent stereotypes may serve as a deterrent for people to be recruited into the profession, may be an important part of the explanation for the low self-esteem of social workers, and may help to promote the public's view that professional social workers are not experts. As a result, the public may be reticent to provide the deserved salary, status, and respect accorded to experts. The public usually does not view social workers as power brokers, and the result may be that there are barriers to the attainment of power.

How then, with the diversity of jobs, skills, roles, experiential backgrounds, and demographic descriptors of real-life social workers, can these narrow and stereotypical misconceptions of social work still persist? Further, why is a profession so singularly devoted to enhancing social functioning and well-being, improving the quality of life, and reducing discrimination so negatively labeled? Why, when BSW and MSW social workers hold college degrees, can segments of society continue to believe that we have no skills, or that social work jobs can be done by just about anyone?

How ironic, that the labels "do gooders" and "bleeding hearts," which certainly might connote people who deeply care, have been used pejoratively. Even more damaging, social workers and the social work profession sometimes have taken these negatives to heart themselves, thus reducing their self-esteem, questioning their abilities, and allowing the ranking of the profession to be reduced.

Let's return to the conference and the luncheon speaker for some insight on these issues.

"I am Sheila, social worker and city councilperson. I have recently been reelected to my third term in office and as some of you may know, I have always referred to myself during campaigns and while in office as a social worker. It almost lost me my first campaign, but I turned it around. Well, enough about me.

"Is our public image so important? Is it only self-serving? No, I don't believe so. If we don't recruit the top people into the profession, it will help to perpetuate a stereotype of a profession less competent, less confident, and less capable. If we have a group of professionals who, despite their competence, have low self-esteem, they may continue to project that image to the public—'I'm not sure of what I'm doing; and, maybe, I am less capable of making important and critical decisions than medical doctors, psychologists, psychiatrists, school teachers and counselors, and attorneys.' If we can't demand competitive salaries and demand the respect that our profession is owed, won't our clients suffer?

"Our clients, vulnerable, often confused, many times in crisis, certainly do not deserve second-class services. And although they certainly do not receive second-class services from professional social workers, it may be easy for them to question the quality of those services if the professionals who deliver them are belittled by the public.

"As professional social workers, with an obligation to empower others, we seem to have been somewhat remiss in empowering ourselves. Labeled as altruists, we are overly sensitive to attacks about self-interest. I get angry about that double bind. There are many professions that proclaim altruistic motives: medical doctors, nurses, attorneys, teachers, psychologists, social workers. And many of these professions are well paid for that altruistic service and are not apologetic for that.

"We, too, need to stop being apologetic when we ask for salaries commensurate with our training; when we ask state legislatures to publicly sanction our education via legal regulation in order to protect our clients. We need to refuse to take the rap when the media mislabels and blames social workers for mistakes.

"I am proud to be a social worker. I tell the media, my constituents, and groups that I address that I am a social worker. That empowers me and I hope, indirectly, it empowers others.

"There are a variety of explanations for this image and, thankfully, some solutions. I have been asked to talk about some of the reasons for the negative image and then turn to our panelists for solutions."

The Reasons behind the Image

There are an array of possible explanations for the initiation and persistence of some of these negative and stereotypical public images of professional social workers. It is unimportant to determine first versus second cause; in fact, the very multiplicity and mutuality of these causes are the blame.

We have chosen to group the explanations that we see for this negative, stereotypic image into four categories: (1) social work practice; (2) social work settings; (3) social work labor force; and (4) professional criteria.

Social Work Practice

The Unloved Clients   We know that one explanation for the poor public image is our clients: the groups unable to take care of themselves; the groups scorned by the rest of society; the groups publicly mandated to be served. Although the client population for social work services is diverse and has become more diversified over the last several decades of expansion of services, expansion of insurance coverage, and entry into new fields of practice, the persistent stereotype, and perhaps even the ideal client given the history of the profession is the "underdog."

Social work, more than other professions, can become contaminated in the public mind simply through an association with a low income, and/or vulnerable, and/or dangerous, and/or disturbed clientele. The criminals, the child abusers and molesters, the drug pushers and users, the HIV infected, the homeless and hungry—social work's client population—are so often feared and despised by the rest of society that social workers, in turn, become the displaced targets for that fear and/or hatred.

Paradoxically, it is around these clients and these social problems that social workers are expected to be agents of social control. We are expected to provide enough service to protect the population and to prevent violence and revolution. Simultaneously, we are often urged to be agents of social change and faulted if we do not successfully advocate to change the conditions that create and foster these problems.

Dirty Business   Social work also gets pejoratively labeled because of the tasks that social workers are sometimes forced to perform. Social workers "take kids away from their parents." Social workers "place people in nursing homes instead of returning them to their home." Social workers "coddle" criminal offenders and drug abusers. Social workers "encourage" people to have abortions.

There is irony here because these are publicly mandated functions. The tasks arise from a complex of often competing societal values, which change with economic conditions, professional philosophies, and political ideologies. For example, the ongoing debate between children's rights and parents' rights leaves the public servant (the social worker) in the middle. To protect the rights of children, in many cases the obvious solution is to remove at-risk children from their homes. Yet, to preserve families and support parental rights, the response must be to maintain children in their own homes.

Similarly, consider the critical and complex decision of whether to return an elderly and/or chronically disabled person to living alone—without adequate community support—or to place that individual in a residential facility. A decision must be made between an individual's autonomy and self-determination and the appropriate and necessary care.

Welfare   Public opposition to welfare and most other publicly funded and delivered social services is strong in this country, and that opposition has been renewed in the last decade. The continued strength of the work ethic, the strong belief in the market economy, and the erroneous stereotypes of who constitutes the "welfare rolls," continue to undermine public welfare services and its workers.

The notions that social workers are discouraging able-bodied people from finding employment, that the welfare system encourages women to have children, and, that there are generations of welfare recipients have never been eradicated. From the welfare raids in the mid-1950s to the current Family Assistance Plan for workfare, the underlying skepticism continues. As a result, the individuals who do the work of this highly suspect system are typically undervalued.

Social Work Settings

Host Settings Much social work is practiced in *host settings*. Social work programs, and social workers, are often found in organizations such as hospitals, mental health clinics, probation departments, school systems, and nursing homes. More often than not in these settings, the profession in charge, both in terms of management and total numbers of employees, is something other than social work: medicine, psychiatry, clinical psychology, educational administration, criminal justice, or nursing.

The obvious outcome of this phenomenon is to subordinate social workers and social work departments to another discipline or profession. This organizational arrangement reflects the assumption that social workers are less able than other professionals to be in positions of administrative control and authority; that is, to perform their own functions without higher order supervision and monitoring, and to be anything other than ancillary to that setting.

Public Employees The anti-welfare state mentality also provides us with a hierarchy of valued employment. Private employment is typically valued more than public employment; consequently, private practitioners enjoy a higher status and frequently receive higher compensation. Professions like nursing and teaching, a high percentage of whose members are public sector employees, are less valued and less well-compensated.

"Bureaucrat" is a more pejorative term than "corporate employee." Public civil service often bases rewards on time-in-rank rather than meritorious performance. Public employment suggests less autonomy of practice; the public managerial model tends to look more like that used with technical employees rather than professional workers.

We can read daily of the struggles of most public school systems to retain excellent teachers; the national nursing shortage has been an issue for several years. Both medicine and law find it more difficult to recruit into their own public sectors—public health departments and public hospitals, for example, or district attorney's offices. To be a professional is to be able to practice autonomously. To be a public employee is, by definition, to be part of a bureaucratic structure with limited autonomy.

Social Work Labor Force

The Nonprofessionals Another variable that is part of the equation for social workers is the large number of people in the social service labor force who are not professionally educated. This may include persons with other higher education degrees but without professional social work education, as well as those with no formal education beyond a college degree. Consequently, the public's view, obtained through print or electronic media, or obtained through direct and real-life experience, often depends on descriptions of skills, tasks and actions, and judgments made by nonprofessionals. Newspaper reports about social workers often use that term in a nonlegal or nonprofessional sense.

As we described in Chapter 12, the cyclical nature of personnel practices in many public social services has contributed in recent decades to declassification. If individuals, irrespective of education and training, can call themselves a social worker, how can the public determine who is really qualified?

An estimated 450,000 people in the labor force are labeled social workers, and only 200,000 have actually earned social work degrees (June Hopps and Elaine Pinderhughes, 1987). In many states, less than one-quarter of the children's protective services labor force and the criminal justice labor force are professionally educated, yet these state employees and direct line workers are in some of the most critical positions to make fundamental life decisions—social work decisions—for children.

Female-Dominated Field An abundance of literature suggests that female-dominated professions such as nursing, teaching, and social work share a common status: the devalued status of females in Western society. These professions are seen as nurturing professions, rather than technical and scientific ones, which suggests an inherent hierarchical bias. The issues surrounding women's work have to do with its often voluntary nature (historically and currently); the fact that women are typically seen as temporary members of the labor force because of their need to "dropout" for child bearing; and that women have been employed in subservient positions (nurses to doctors; teachers to principals; caseworkers to executives).

Women pioneered social work and occupied early leadership positions, but men entered the administrative positions in both

practice and in education with the age of scientific management—
the large-scale, public-sector agencies created in the late 1950s and
1960s. Another issue, for which no reliable data exists, is the perception that women lack a *career* orientation (Diane Kravetz and Linda
Jones, 1982, pp. 79–81; Karen Haynes, 1989, pp. 20–29). The perception that many women in social work want part-time and/or
temporary jobs to enhance family incomes, or to provide some additional out-of-the-home interaction suggests that many female social workers do not have a long-term career orientation, and may
well reduce the perceived need for salary equity and promotional
opportunities.

Charity Workers   Social work quite clearly originated in religious
and charitable movements. As a consequence, individuals within
these early movements were neither professionally trained nor specifically educated. They were, in the best sense of the term, "do
gooders" who used no specific methodologies other than care and
concern. No one paid charity workers; they did it out of altruism,
and many of them were in fact wealthy women who may not have
needed payment. For the most part, it was societally unacceptable
for women to do paid work.

Throughout ancient as well as present times, organized religion has played an important role in the charity movement.
Whether it was viewed as a way to salvation for the individual or as
a socially desirable act, individuals volunteered their service in behalf of others; this meant the deserving poor—the widows, orphans, the frail elderly—or the impoverished. Charity workers were
benevolent volunteers, not professionally trained persons. Unfortunately, with the recent reduction in public dollars and the resurgence of privatization with its dependence on volunteers, this perpetuates the myth that social workers are motivated by conditions
other than career or salary.

Professional Criteria

Legal Regulation.   Until the 1970s the profession of social work in
the United States lacked public sanction (see chap. 12). Social work
employment was unregulated, and the title of social worker was
unprotected. The state battles to achieve both title protection and
protection of practice have been hard fought. Just over two decades

later, legal regulation has finally been achieved at some level in every state.

A profession that has to fight to convince the public, specifically legislators, of the need to require education and training to perform societally mandated functions, is clearly one that lacks empowerment. Even in those states where licensure of social work practice has been achieved, the statute has often had to exempt public employees, which significantly reduces the effectiveness of the law and any ability to help the public identify social workers.

Specialization. Unfortunately, the trend toward increasing specialization for social workers has sometimes enhanced the status, compensation, and public image of individuals but may have disadvantaged the total profession. An unanticipated consequence of specialization has been the creation of labels; social work specialists no longer identify themselves as social workers, but rather as marriage counselor, family therapist, social psychotherapist, child advocate, neighborhood organizer, consultant, or programs evaluator. Although subspecialization labeling can be useful in describing the specifics of a job, a target client population, or a functional area, it does not help to unify the profession or to provide a uniform and professional image to the public.

Medical doctors use specialty labels without the generic, such as pediatrician, internist. A better model for social workers might be nurses who use both generic and specialist terms together (pediatric nurse, surgical nurse) or attorneys who tend to use the generic label first and then a specialty label if and when appropriate (attorney specializing in family law).

Accountability. Until recently, the adage "good people do good works" meant that social work did not need to be accountable for its practice outcomes. Only since the mid-1970s has social work increasingly been asked to justify its existence, to measure its services, to document its methodology and its success. Unfortunately, many social workers lack the training in research and evaluative methods to effectively ask and answer those questions.

As we noted in Chapter 12, the outcomes of our services are neither easily nor inexpensively measured. Have we prevented domestic violence? Have we reduced family stress and conflict? Have we improved the living conditions of a frail elderly person? Such questions are dependent on reliable and valid measures of complex constructs.

It is important to note that the preferred outcomes of many services are also long-term—stopping recidivism, primary prevention, or long-term cures. Society in general, and legislators and funders in particular, want quick solutions.

The moderator thanks the speaker and quickly notes, "Well, that may feel a bit heavy, but we will hear about solutions next. We know that a problem must be identified and the client engaged before an effective solution can be reached. So, although the identification of our image problems may be initially discouraging, it's the healthy first step toward our collective remedy."

Solutions

Unfortunately, there are no easy, "quick fix" solutions to many of these public image problems, or they would not so persistently exist in the 1990s. However, a number of solutions, many already in use across the country, can move us closer to overcoming stereotypes and eroding myths.

Individual Strategies

Call Yourself a Social Worker. *"I am Luz, social worker, and executive director of our local mental health clinic. I didn't always identify myself that way, but recently, the first MSW commissioner of our state Department of Mental Health and Mental Retardation addressed this issue at the state's NASW conference. He noted that much earlier in his career he had obtained an MBA after his MSW and had purposively used the MBA descriptor as he began his rise from executive director of a community mental health center to commissioner in another state. He remarked that he found it somewhat ironic that the higher up he moved and the longer he stayed there, the more important he felt the social work descriptor had become. He noted that earlier he had wanted to portray himself as a 'scientific manager' and the MBA was useful, but he increasingly realized that there was not much science in management and that indeed the most important parts of management were the human relations skills and the values. At the end of his speech, he proclaimed, 'I am proud to be a social worker and I call*

I Am a Social Worker!

By Beverly McPhail

There are many wonderful characteristics to be found among social workers, but one of the lesser known, and most unusual qualities, is the ability to remain incognito. Think about it for a minute. When is the last time you met another social worker? Although you may have met child advocates, counselors, managers, clinicians, family therapists, psychotherapists, legislators, or community organizers, in reality many of these people are unidentified social workers. Social workers too often hide their social work background from clients and colleagues alike.

Of course, it is difficult to blame social workers for not speaking proudly about their professional roots since the image of social work is often tarnished. Too often the public perception of a social worker is either a naive "do-gooder" or an uncaring child welfare worker. I remember once

chatting with a neighbor whose son was due to start classes at the University of Texas within the week. Upon my inquiry about his major, his mother explained that since he had a desire "to help people," he had chosen pre-medical studies. I suggested he check into the school's social work program. The mother quickly grimaced and stated that her son wanted a profession with a little more status.

Well, no wonder social workers go undercover! Who wants to be identified with a profession with low status, little prestige, and poor economic compensation? However, this dilemma is a bit like the chicken and the egg. Which came first? Did social work have a poor reputation and so we stopped identifying ourselves as social workers; or, did we stop identifying ourselves as social workers and then develop a poor image?

The question of which came first is probably a moot point. A better question may be: what can we do about our image? Perhaps we can adopt from the gay community the practice of "outing." That is, we can publicly identify prominent people in the mental health field who are respected "clinicians" and "therapists" as the social workers they are. However, this practice seems in direct contradiction to our value of self-determination.

Another answer may be for each social worker to start identifying themselves to their clients, colleagues, and friends as social workers. Social workers can start educating people about the social work profession. If the only time that social workers are publicly identified is when an overworked, underpaid child welfare worker comes under attack, then our image problem will persist. However, if all social

myself a social worker and it is my social work training that has been most meaningful in my managerial jobs.' The audience, almost as one, rose to their feet. I realized that he had given the audience empowerment, pride, identity, and unity all from that very simple statement."

workers claimed our social work education, title, and ideology, our image would be sure to change. For if the public learned about the variety of places we work—in the schools, legislatures, mayor's office, hospitals, social service agencies, hospices, grass-roots organizations—their perception of social work would expand. And, if our colleagues came to know that we are successful as therapists, advocates, and clinicians because of our social work approach to client problems, their respect for social workers would grow. And, if our clients learned that our emphasis is not only on social treatment, but on social change, their trust in us would increase. And, if the world saw our committed work in dealing with the major social problems of our times, such as homelessness, domestic violence, suicide, and teenage pregnancy (to name just a few), their appreciation for our frontline involvement would increase.

Some would argue that the semantics of what we call ourselves isn't important. They may argue that what we are called is less important than what we do. Yet, if social workers are to assist clients, we must first become advocates for ourselves. We cannot empower clients if we as a profession are not empowered. And social workers cannot become empowered unless we start proudly identifying ourselves as social workers. As social workers, we have a unique perspective to offer the community that other professions do not possess. With our focus on activism and change, social workers are committed to prevention as well as treatment. Our profession has a proud history of advocating for the powerless. The early social workers paved the way for how citizens of the United States look at, and deal with, social problems. Social workers need to reaffirm our proud traditions and seek to carry them into the next century, for we are truly a profession that has made the world a better place in which to live.

So, the next time someone asks you what you do for a living, tell them you are a social worker. The particular job title or specific work responsibilities can follow. Explain your educational background and the unique social work ideology. For those of you who haven't used the term in years, your voice may be a little rusty at first. Practice saying it in front of the mirror until your voice becomes louder and stronger. "I am a social worker . . . I AM A SOCIAL WORKER!" Or, join the new twelve-step program, SWA—Social Workers Anonymous. Or, read the dramatic new bestseller by a recovering therapist who reclaimed her social work roots, "Incognito No More!" These techniques work for our clients—who knows, they might work for us, too.

For those who do not recognize the name, Beverly is an active member of NASW/Houston Unit, and a much-published opinion writer for the Houston Post. She is also a social worker who does not have the ability to "remain incognito."
SOURCE: Houston Unit NASW Newsletter, *guest editorial, October 1991.*

Ryan provides another example. "Several years ago at a profes-sional conference, it was surprising to see the incredible affect made by the conference chair. She opened the conference by introducing herself as a social worker first, then noted her position. Every other speaker at that conference, and every year since that date at that same conference, people have introduced themselves as social workers, first, and then added any additional professional description. Conference attendees remarked at the pride and unity they felt. From then on, I began to identify myself as Ryan, social worker and senatorial aide."

This is an easy solution, but, unfortunately, one infrequently employed. The very nature of the negative public image makes many of us deny our training and our profession, and each time we do, we contribute to the myths and stereotypes. Whether it be at a professional conference, to the media, on an airplane or at a private party, calling ourselves social workers, proudly and continuously, will educate the public and enhance our image.

Correct the Negative Stereotypes. *"Media watch groups are a terrific strategy,"* Molly offers. *"Our local NASW group developed one several years ago and with much more consistency and far greater power we have corrected the media for its incorrect use of the term social worker, for pejorative stereotypes of our clients, and for incorrect and biased viewpoints about social services. In fact, we have reporters now calling us first so that they don't make a mistake."*

Etta chimes in, *"I once got so angry about an issue that I wrote a response and showed it to a colleague of mine. She suggested that I send it to the newspaper. I thought, they'll never print this. But they did and I felt extremely pleased that I didn't just sit back and let one side of the debate get aired. I write Op Eds (Opposite the Editorial page) frequently and they often are published."*

A second extremely important strategy is to consistently provide commentary against the commonly held myths and inaccuracies about our profession. We corroborate these misconceptions when we remain silent in the face of these allegations just because we are fearful that we might have insufficient evidence, facts, and knowledge in the face of ignorance, prejudice, and bias. Our professional mandate should require us to take this stance. Not righting the inaccuracies is tantamount to maintaining mistruths. To be concerned that we do not have sufficient facts to speak out is to accept the stereotype of our ignorance and to believe that the people who speak against us have more and greater knowledge about what we do.

Educate the Public. *"I used to just accept the public's ignorance about what social workers do and believe that there was nothing I could do to change it,"* Carlos, barrio organizer, begins. *"It seemed like too overwhelming a task for one person. Then, sitting at a school board meeting, I asked some people how they knew so much about welfare mothers. They answered that they read it in the papers. Then and there it hit me, I could write to the papers and get some of my colleagues to do the same. Maybe the public was in need of education. I realize that it's not that easy, but if people have only one side of an issue, that's the side they're likely to adopt."*

Thus, you do not have to wait until something negative or incorrect is written, you can educate the public with stories about the positive outcomes of services, the real stories of our clients. You may need to become more sensitive to timing of stories, or "news pegs," but it can be extremely effective.

Support Your Professional Associations. *"I didn't keep up my membership in the NASW for a while because there were several other specialty organizations that provided me with journals and continuing education opportunities that I felt were much more important. Recently, as the NASW became more active in the initiation and lobbying for progressive social legislation, I realized that there were other important reasons to lend my support. I can specifically remember when the NASW responded to President Reagan's AIDS commission report by noting that the statement 'blanket exceptions to confidentiality might be applied' to 'certain categories of people' was in conflict with NASW's ethics code. Social workers are involved with AIDS from the day patients are tested through their loved ones' grieving after they die, yet the report barely acknowledged social workers' roles. What other professional organization is obligated to take these public stands? How can we ignore our professional association and then criticize it for what it isn't doing?"* Nancy, family counselor, asks the group.

A final individual strategy is to join and support professional organizations. We cannot win these battles alone. Whether our goals are to improve practice, to begin new services, or to enhance our profession, part of the strategy includes our individual commitment to be part of a collective effort.

Organizational Strategies

Sell Yourself and the Profession. *"I used to let the language of job descriptions exclude me,"* Julie, director of the Early Adolescent Program at the Children's Museum, speaks up. *"An ad that read MBA preferred used to be a signal to me not to even apply. Even an ad that didn't specify social work education provided a barrier in my own*

Those on Welfare Catch Epithets While Rest Getting Flowers

The Mothers We Love to Hate

By Beverly McPhail

It's Mother's Day and mothers all across the nation are being honored. Flowers, breakfast in bed, and praises extolled from pulpits will be the common experience for many mothers today.

Rhetoric will flow calling mothers the backbone of our families and our society. The sacrifices mothers make for their children and families will be praised and some moms will get a day of well-deserved rest. Gifts of candy, jewelry, and nursery school crafts will abound to honor that woman who spends so much of her life in service to others.

President Bush and other politicians will include a note in their speeches about the contributions mothers have made to our country.

And yet one group of mothers will not be the beneficiaries of such high praise and commendation. This group of mothers will not receive the admiration of most Americans, but will instead receive their condemnation. This group of women are the mothers Americans love to hate. They are welfare mothers.

Although most Americans do not personally know a welfare mother, most Americans purport to know all about her.

She is a parasite, a sponge, a woman undeserving of our respect and praises, even on Mother's Day. She is a lazy woman who stays home and has children at the taxpayer's expense. She has five, six or seven children and should be forced to have her tubes tied.

She's on welfare for years and is a major drain on our country's resources. She's the scourge of democracy and the blame for all the major social problems of our times, including increased crime, drug use, and the deficit.

This cruel stereotype of the welfare mother is totally untrue and unsupported by statistics. In fact, the welfare mother myth and reality are quite different.

In Region 11 of the Texas Department of Human Services (TDHS), which consists of thirteen counties including Harris County, there are 56,068 single-parent households receiving Aid to Families with Dependent Children (AFDC). In these families, the average number of children is 1.9. The average mother stays in the program for two years. The average mother with two children receives $180 a month in AFDC payments compared to California where similar families receive over $500 a month.

Texas ranks 48th in the nation in the amount of payments made to poor women and their children. The only states that pay less are Mississippi and Louisiana.

Of all the mothers receiving assistance in Region 11, 11 percent are involved in the innovative job training program which works to help women receive their GED and gain employment.

However, it is not laziness or lack of motivation that keeps this percentage so low, it is lack of funds. Many women are unable to participate because TDHS doesn't receive enough money to provide day care and transportation to enable more women to participate in the program.

Chuck Adams, public information officer for TDHS, reports that most of the women are working to get off of welfare. "That's the good news," he states, "Women can increase their self-esteem and education is the key."

Although education is the key in his mind, punishment seems to be the answer for many more Americans.

New Jersey recently passed a law which reduces a woman's benefits if she has additional children while on welfare. Texas doesn't have such sanctions for women who have more children, but an extra $57.00 a month for each additional child is hardly an incentive to have more children.

Since the average mother on welfare has two children, sanctions like those of New Jersey would affect only a very small percentage of women. Of course, when you rank 48th out of 50 states in amount of benefits paid, there is not too much room for cutting benefits.

More punitive measures are being proposed across the nation in addition to other so-called reforms. Texas already has workfare provisions, which are increasing in popularity in other states. In Texas, if a

woman does not participate in the job program when transportation and child care can be provided, she is "sanctioned" and her benefits are cut. But the number of women who refuse job training is exceeded by the number of women who want the training and are refused help due to lack of funding.

The system is at fault, not the women.

Yes, there are some people who are unmotivated, do as little work as possible, are unfit parents and might even be called lazy. Unfortunately, these characteristics can be observed in many Americans in schools, offices and neighborhoods across the nation and cannot be attributed solely to women receiving welfare.

In a recent national radio address, President Bush came down hard on mothers receiving assistance, stating they "have certain responsibilities to seek work, or get education, and training that will help them get a job." That's a Catch-22 for many mothers who would like to do just that, but can't due to lack of program funding.

Another contradictory message we send welfare mothers is to reduce the number of children they have. Yet no provisions are made for birth control or

abortion services through Medicaid.

Additionally, Bush addresses the responsibilities of welfare mothers but never mentions the fathers of their children. The term "welfare father" doesn't even exist in our vocabulary.

So why do Americans love to hate welfare mothers? Chuck Adams points to the fact that this is an election year and that the country is in a recession as a double rationale. The laid-off auto worker needs to be angry at someone and welfare mothers make a convenient scapegoat. Politicians' criticizing welfare mothers is a guaranteed vote-getter similar to showing the revolving prison door letting out African American convicts.

Both pictures play to the worst stereotypes Americans hold, attempting to arouse fear and prejudice and steer us away from the issues and statistics which often paint a far different picture.

Welfare mothers are by definition female and poor. Of all groups in America today they are probably the most unempowered. It's easy to attack welfare mothers, for they don't have the resources to fight back.

Welfare mothers are too busy to organize. They are trying to survive.

Focusing on welfare mothers as the cause of all social problems in America today is easier than trying to understand and solve the complexities of the real problems.

It's easier to bash the Japanese than to change the way Americans do business. It's too complex to understand how Charles Keating cost taxpayers billions of dollars due to his financial wheeling and dealing.

It's easier to imagine women having babies at taxpayers' expense.

A welfare mother is actually a woman who has dreams, hopes, and aspirations like everyone else. Yet her feelings and life experiences are ignored and invalidated and she is defined by the assistance she receives. "Welfare mother" is a term that dehumanizes and objectifies a person.

Women receiving assistance aren't the stereotypical women that they are suggested to be. They are women who happen to be poor and mothers. "Most women are a man away from welfare" is a statement that rings true for many women, and yet Americans don't want to believe it. It's easier to ascribe to these mothers such attributes as lazy and parasitic, rather than acknowledge they are victims of circumstances that can befall any woman.

When fathers desert their families, refuse to pay child support, and there is not national health care insurance, many women have little resources and support. When society continues to pay women less than men and most job openings for women continue to be menial and low-paying, women can easily become trapped.

Suffering the dual oppression of sexism and classism, and—for women of color—racism, it is a wonder these women are able to get off welfare at all.

Instead of holding them up for ridicule and contempt, researchers should be studying how some of these mothers pull themselves up and get off welfare in two years against tremendous odds and society's begrudging assistance.

Many of these mothers deserve our understanding and respect, not our contempt.

Happy Mother's Day.

SOURCE: Houston Post, *10 May 1992.*

---

mind to my application. An important mentor convinced me to jump in, and sell myself. It worked and what I realize now is that it also helps to sell our profession. Now, I create the job descriptions."

George, union dispute mediator, adds, "My position was not even advertised in any of our regular professional newsletters. It certainly didn't include credentials for social work. But, with years of family counseling in my background, and the knowledge that alot of social work is mediation, I applied. I really had to sell myself, but I got the position. Since then, dispute resolution centers have come into existence in my community and I am involved in alot of mediation training."

One strategy is to get organizations, particularly large-scale ones, to view social work education as appropriate preparation for management. With the emergence of accountability issues in the mid-1970s, we witnessed the trend of catapulting MBAs and MPAs into executive positions with the idea that they had more of the organizational, managerial, budgeting, and accounting skills than MSWs. These skills are necessary, but to have them without an understanding of the values of professional service, the theories and techniques utilized to intervene, and the person-in-environment approach, is to be unable to manage social services well. It is not surprising that the bottom line becomes the top priority when we abdicate leadership responsibilities. To minimize the human relations skills and the importance of values to an organization, both of which are achieved through social work training, is also to undersell ourselves and our profession.

Market Your Organization. *"Marketing doesn't have to be all that expensive,"* Barbara, Employee Assistance Program supervisor, *says emphatically. "I serve on the board of a rather small not-for-profit agency in my community. Not only are they small, with a very small budget, but they aren't well known. The board was really feeling in a bind. How could we fundraise in a community that really didn't know what we did or that we existed at all. On the other hand, how could we squeeze money to pay for expensive marketing?*

"The board was ready to give up, so I decided to take on the challenge. You know what I found out? There are some terrific public relations firms who want to do some pro bono work. I found a group who did an excellent Public Service Announcement and a 15-minute video for free. Of course their name is now identified with those products, so they 'won' also."

Someone in the audience speaks up. "My agency realized that it had to rethink its name because it had expanded services and changed clientele over time. We realized that the right name and name recognition is both important for our clients to get to the right place and for funders to see us as an important player in our community. We also found a public relations firm to help us test out new names on our community. Once we changed our name, we had to hire someone to redo our agency logo and letterhead. Was it worth it? You bet."

Another organizational strategy is to undertake, in a much more planned fashion, public relations efforts. Although most social service agencies are fiscally constrained and find themselves understaffed, the logic of placing some resources into public relations and marketing is part of a longer term strategy of improving our image. This is not to suggest that half of an agency's budget be allocated to wide-scale marketing campaigns, but it is supportive of improving the public image of the agency and services, which will directly improve the public image of social work and quite likely enhance the capacity of an agency to raise community funds.

Publicize Your Successes. *"I used to get tired of all the forms we had to use in our agency," Judy, Children's Protective Service worker, shares. "Finally, a new executive was hired and she must have heard that we were frustrated with all the paperwork. She began meeting with small groups of us to explain why and how she used that infor-mation. I knew that we had to give some of it to the state to account for what we were doing. I didn't know that it had been used to argue for more staff; that it was important to maintain information to give the media when they were certain we were inept and underworked. She said that she intended to begin to prepare and distribute an annual report for public distribution. She also said that she wanted to create a committee to see how some of it could be used for worker merit review. I still found it time consuming, but I could connect it to our service mission."*

Increasingly, social workers and social service agencies are utilizing research methodologies and collecting data to improve practice. Sharing this information in public forums as well as in professional research journals is essential to public education and for our professional image.

Large-Scale Efforts

Validation Studies. *Patricia Sue, executive director of the Campfire Girls, speaks. "You need to be careful about how you try to validate that social work education is essential for certain positions. I wanted to professionalize our staff and requested that my board authorize me to convert many positions as they became vacant to require a BSW. The board wanted to determine whether they really needed profes-sional social workers and developed a plan to answer that question.*

"Their plan consisted of doing a task analysis of the tasks cur-rently performed by our staff (mostly nonprofessionals). I objected, explaining that they wouldn't get a description of the tasks and skills necessary to do the job, but a description of what tasks were being performed. Most of the board felt that it was easier to do this induc-tively rather than deductively. It was a struggle, but I finally convinced them to do it my way."

Validation studies began approximately at the same time as the push for legal regulation in the United States (the early 1970s) and are not only essential to prevent further declassification but to validate social work credentials for human service jobs (Robert Teare, 1987). These validation studies are important because they provide the research to support our profession's contention that it takes extensive education to provide many social service tasks. Moreover, these studies are necessary to provide the necessary delineation between paraprofessional and professional job positions.

Legal Regulation. *"I got tired of hearing that our state professional association's first lobbying priority was licensure until it became clear that without licensing, insurance companies wouldn't reimburse mental health counseling services provided by social workers," Luz notes. "Because social workers make up the largest professional group in the mental health field, the potential reduction in service providers, a limited choice of professional expertise, and higher cost of services would all negatively impact our clients. At that point, I jumped on the bandwagon and wrote letters to my state representative and provided testimony in support of social work licensure."*

A strategy that needs to be continued is the pressure to retain legal regulation of social work practice. Although all states have now passed some form of legal regulation of social work practice, many states want to remove the certification or registration requirement. In the states in which public employees are exempted, their statutes need to be strengthened to cover the public sector of the labor force in licensure. In states where regulation faces "sunset" laws (laws requiring a review and reaffirmation of a statute), renewed advocacy is essential.

There are inherent professional conflicts in this strategy given the criticisms of the self-serving and exclusionary nature of legal regulation. However, in addition to the issue of image, legal regulation is mandatory for insurance carriers to cover social worker's services.

Educating Entertainers. *"When I read about the creation of the NASW Communications Network (NCN) in 1988, I thought that this was a frivolous project," Bill, AIDS activist, admits. "But when NCN got actor Dennis Weaver to do a public service announcement on AIDS for the NASW's national campaign, I was impressed. Later, when I read who in the entertainment industry had been given a 'Si' award, I realized that these awards—by choosing shows, entertainers, and directors who accurately portrayed the life and problem of social work*

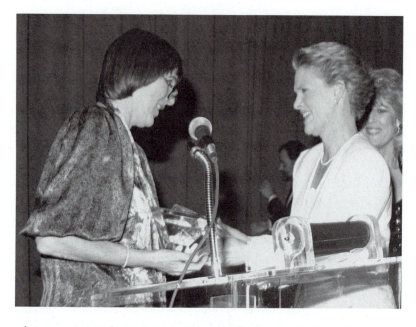

NCN founder and president Suzanne Dworak-Peck presents a "Si" (Social Issues) award to Sharon Gless, star of television's *The Trials of Rosie O'Neill* and *Cagney and Lacey*. Also pictured is Meredith MacRae, event emcee. NCN (NASW Communications Network, Inc.) is an independent nonprofit corporation.

clients or social workers—promote better understanding by the entertainment industry while providing the public with better and more sensitive information. I realized that this was a very smart group to target because through educating them and then rewarding them for their accuracy, the wider public had indirectly been targeted. I know in the area of AIDS, there has been more and better fiction and nonfiction coverage."

The idea behind the NCN was to work with the entertainment industry to educate writers in the television and movie arena so that social workers and our clients are portrayed in a realistic light. This large-scale effort to turn our public image around by building "a foundation for a relationship with the entertainment industry that will help us open doors and foster a better understanding of social issues" (Suzanne Dworak-Peck, 1988). Annually, since 1989, the NCN gives "Si" awards to writers, actors, and directors, who portray social workers accurately and take on important social issues.

Summary

This chapter began with a delineation of the commonalities of our professional identity, which transcend interventive method, field of practice, or organizational role. It is our contention that the professional identity of social workers cannot be discussed without an examination of the public's image of our profession, so explanations for the various public images were provided. The chapter ends with a variety of strategies for continuing to enhance this image. These strategies include individual, organizational, and professional suggestions.

We have come a long way since the charity workers of a century ago. We have progressed even farther when one remembers that formal training is an even more recent development. With about two decades of formalized efforts to regulate our practice, all states have now enacted legislation.

Social work practice has become diversified and specialized in the last quarter century, so the fact that we have to identify who we are and what we do really should be no surprise. Social work education did not add a professional entry level of education until 1974.

Although our image may be somewhat tarnished and inaccurate, this can be remedied with some polishing and information dissemination. The image cannot be all bad because enrollments in social work programs have continued to rise since the latter half of the 1980s. NASW membership has risen during this time period as well and labor force projections indicate an increasing demand for social workers in the future.

References

Dworak-Peck, Suzanne. "NCN Project is Building Relationship with Media." *NASW News*, Vol. 35 (May 1988): 6.

Haynes, Karen S. *Women Managers in Human Services*. New York: Springer Publishers, 1989.

Hopps, June G., and Elaine B. Pinderhughes. "Profession of Social Work: Contemporary Characteristics." In *Encyclopedia of Social Work*, 18th ed., 351–366. Edited by Anne Minahan. Silver Spring, MD: NASW, 1987.

Kravetz, Diane, and Linda E. Jones. "Career Orientations of Female Social Work Students: An Examination of Sex Differences." *Journal of Education for Social Work*, Vol. 18, No. 3 (1982): 77–84.

Teare, Robert. *Validating Social Work Credentials for Human Service Jobs: Report of a Demonstration*. Silver Spring, MD: NASW, 1987.

CHAPTER 14

The Future of Social Work

Introduction

"And for your last assignment in this class, I want you to come prepared to talk about the future of social work, and your future in social work in the twenty-first century. We've spent time during this semester discussing the long and rich history of our practice and of our profession. We've examined the values, knowledge, and method base of social work. And, more recently, we've talked about professional issues and professional identity. Now I want you to take what you have heard and project a decade ahead to the profession's future and to your own.

"I want to give you something to think about, so I thought that I'd share some of the trends and projections that have been made about the future in general. These may help you as you envision the upcoming decade."

The Trends

Over a decade ago, John Naisbitt published *Megatrends: Ten New Directions Transforming Our Lives,* which described certain trends and their implications for the future. For the most part, Naisbitt's trends reflected shifts already taking place that he predicted would continue, including:

1. From an industrial to an informational society.

2. From a forced technology to one that matches high technology with high touch.

3. From a national to a global economy.

4. From short term to long term perspectives.

5. From centralized to decentralized decision making.

6. From institutional help to self help.

7. From representative democracy to participatory democracy.

8. From hierarchical structures to networks.

9. From powerful northern industrial cities to powerful southern and western cities.

10. From either/or choices to multiple option choices.

The book ends optimistically, defining the transitional time as one "filled with opportunity. If we can learn to make opportunity our friend, we can achieve much more than in stable eras. . . . We have extraordinary leverage and influence—individually, professionally, and institutionally—if we can only get a clear sense, a clear conception, a clear vision, of the road ahead. . . . What a fantastic time to be alive!" (John Naisbitt, 1982, p. 283).

Needless to say, we have all witnessed the impact of these changes during the last decade. By the 1980s, the information revolution that began in the mid-1950s, had allowed the introduction and adaptation of information technology to the home and to mobile offices. Microcomputers, cellular telephones, FAXs, and interactive personal services available via modem allow us to purchase goods and services and to access current international news and electronic encyclopedia. Certainly the presence of multinational corporations and the creation of a European Common Market illustrate the emergency of a global economy. And Xerox's announcement in 1981 that it was in "the automated office business"—although such business represented only 5 percent of its current sales—suggests a shift from short-term, bottom-line thinking to a longer term perspective.

In the profession of social work, health promotion and personal support related strategies are increasingly common. Self-help support groups for a wide range of problems or concerns have proliferated as more people seek to get their own houses in order. Health and recreation programs are popular for general fitness, for employee productivity, and for their perceived benefits to mental health.

Hospices, wellness programs, and home health care have opened new avenues of service delivery in the health care arena and mediation and family preservation services require new skills and different expectations of the client systems in the child and family arena.

John Naisbitt and Patricia Aburdene (1990) also forecasted new trends:

1. The booming global economy of the 1990s.
2. A renaissance in the arts.
3. The emergence of free market socialism.
4. Global lifestyles and cultural nationalism.
5. The privatization of the welfare state.
6. The rise of the Pacific Rim.
7. The decade of women in leadership.
8. The age of biology.
9. The religious revival of the new millennium.
10. The triumph of the individual.

Think about how many of these have already begun. The demise of the Soviet Union and the restructuring of the economy; the emergence of Japan as a leader in international trade; the Moral Majority's sophisticated and successful use of the media; and the emergence of biotechnology have already occurred.

For social work in particular, the privatization of the welfare state, the ethical considerations raised by biotechnical advances, and the increased presence of women in leadership will all affect our practice. Let's examine a few of these trends in more depth.

Demographic Trends

Because the population, and consequently the work force, will grow more slowly than at any time since the 1930s, the average age of the population and the work force will rise. Unemployment should decline, and industry will have more experienced workers with increased income and savings per worker. On the other hand, a smaller labor pool may mean that businesses will lose their competitive edge.

More women, more minorities, and more immigrants will enter the work force. Predictions suggest that two-thirds of all new entrants into the work force in the 1990s will be women and that 61 percent of all women of working age will be employed by the year 2000. An additional 29 percent of the new entrants into the labor force will be minorities, and 66 percent or more of the immigrants of working age are likely to join the labor force.

This suggests that the demographic makeup of the work force

will be much different in 2000 than it is today. Minorities, women, and immigrants will make up more than five-sixths of the new additions to the work force. Additionally, these new entrants into the labor force will bring with them a different set of demands—for day care, pregnancy leaves, part-time, flex-time, and at-home jobs. Similarly, attention to high school completion, recruitment of minorities into higher education, and vocational education will be even more essential (*Workforce 2000*, 1987).

A Service Economy

The movement of production from goods to services will also continue. The service industries differ from other goods producing industries in that they produce economic value without a tangible product. Although some services, such as transportation, may add value to manufactured goods because they are made more accessible, other services such as education and social services, create value that is largely independent of a goods producing economy (*Workforce 2000*, p. 21).

There is no single and accurate stereotype of service industries. Services are often stereotyped as low productivity and low wage industries, for example, the fast-food industry. However, the health care industry with the presence of both capital and technologically intense systems, also suggests extensive knowledge and training and high wages. Therefore, improved productivity in the new service industry will probably require higher order skills.

Technology

Additionally, increases in telecommunications will continue so that in-home shopping and banking will be increasingly part of the future. On-line weather, current news, and encyclopedias are already easily and relatively inexpensively available in homes.

The global economy is already here. Increasingly, available goods produced in less developed countries are sold in the United States, and goods produced in the United States are sold internationally. The global economy continues to push our nation from a goods producing to a service producing economy.

The "Third Industrial Revolution," or robotics, brings with it the specter of people being replaced by machines and the challenge of meeting a declining labor force with labor-saving machinery. It further suggests more at-home work possibilities, suggesting more flexible work time and the opportunities for more, or at least different, family and leisure time.

Women in Leadership

Already more women have assumed leadership positions. This trend has resulted because women have reached a "critical mass" in most of the white-collar professions, making it more and more difficult to deny them upper management roles (John Naisbitt and Patricia Aburdene, 1990, p. 223). More women are educating themselves for these positions; women are becoming a larger proportion of the labor force in general and of the midmanagerial labor force in particular.

In addition, the managerial paradigm appears to have shifted from a paradigm of *control* to a paradigm of *modeling* and *encouragement*. This new paradigm is more congruent with the feminist perspective. With fewer new recruits, leadership in the work force will mean obtaining and sustaining commitment and loyalty, supporting employees through lifelong learning programs, and nurturing their capacities for self-motivation and personal/professional growth.

As Patricia Aburdene and John Naisbitt (1992) note, the global village is watching women in Third World villages and on inner-city streets confront and solve tough problems. The 1992 election continued to see the increase of women in the political arena. Four additional females joined the two already serving in the U.S. Senate. Both of the senators elected in California were female; one was the first black female ever elected to the U.S. Senate.

Around the world the list of female presidents and prime ministers grows. Even two Moslem countries in Asia have elected women leaders, which was unimaginable just a few years ago (Patricia Aburdene and John Naisbitt, 1992, p. 311).

The Practice of Social Work

As we have already indicated, the practice of social work has changed dramatically over the past century. Social work has moved from a cause to a profession; from single-level educational preparation to multiple levels of professional preparation; and from a fairly narrow psychodynamic perspective to a breadth of theories and their relevant interventive strategies. The person-in-environment perspective has helped our profession to re-focus and to differentiate ourselves from other helping professionals, and the use of behavioral and cognitive approaches has broadened the practice skills.

Despite fears that the Reagan era's federal cutbacks would severely diminish the social work labor force and the consequent effectiveness of social work, this has not happened. In fact, the Department of Labor employment projections forecast at minimal, a total of 90,000 new social work positions by 1995 (U.S. Department of Labor, 1986). This would mean approximately 410,000 social work positions by 1995.

The majority of the social work labor force (85 percent) are still employed in formal organizations—public, not-for-profit, or proprietary—despite the movement of the last decade toward private or group practice. Mental health, children's services, health, and family services, in that order, represent the four largest arenas of practice, representing approximately 33 percent, 17 percent, 13 percent, and 13 percent respectively (NASW, 1987).

The shift into private practice in the past decade has created controversy, because potentially it represents an abandonment of the more traditional public sectors of social work practice; however, it currently represents a relatively small but important segment of social work practice. Serving diverse client populations in multiple arenas, both private and public, can only further strengthen the demand for and therefore the future of social work practice.

Social Work Educational Trends

For almost 75 years, the MSW was the sole professional social work degree in the United States. However, today there are almost as many social workers trained in bachelor's programs as in masters' programs. As was noted in Chapter 11, the initiation of BSW programs in the mid-1970s has more than doubled the number of students annually enrolled in social work programs. In 1991 there were 56,655 students enrolled in BSW programs nationally and 20,490 enrolled in MSW programs. Doctoral education in social work has increased simultaneously, and probably in part due to this growth in BSW programs. Over the same period, there has been rapid increase, both in the number of doctoral programs offered as well as in the number of doctoral degrees granted. There were 2,111 students enrolled in doctoral social work education during this same time period (CSWE, 1992).

Changing Roles and New Arenas of Practice

Given the changing and expanding practice arenas, the changing national demographics and the continued emphasis on technology, social workers' roles are likely to become even more diversified than ever. With the need to increase publicly supported day care on one end of the lifespan, and the need to improve the options for the well elderly on the other, social workers, particularly BSWs, will find increasing employment arenas in these fields.

The problems of substance abuse and its interrelatedness with high school drop-outs, teen pregnancy, and domestic violence will enhance and probably expand services in public schools, juve-

Governor of Arkansas Bill Clinton speaks at Henry Street Settlement House in New York City during his 1992 campaign for the presidency of the United States.

nile justice, and child welfare in general. Work-based or work-related employee programs will continue to expand as the labor force ages and increased strategies to retain, motivate, and serve that labor force will develop.

These new or expanding arenas of practice will require an entire spectrum of social work roles, from direct service work with individuals, their families, and significant others, to macro roles, including planning for and managing these new and expanding services, providing for their evaluation, and conducting research relative to emerging unmet needs. Mediation will continue to increase as a method in family intervention.

Similarly, with control of social services increasingly returned to state and local levels, the roles for social workers in the policy arena should continue to expand. Social workers will be needed not only as policymakers, but in the political realm in higher education. The NASW recently published a list of social workers in political office. This list, the first of its kind, acknowledges this as a growing arena of practice and probably represents only a fraction of the social workers actually holding political positions across the nation.

The "high touch" versus "high tech" debate continues. Technology is being used more and more to process and categorize information, to reduce the repetitive collection of client data, and as a useful diagnostic aid. The arguments that technology dehumanizes the process and potentially infringes on confidentiality must be heeded, but should not and will not, delay its appropriate utilization. Professionals need to be aware that computers can aid in a number of processes, including diagnosis and assessment, by analyzing risk factors to help predict the best fit between a client's problems, personal characteristics, and appropriate services; but social workers must also realize that although technology may enhance, it cannot replace professional judgment.

Some Emerging Issues

A number of emerging issues have already caught the profession's attention and will continue to be part of our dialogue in the future. Among these is the ongoing balance between professional treatment and volunteerism, or self-help, as methods of intervention. Some issues that are relatively recent to the social work arena have long since been debated and resolved in both education and medicine. For example, the role of volunteers in the medical arena is seldom confused with those of physicians and nurses. Similarly, support groups for patients with specific diseases or for their families do not take the place of, but operate in conjunction with, professional care. In education, volunteer tutors supplement but do not replace teachers in the classroom.

The social work profession is beginning to grapple once again with the issue of chronic care. Hospitals, although central to the health care industry, are increasingly seen as only one of many players. Convalescent and nursing homes, home health care, and outpatient treatment are not just "fads"; they are necessary additions as our general population becomes older. Such alternatives respond to the need for more humane care, as well as to the problem of escalating health care costs.

Whether the issues are adoption, reproductive rights, the right to no treatment, or the right to extensive treatment, social workers will find themselves at the center of a variety of inter- and intraprofessional ethical debates. Ethics, and not solely techniques or technology, will increasingly frame the alternatives of choice and the boundaries of acceptability. Privatization will also continue to be an issue for the profession of social work. Because public policies mandate what private not-for-profit agencies may do, governmental regulations may infringe more powerfully on these agencies than ever before. On the other hand, as social workers and social work agencies move toward marketplace ideologies and the delivery of only those services for which there is financing, a two-tiered service delivery system may emerge.

The Future

"Class, I am now pleased to introduce Professor Peggy Clements, who is chair of the Institute for the Future. I have asked her to share some thoughts with you on our last day about the future of social work."

"Can you imagine what fun and luxury it is to be able to daydream, fantasize, and gaze into my crystal ball with a serious intent and outcome as part of one's job! Imagine being able to read science fiction and high tech stuff for a professional, pragmatic, purpose! I am the executive director of this center (well, if I'm dreaming, I may as well go all the way.) I walk into the center, listening as always to the

low hum, clicks, and beeps of the friendly machines. Before moving to my office, I stop by for a cup of coffee. I say good morning to the coffee machine, so that it can analyze my voice and produce a moderately hot, medium cup of coffee, a little sugar, a little cream—as it has already been programmed.

"Once in my office, I again say good morning to my computer, who then replies, 'Good morning, Peggy, shall I transmit this morning's Silicon Courier? *'Of course, Detra,' I reply. In case you're wondering, Detra is her nickname, shortened from Digital Electronic Transformation Resonator by Apple. Detra calls up the morning edition. Oh, yes, I probably should mention, this was formerly the* Wall Street Journal. *Printed daily papers have been outdated for over a decade. I scroll through the pages and then type in a few key words so that I can briefly review social service stories.*

" 'Here's a list of yesterday's activities,' Detra interrupts, 'Or would you rather see your day's agenda?' 'Today's agenda,' I reply. On the screen flashes a multicolored agenda, including lists of people in meetings, my tasks, as well as time and place, color coded by importance. Fortunately, the only red agenda item today is my midafternoon briefing to the legislative human services committee on future service needs. 'Let's see the activity list now.' That list flashes up and I quickly review it.

"I press a key to indicate I'm finished (Detra hasn't learned to read my mind yet) and the screen automatically displays the state map with dots indicating client locations. Just to be sure, I call up an overlay of spatial distributions of activities for the year to date. No significant differences. Next several graphs appear comparing yesterday's volume to the previous day's and by the same day last week, and lastly by this day last year. Stats compare favorably.

"Before you become too impressed with this output, let me emphasize what was not collected. You may have wondered why no additional client demographic information was collected and concluded that either I don't know what important client information is, or I was sloppy in my listing. Wrong on both counts. No additional information was collected because it was unnecessary. Detra communicates with the states' mainframe computer daily and given basic client data, can then routinely collect age, sex, occupation, and income data. Also, don't feel too sorry for Detra, this task took her only seconds. Because Detra's memory is much better than mine, the statistical comparisons are an easy function, but provide twice daily monitoring of client vol-

ume and client location so that I can pinpoint trouble, or change staffing patterns rapidly.

"Having noticed that one worker, Kristin, seems to have a disproportionately low client load, I type in my inquiry. On the screen is displayed our weekly task allocations, which graphically indicates that Kristin's is filled with legislative briefs. 'Let me see this.' I touch the screen at the legislative briefs line (the touchscreen concept has been developed for years) and immediately displayed is a list of briefs due tomorrow that have been Kristin's responsibility. 'Thanks, Detra, would you contact Kristin for me?'

"I press the sight enhancer function key and within moments, Kristin's face appears on the screen. 'Sorry to bother you at this time, but I want to know who you think can help you finish up those two briefs on foster placements and health status indicators.' (Note, even in the future, computers cannot make all decisions.) 'Well, in this instance, a final review of the data for any additional analysis is what is necessary. Consequently, I think Mary should be the choice.' 'Thanks, I'll see you next week.'

"All workers have home computers linked to Detra and rotate working at home and in the office. Before calling Mary, I look around the office and my mind wanders back some years when we first introduced the home work station. Everyone wanted to work at home all the time. What flexibility! It would eliminate commute time (greatly reduced from now, I might add, with monorails, people movers, high speed intercity trains and programmable cars), it would give people greater flexibility to connect with their children, friends, significant others.

"And so I decided that all we needed were weekly reports summarizing activities and highlighting future issues communicated from the central computer (I didn't call her Detra then); monthly staff meetings via videocommunication; and biannual staff meetings where we would meet face-to-face. Greeted with great enthusiasm, everyone packed up their data and floppy disks, their plants, pictures, posters, and other memorabilia to reestablish themselves in this pleasant home environment.

"After the first two months went by, I began to notice some strange behaviors. Workers were dropping by the office on their way to do an errand (remember that lots of errands no longer have to be run because one can dial up store lists, call up pictures of merchandise, ask questions about whether this dress or suit runs small or large, and *order for home delivery). So, I began to ask questions. I had also begun to notice, that with no one else around, I had found a name for my computer (Detra) and was using more voice and touchscreen commands than keyboard. Strange, no?*

"Well, it appeared that in our very high tech, efficient world touch was sorely missed. People still didn't want to come to the office daily, but, although it was hard for us to say, we did want to come in at periodic intervals. We acknowledged that while we could quickly get all the information we needed; that although we could see each other via video when we wanted to talk, these planned, formal, and technological encounters didn't satisfy our needs to see people directly, and to pat them on the back (or be patted, literally); that is, to touch them. It also appeared that, organizationally, we were lying dormant with respect to creative ideas. We didn't spontaneously bump into each other at the coffee machine, in the restrooms, or in the elevator and start a rather innocuous conversation resulting in a brainstorm.

"So, we instituted a staffing plan that included a rotation between work and home. A core of staff representing all subunits was always in the office. The entire staff would be in only a few days each month. And, we haven't budged from that plan since.

"My reverie is broken by Detra's interruption: 'Major fire downtown—six buildings blazing! Shall I alert the surrounding buildings and check that the Red Cross and Disaster Relief agencies have been contacted.' 'Yes, and when you're finished, give me a list of volunteers available at this time of the day in the vicinity.' While waiting momentarily for this list, I try to remember how slow and labor intensive just these few tasks would have been. Of course, we might not have even been called, or at least not for critical minutes. Getting simultaneous transmission of police/fire/ambulance emergency calls has not only saved lives and property, but assured our central place (and stable funding) within the state.

"The screen flashes up a list of 22 volunteers. I type in a command for these 22 to be divided, as previously agreed, to the 3 workers currently listed for this task. They will then personally call these volunteers immediately with a set of instructions commonly agreed on by the two agencies and the fire department. I learned, tragically, many years ago, that even willing and committed volunteers respond faster and more effectively if they are personally contacted by a staff person with whom they are acquainted.

"I know that once the fire trucks have returned, Detra will be notified as to the extent of damage, as well as of lives and property

saved. The Red Cross and the Disaster Relief agencies will also input information to Detra. She'll then compile it, do some basic statistical analyses, and send it to our public relations staff person for editorial comments and the individual flair. A model article will be transmitted. This way, coverage of our agency's efforts will be in all local media for this evening's distribution. You can't, even in the future, keep the agency name in the news too much.

"I begin my preparation for this afternoon's legislative committee briefing. What the committee has specifically requested is a state-wide description of human services provided by categories. The committee also wants the total, unduplicated number of clients served in the state, an average cost of delivering all services per client, as well as a per capita population allocation. As you may have already guessed, I will also provide for display, maps showing the spatial pattern of service users, color coded for the state's standardized major categories of service.

"I type in a message to Brenda, our research and statistics whiz, to compile, analyze, and transmit to me by noon. She's not working for another hour, so I hit one more key to assure that this will be the first message she receives. Now on to the second set of data that they need. Using the same classification, I am supposed to present a compilation of current unmet needs, as well as a five-year forecast of human service needs. Detra can handle both of these tasks quite rapidly with a few touches of the keys to instruct frequency distributions, bar graphs, and the spatial patterns of needs.

"The last data set that I will use comes from our recent cable poll requesting that the citizenry of our state rank what they, personally, view as unmet needs within their community, and what they think, generally, the government should be providing. I can remember when cable TV was first initiated and then later, the interactive mechanisms of the 'QUBE' system and the forecasting (was it back in 1982?) of a civic communication cooperative. More than 10 years later, nationally developed civic broadcasting began, which included cable town meetings, electronic polling and voting, and computerized information services as free public utilities. Clearly this civic videotex service not only provides the 'simple information' on all community and statewide services, but the ability to poll the citizenry on public views.

"I call up this data set immediately, before I determine what analysis should be done, or the presentation style. I am delighted (and relieved) to immediately note that 65 percent of all of our state's families have responded, and that they are geographically representative. I

am also not surprised to see that the perceived future need will continue to be independent, but supervised, living units for the aged—now defined as those over 75.

"That reminds me to talk to our ombudsperson about the public health violations in some of these housing units. Another smile crosses my face. I can still recall, although more faintly now, when class advocacy was not a paid for and central function of every social service system.

"I shall not bore you with the rest of my day, because it consists of some routine and not very new tasks. Two workers become ill, and our personnel director, with the help of Detra, recruits replacements. I begin work on merit salary and promotion recommendations, certainly using computerized information, but still relying on practice wisdom, intuition, and a personal assessment of motivation still not amenable to numerical quantification. See, some things won't be conquered by high technology.

"Now let me close by celebrating that high tech will always need touch. And, as I remind Detra daily, I can serve clients without her, but not she, without me. And only you can keep the human touch in human services."

There's silence for a few moments and then David speaks up. "You know, much of what you predicted goes along with my own fantasy that more of social service expenditures will be for public education and for prevention. I predict that there will be an increasing need for social workers in the public policy and political arena. I hope that social workers' roles really will be a bit less in remediation and rehabilitation."

Lisa jumps in. "I wrote about the role of social workers in school systems. I would like to believe that every school would have a social work department. That no new student, at any age or grade, would be admitted to a school without an interview by a social worker to assess the total needs of the student. That social workers would be linked, electronically, to the data bases of all social services so that in referring students and their family, the social worker would know eligibility requirements, fees, hours, and waiting lists. The worker could program the computer to schedule follow-up meetings to evaluate the student's needs and the service delivery effectiveness."

Tricia, with emotion in her voice, says, "I envisioned a future where no child would be lost in a foster care system. Where all children would have permanent homes with financial support, and when necessary, counseling, job training, and day care. A system in which all workers would have adequate training, good salaries, and positive public images."

Jason speaks hesitantly. "I was talking to my father the other night about this assignment and my prediction of a greater role for social workers in the corporate arena. Even he agreed that workers need help to get through life's problems like divorce and death. Making placement decisions regarding elderly parents can provide pain for many families and just raising children can be difficult without anyone to consult about what's normal these days. I told him that social workers could also help people prepare for job transitions to new areas of skill, to new geographic locations, and for retirement. You know what? He agreed about these increasing roles of social workers! My father!"

Conclusion

The professor thanks the guest lecturer and commends the students on the innovativeness and thoughtfulness of their assignments. She concludes:

"Although still considered a relatively young profession, social work has now achieved sufficient maturity to have received public sanction via legal regulation of practice; professional maturity through the granting of two professional practice degrees; to have become an important collaborator with a number of professions and disciplines; and to continue to be not only important service delivers, but increasingly policymakers and administrators in social services. The social work paradigm of person-in-environment will continue to be increasingly necessary with the complex specializations and the fragmentation of service delivery.

"It will continue to fall to social work to differentiate between rights and luxuries, to advocate equal access for all, to define the limits of marketplace factors, and to monitor the nation's progress on its domestic agenda.

"As transformed as any society may become, and as improved and humane as that society may strive to be, there will always be life crises and catastrophes; there will always be personal and interpersonal stresses; and there will always need to be professionals who can be the buffers, the interpreters, and the solution seekers for others: There will always be a need for social work.

"Consequently, there is no question of a future for social work; the question is whether your *future is in social work. I wish you well in whatever you choose to do."*

The professor watches them leave the classroom for the last time and slowly returns to her office, and sits, staring out of the window.

Where will they be in another decade? What will social work practice really look like?

References

Aburdene, Patricia, and John Naisbitt. *Megatrends for Women.* New York: Villard Books, 1992.

Council on Social Work Education (CSWE). *Statistics on Social Work Education in the United States: 1991* Washington, D.C.: CSWE, 1992.

Naisbitt, John. *Megatrends: Ten New Directions Transforming Our Lives.* New York: Warner Books, 1982.

Naisbitt, John, and Patricia Aburdene. *Megatends 2000: Ten New Directions for the 1990s.* New York: William Morrow, 1990.

The National Association of Social Workers (NASW). *Salaries in Social Work: A Summary Report on the Salaries of NASW Members, July 1986–June 1987.* Silver Spring, MD: NASW, 1987.

U.S. Department of Labor. Bureau of Labor Statistics. *Employment Projections for 1995: Data and Methods,* bulletin 2253. Washington, D.C.: Government Printing Office, 1986.

Workforce 2000: Work and Workers for the 21 Century. Indianapolis, IN: Hudson Institute, 1987.

Appendix: NASW Code of Ethics

Preamble

This code is intended to serve as a guide to the everyday conduct of mem-bers of the social work profession and as a basis for the adjudication of issues in ethics when the conduct of social workers is alleged to deviate from the standards expressed or implied in this code. It represents stan-dards of ethical behavior for social workers in professional relationships with those served, with colleagues, with employers, with other individuals and professions, and with the community and society as a whole. It also embodies standards of ethical behavior governing individual conduct to the extent that such conduct is associated with an individual's status and identity as a social worker.

This code is based on the fundamental values of the social work profes-sion that include the worth, dignity, and uniqueness of all persons as well as their rights and opportunities. It is also based on the nature of social work, which fosters conditions that promote these values.

In subscribing to and abiding by this code, the social worker is ex-pected to view ethical responsibility in as inclusive a context as each situa-tion demands and within which ethical judgment is required. The social worker is expected to take into consideration all the principles in this code that have a bearing upon any situation in which ethical judgment is to be exercised and professional intervention or conduct is planned. The course of action that the social worker chooses is expected to be consistent with the spirit as well as the letter of this code.

In itself, this code does not represent a set of rules that will prescribe all the behaviors of social workers in all the complexities of professional life. Rather, it offers general principles to guide conduct, and the judicious appraisal of conduct, in situations that have ethical implications. It provides the basis for making judgments about ethical actions before or after they occur. Frequently, the particular situation determines the ethical principles that apply and the manner of their application. In such cases, not only the particular ethical principles are taken into immediate consideration, but also the entire code and its spirit. Specific applications of ethical principles must be judged within the context in which they are being considered. Ethical behavior in a given situation must satisfy not only the judgment of the individual social worker, but also the judgment of an unbiased jury of professional peers.

This code should not be used as an instrument to deprive any social worker of the opportunity or freedom to practice with complete professional integrity; nor should any disciplinary action be taken on the basis of this code without maximum provision for safeguarding the rights of the social worker affected.

The ethical behavior of social workers results not from edict, but from a personal commitment of the individual. This code is offered to affirm the will and zeal of all social workers to be ethical and to act ethically in all that they do as social workers.

The following codified ethical principles should guide social workers in the various roles and relationships and at the various levels of responsibility in which they function professionally. These principles also serve as a basis for the adjudication by the National Association of Social Workers of issues in ethics.

In subscribing to this code, social workers are required to cooperate in its implementation and abide by any disciplinary rulings based on it. They should also take adequate measures to discourage, prevent, expose, and correct the unethical conduct of colleagues. Finally, social workers should be equally ready to defend and assist colleagues unjustly charged with unethical conduct.

The NASW Code of Ethics

I. The Social Worker's Conduct and Comportment as a Social Worker
   A. Propriety—The social worker should maintain high standards of personal conduct in the capacity or identity as social worker.
      1. The private conduct of the social worker is a personal matter to the same degree as is any other person's, except when such conduct compromises the fulfillment of professional responsibilities.
      2. The social worker should not participate in, condone, or be associated with dishonesty, fraud, deceit, or misrepresentation.

3. The social worker should distinguish clearly between statements and actions made as a private individual and as a representative of the social work profession or an organization or group.

B. Competence and Professional Development—The social worker should strive to become and remain proficient in professional practice and the performance of professional functions.

1. The social worker should accept responsibility or employment only on the basis of existing competence or the intention to acquire the necessary competence.

2. The social worker should not misrepresent professional qualifications, education, experience, or affiliations.

C. Service—The social worker should regard as primary the service obligation of the social work profession.

1. The social worker should retain ultimate responsibility for the quality and extent of the service that individual assumes, assigns, or performs.

2. The social worker should act to prevent practices that are inhumane or discriminatory against any person or group of persons.

D. Integrity—The social worker should act in accordance with the highest standards of professional integrity and impartiality.

1. The social worker should be alert to and resist the influences and pressures that interfere with the exercise of professional discretion and impartial judgment required for the performance of professional functions.

2. The social worker should not exploit professional relationships for personal gain.

E. Scholarship and Research—The social worker engaged in study and research should be guided by the conventions of scholarly inquiry.

1. The social worker engaged in research should consider carefully its possible consequences for human beings.

2. The social worker engaged in research should ascertain that the consent of the participants in the research is voluntary and informed, without any implied deprivation or penalty for refusal to participate, and with due regard for the participants' privacy and dignity.

3. The social worker engaged in research should protect participants from unwarranted physical or mental discomfort, distress, harm, danger, or deprivation.

4. The social worker who engages in the evaluation of services or cases should discuss them only for professional purposes and

only with persons directly and professionally concerned with them.

5. Information obtained about participants in research should be treated as confidential.

6. The social worker should take credit only for work actually done in connection with scholarly and research endeavors and credit contributions made by others.

II. The Social Worker's Ethical Responsibility to Clients

F. Primacy of Clients' Interests—The social worker's primary responsibility is to clients.

1. The social worker should serve clients with devotion, loyalty, determination, and the maximum application of professional skill and competence.

2. The social worker should not exploit relationships with clients for personal advantage.

3. The social worker should not practice, condone, facilitate, or collaborate with any form of discrimination on the basis of race, color, sex, sexual orientation, age, religion, national origin, marital status, political belief, mental or physical handicap, or any other preference or personal characteristic, condition, or status.

4. The social worker should avoid relationships or commitments that conflict with the interests of clients.

5. The social worker should under no circumstances engage in sexual activities with clients.

6. The social worker should provide clients with accurate and complete information regarding the extent and nature of the services available to them.

7. The social worker should apprise clients of their risks, rights, opportunities, and obligations associated with social service to them.

8. The social worker should seek advice and counsel of colleagues and supervisors whenever such consultation is in the best interest of clients.

9. The social worker should terminate service to clients, and professional relationships with them, when such service and relationships are no longer required or no longer serve the clients' needs or interests.

10. The social worker should withdraw services precipitously only under unusual circumstances, giving careful consideration to all factors in the situation and taking care to minimize possible adverse effects.

11. The social worker who anticipates the termination or interruption of service to clients should notify clients promptly and

seek the transfer, referral, or continuation of service in relation to the clients' needs and preferences.

G. Rights and Prerogatives of Clients—The social worker should make every effort to foster maximum self-determination on the part of clients.

1. When the social worker must act on behalf of a client who has been adjudged legally incompetent, the social worker should safeguard the interests and rights of that client.

2. When another individual has been legally authorized to act in behalf of a client, the social worker should deal with that person always with the client's best interest in mind.

3. The social worker should not engage in any action that violates or diminishes the civil or legal rights of clients.

H. Confidentiality and Privacy—The social worker should respect the privacy of clients and hold in confidence all information obtained in the course of professional service.

1. The social worker should share with others confidences revealed by clients, without their consent, only for compelling professional reasons.

2. The social worker should inform clients fully about the limits of confidentiality in a given situation, the purposes for which information is obtained, and how it may be used.

3. The social worker should afford clients reasonable access to any official social work records concerning them.

4. When providing clients with access to records, the social worker should take due care to protect the confidences of others contained in those records.

5. The social worker should obtain informed consent of clients before taping, recording, or permitting third party observation of their activities.

I. Fees—When setting fees, the social worker should ensure that they are fair, reasonable, considerate, and commensurate with the service performed and with due regard for the clients' ability to pay.

1. The social worker should not accept anything of value for making a referral.

III. The Social Worker's Ethical Responsibility to Colleagues

J. Respect, Fairness, and Courtesy—The social worker should treat colleagues with respect, courtesy, fairness, and good faith.

1. The social worker should cooperate with colleagues to promote professional interests and concerns.

2. The social worker should respect confidences shared by colleagues in the course of their professional relationships and transactions.

3. The social worker should create and maintain conditions of practice that facilitate ethical and competent professional performance by colleagues.

4. The social worker should treat with respect, and represent accurately and fairly, the qualifications, views, and findings of colleagues and use appropriate channels to express judgments on these matters.

5. The social worker who replaces or is replaced by a colleague in professional practice should act with consideration for the interest, character, and reputation of that colleague.

6. The social worker should not exploit a dispute between a colleague and employers to obtain a position or otherwise advance the social worker's interest.

7. The social worker should seek arbitration or mediation when conflicts with colleagues require resolution for compelling professional reasons.

8. The social worker should extend to colleagues of other professions the same respect and cooperation that is extended to social work colleagues.

9. The social worker who serves as an employer, supervisor, or mentor to colleagues should make orderly and explicit arrangements regarding the conditions of their continuing professional relationship.

10. The social worker who has the responsibility for employing and evaluating the performance of other staff members, should fulfill such responsibility in a fair, considerate, and equitable manner, on the basis of clearly enunciated criteria.

11. The social worker who has the responsibility for evaluating the performance of employees, supervisees, or students should share evaluations with them.

K. Dealing with Colleagues' Clients—The social worker has the responsibility to relate to the clients of colleagues with full professional consideration.

1. The social worker should not assume professional responsibility for the clients of another agency or a colleague without appropriate communication with that agency or colleague.

2. The social worker who serves the clients of colleagues, during a temporary absence or emergency, should serve those clients with the same consideration as that afforded any client.

IV. The Social Worker's Responsibility to Employers and Employing Organizations

L. Commitments to Employing Organization—The social worker

should adhere to commitments made to the employing organization.

1. The social worker should work to improve the employing agency's policies and procedures, and the efficiency and effectiveness of its services.
2. The social worker should not accept employment or arrange student field placements in an organization which is currently under public sanction by NASW for violating personnel standards, or imposing limitations on or penalties for professional actions on behalf of clients.
3. The social worker should act to prevent and eliminate discrimination in the employing organization's work assignments and in its employment policies and practices.
4. The social worker should use with scrupulous regard, and only for the purpose for which they are intended, the resources of the employing organization.

V. The Social Worker's Ethical Responsibility to the Social Work Profession

M. Maintaining the Integrity of the Profession—The social worker should uphold and advance the values, ethics, knowledge, and mission of the profession.

1. The social worker should protect and enhance the dignity and integrity of the profession and should be responsible and vigorous in discussion and criticism of the profession.
2. The social worker should take action through appropriate channels against unethical conduct by any other member of the profession.
3. The social worker should act to prevent the unauthorized and unqualified practice of social work.
4. The social worker should make no misrepresentations in advertising as to qualifications, competence, service, or results to be achieved.

N. Community Service—The social worker should assist the profession in making social services available to the general public.

1. The social worker should contribute time and professional expertise to activities that promote respect for the utility, the integrity, and the competence of the social work profession.
2. The social worker should support the formulation, development, enactment and implementation of social policies of concern to the profession.

O. Development of Knowledge—The social worker should take responsibility for identifying, developing, and fully utilizing knowledge for professional practice.

1. The social worker should base practice upon recognized knowledge relevant to social work.
2. The social worker should critically examine, and keep current with emerging knowledge relevant to social work.
3. The social worker should contribute to the knowledge base of social work and share research knowledge and practice wisdom with colleagues.

VI. The Social Worker's Ethical Responsibility to Society

P. Promoting the General Welfare—The social worker should promote the general welfare of society.

1. The social worker should act to prevent and eliminate discrimination against any person or group on the basis of race, color, sex, sexual orientation, age, religion, national origin, marital status, political belief, mental or physical handicap, or any other preference or personal characteristic, condition, or status.
2. The social worker should act to ensure that all persons have access to the resources, services, and opportunities which they require.
3. The social worker should act to expand choice and opportunity for all persons, with special regard for disadvantaged or oppressed groups and persons.
4. The social worker should promote conditions that encourage respect for the diversity of cultures which constitute American society.
5. The social worker should provide appropriate professional services in public emergencies.
6. The social worker should advocate changes in policy and legislation to improve social conditions and to promote social justice.
7. The social worker should encourage informed participation by the public in shaping social policies and institutions.

SOURCE: National Association of Social Workers, Inc. *Social Work Speaks: NASW Policy Statements,* 2nd ed. Silver Spring, MD: NASW, 1991.

INDEX

Photo and Illustration Credits

Chapter 1: Opener and all photos by Gerald J. Miller.

Chapter 2: Opener, Fotomas Index, Kent, England. P. 55, Addams: frontispiece from *Proceedings of the [1910] National Conference of Charities and Correction* (Fort Wayne, IN: Archer Printing, 1910), Social Welfare History Archives, University Library, University of Minnesota; Rankin and Starr: Sophia Smith Collection, Smith College; Tubman and Truth: Schomburg Center for Research in Black Culture, Special Collections, New York Public Library. P. 63, Jane Addams Memorial Collection, Special Collections, The University Library, University of Illinois at Chicago.

Chapter 3: Opener, Coalition for the Homeless, New York, NY. P. 87, photo by Y. R. Okamoto, reprinted courtesy of Lyndon Baines Johnson Library, Austin, TX. P. 94, courtesy of Sarah Weddington.

Chapter 4: Opener, photo by Cewzan Grayson, reprinted courtesy of Social Services Employees Union Local 731, AFSCME, New York, NY. P. 117, March of Dimes Birth Defects Foundation, White Plains, NY. Pp. 119, 129, United Way of America, Fairfax, VA.

Chapter 5: Opener, United States Department of Health and Human Services. P. 149, National Park Service, Ellis Island Immigration Museum. P. 158: blind boy, Perkins School for the Blind, Watertown, MA; other photos, United Way of America, Fairfax, VA. P. 164, United States Department of Justice Immigration and Naturalization Service.

Chapter 6: Opener, New York Coalition for the Homeless, New York, NY. P. 189, photo by George Hirose, reprinted by courtesy of the Henry Street Settlement House, New York, NY.

Chapter 7: Opener, United States Department of Health and Human Services. P. 213, photo by Tom McKitterick, Impact Visuals. P. 220, courtesy of Senator Barbara Mikulski.

Chapter 8: Opener, United Way of America, Fairfax, VA. P. 247, frontispiece from Joanna C. Colcord, ed. *The Long View: Papers and Addresses by Mary Richmond* (New York: Russell Sage Foundation, 1930), Social Welfare History Archives, University Library, University of Minnesota. P. 253, courtesy of St. Vincent's Hospital—Westchester, Harrison, NY. P. 258, Schomburg Center for Research in Black Culture, Special Collections, New York Public Library.

Chapter 9: Opener, New York Coalition for the Homeless, New York, NY. P. 288, Linn County Case Management Program, Cedar Rapids, IA. P. 290, photo by Tom McKitterick, Impact Visuals.

Chapter 10: Opener, NYNEX. P. 307, Art Stein/Planned Parenthood Federation of America, Inc.

Chapter 11: Opener, Henry Street Settlement House, New York, NY. P. 322, YMCA of the USA Archives, University of Minnesota Libraries. P. 330, Smith College Archives, Smith College, Northampton, MA.

Chapter 12: Opener, photo by Tom McKitterick, Impact Visuals. P. 353, Linn County Case Management Team, Cedar Rapids, IA.

Chapter 13: Opener and p. 380, photo by Gerald J. Miller. P. 402, NASW Communications Network, Los Angeles, CA.

Chapter 14: Opener, photo by Michael D. Sullivan, United States Department of Health and Human Services. P. 411, photo by Kristen Johnson, Henry Street Settlement House, New York, NY.